# Direct Foreign Investment
# in Asia's Developing Economies
# and Structural Change
# in the Asia-Pacific Region

# Direct Foreign Investment in Asia's Developing Economies and Structural Change in the Asia-Pacific Region

EDITED BY

## Eric D. Ramstetter

Westview Press

BOULDER • SAN FRANCISCO • OXFORD

Published in 1991 in the United States of America by Westview Press, Inc., 5500 Central Avenue, Boulder, Colorado 80301-2847, and in the United Kingdom by Westview Press, 36 Lonsdale Road, Summertown, Oxford OX2 7EW

Library of Congress Cataloging-in-Publication Data
Direct foreign investment in Asia's developing
economies and structural
    change in the Asia-Pacific region / edited by
Eric D. Ramstetter.
        p.   cm.
    Includes bibliographical references.
    ISBN 0-8133-1079-2
    1. Investments, Foreign—Asia.   2. Investments, Foreign—Pacific Area.   3. Asia—Economic
policy.   4. Pacific Area—Economic policy.
I. Ramstetter, Eric D., 1956–
HG5702.D57   1991
332.6′73′095—dc20                                                                      91-19335
                                                                                            CIP

Printed and bound in the United States of America

The paper used in this publication meets the requirements
of the American National Standard for Permanence of Paper
for Printed Library Materials Z39.48-1984.

10      9      8      7      6      5      4      3      2      1

# Contents

# Tables

# Preface and Acknowledgments

This book is the result of a project organized by the Institute for Economic Development and Policy (IEDP, formerly the Resource Systems Institute) of the East-West Center (EWC). The expressed goal of the project was to produce a monograph evaluating the extent to which direct foreign investment (DFI) in developing countries is related to structural change in the Asia-Pacific region. This project is part of the continuing work on DFI in the IEDP following the publication of *Direct Foreign Investment and Export Promotion: Experiences and Policies in Asia* (edited by Seiji Naya, Vinyu Vichit-Vadakan, and Udom Kerdpibule, Honolulu and Kuala Lumpur: East-West Center and Southeast Asian Central Banks Research and Training Centre) in 1987. A subsequent DFI project is also in its initial stages at this writing.

This book has three distinguishing features. First, it attempts to integrate analyses of structural changes in major source countries and selected host countries in order to facilitate increased understanding of the channels through which investing and host countries interact in the Asia-Pacific region. Second, although the degree of analytical sophistication is still severely limited by data availability problems, the contributors to this monograph have been able to substantially extend previous analyses over longer periods of time and provide new analyses of changes over time that were not previously possible. The longer time horizon is in turn particularly valuable in the study of longer-term structural issues, which are the focus of this monograph. Third, the analyses are oriented toward understanding the implications of past relationships for future adjustment. Recently, there have been important and large changes in the region's economies—for example, the appreciation of the yen and the new Taiwanese dollar, which will have important effects on future structural changes in the region. Although quantitative analyses of the role DFI has played after the mid-1980s have been limited by lack of data, the contributors to this monograph have been careful to interpret past relationships in the context of recent events.

This volume is authored by a group of economists and as a result is largely oriented toward stimulating discussion among economists. However, it should also be stressed that the theoretical and statistical analyses used in the volume are generally not very abstract. Thus, the volume should also be of use to researchers in fields outside of economics and to public policymakers. In an educational setting, the volume could serve as a useful supplement or perhaps even as a main text in graduate level or advanced undergraduate level seminars on international economics, economic development, and/or the Asia-Pacific economy.

Finally, I would like to stress that this project has been a collective effort from the outset and I would like to thank a number of individuals for their contributions. Seiji Naya, IEDP Assistant Director William E. James, and Chung H. Lee have all provided important assistance with the design and coordination of the project. Robert E. Lipsey also gave key advice about research design in the early stages of the project. In the latter stages, Janis Togashi thoroughly edited several copies of the manuscript and contributed greatly to its improvement. Cynthia Nakachi provided crucial typing expertise through several revisions of the manuscript. She and other IEDP staff (Mendl Djunaidy, Jeni Miyasaki, and Ann Takayesu among others) also helped with the arrangements for the March 1989 working meeting at which first drafts were presented and discussed. I also wish to thank all EWC staff members who contributed directly and indirectly to this project but are not named here.

*Eric D. Ramstetter*

# PART ONE

## Issues and Theory

# 1

# Direct Foreign Investment and Structural Change in the Asia-Pacific Region: The Issues

*Seiji Naya and Eric D. Ramstetter*

### Goals of the Study

The relatively rapid economic growth experienced in the postwar period in Japan, the newly industrializing countries (NICs) of Asia Hong Kong, Korea, Singapore, and Taiwan), and the four larger Association of Southeast Asian Nations (ASEAN-4: Indonesia, Malaysia, the Philippines, and Thailand), have been very important elements in what several observers have referred to as the transition to a Pacific Century (e.g., Oshima 1987, Ch. 12). Although the degree of this shift and its implications are sometimes exaggerated, it is clear that economic growth in these Asian economies has far outstripped the world average in the last two decades. Moreover, this growth has been accompanied by large changes in the structure of economic activity in these countries with manufacturing industries in particular becoming more important in several economies. Within manufacturing itself, there were also large changes in the structure of activity, especially in the NICs, Japan, and the United States, where technological advances and rationalization of production lines (often relocated to less developed countries like the ASEAN-4) led to greater emphasis on research and development (R&D) and capital-intensive activities in a number of industries. These structural changes were in turn closely related to large changes in international patterns of comparative advantage and thus had important impacts on economies outside of Asia. Structural changes in other regions affected Asia in an analogous manner, but because Asian structural changes were in many ways the most rapid, they have more often been viewed as the causes of changes in other regions.[1] Furthermore, the pace of structural change in Asia accelerated markedly in the mid-1980s with currency appreciation leading to large adjustments in Japan, Korea, and Taiwan. These adjustments have in turn had significant impacts on a number of Asia's developing economies, especially Thailand and the other ASEAN-4 economies, as numerous labor-intensive production lines were relocated from Japan and Taiwan, among other countries, to lower-cost locales.

An important element in the migration of production lines in developing Asia has been the multinational corporation. Direct foreign investment (DFI) by multinationals from the United States, Japan, Europe, and recently the Asian NICs, has been significant in each of the NIC and ASEAN-4 economies, and in a number of industries, foreign multinationals have played crucial roles in stimulating growth. Some have claimed that outward investment to Asia from the United States has contributed to the decline of several U.S. industries; the debate on a DFI-induced hollowing out of the Japanese economy is conducted in a similar vein. However, to date, there has been little research which focuses on quantitative analysis of DFI's effects on industrial structures in either the host or the investing economies.[2] The primary purpose of this volume is to fill this lacuna and measure some of these effects and analyze their implications.

In the past, there have been numerous studies of the effects of DFI on the NIC and ASEAN-4 economies (e.g., Galenson 1985; UN 1985; Naya, Vichit-Vadakan, and Kerdpibule 1987), of the effects of U.S. DFI abroad on the U.S. economy (e.g., Bergsten, Horst, and Moran 1978; Lipsey and Weiss 1981, 1984; Blomström, Lipsey, and Kulchycky 1988), and a few studies of the effects of Japan's DFI abroad on the Japanese economy (e.g., Goto 1988). However, there has been no study that integrates empirical analyses of DFI's effects on the host and investing economies in the Asia-Pacific region. A second goal of this project has thus been to integrate these interrelated analyses into one comprehensive volume. Another shortcoming of many previous studies of DFI in the Asia-Pacific region has been the limited time horizon that existing data have provided. In this volume, the authors have been able to markedly increase the time horizons in a number of analyses, thus affording a more dynamic perspective of the issues involved.

## Structural Change: What Is It and What Are the Problems?

What is meant by structural change or structural adjustment? Simply put, these terms refer to the process by which the distribution of a given economic phenomenon changes across activities.[3] For example, structural change can refer to changes in the industry-wise distributions of production, employment, exports, and other economic activities. The terms can also refer to intraindustry structural changes in factor intensity or technology or economywide structural changes in the distribution of income between saving and consumption. In short, since there are numerous dimensions to the distribution of economic activities, it is clear that no single definition of structural change exists. This volume concentrates on the industry dimension; that is, the distribution of production, employment, trade, and other activities, across industries. However, other dimensions will also be employed at various times and it is thus extremely important for the reader of this volume to first identify the type of structural change that is being discussed.

What are the problems posed by structural change? From the perspective of the distribution of activities across industries, problems emerge because structural change forces the migration of economic resources between industries and such migration is costly. For example, production costs in several firms in the U.S. steel industry, the

Japanese garments industry, and the Korean rice industry have risen above world levels in the last decade. The firms in these industries have two options; they can either increase productivity and reduce costs, or cease production. In the latter case, workers and capitalists would both face large adjustment costs, at least in the short run, as they must all find new jobs. Moreover there can be large losses even in the former case if, for example, increased automation and reductions in the labor force are required to increase productivity. However these industries may also benefit from the changes. If their competitive positions are improved, they may as a result be able to expand and attract additional workers and capital. Yet even if this expansion is adequate to absorb all of the resources left unemployed in the former three industries, medium-term problems may remain since resources used in production of U.S. steel may be less productive than they are in producing U.S. rice, resources used in producing Japanese garments may be less productive than they are in making steel, and resources used to grow Korean rice may be less productive than they are in producing garments.

Three principles must be stressed here. First, the causes of structural change are generally long run in nature. A basic cause of structural change is changes in the relative cost structures among industries and countries. In turn, changes in relative cost structures often result from changes in factor endowments and technology. Another basic cause of structural change is changes in demand patterns, with per capita income levels being perhaps the most important determinant in this respect. Since perceptible changes in per capita incomes, factor endowments, and technology generally take a substantial period of time (5–10 years or more), structural change is best viewed as a result of the interaction of long-term factors.

Second, if economic institutions (markets, firms, and governments) are successful in promoting the migration of productive resources from industries characterized by relatively low factor productivity (and low factor rewards) to industries with relatively high factor productivity (and high factor rewards), the reallocation of productive resources will generally be welfare-improving. As a result, it is argued that structural change, although a result of long-run economic forces, presents few long-run problems if markets are reasonably competitive or if economic institutions ensure that economic agents receive price signals based on the principle of relative scarcity.

Third, the problems created by structural change are primarily reflected in the short-and medium-term costs incurred by economic agents during the process of adjustment. These costs are incurred largely because adjustment implies the reallocation of quasi-fixed physical and human capital, the existing stocks of which are a result of discrete investment decisions taken previously. For example, once an automobile factory is built, it generally becomes more costly to liquidate the factory and use the assets generated to construct a semiconductor factory than it is to raise new financial capital for the same purpose. A similar logic applies to the development of human capital; once workers have been trained in producing steel, it is more costly to retrain them to assemble semiconductors than it is to train unskilled workers to assemble semiconductors since the wages paid during the training period must generally be higher in the steel workers' case. In other words, the reallocation of productive resources, which may take time to create, is in general a costly process. The costs incurred vary widely and depend greatly on a number of factors including the productive resource, the technology, and the institutions involved.

The fact that the costs of adjustment can vary depending on the institutions involved leads one to ask which institutional arrangement is optimal in the sense that adjustment costs are minimized. This question, as applied to international adjustments, is a major focus of this study. Three institutions are suggested to be the most important in the international reallocation of resources that is necessitated by the process of structural change: markets, firms, and public institutions (e.g., government). In other words, it is possible to have market-coordinated interfirm adjustment, multinational-coordinated intrafirm adjustment, and public institution-coordinated inter- and intrafirm adjustment.

In general, the efficacy of each of these institutions differs depending upon the industry and the country involved. In the case of multinational-coordinated adjustment, some literature argues that DFI's role is welfare-reducing because multinationals lead to deindustrialization in industrialized countries and exploitation of labor in developing countries, among other undesirable practices (e.g., Peet 1987). The critics of multinationals often advocate greater public institution-coordinated adjustment. However, in this volume, the view that DFI by multinationals has the potential to reduce the costs of international adjustment where corporate networks operate more efficiently than arm's-length markets or public institutions is emphasized. Focus is on the comparison of market-coordinated adjustment and multinational-coordinated adjustment, though it is clear that public institutions have important roles to play in international adjustment, especially when supplies of public goods (e.g., infrastructure, a clean environment) are affected and externalities exist. Yet we and several of the authors in this volume share a large skepticism about the efficacy of attempts to increase public control over reasonably competitive private markets and firms beyond the measures that are deemed necessary to secure adequate supplies of public goods and compensate for externalities. Moreover, since the focus of this volume is the effect of DFI on industrial adjustment in market economies, the more relevant alternative to multinational-coordinated adjustment is generally thought to be market-coordinated adjustment.

There are then two distinct analytical problems: (1) determining the role of multinationals in adjustment, and (2) evaluating the relative efficiency of multinational-coordinated adjustment. A large part of this volume is devoted to the former problem since its solution is a prerequisite for the latter's treatment and because we know of no previous comprehensive treatment of the DFI-structural change relationship in the Asia-Pacific region. Inferences about the relative efficiency of multinational-related adjustment are also made where possible but these inferences are by no means definitive conclusions, especially since an unambiguous evaluation of the costs of either multinational-coordinated adjustment or market-coordinated adjustment could not be made.

However, with regard to the relative efficiency of adjustment through multinationals, a couple of general observations are pertinent to all studies. First, theory tells us that the very existence of a multinational indicates that international intrafirm coordination of economic activities (and hence adjustment) is more efficient than international interfirm coordination, at least in some respects.[4] Second, although it is very difficult to unambiguously measure whether adjustment costs are indeed reduced or increased by the presence of multinationals, there are some indications that the presence of multinationals may facilitate smoother adjustment. If the U.S.-Asia relationship is taken as an example, casual observation indicates that U.S. adjustment to increased import competition has been most difficult in industries like textiles and apparel, metals, and automobilies where U.S. multinational participation has been minimal in Asia. In contrast, adjustment has been substantially easier in chemicals and electronics, two industries in which U.S. multinational activity has been quite high in Asia. This observation reflects the sentiment of Helleiner (1981) who suggested that U.S. industries characterized by large multinational involvement were less likely to seek protection from foreign imports. Of course, even if one accepts that industries characterized by a high degree of multinational activity in trading partners have fewer adjustment problems, it does not necessarily follow that increased multinational activity will facilitate smoother adjustment in troubled industries. For this reason, it is extremely important to identify the conditions under which adjustment through multinationals is likely to be beneficial. This book attempts to illuminate some of the issues involved in this regard.

## The DFI-Structural Change Relationship:
## Modes of Analysis

There are many ways in which an analysis of the issues that are dealt with in this study can be done. First, despite the drawbacks sometimes involved, theorizing about the economic relationships involved is indispensible to any economic study; thus, some theorizing is included in this volume. Moreover a lot of work has been done on the conceptual frameworks that were used in the empirical studies which form the core of this study, though this conceptualizing hardly constitutes a formal theory.

As for the empirical studies themselves, a number of modes are employed. First, the host country was chosen as the basic accounting unit in the study of the inward DFI-structural change relationship in host developing economies. Of course, the DFI-structural change relationship may also differ depending on the investing economy involved and such differences are mentioned where relevant.[5] Nonetheless differences between domestic firms and multinationals, not among different types of multinationals, are the primary focus of this study. Second, in an analogous manner, the investing country was chosen as the basic accounting unit in the study of the outward DFI-structural change relationship in Japan and the United States. In contrast to the first type of study, distinguishing among DFI destinations is a major concern of these studies as they focus on DFI in the NICs and the ASEAN-4. Third, two integrated analyses of the issues in both host and investing countries, the first utilizing the industry dimension as its basic accounting unit and the second employing a variety of basic accounting units, are presented in this volume.

This study is organized into five parts. Part I introduces the reader to the topics taken up (this chapter) and presents a theoretical exposition of some of the issues involved (Chapter 2). The theoretical presentation is especially important because it serves to provide a framework from which to view the subsequent empirical studies and because it helps to clarify issues which empirics alone would leave ambiguous. Parts II and III contain studies of inward DFI and structural change in selected ASEAN-4 economies (Indonesia in Chapter 3 and Thailand in Chapter 4) and

NICs' economies (Korea in Chapter 5 and Taiwan in Chapter 6), respectively. Part IV focuses on outward DFI and structural change in the two major investors in the region, Japan and the United States. Finally, Part V provides an integrated perspective with one study (Chapter 9) focusing on an industry-by-industry analysis of DFI's role in determining the regional division of labor and the other study (Chapter 10) providing an integrated view of DFI's role in structural changes in the United States, Japan, and Asia's developing economies. The concluding chapter summarizes the major conclusions of the studies in the volume and offers some suggestions for future research.

Finally, a number of points are relevant to all studies. First, there is a strong focus on the DFI-structural change relationship within manufacturing, though implications for shifts among manufacturing, primary production, and services are also noted as relevant. Second, there is strong emphasis on analyzing the real activity of multinationals as reflected in the heavy use of indicators such as employment, trade, value added, and factor intensity. Less concern is given to the financial activities of multinationals, since the financial activities may or may not reflect real activity, especially in tax havens such as Hong Kong. Third, although the data do not usually permit extension of detailed analysis beyond the mid-1980s, the authors are all highly conscious of the important changes that have occurred since 1985 and have made efforts to include discussion of related issues as appropriate. The most important of these changes are: (1) currency realignments, (2) continuing macroeconomic disequilibria and strong protectionist sentiment in the United States, and (3) the growing importance of the NICs, especially Taiwan, as a major source of DFI in the Asian region.[6] In short, this volume represents a collection of thorough and forward-looking papers which will be of use to students of DFI, structural change, and the Asia-Pacific region.

### Notes

1. See Oshima (1987) for a recent survey of Asian economic growth and structural changes. Hughes (1987), Ichimura (1988), and James, Naya, and Meier (1987), focus more narrowly on growth and structural changes in developing economies, while Balassa and Noland (1988), Komiya (1988), and Shinohara (1982, 1986) analyze Japan's performance in detail. Finally, Baldwin (1986, 1988), Feldstein (1988), Krugman (1986), and Stern (1987) are among the growing number of studies which focus on the reactions of the United States to increased import competition, much of it coming from Japan and Asia's developing economies.

2. Of course a number of studies do provide a wealth of information which is helpful in this respect and we shall draw heavily on relevant studies as necessary in this volume. However the focus on structural change itself is somewhat novel.

3. Here we have defined these terms synonymously but we should also note that structural adjustment is often used in a manner which implies that the changes involved are the result of active adjustments by economic agents. However, in that both terms refers to changes in the distribution of economic activities, the positive economic phenomenon referred to by each term is essentially the same.

4. This point is especially emphasized by those who argue that internalization of arms-length transactions is the major reason for the existence of multinational firms (Rugman 1980, 1985).

5. Kojima (1978, 1985), Lee (1979, 1983), and Ramstetter (1987) are examples of studies which focus on the differences and similarities of impacts imparted by DFI from different investing countries.

6. Taiwan's net DFI abroad on a balance-of-payments basis went from US$80 million or less annually through 1986 to US$704 million in 1987 and US$4,120 in 1988. In comparison, Japanese outflows did not exceed US$3,000 million until 1981 and averaged US$4,349 million in 1981–1983 (Republic of China, Central Bank of China, various years; Japan, Bank of Japan, various years).

# References

Balassa, Bela, and Marcus Noland. 1988. *Japan in the World Economy*. Washington, D.C.: Institute for International Economics.

Baldwin, Robert E. 1986. *The Political Economy of U.S. Import Policy*. Cambridge: MIT University Press.

Baldwin, Robert E., ed. 1988. *Trade Policy Issues and Empirical Analysis*. Chicago: University of Chicago Press.

Bergsten, C. Fred, Thomas Horst, and Theodore H. Moran. 1978. *American Multinationals and American Interests*. Washington, D.C.: Brookings Institution.

Blomström, Magnus, Robert E. Lipsey, and Ksenia Kulchycky. 1988. U.S. and Swedish Direct Investment and Exports. In *Trade Policy Issues and Empirical Analysis*, edited by Robert E. Baldwin. Chicago: University of Chicago Press.

Feldstein, Martin, ed. 1988. *The United States and the World Economy*. Chicago: University of Chicago Press.

Galenson, Walter, ed. 1985. *Foreign Trade and Investment: Economic Development in the Newly Industrializing Asian Countries*. Madison: University of Wisconsin Press.

Goto, Junichi. 1988. *Kokusai Rōdō Keizai Gaku: Bōeki Mondai Heno Atarashii Shiten* [International labor economics: toward new perspectives on trade problems]. Tokyo: Toyo Keizai.

Helleiner, G. K. 1981. *Intra-Firm Trade and the Developing Countries*. New York: St. Martin's Press.

Hughes, Helen, ed. 1987. *Explaining the Success of Industrialization in East Asia*. Canberra: Australian National University.

Ichimura, Shinichi, ed. 1988. *Challenge of Asian Developing Countries*. Tokyo: Asian Productivity Organization.

James, William E., Seiji Naya, and Gerald M. Meier. 1987. *Asian Development*. Madison: University of Wisconsin Press.

Japan, Bank of Japan. Various years. *Balance of Payments Statistics Monthly*, March 1966–March 1988 issues. Tokyo: Bank of Japan.

Kojima, Kiyoshi. 1978. *Japanese Direct Foreign Investment: A Model of Multinational Business Operations*. Tokyo: Tuttle.

————. 1985. Japanese and American Direct Investment in Asia: A Comparative Analysis. *Hitotsubashi Journal of Economics* 26(1): 1–35.

Komiya, Ryutaro. 1988. *Gendai Nihon Keizai: Makuroteki Tenkai to Kokusai Keizai Kankei* [The modern Japanese economy: macro perspectives and international economic relations]. Tokyo: University of Tokyo Press.

Krugman, Paul R., ed. 1986. *Strategic Trade Policy and the New International Economics*. Cambridge: MIT University Press.

Lee, Chung H. 1979. United States and Japanese Direct Investment in Korea: A Comparative Study. *Journal of Economic Development* 4(2): 89–113.

_____ . 1983. International Production of United States and Japan in Korean Manufacturing Industries: A Comparative Study. *Weltwirtschaftliches Archiv* 119(4): 744–53.

Lipsey, Robert E., and Merle Y. Weiss. 1981. Foreign Production and Exports in Manufacturing Industries. *Review of Economics and Statistics* 63(4): 488–94.

_____ . 1984. Foreign Production and Exports of Individual Firms. *Review of Economics and Statistics* 66(2): 304–308.

Naya, Seiji, Vinyu Vichit-Vadakan, and Udom Kerdpibule, ed. 1987. *Direct Foreign Investment and Export Promotion: Policies and Experiences in Asia.* Honolulu and Kuala Lumpur: East-West Center and Southeast Asian Central Banks Research and Training Centre.

Oshima, Harry T. 1987. *Economic Growth in Monsoon Asia.* Tokyo: University of Tokyo Press.

Peet, Richard, ed. 1987. *International Capital and Industrial Restructuring.* Boston: Allen and Unwin.

Ramstetter, Eric D. 1987. The Impacts of Direct Foreign Investment on Host Country Trade and Output: A Study of Japanese and U.S. Direct Foreign Investment in Korea, Taiwan, and Thailand. In *Direct Foreign Investment and Export Promotion: Policies and Experiences in Asia,* edited by Seiji Naya, Vinyu Vichit-Vadakan, and Udom Kerdpibule. Honolulu and Kuala Lumpur: East-West Center and Southeast Asian Central Banks Research and Training Centre.

Republic of China, Central Bank of China. Various years. *Balance of Payments, Taiwan District, Republic of China,* 1958–1982 Summary and March 1981–March 1989 issues. Taipei: Central Bank of China.

Rugman, Alan M. 1980. Internalization as a General Theory of Foreign Direct Investment: A Reappraisal of the Literature. *Weltwirtschaftliches Archiv* 116(2): 365–69.

_____ . 1985. Internalization is Still a General Theory of Foreign Direct Investment. *Weltwirtschaftliches Archiv* 121(3): 570–75.

Shinohara, Miyohei. 1982. *Industrial Growth, Trade, and Dynamic Patterns in the Japanese Economy.* Tokyo: University of Tokyo Press.

_____ . 1986. *Nihon Keizai Kogi: Deta de Kataru Keizai no Dainamizumu* [Lectures on the Japanese economy: economic dynamism according to the data]. Tokyo: Toyo Keizai.

Stern, Robert M., ed. 1987. *U.S. Trade Policies in a Changing World Economy.* Cambridge: MIT University Press.

United Nations (UN). 1985. *Patterns and Impact of Foreign Investment in the ESCAP Region.* New York: United Nations.

# 2

## The Theory of
## the Multinational Enterprise:
## A Common Analytical Framework

*James R. Markusen*

### Introduction

There exists today a large literature on the multinational enterprise. Much of this literature is empirical and/or policy-oriented, and tends to deal either with broad aggregate measures of direct foreign investment (DFI) or highly specific case studies. The theoretical work often seems to suffer from a degree of informality that makes it hard to clearly understand the connection between assumptions and conclusions. Other (generally more formal) theoretical work deals with very specific models which seldom seem to apply to a "majority" of cases. In my opinion, the consequence of these observations is that both the empirical and the theoretical literature are less than satisfactory in answering the following basic questions: (1) Why do multinationals exist at all? (2) What are the positive and normative consequences of multinationals as opposed to other market structures? (3) How do multinationals contribute to structural change?

The purpose of this paper is to draw together ideas from the empirical and theoretical literature into a common conceptual and analytical framework for understanding the multinational firm. The specific purpose of this project is of course to deal with the multinational as applied to developing (primarily the ASEAN-4: Indonesia, Malaysia, the Philippines, and Thailand) and newly industrialized countries (NICs: Hong Kong, Korea, Singapore, and Taiwan) of the Pacific basin, and to their major source countries (the United States and Japan). As will become clear, I do not believe that there is or should be a different theory of the multinational for different countries. Indeed, such a country-specific theory would not be a theory at all in the usual sense of the term. Therefore, presentation of the theory is on a general level for most of the paper. On the other hand, I most certainly do believe that certain aspects and implications of the theory are more relevant to developing economies and the NICs. A very important example is that there has been a great deal of export-oriented DFI in the Pacific basin, whereas inward DFI into Europe is primarily import substituting. Thus the analysis of the host and home (source) countries should concentrate on this wherever possible. Other relevant differences will be discussed.

With respect to structural change which is the principal focus of this volume, the paper suggests four broad findings:

1. The multinational is a facilitating institution which helps to organize world production to optimally exploit comparative advantage
2. The multinational is, by nature, a major vehicle for transferring technical and managerial skills
3. The public-goods nature of the latter implies spillovers and long-term structural changes to the host economies
4. Under plausible assumptions, multinationals make socially efficient decisions as to the location of production so that the decision to move production from home to host country is welfare improving for both countries although this does not imply that price and output decisions are socially optimal

The paper is organized as follows. In the next section, some of the existing empirical and theoretical literature is discussed. Then a general conceptual model of the multinational is presented, and the positive and normative consequences of this model are examined. The model is static, but attempts are made to draw inferences from the basic conceptual framework for structural change issues. This is not an easy task because the formal literature has, by and large, never investigated the links between DFI and structural change. Following this discussion, a simple analytical version of the model is given and some welfare analysis is presented.[1] The policy implications of the welfare analysis are then discussed and the major conclusions of the paper are summarized.

## Empirical and Theoretical Foundations

The most basic question that any theory of the multinational must answer is why multinationals exist at all. Why are markets not served by exports from foreign firms or by production by locally owned firms? Trade barriers such as tariffs and transport costs obviously lead to the displacement of imports; but if there are costs to doing business abroad and if finance and technology is equally available everywhere (as generally assumed in neoclassical trade theory), the domestic production generated by trade barriers will be by local firms, not by foreign multinationals. Simple scale economies in production will not help either. Scale economies of the traditional neoclassical variety lead to geographical centralization of production, not decentralization which is the hallmark of the multinational. Thus, a successful theory of the multinational must explain not only why production is occurring in a country, but also why that production is carried on by foreign-owned firms. If a theory cannot do this, we cannot have any confidence in the predictions of that theory.

The vast literature on the multinational arrives at a consensus on only a few issues. There is however some, but not unanimous, support for John Dunning's "eclectic" view as to the necessary conditions under which a firm will undertake DFI (Dunning 1977, 1981). Under this view, sometimes referred to as the OLI (ownership, location, internalization) paradigm, three conditions are necessary. First, the firm must have an ownership advantage such as proprietary rights to a product or a production process that allows it to compete successfully with foreign companies. Second, the foreign country must have a location advantage for production, such as tariff or transport cost barriers to imports or low factor prices, that leads the multinational to produce in that market rather than service it by exports. Third, there must be an internalization advantage that leads the multinational to buy or create a foreign subsidiary rather than license production and/or distribution of a product to a foreign firm.

There is some dissent to this view. For example, Rugman (1981, 1985, 1986) focuses on internalization as the key element and Casson (1986) suggests that the ownership advantage is relevant to the theory of the firm (as in what makes a successful firm) but not to the theory of the multinational in particular. At the great risk of becoming involved in this debate, I find Dunning's eclectic approach to be useful in the present context. We are more interested in the two questions of whether a product is provided to a foreign market and whether it is provided by exports or by foreign production, and less interested in whether the production in the host country is by a subsidiary or by a licensee of the home firm. The former two questions relate to the O (ownership) and L (location) of the Dunning paradigm, while the latter relates to the I (internalization) of the paradigm that completes the triad.

The OLI framework does not by itself tell us what types of ownership advantages firms have. It is here that we turn to the empirical literature. Important differences in the degree of multinational activity across industries have long been observed. In some industries, multinationals account for a major share of total output while in other industries this share is minor. It has also been shown consistently that the degree of multinationality in an industry is closely related to such variables as research and development (R&D) expenditure as a percentage of sales, marketing expenditures as a percentage of sales, and the ratio of white-collar (professional/technical) workers to blue-collar production workers (Caves 1982). A number of authors have documented the fact that DFI is preferred by firms which have new and/or technically complex products, or products/services relying on careful quality control and reputations (Caves and Murphy 1976; Conklin and St. Hilaire 1988; Davidson and McFetridge 1984; Mansfield and Romeo 1980; Wilson 1977). Within individual industries, Beaudreau (1986) has shown that firms with more accumulated experience have a higher level of multinational activity.

These empirical results give rise to the concept of knowledge-based, firm-specific assets (FSAs). These are proprietary assets of the firm embodied in such things as the human capital of the employees, patents or otherwise exclusive technical knowledge, copyrights or trademarks, or even more intangible assets such as management know-how or the reputation of the firm. There are two good reasons why these knowledge-based assets are more likely to give rise to DFI than physical capital assets. First, knowledge-based assets can be transferred easily back and forth across space at low cost. An engineer or manager can visit many separate production facilities at relatively low cost. Plant and equipment, on the other hand, do not have this portability. Second, knowledge often has a jointness or "public goods" characteristic in that it can be supplied to additional production facilities at very low cost.

For example, blueprints for new products or production processes, which are a knowledge-based asset, can be provided to additional plants without reducing the value of the blueprints to the initial plants. Blueprints are thus a joint input into all plants. Trademarks and other marketing devices also have this property. Assets based on physical capital such as machinery tend not to have this property. That is, physical capital usually cannot yield a flow of services in one location without reducing its productivity in other locations.

The joint input characteristic of knowledge-based assets has important implications for the efficiency of the firm and in turn for market structure. These implications are summarized in the notion of economies of multiplant production where a single two-plant firm has a cost efficiency over two independent single-plant firms. For example, the multiplant firm (i.e., the multinational) need only make a single investment in R&D, while two independent firms must each make the same investment. The latter industry structure therefore involves the duplication of FSAs. Cost efficiency will then dictate that multinationals (multiplant firms) will arise as the equilibrium market structure in industries where FSAs are important. As was pointed out, this is the empirical observation.

The converse proposition should also be emphasized. Scale economies based on physical capital intensity do not by themselves lead to DFI. This type of scale economy implies the cost efficiency of centralized production rather than geographically diversified production as noted earlier. Of course, some industries with a high physical capital intensity may also be industries in which FSAs are important. We often find this with respect to the marketing and servicing of output. For example, many Japanese multinationals in manufacturing industries in fact do little manufacturing in North America, preferring to concentrate this phase of their operations in Japan. Their subsidiaries in North America are largely and often exclusively involved in wholesaling, marketing, and servicing the firms' products. Thus knowledge-based scale economies (multiplant economies) may dominate in certain phases of operation while plant scale economies (single-plant economies) may dominate in other phases.

The proposition that multinationals tend to be firms in which knowledge-based capital is important also fits very well with the empirical observations related to the newness, technological complexity, and quality/reputation aspects of products. The same public-input characteristic of knowledge-based capital which is the basis for multiplant economies also leads to moral hazard and adverse selection issues. These issues then lead firms to internalize the problems involved by undertaking DFI. Assets with public good characteristics can be easily dissipated by agent opportunism. Technical and other trade secrets passed to a subsidiary or a licensee by a home firm can be easily lost. If an engineer can supply technical knowledge to a branch plant or a licensee at low cost, it is likely that a licensee can peddle the technology to third parties at low cost. A similar problem occurs with servicing and with the asset "reputation" for product quality. Licensees have a strong incentive to shirk on product quality or servicing in order to capture short-run profits. Although there can be problems of opportunism within firms, most scholars believe that these problems are less severe with a subsidiary than with a licensee. Hence the existence of knowledge-based assets tends to rule out licensing or other arm's-length arrangements, reinforcing the correlation between these assets and multinationality.

Let us therefore assume that multinationals are firms which possess, in at least some of their operations, FSAs. What then is the real trade flow across borders that is generating a stream of returns for the multinational firm? The latter is observable while the former generally is not (in some cases the multinational does of course supply financial capital to the foreign subsidiary, while in other cases funds are borrowed locally). In my opinion, multinationals are in the business of supplying the services of the firms' FSAs to foreign subsidiaries. These services include management, engineering, marketing, and financial services which are based on human capital. They also include the services of patents and trademarks which are other knowledge-based assets. Subsidiaries import these services in exchange for repatriated profits, royalties, or direct service charges.

If we accept the notion of FSAs as the cornerstone of the theory of the multinational, several implications for the balance-of-payments (BOP) accounts and our qualitative understanding of trade follow directly. This theory implies that a major component of the trade between parent firms and subsidiaries is management, engineering, and other services as just mentioned. If these assets were traded at arm's length, they would be classified in the BOP statistics as trade in producer services. Yet because they are traded within the firm, they are often classified quite separately as returns to or payments for DFI. The BOP statistics are, in other words, kept on the basis of the mode of transaction (arm's-length versus intrafirm) rather than on the basis of the economic content of the transaction. While this is appropriate for certain purposes, it is not helpful for understanding the content of real trade flows. In particular, this accounting method does not make it obvious that host countries are receiving anything at all in exchange for the profits being repatriated by multinationals. Ideally, returns to DFI would be broken down into such things as payments for management and engineering services, and pure monopoly profits. But since these transactions are intrafirm, it is hard to see how any reliable statistics can be developed (a problem that relates closely to the transfer pricing literature).

The same argument suggests that the book value of DFI investments, which is basically a valuation of investment in plant and equipment, reveal only limited information about the true value of the investment. To the extent that a major feature of DFI is the transfer of technology, management know-how, marketing networks, and so forth, recorded values of DFI may seriously underestimate the true economic value (measured as the opportunity cost to the host country of undertaking the project itself, including development of the necessary FSAs).

Note at this point that nothing has been said regarding import-substituting versus export-oriented DFI. This omission is deliberate since the general theory that has just been developed is believed to be independent of the direction of trade in the multinationals' final output. The theory applies to both export and import-competing industries, and indeed to nontraded industries (e.g., hotels) as well. The theory explains what types of firms and industries are likely to be dominated by multinationals. "Types" in this theory clearly refer to the nature of the firm's technology and product, particularly the importance of knowledge-based capital, rather than to a classification according to the direction of trade. Other things equal, there is no particular reason to believe that multinationals in a host country are primarily import substituting or export oriented. This agnosticism is reflected in the data of Naya and

Ramstetter (1988) which showed that multinationals are heavily engaged in trade, but not necessarily more in exporting than in importing.

Other things are, of course, not equal. Empirically, DFI in the ASEAN-4 and the NICs is much more balanced than DFI in the industrialized economies, the latter being primarily import substituting. It is my view that, among industries characterized by knowledge-based assets, the direction of trade associated with the output of the industry is determined by the traditional comparative advantage and tariff-transport cost variables. Europe, for example, offers U.S. and Japanese firms few advantages based on comparative advantage such as low wages, low cost of capital, or the availability of skilled workers. At least until very recently, entry of U.S. and Japanese firms into the European market was generally to avoid tariff, quota, transport, and other distance-related costs. This DFI was accordingly primarily import substituting.

It is reasonable to generalize that the ASEAN-4 and NIC economies, on the other hand, offered advantages based on comparative costs. Low wages and a comparatively educated and disciplined work force are likely the primary advantages. Further, these economies tend to lack the talent and resources needed to develop their own knowledge-based assets in a way that exploits their comparative advantage. These economies may thus have a potential comparative advantage in labor-intensive manufactured goods and natural-resource products, but a potential that cannot be exploited by indigenous entrepreneurs. Key assets or inputs are missing, and I suggest that these key inputs are the same knowledge-based assets that have been discussed. Machinery can be bought, but the managerial and technical expertise needed to use it properly is difficult to transfer at arm's length and is very costly to develop at home.

My view is thus that multinationals arise in industries which have certain technological and informational characteristics, but that the trade orientation of multinationals in a particular country is determined by more traditional principles of comparative advantage and trade barriers. There is no strong a priori reason for supposing that DFI is either a complement or a substitute for trade in the absence of knowing the factor endowment and trade barriers of the country in question.

Note that this argument does not suggest that multinationals do not fundamentally affect the structure of production and trade. As noted above, a developing country in particular may have many of the ingredients necessary to produce and export a particular class of goods (e.g., electronic goods or components), but the country may lack key technical and managerial skills. The entry of the multinational firm into such a country provides the missing ingredients and leads to the production and export, possibly on a very large scale, of goods that were previously imported and/or not produced. Furthermore, to the extent that the knowledge-based capital eventually becomes incorporated into the human capital of the host country's work force, the multinational permanently changes the factor endowment of the host country. The trade orientation of the multinational depends on local comparative advantage factors and on trade barriers, but it is perfectly consistent to say that the multinational itself can lead to substantial structural changes and to a shift in revealed comparative advantage (i.e., which goods are actually exported). It is further possible that due to local learning, the shift is permanently embodied in local workers such that the new production configuration would be maintained even if the multinational exited the country. Again, this is an important implication of knowledge-based capital that is not valid for physical capital. Students are eventually able to read without their teacher, but machinery repatriated with its owner no longer yields a flow of services in the host country.

Now let us consider the implications that such a model has for the welfare effects of DFI. First, let me reiterate one of the main points of the above analysis in a way that states the conclusion in a manner that is more useful for welfare analysis: The multinational must be providing value to the host country in the form of managerial, technical, and other services; if the multinational was not doing so, the costs of doing business abroad would mean that the multinational could not exist and we would not observe DFI. The existence of these costs are prima facie evidence that the multinational is providing the host country with productive services at a lower cost than the host country could if it were to provide those services itself. The multinational thus provides the host country with producer services, the value of which can be measured by the cost that the host country would have to incur if it had to develop the managerial, technical, or marketing expertise itself. From a technical or cost point of view, the multinational unambiguously makes the host country better off.

Even ignoring the often-debated political and social ramifications, (topics which are beyond the scope of this paper), the technical aspect of DFI is not the only one that must be considered. A theoretical prediction of the model developed is that by nature of the fact that multinationals possess proprietary firm-specific assets, multinationals inherently tend to be found in imperfectly competitive market structures. Perfectly competitive market structures are found in situations in which firms do not have special advantages (there are of course situations in which Ricardian rents exist, as in well-located land); but if there are even small costs of doing business abroad as just discussed, then the foreign firms are forced out in competitive markets. This theoretical prediction is strongly supported by empirical evidence which shows a high correlation between the degree of multinationality and the concentration in an industry.

Imperfect competition implies the existence of monopoly profits, and with monopoly profits comes the issue of who captures these profits. In the absence of a multinational in a host country, either the good in question is not produced at all (which would typically be the outcome in the less developed countries) or it is produced by a domestic oligopoly (monopoly for simplicity). In the first instance, there are no monopoly profits. Since the multinational firm must bid resources away from the other sectors, the national income of the host country must rise with the entry of the multinational. If the good is produced by a domestic monopolist in the absence of the multinational, the situation is less clear. The multinational takes over the market by virtue of technical efficiency as discussed above. However the multinational captures rents that would otherwise have gone to the domestic entrepreneur and entered into the domestic income stream. It is possible to construct situations where the profit transfer from the domestic firm to the multinational firm is larger than the efficiency gain from the latter such that the host country is worse off under the multinational.[2]

How likely such a welfare-reducing scenario might be is unclear. What we can say is that such a scenario is less likely as (1) the multinational firm is much more efficient than the domestic firm, and (2) there is competition among multinationals for entry into the host country such that the multinationals' profits are smaller. My personal conjecture is that the welfare-reducing scenario is very unlikely in smaller, developing economies. These economies often cannot support production of the goods in question in the absence of multinational firms, which leads to the welfare-increasing scenario. When production by domestic firms can be supported, it is likely to be the case that the firm-specific costs incurred are large relative to the size of the market such that the degree of cost inefficiency of the domestic firms is high. Both statements are less likely to be true for the NICs.

Note that these comments on welfare are independent of the trade orientation of the multinational company. As in the case of the positive analysis, the normative implications of the general model are valid for export-oriented, import-competing, and nontraded industries. Two caveats on import-substituting investment should, however, be noted. Suppose that the multinational enterprise enters a market due to a very high tariff. Now there is a loss of tariff revenue which is very much like the loss of monopoly profits to a domestic firm. Thus the multinational firm could be welfare reducing due to the shifting of rents from the domestic government to the foreign firm. Even if this is not the case, it might still be true that the multinational firm is welfare reducing, not with respect to the tariff-ridden equilibrium, but with respect to free trade. Thus when the initial equilibrium is distorted, as is often the case in developing countries, the import-substituting multinational may be welfare increasing relative to the initial equilibrium but welfare reducing relative to some other alternative such as free trade. One can certainly find many cases in which an import-substituting multinational would not have entered in a free-trade situation, suggesting that the price the multinational charges must exceed the world free-trade price. In such a case, consumer surplus in the host country must be lower with the multinational firm, and with no compensating gains (such as profits), welfare will be lower relative to free trade.

## Multinationals and Structural Change

As noted in the introduction, there has been very little formal work connecting the theory of the multinational with issues of structural change. This is unfortunate insofar as this connection is the principal focus of this volume. Nevertheless the general conceptual view presented in the preceding section has a number of interesting and straightforward implications for the multinational-structural change relationship. Several of these implications are explored in this section, with particular emphasis on relationships which I believe will stand up to formal theorizing. A more thorough analysis must await further theoretical analysis.

One of the most interesting implications of the general conceptual model was hinted at in the previous section. It is easy to conceive of situations where exogenous changes in key economic variables are, through the vehicle of the multinational, translated into the production of new products in developing countries and to changes in the direction of trade in those products. Furthermore such structural changes cannot come about without the presence of multinationals in these cases. Thus the multinational enterprise is an institution that facilitates structural adjustment, although by itself this does not guarantee a welfare improvement.

To illustrate the multinational's ability to facilitate structural change, consider a very simple, but entirely plausible, situation. Suppose there is a commodity X, which is consumed largely in a high-income country, country H, and scale economies prevent commodity X from being produced in more than one country. The commodity is labor intensive in production at the margin, but requires in addition one unit of sophisticated technical-managerial know-how. There is a second (low-income) country, country J, which has a lower wage rate than country H but which does not possess any endowment of know-how. Initially assume that the wage rate differences are insufficient to compensate for the cost of transporting commodity X to country H. Thus commodity X is produced only in country H and the issue of producing the good in country J does not arise.

Now assume that the wage difference grows or the transport cost falls until it becomes optimal to produce commodity X in country J and ship it to country H if we focus only on marginal production costs. Without the institution of the multinational firm, it is difficult to shift production to country J. In some cases, it may be possible to sell or license the technology to a firm in country J, but in many cases, the know-how is embodied in the employees of the original firm or moral hazard and adverse selection problems make licensing infeasible. Thus the feasible alternatives are for the firm to keep production in country H, or to set up a subsidiary in country J. If the latter cannot occur due to an inability on the part of the firm or due to policies in either country, structural change does not occur. The ability of the firm to set up a subsidiary (i.e., become a multinational firm) leads to structural change in which (1) the production of a new product is introduced into country J, (2) the direction of trade in commodity X is reversed, and (3) world production is consistent with comparative advantage and world production efficiency. The multinational firm is a "facilitating institution" which allows the world to adjust production to optimally exploit changing patterns of comparative advantage. The welfare consequences of this structural change are not obvious (e.g., does the multinational make the socially efficient choice of location decision); a discussion of this aspect is postponed until the next section.

A second major dynamic issue of structural adjustment arises from the concept of knowledge-based capital. We noted earlier that knowledge-based capital has a public good or jointness property to the extent that it can be incorporated into additional production facilities at low or potentially zero marginal cost. It was also noted in this context that the same property may imply that the knowledge assets may be easily dissipated through agent opportunism, and hence there is a strong incentive for the firm to transfer these assets internally through DFI.

It can be argued that in many instances it is difficult to prevent knowledge from being transferred to the local employees of the firm who work with and observe the technical and managerial techniques of the firm. The most obvious cases are those industries in which the knowledge or techniques are embodied in the workers themselves and thus must be transferred or taught to the workers in the host country. After some initial learning period, the workers become capable of opening a rival firm, or of transferring their knowledge to new firms in related industries. This becomes a positive externality effect for the local economy arising from the presence of the multinational. As a result, the host country economy becomes more diversified as time goes by. This implication of the general theory receives support in Schive and Tu (this volume), which notes that foreign firms' local content has risen significantly over time, and that subsidiaries which have been established longer have higher local content.[3]

A third issue of structural adjustment follows directly from the second. If the knowledge-based capital of the firm is embodied in the human capital of its workers (for example, if blueprints or procedures are memorized), then the workers may be a threat to their own firm. This notion, which has been examined by Beaudreau (1986) and others, suggests that one possible consequence of knowledge-based capital is that in subsequent time periods the firm may be forced to pay higher wages to the relevant employees. This process could force average costs up to meet prices thereby reducing pure economic profits to zero. This is in turn a sufficient condition for the host country to be better off with the multinational than with a national firm in succeeding time periods. The multinational company might choose to exit or sell out after the domestic entry threat becomes clearly viable. If the multinational is an exporting firm and no exports existed before the firm arrived, then the multinational leaves the direction of trade permanently reversed since the knowledge-based capital of the country becomes a permanent part of the factor endowment of the host country once it is transferred to domestic workers. While this discussion is somewhat speculative, it is not inconsistent with a number of the other papers in this volume that find that multinational enterprises are accounting for a declining fraction of new investment in the Pacific region.

In summary, issues related to the public good or jointness property of knowledge capital, in particular, the inability of multinationals to prevent transfer of knowledge to host country workers, may have greater implications for structural changes generated by multinational enteprises than issues related to the potential of the multinational to directly affect the patterns of comparative advantage.

It should be noted, however, that the arguments regarding structural change do not have clear and obvious welfare implications. The arguments do suggest that the flow of welfare will increase once employees in the host country have acquired the new knowledge and skills. If individual workers are assumed to have perfect foresight, then equilibrium wages may be forced down in the initial learning period as workers compete for jobs which are expected to impart valuable skills. Thus the welfare gains in the later period are to some extent dissipated by the low wages in the earlier period, and the intertemporal effect is unclear. While it would be difficult to provide clear empirical support for this scenario, from the point of view of positive economics, the entry of the multinational firm has in this case permanent long-run consequences in changing the production mix and the pattern of comparative advantage in the country. As noted earlier in this paper, physical capital does not bestow this type of externality.

One caveat to this generally optimistic picture is provided in a paper by Horstmann and Markusen (1987). In this paper, countries are assumed to be initially of different size in a growing world. One country achieves minimum size to support the production of a good first, and then becomes the home country to a new firm that has invested in the development of knowledge-based assets. It can now open branch plants in foreign countries for only the plant-specific cost. As the foreign market grows, the first entrant can profitably invest in a branch plant before any domestic entrant can do so since the latter must invest in both the firm-specific and the plant-specific costs. The first entrant can thus preempt new entrants if fixed costs are sunk (i.e., plant and equipment cannot be liquidated). Horstmann and Markusen show that although the multinational firm (the first entrant) will not always choose the option to preempt, when the multinational does preempt, the sunk cost assumption makes a welfare-reducing scenario somewhat more likely. Now, even if the potential domestic firm becomes the most competitive after a certain time period, it cannot enter (assuming the market cannot support two firms) because it knows that the incumbent multinational firm will not exit. In this case, there is a large loss of profits to the host country and the country's welfare is lower under the multinational. Horstmann and Markusen show that this scenario cannot occur if, as in the static analysis, there is competition among multinationals for entry such that entry first occurs when the present value of profits are zero. The fact that the present value of profits is zero for the multinational firm that has invested the firm-specific cost implies that the present value of profits are negative for a potential domestic entrant. This turns out to be a sufficient condition for the present value of the income stream of the host country to be higher with the multinational firm than with the domestic firm. Once again, we have the intuitive result that competition among multinationals is a sufficient condition for multinational enteprises to be welfare improving for the host country. The Horstmann and Markusen study also ignores the possibility of learning by the employees of the multinational enterprise as discussed above, which puts a severe constraint on the multinational enterprise's ability to exercise market power in the long run.

A final dynamic implication which can be drawn from our knowledge-based capital view of multinationals concerns the issue of appropriate technology. There seems to be a view that multinational enterprises often transfer "inappropriate" (e.g., capital-intensive) technologies that impede the development of developing economies. The knowledge-based capital view stresses the fact that the physical capital intensity as well as other aspects of a production process closely reflect the knowledge-based capital and learning experience of the firm. I believe that the smooth isoquants of neoclassical economics are a bit of a myth and often a major distortion. Facing certain factor prices in their home country, firms invest in learning best-practice technologies for those factor prices. They achieve one point on the neoclassical isoquant through these investments and their accumulated experiences. The firm then cannot simply move costlessly to another point on that isoquant when it opens a branch plant in a low-wage host country. The firm does not know a best-practice labor-intensive technique and would have to incur a possibly large fixed cost to develop one. Given these fixed costs of developing a technique, it is perfectly reasonable to suppose that a known capital-intensive technique may be cheaper to introduce than to develop a new labor-intensive technique. The lower marginal cost of the latter may be outweighed by the fixed costs of development. Thus, the factor intensity of a technique does not tell us its cost effectiveness. Knowledge-based, firm-specific assets may, in other words, be partly specific to the products and the production processes that the firm has developed for high-wage, high-income markets.

## Welfare Analysis for the Home and Host Countries

Consider a model where two goods ($X$ and $Y$) are produced from a single factor, labor ($L$), which is in inelastic supply at any point in time ($L = L_X + L_Y$) and is internationally immobile. $Y$ is produced with constant returns by a competitive industry and units are chosen such that $Y = L_Y$. $Y$ is used as the numeraire so that the wage rate in terms of $Y$ is equal to one. To begin producing $X$, a firm must incur the once-and-for-all sunk costs of $F$ (firm-specific cost) and $G$ (plant-specific cost) in terms of $Y$ (or $L$). Additional plants may be opened for the cost of $G$ only. $F$ is thus intended to represent the knowledge-based capital that is a joint input or public good within the firm. $F$ could be thought of as an R&D investment necessary to design a product or a production process. Once the design is produced, it can be costlessly incorporated into additional plants. This leads to multiplant economies of scale where a two-plant firm incurs $F$ only once, while two one-plant firms must each incur $F$. The fact that the services of $F$ can be costlessly extended to additional plants does not, of course, imply that these services are of no value to the additional plants.

Let $MC$ denote the marginal cost of producing $X$ and assume that this is constant and identical in each of the two, the home and the host, countries. The home country has an existing $X$ producer that may export to or open a branch plant in the host country. The host country may open its own firm, or obtain $X$ from the home country either by imports or from a branch plant. The total cost of producing $X$ is the marginal cost times output, plus the relevant fixed costs ($F + G$ for a new firm or just $G$ for a branch plant). The average cost ($AC_H$) of producing $X$ in the host country in its own new firm ($AC_H^N$) or in a branch plant ($AC_H^B$) are total cost divided by output $X$ and are given respectively as,

$$AC_H^N = MC + G/X + F/X; \quad AC_H^B = MC + G/X \tag{2.1}$$

Average costs are decreasing in output for both the new firm and the branch firm. It is clear that branch plant production is more technically efficient due to the exploitation of the joint input nature of $F$, but whether or not this technical efficiency outweighs possible market power distortions requires further analysis.

Consider the equilibrium in which the host country has no involvement with the home country versus an equilibrium in which a multinational firm produces $X$ in the host country and repatriates whatever profits it earns. Let $M$ refer to equilibrium quantities when the multinational firm is producing with a branch plant and let $A$ refer to the host country autarky outputs and prices. Consider first the host country. The revealed preference criterion for the host country to be better off with the multinational firm than in autarky is,

$$C_{YM} + p_M C_{XM} > C_{YA} + p_M C_{XA} \tag{2.2}$$

where $C_{ij}$ is consumption of the $i$th good ($i = X, Y$) in the $j$th equilibrium ($j = A$, $M$), and $p_j$ is the relative price ratio ($X$ to $Y$) in the $j$th equilibrium in the host country. In autarky, we have the market-clearing conditions that supply equals demand for each good,

$$c_{YA} = Y_A \; ; \; c_{XA} = X_A \tag{2.3}$$

At the multinational equilibrium, we must have the balance-of-payments constraint that the value of consumption equals the value of production minus repatriated profits at multinational prices $R$. This constraint is given by,

$$c_{YM} + p_M c_{XM} = Y_M + p_M X_M - R \tag{2.4}$$

Substituting equations (2.3) and (2.4) into equation (2.2), the condition for gains becomes,

$$Y_M + p_M X_M - R > Y_A + p_M X_A \tag{2.5}$$

Now subtracting the total labor endowment, $L = L_{XM} + L_{YM} = L_{XA} + L_{YA}$, from both sides of equation (2.5),

$$(Y_M - L_{YM}) + (p_M X_M - L_{XM}) - R > (Y_A - L_{YA})$$
$$+ (p_M X_A - L_{XA}) \tag{2.6}$$

The assumption of competition in good $Y$ implies that profits in $Y$ are zero; i.e., $(Y_M - L_{YM}) = (Y_A - L_{YA}) = 0$, so that equation (2.6) reduces to,

$$(p_M X_M - L_{XM}) - R > (p_M X_A - L_{XA}) \tag{2.7}$$

Assume as in the previous section that the host-country government imposes no taxes. In this case, the left-hand side of equation (2.7) is always zero. That is, the multinational firm repatriates all profits so that $(p_M X_M - L_{XM}) = R$. The sufficient condition for gains in equation (2.7) thus reduces to,

$$(p_M X_A - L_{XA}) < 0 \tag{2.8}$$

A sufficient condition for the free-market solution to improve on autarky is thus that the present value of profits from producing the autarky outputs at multinational equilibrium prices is negative. One condition that is sufficient for equation (2.8) to hold is that there is enough competition among multinationals to drive price down to average cost. If this condition is met and both $X$ and $Y$ are normal goods in consumption, then $p_M$ must be less than $p_A$. The reason is that if a domestic firm charged $p_M$ in autarky, it would have to be producing more $X$ (and therefore less $Y$) than at the multinational-firm equilibrium in view of the host-country firm's higher fixed cost if the latter is to earn non-negative profits. But at this production configuration of more $X$ and less $Y$, the demand price will be below $p_M$ and thus a price of $p_M$ or lower cannot be an equilibrium price in autarky. Equivalently, the autarky output of $X$ will be less than the amount that must be produced to break even at price $p_M$. This in turn implies that equation (2.8) holds. Average cost pricing by the multinational is sufficient for the host country to gain.

Now we turn to the host (source) country. The algebra of equations (2.2) through (2.7) can be used here by simply changing the sign of $R$. For the moment, $p_M$ will refer to either the price ratio when the multinational firm chooses to invest abroad or when it chooses to export. The home-country version of equation (2.7) then becomes,

$$(p_M X_M - L_{XM}) + R > (p_M X_A - L_{XA}) \tag{2.9}$$

This can be written as,

$$(p_M - L_{XM}/X_M)X_M + R - (p_M - L_{XA}/X_A)X_A > 0 \tag{2.10}$$

But $L_{ij}/X_j$ is just the average cost of producing X, $AC_{ij}$. Equation (2.10) can then be written as,

$$(p_M - AC_{XM})X_M + R - (p_M - AC_{XA})X_A > 0 \tag{2.11}$$

In this simple model, $AC_{ij}$ is decreasing in commodity X. Thus if $X_M > X_A$, then $AC_{XM} < AC_{XA}$. But the latter in turn implies that $(p_M - AC_{XM}) > (p_M - AC_{XA})$, so that $X_M > X_A$ is sufficient for equation (2.11) to be positive ($R$ must be nonnegative by assumption).

The expansion of domestic production of commodity X is a sufficient condition for the home country to be better off by allowing its domestic producer to export or invest abroad. Consider exporting first. The intuition behind this result is a familiar one from public finance theory. Because of the fixed cost of producing X, the price charged must exceed the marginal cost of production, $(p - MC) > 0$. Price indicates the value of an additional unit of the good in consumption while MC indicates the cost of the resources needed to produce an additional unit. With price in excess of marginal cost, additional units of X produced generate a surplus of $(p - MC)dX$. Exports of X thus generate a gain for the domestic economy independently of employment arguments.

Now suppose instead that the multinational firm wishes to export only the services of its firm-specific asset $F$ and produce X abroad. Domestic production of X will almost certainly be less than at the exporting equilibrium just derived and could possibly be less than in autarky (i.e., the multinational could repatriate some of the foreign production to serve the domestic market). Could the home country be worse off as a consequence of the outward DFI? The answer is no. Let $R_M$ denote the multinational firm's profits on its domestic production at the free-trade equilibrium (whether exporting, producing both at home and abroad, or even serving the domestic market by imports from its foreign plant; $R_M$ is zero in the last case). Let $R_{AM}$ denote the multinational firm's profits on its domestic production in autarky, but evaluated at free-trade prices. More formally,

$$R_M = (P_M - AC_{XM})X_M \; ; \; R_{AM} = (P_M - AC_{XA})X_A \qquad (2.12)$$

Equation (2.11) can then be written as,

$$(R_M + R) - R_{AM} > 0 \qquad (2.13)$$

The first two terms in equation (2.13) are the multinational firm's total profits at the free-trade equilibrium. The first is profits on domestic production (which may include export sales) and the second is profits repatriated from the foreign subsidiary. If the multinational firm is a rational maximizer, it will not undertake exporting or DFI unless the sum of these two terms exceeds $R_{AM}$ (i.e., profits from domestic plus foreign operations are revealed as preferred to autarky profits). Thus the home country is better off with foreign operations than in autarky.

It cannot be established in general whether the country as a whole is better off if the multinational firm chooses DFI over exporting or vice versa. That is, the multinational may not always make the socially efficient choice of exporting versus DFI. However, under reasonable assumptions, the multinational does make the socially efficient choice. Again let $M$ denote the DFI option and let $E$ denote the exporting option. The simple autarky market-clearing condition in equation (2.3) must be replaced by the balance-of-payments condition,

$$C_{YE} + P_E C_{XE} = Y_E + P_E X_E \qquad (2.14)$$

This can also be written as,

$$C_{YE} + P_M C_{XE} + (P_E - P_M)C_{XE} = Y_E + P_M X_E$$
$$+ (P_E - P_M)X_E \qquad (2.15)$$

or

$$C_{YE} + P_M C_{XE} = Y_E + P_M X_E + (P_E - P_M)(X_E - C_{XE}) \qquad (2.15')$$

Let $R_{EM}$ denote the profits on export sales evaluated at DFI prices. The same procedure as used in equations (2.5) and (2.6) can then be used to get the equivalent of equation (2.7),

$$Y_M + P_M X_M + R > Y_E + P_M X_E + (P_E - P_M)(X_E - C_{XE}) \qquad (2.16)$$

which implies,

$$(R_M + R) - R_{EM} > (P_E - P_M)(X_E - C_{XE}) \qquad (2.17)$$

Rationality on the part of the multinational firm will again imply that $(R_M + R)$ $\geq R_{EM}$. But we now have the additional term on the right-hand side of equation (2.17) which is a terms-of-trade effect. Given that $(R_M + R) > R_{EM}$, the inequality in equation (2.17) will hold and the country will be better off with DFI than exporting if this last term is negative. Since $(X_E - C_{XE}) > 0$ by the assumption that X is exported, the right-hand term will be negative if $(p_E - p_M) < 0$. That is, a sufficient but not necessary condition for the home country to be better off with outward DFI than with exports is that the export price, $p_E$, is less than the DFI price, $p_M$.

One factor which leads to $p_E < p_M$ is a foreign tariff that forces down the price received when exporting but not when serving that market by a foreign branch plant. Transport costs would have a similar effect. These factors are reasonably common and are indeed two important forces that motivate DFI in the first place. More rigorously, assume that to engage in DFI, the home firm must make a fixed-cost investment, G, in a foreign plant. If the marginal costs at home and abroad are the same and constant as have been assumed, then the home firm will only invest abroad if the price it can charge, $p_M$, exceeds the net price it receives from exporting, $p_E$. Thus the observation of DFI implies that $(p_E - p_M) < 0$, and the inequality in equation (2.17) holds. If the home firm chooses DFI, then the home country must be better off than if the firm was forced to choose exporting which is in turn preferred to autarky. The multinational firm chooses the socially efficient (from the home country's point of view) mode of serving the foreign market.

## Policy Analysis

There have of course been entire books written on various policy-related aspects of multinationals. Taxation has been of principal economic interest, while the social and political consequences of DFI has occupied many pages in the work of authors from many disciplines. Technology transfer and other externalities are other areas of great importance. It is far beyond the scope of this paper to provide any comprehensive analysis of public policy and DFI. However a few important points are derived from the above model.[4]

An extremely important point which has been underemphasized in the literature is that multinationals are endogenous. A firm may choose to serve a certain host market by exporting to it, by opening a subsidiary (become a multinational firm), or by licensing a foreign firm; and, of course, it may choose not to serve that market at all. In the case of export-oriented DFI, the choice is typically the more narrow option of a subsidiary versus nothing at all.

The fact that these discrete choices exist has probably been appreciated more in the policy literature than the theory literature. Until recently, theorists have been more or less captured by marginal analysis and competitive equilibrium, neither of which is well suited to the discrete choices just mentioned. Some of the more formal policy analyses seem to fall into this trap as well. For example, in the transfer pricing literature, the effects of differences in taxation between countries on the marginal pricing and output decisions of multinationals are assessed. However I do not recall reading any analyses in which the existence of the multinational firm and its ability to rearrange production and plants internationally have been explicitly incorporated.

There is some reason to suspect that the discrete choices of location and production mode are much more important than the marginal price and output effect of taxation. Certainly some simple simulations in Horstmann and Markusen (1990) illustrate this possibility. Thus for the remainder of this section, attention will be devoted to certain possible effects of public policy on DFI and therefore on production, trade, and welfare. Note that the global analysis of the previous two sections is very much in this spirit. Once again, in the general spirit of this project the focus will be on the host country.

Host-country policies can be used either to directly encourage or discourage DFI. Both types of policies have been observed in the developing countries and in the NICs, and often the two types of policies occur simultaneously in a country. Other policies which are not primarily DFI policies also have a substantial impact on the DFI decision. These include tariffs, quotas, exchange controls, and domestic taxation policies.

First, let us consider policies which encourage the entry of multinationals into the host country, including "carrot" policies such as subsidies or tax holidays, and "stick" policies such as high tariffs or quotas in the case of import-substituting DFI. Assume initially that a good is being imported from a foreign country and a policy designed to attract a foreign firm is being contemplated. Note that whether that firm will be solely import substituting or will export (i.e., reverse the direction of trade) is not necessarily important). In traditional competitive (full-employment) models, a policy that attracts a foreign firm is always welfare reducing for a country with no monopoly power in trade. Prices give correct signals of costs and resource scarcity, and firms choose locations as well as outputs efficiently. However, with large fixed costs and imperfect competition as in the model developed in this paper, this conclusion does not necessarily follow. Assume, for example, that the marginal costs of production in the home and host countries are the same. If there are transportation costs, the price of the product will be higher in the host country when it imports the good than if it were produced domestically. But the fixed costs of opening a plant may be so high as to deter the multinational firm from DFI; that is, the lower unit costs of serving the host country are less than the fixed costs of opening a branch plant. If a tariff or quota were established, it would change the balance of this decision and may induce the multinational firm to open a plant. Price to domestic consumers will then fall and the host country is unambiguously better off.

A key assumption behind this result is that the marginal cost of production in the host country is less than the marginal cost plus transport cost from the home country; thus the price falls when the multinational firm enters. If this is not the case, then inducing the multinational to enter the host country is welfare reducing. This case is interesting since it provides a situation where the initial equilibrium market structure is not optimal from the point of view of the host country, even though that country has no influence over world prices. In other words, this example illustrates how fixed costs and discrete decision making can lead to policy implications that differ significantly from those derived from traditional competitive analysis.

Now consider policies which prohibit DFI, and assume that the initial equilibrium involves a multinational monopolist producing in the host country. Note that this situation is not simply the reverse of the scenario that was considered previously. If the multinational is forced out, the host country may import the good in which case we do have the reverse situation; but the host country may instead find that it does not have access to the good at all (transport costs are prohibitive) or the good may be produced by a domestic monopolist.

Which of these alternatives is chosen to replace the multinational may make a major difference to the welfare conclusions. As just noted, the case of the substitution of imports for DFI has been discussed above. In the case where the good is no longer available at all, it is hard to see how the country can possibly be better off unless, perhaps, the multinational was distorting domestic factor markets. There must be a consumer surplus loss from the disappearance of the product, and there is no offsetting gain in profits or government revenue. If an inefficent domestic monopolist replaces the multinational firm, then we have the situation discussed in previous sections. The capture of profits by the domestic firm, profits that would otherwise have gone to the multinational, may or may not outweigh the loss of productive efficiency.

I wish to avoid a taxonomy of situations and outcomes. Nor am I prepared to guess as to which types of scenarios are more likely than others. Indeed I believe that no intelligent guesses can be made without country-and industry-specific information. My goal is simply the modest one of convincing the unbelieving to supplement, if not supplant, the marginal analysis of public policies with a discrete or global analysis that explicitly takes into account the existence of location decisions and large firm-specific fixed costs.

The dynamic and structural issues previously discussed also have interesting implications for public policy. The first of these issues concerns first-mover advantages and preemptive entry. A firm which has already invested the firm-specific costs in order to enter the industry in the home country has a cost advantage over (potential) new firms in entering foreign markets. As noted above, one interesting case occurs when the multinational produces at the same marginal cost in the home- and host-country markets. In this case, the host country benefits by the entry of the multinational firm relative to importing the good or to not having the good at all since the equilibrium price with the multinational will be lower. However, the multinational enterprise will not necessarily be willing to enter the country because the fixed costs of a branch plant may outweigh the saving in transport costs.

An implication of this particular scenario is that there is a positive welfare effect from public policies that encourage entry of the multinational. In the case of import-substituting investment, high trade barriers encourage such a shift in the mode of serving the country. Early entry by the multinational enterprise (i.e., entry before the country's market is large enough for the multinational firm to voluntarily enter) increases welfare during the intervening time period and begins the process of structural change at an earlier date. That is, any learning and knowledge accumulation processes induced by the multinational enterprise are begun at an earlier date. Thus in cases where the multinational is deemed to be beneficial in the static sense, the development process is accelerated in the dynamic sense by encouraging early entry.

A qualification to this argument arises due to the existence of sunk costs as detailed above. If investments cannot be liquidated easily, then the first-mover advantage of the multinational can later turn into a barrier to entry by domestic firms (Horstmann and Markusen 1987). Even if potential domestic firms become equally or more competitive, they cannot undercut the multinational except by pricing all the way down to marginal cost. Further, the threat to continue pricing at marginal cost is not very credible. In such a situation, the multinational deters entry and at the same time continues to enjoy monopoly profits.

In this case, what is called for is some sort of industrial organization policy that explicitly attacks the entry-deterrence problem. In broad general terms, the policy might consist of aid to potential domestic entrants or measures directed at the multinational enterprise. The problem with the former set of policies is that policy should be careful not to encourage the existence of too many firms in an increasing-returns industry. Policies directed at the multinational enteprise could include "carrot" policies such as supporting a local buyout of the multinational firm. "Stick" policies such as taxation can also be used but there is the possibility that the host country will damage its reputation for future DFI. In any case, the principal point is that the existence of sunk costs implies that an initially beneficial DFI may eventually come to constitute a detrimental barrier to entry of domestic firms.

Another point considered above is the possibility of learning and knowledge accumulation by locals. If multinational enterprises are generally associated with the existence of knowledge-based assets that are joint inputs across plants, this same jointness property may imply that the knowledge-based capital is easily acquired over time by the host-country employees of the multinational firm. This is probably a very powerful effect in many circumstances and deserves to be considered very seriously. As noted above, Peter Murrell's work on Eastern European firms suggests that the lack of involvement in those countries by Western multinationals has severely curtailed the ability of Eastern European economies to produce in high-tech sectors. The costs of developing the relevant technologies on one's own is generally prohibitively expensive for smaller, middle-income countries.

With respect to public policy, one extreme view is that there is no externality at all and thus, no special role for government policy is called for. The argument is that workers of the multinational firm foresee their private benefits from the accumulation of skills and fully internalize this effect by signing contracts with the multinational firm for lower wages than they could obtain elsewhere. However, to the extent that there is less than full internalization of the learning externalities, there is a positive role for public policy in encouraging the entry of multinational enterprises. On the other hand, there may be negative externalities associated with the entry of multinationals into developing countries. Disruptions of social traditions and political institutions are two examples that are often mentioned, though these effects are beyond the scope of this paper. My purpose here is, once again, to draw out the implications of the knowledge-capital model of the multinational firm for public policy.

A final dynamic and structural consideration mentioned above is the issue of "appropriate" technologies. Specific techniques require large investments in R&D and learning-by-doing, and a particular technique, like a particular product, embodies the knowledge-based capital of the firm. To develop new techniques which are optimal at the margin for different sets of factor prices may require large fixed costs. Thus it cannot be concluded that the application of capital-intensive methods developed in the multinationals' home country are "inappropriate" in a labor-abundant, capital-scarce economy.

What are the implications for public policy? The simplest answer, and one containing a lot of truth, is that it should not be an issue at all. There is no particular reason to believe that the multinational enterprise does not make a socially efficient choice between the fixed costs of developing a new labor-intensive technique and the lower unit costs that such a technique would offer. One exception occurs if it is believed that there are substantial learning externalities associated with the multinational firm, both within that industry and within the general economy. In this case, there may be different costs and benefits to the host country associated with alternative technologies that are not internalized in the multinationals' decision making. Another factor to consider in a rapidly developing economy is whether or not the inappropriate capital-intensive technologies today will continue to be inappropriate in ten years time.

## Summary and Conclusions

The purpose of this paper is to draw on the existing empirical and theoretical literature on multinationals in order to generate a common analytical framework for understanding the positive and normative consequences of direct foreign investment. Insofar as there are wide ranges in the degree to which an industry is dominated by multinational enterprises, the first question must inevitably be what sort of technological or other characteristics are important determinants of multinationality. The empirical literature strongly suggests that multinational firms are associated with the existence of knowledge-based assets. The services of these assets are easily provided across long distances, and they have a jointness or public goods aspect in that they can be provided to additional plants at no cost to existing plants. Knowledge-based assets give rise to multiplant economies of scale and support multinationals as equilibrium market structures.

Although there are many other aspects to multinationals (as evidenced by the volume of research on them), this paper has largely confined itself to the more modest task of drawing out the implications of the knowledge-based capital model for the economic structure and welfare of the host and home countries. The paper presented a model in which the multinational firm transfers the services of knowledge-based, firm-specific assets to a host country. The host country benefits from this since it does not have to make the costly investments necessary to develop that capital itself. The positive consequences of the model include a study of the trade orientation of the multinational firm and the dynamic effects due to knowledge accumulation in the host country. Normative analysis for the host country focuses on the trade-off between the technical advantages offered by the multinational enterprise and the greater degree of market power which is almost always associated with multinationals. Normative analysis for the home country focuses on the choice between serving a foreign market by exports or by a branch plant, possibly exporting back to the home country in the latter case (i.e., "exporting jobs"). Dynamic learning externalities are discussed although they are not incorporated into the formal model. Nevertheless, even these factors are not ad hoc considerations but follow directly from the notion of knowledge-based capital transferred by the multinational. Thus the basic model provides a common conceptual and analytical framework for dealing with a wide range of issues.

As noted in the introduction, four broad conclusions are suggested which are relevant to issues of structural change: (1) Multinationals are facilitating institutions which are able to exploit changes in exogenous variables so as to organize world production to optimally exploit comparative advantage; (2) The knowledge-based capital model suggests that multinationals are, by nature, major vehicles for transferring technical and managerial skills; (3) The public goods nature of knowledge-based capital implies spillovers and permanent structural change in host economies; and (4) Under plausible assumptions (competition among multinationals, lower marginal cost in host economies), multinational enterprises locate production in a socially efficient manner from the point of view of both host and home countries.

## Notes

1. Readers interested only in a nonanalytical summary may wish to skip the description of the model and jump directly to the policy analysis that follows.

2. A simple case is presented in Horstmann and Markusen (1989).

3. This view also receives empirical support from work by Peter Murrell (1990) which contrasts Eastern European economies with Western Economies with similar per capita income levels. Almost without exception, the former do not permit DFI by Western multinationals while the latter do. As a consequence, Murrell notes that the Eastern European countries are much less able to compete in high-tech sectors. Murrell attributes this to the fact that the knowledge-based capital used to produce in these sectors is easily transferred by multinational enterprises, but is prohibitively costly for small economies to develop for themselves.

4. A more formal discussion of the points that follow can be found in Horstmann and Markusen (1990).

## References

Beaudreau, Bernard. 1986. Managers, Learning and the Multinational Firm: Theory and Evidence. Ph.D. diss., University of Western Ontario.

Casson, Mark. 1979. *Alternatives to the Multinational Enterprise.* New York: Holmes and Meier Publishers.

————. 1986. *The Firm and the Market: Studies on Multinational Enterprise and the Scope of the Firm.* Oxford: Basil Blackwell.

Caves, Richard. 1982. *Multinational Enterprise and Economic Analysis.* Cambridge: Cambridge University Press.

Caves, Richard, and William Murphy II. 1976. Franchising: Firms, Markets, and Intangible Assets. *Southern Economic Journal* 42(4): 572–86.

Conklin, David, and France St. Hilaire. 1988. *Canada's Trade in High Technology: The Case of Information Technology.* Halifax: Institute for Research on Public Policy.

Davidson, W. H., and Donald McFetridge. 1984. International Technology Transactions and the Theory of the Firm. *Journal of Industrial Economics* 32(3): 253–64.

Dunning, John. 1977. Trade, Location of Economic Activity and the MNE: A Search for an Eclectic Approach. In *The International Allocation of Economic Activity*, edited by

Bertil Ohlin Hesselborn and Per Magnus Wijkman. New York: Holmes and Meier Publishers.

———. 1981. *International Production and the Multinational Enterprise*. London: Allen and Unwin.

Eastman, Harry, and Stefan Stykolt. 1967. *The Tariff and Competition in Canada*. Toronto: Macmillan.

Grubel, Herbert. 1974. Taxation and the Rates of Return from Some U.S. Asset Holdings Abroad, 1960–1969. *Journal of Political Economy* 82(3): 469–87.

———. 1977. *International Economics*. Homewood, Ill.: Irwin.

Helpman, Elhanan. 1984. A Simple Theory of International Trade with Multinational Corporations. *Journal of Political Economy* 92(3): 451–71.

Horstmann, Ignatius, and James R. Markusen. 1987. Strategic Investments and the Development of Multinationals. *International Economic Review* 28(1): 109–21.

———. 1989. Firm-Specific Assets and the Gains from Direct Foreign Investment. *Economica* 56(221): 41–48.

———. 1990. Endogenous Market Structures in International Trade. *Journal of International Economics*, forthcoming.

Kravis, Irving B., and Robert E. Lipsey. 1986. Production and Trade in Services by U.S. Multinational Firms. New York University Working Paper.

Mansfield, Edwin, and Anthony Romeo. 1980. Technology Transfer to Overseas Subsidiaries by U.S. Based Firms. *Quarterly Journal of Economics* 95(4): 737–50.

Mansfield, Edwin, Anthony Romeo, and Samuel Wagner. 1979. Foreign Trade and U.S. Research and Development. *Review of Economics and Statistics* 61(1): 49–57.

Markusen, James R. 1981. Multinationals, Multiplant Economies, and the Gains from Trade. *Journal of International Economics* 16(3/4): 205–26.

———. 1989. Service Trade by the Multinational Enterprise. In *Multinational Service Firms*, edited by Peter Enderwick. London: Routledge.

Markusen, James R., and James Melvin. 1984. *The Theory of International Trade and Its Canadian Applications*. Toronto: Butterworths.

Murrel, Peter. 1990. *The Nature of Socialist Economies: Lessons from Eastern Europe Foreign Trade*. Princeton: Princeton University Press.

Nicholas, Stephen. 1983. Agency Contracts, Institutional Modes, and the Transition to Foreign Direct Investment by British Manufacturing Multinationals Before 1939. *Journal of Economic History* 43(3): 675–86.

Naya, Seiji, and Eric Ramstetter. 1988. Direct Foreign Investment in Asia's Developing Economies and Trade in the Asia-Pacific Region. Paper presented at the Conference on Economic Cooperation Through Foreign Investment in the ESCAP Region, 20–23 September, Beijing, China.

Niosi, J. 1985. *Canadian Multinationals*. Toronto: Between the Lines.

Rugman, Alan M. 1981. *Inside the Multinationals: The Economics of Internal Markets*. New York: Columbia University Press.

———. 1985. Internationalization is Still a General Theory of Foreign Direct Investment. *Weltwirtschaftliches Archiv* 121(3): 570–75.

———. 1986. A Transaction Cost Approach to Trade in Services. School of Management, University of Toronto Working Paper.

Statistics Canada. 1986. *Canada's International Trade in Services—1969-1984*. Ottawa: Ministry of Supply and Services Canada.

Teece, David. 1976. *The Multinational Corporation and the Resource Cost of International Technology Transfer*. Cambridge, Mass.: Ballinger.

Wilson, Robert. 1977. The Effect of Technological Environment and Product Rivalry on R&D Effort and Licensing of Inventions. *Review of Economics and Statistics* 59(2): 171–78.

# PART TWO

# Inward Investment
# and Structural Change
# in Developing Economies

# 3

## Foreign Firms and Structural Change in the Indonesian Manufacturing Sector

*Mari Pangestu*

### Introduction

Direct foreign investment (DFI) has played a major role in Indonesia's industrialization since 1967 (the new-order period) under the Soeharto government. Indonesia has undergone the usual stages of industrialization moving from import substitution in final consumer goods to import substitution in intermediate and capital goods, and more recently to export-oriented expansion. Since oil is very important in the Indonesian economy, changes in oil prices have played a key role in stimulating these structural changes. Indeed the recent push towards exports was largely a response to the fall in oil prices.

The aim of this paper is to examine the role of DFI in structural changes occurring in the Indonesian manufacturing sector.[1] To this end, the paper focuses on evaluating DFI patterns as well as foreign firm production, employment, and export activities. However, before proceeding with the analyses, it is helpful to take a closer look at the structural changes Indonesia has gone through since 1967.

### Structural Change and Policies in Indonesia

It is helpful to divide recent Indonesian economic history into three periods: the stabilization period (1967–1972), the oil boom years (1973–1982), and the period of declining oil prices (1982–1989). At the end of the old-order period under Soekarno (pre-1967), Indonesia suffered from high rates of inflation, low levels of trade, foreign exchange reserves close to zero, a domestic manufacturing sector operating at an estimated 20–30 percent of capacity, and a badly damaged economic and physical infrastructure. At this time, the manufacturing sector was comprised of standard consumer goods such as textiles and a few agricultural processing industries such as rice milling. Moreover, economic policies were heavily interventionist.

In contrast, the new-order government extensively liberalized the economy in the stabilization period. Trade and industrial policies became less restrictive. As the main emphasis of policy was to provide basic needs (clothing and food), import substitution was promoted in consumption goods industries, with protection concentrated in the textiles and food processing industries. An open-door policy towards foreign investment was adopted for most industries and the 1967 Foreign Investment Law sought to encourage private investment in priority sectors by offering tax holidays, exemptions on import duties and sales taxes for imports of machinery and equipment, accelerated depreciation, guaranteed repatriation of capital and profits, and provisions for carrying forward losses. Foreign banks were allowed to open branches in Indonesia (although this industry was subsequently closed to DFI in 1969). Initially there were no restrictions on foreign equity and employment of expatriates, and 100 percent foreign ownership was allowed. The only restriction foreign investors faced was that they were not allowed to distribute their own products in the domestic market.

In the oil boom period, the increase in oil prices provided Indonesia with a large source of funds; indeed oil dominated the economy and accounted for 60 percent of government revenues and 70 percent of total exports. Policy emphasis shifted toward import substitution in raw materials processing, intermediate goods, and finally capital goods. Anticipation of higher oil revenues after the second oil boom led to a further focus on industrial diversification and creation of backward linkages. Social objectives such as employment creation, achieving an equitable distribution of income, and increasing participation of the weak sector[2] also became increasingly important. In 1978 there was a devaluation to reverse the deterioration in the price of tradeables relative to nontradeables which resulted from government spending of oil revenues or the so-called Dutch disease effect. However, while relief was temporarily afforded, the devaluation did not increase nonoil exports significantly because of continued high inflation and the second oil boom which followed soon after the devaluation.[3] Furthermore the devaluation was not accompanied by deregulatory measures that were sufficient to reduce the anti-export bias which resulted from high levels of effective protection that varied widely across sectors. On the other hand, the export duty drawback scheme that was introduced in 1978[4] worked as an export subsidy, and the phasing out of log exports in 1980–1986 stimulated exports of processed wood products.

During the oil boom period, foreign investment regulations became more restrictive: (1) Indonesian equity shares had to be increased to 51 percent within a ten-year period; (2) the list of "closed sectors" was extended; (3) tax incentives were reduced; and (4) there were increased restrictions on employment of expatriates. On the other hand, there were some improvements in administrative procedures, including the publication of the investment priority list and the establishment of a "one-stop" service center at the Board of Investment.[5] The increased restrictiveness was highly related to to the violent anti-Japanese riots that accompanied the visit of Prime Minister Tanaka in 1974.[6]

Since 1982 declining oil prices have resulted in drastically reduced export and government revenues while the appreciation of non-U.S. dollar currencies (especially the yen) since 1985 has increased debt service payments markedly. The pressures resulting from these changes have contributed to major changes in economic policies and economic structure in Indonesia. The government's first reaction to the economic crisis that was brought about by the fall in oil prices was to cut government expenditure, raise nonoil government revenues, and implement a restrictive monetary policy with growth declining as a result. However these moves represented more than simple demand management as the tax system was overhauled in 1984[7] and the banking sector was deregulated to some extent in 1983. The rupiah was also devalued in 1983 in order to increase the revenues from oil in rupiah terms as well as to increase nonoil exports. As in 1978, nonoil exports did not increase significantly; this was due to the subsequent inflation and the lack of complementary trade and industrial reforms. However another 45 percent devaluation in September 1986 was followed by a large increase in nonoil exports as inflation was controlled and the trade, industrial, transportation, and financial sectors were markedly deregulated following the devaluation. For example, many nontariff import barriers were replaced by tariffs and several investment barriers, such as complicated licensing requirements, were reduced or removed. These and other related reforms have greatly increased competitive pressures in Indonesian manufacturing.

On the DFI side, one-stop service was extended to the regional boards of investment in 1984 and investment licensing procedures were simplified in 1985. Tariff reforms and a drastic overhaul of the customs system were undertaken in 1985 and an improved duty drawback scheme for foreign investors was announced in May 1986.[8] Further deregulation came in December 1987 when joint ventures were allowed to export their own products as well as products of other companies. In addition, the export-production ratio that was required of export-oriented investors was reduced from 85 percent to 65 percent. In October 1988, the entry of more foreign banks in the form of joint ventures with a maximum foreign ownership share of 85 percent was allowed.[9] In November 1988, foreign investors were allowed to engage in domestic distribution of their products through joint ventures. In May 1989, a relatively simple list of sectors closed to foreign investment replaced the previous priority list which had become quite complex and restrictive.

Table 3.1 shows that Indonesia's economic growth has been quite respectable for most of the new-order period with real GDP growing 13 percent annually in 1971–1973, 7 percent annually in 1973–1980, and 4 percent annually in 1980–1987. In response to the movements in energy prices, the combined share of oil-related sectors (i.e., mining and quarrying, refinery oil, and liquified natural gas [LNG]) in real GNP increased from 24 percent in 1971 to 30 percent in 1973 before declining to 27 percent in 1980, 22 percent in 1985, and 21 percent in 1987. On the other hand, the share of nonoil-related manufacturing has steadily increased from 5 percent in 1973 to 8 percent in 1980 and 9 percent in 1985–1987. Thus nonoil manufacturing remains a very small portion of real GDP in Indonesia, though its share of GDP has grown rapidly in the last decade.[10]

Looking at exports in the 1980s (Table 3.2), the growth of manufacturing (in nominal terms) is even more significant. Manufacturing's share of total exports was only 2 percent in 1980 but increased to 11 percent in 1985 and 30 percent by 1988. In contrast, the share of oil, gas, and minerals declined from 76 percent in 1980 to 73 percent in 1985 and 46 percent in 1988, while agriculture's share remained relatively constant. On the strength of the rapid growth of plywood exports, resource-intensive exports came to account for the largest share of manufactured exports by 1985–1988 (41–49 percent). This group is followed by labor-intensive manufactures (34–40 percent shares) of which the major items are garments and woven cloth.

Table 3.1 Structural Change in Indonesia's Real Gross Domestic Product, 1971-1987

| Industry | 1971 | 1973 | 1980 | 1985 | 1986 | 1987 |
|---|---|---|---|---|---|---|
| Real GDP (billions of 1983 rupiah) | 33,300 | 42,189 | 66,675 | 80,119 | 83,318 | 86,307 |
| **Shares of real GDP (%)** | | | | | | |
| Agriculture | 34 | 30 | 25 | 24 | 24 | 23 |
| Mining and quarrying | 24 | 30 | 24 | 17 | 18 | 16 |
| Manufacturing | 6 | 5 | 11 | 13 | 13 | 14 |
| Refinery oil | na | 0 | 0 | 1 | 1 | 1 |
| LNG | 0 | 0 | 3 | 4 | 4 | 4 |
| Other manufacturing | na | 5 | 8 | 9 | 9 | 9 |
| Services | 36 | 35 | 40 | 50 | 48 | 46 |
| Electricity, gas and water | 0 | 0 | 0 | 1 | 1 | 1 |
| Construction | 3 | 4 | 6 | 6 | 6 | 6 |
| Transport and communications | 3 | 3 | 4 | 6 | 6 | 6 |
| Public admin. and defense | 5 | 5 | 6 | 8 | 8 | 9 |
| Other services | 24 | 23 | 24 | 25 | 25 | 26 |

na = Not available.

Source: Biro Pusat Statistik (various years b).

Table 3.2  Structural Change in Indonesia's Merchandise Exports, 1980-1988 (percentage)

| Industry[a] | 1980 | 1985 | 1986 | 1987 | 1988 |
|---|---|---|---|---|---|
| Total exports | 23,950 | 18,587 | 14,805 | 17,136 | 19,219 |
| Agriculture | 22.0 | 16.0 | 21.0 | 21.0 | 24.0 |
| Oil, gas, and mineral | 76.0 | 73.0 | 61.0 | 55.0 | 46.0 |
| Manufacturing | 2.0 | 11.0 | 18.0 | 24.0 | 30.0 |
| Share of manufacturing exports | | | | | |
| Resource-intensive | 23.7 | 48.6 | 46.0 | 52.3 | 44.6 |
| Plywood | 13.5 | 46.1 | 42.9 | 48.8 | 40.9 |
| Cement | 5.2 | 1.1 | 1.6 | 1.5 | 1.4 |
| Leather | 1.2 | 0.4 | 0.6 | 1.2 | 1.2 |
| Other resource-intensive | 3.8 | 1.0 | 1.0 | 0.8 | 1.1 |
| Labor-intensive | 57.1 | 38.4 | 40.1 | 33.5 | 38.6 |
| Garments | 19.5 | 16.6 | 19.9 | 15.3 | 14.4 |
| Woven cloth | 8.5 | 11.1 | 10.9 | 9.9 | 10.3 |
| Yarn | 0.6 | 0.6 | 0.8 | 2.2 | 2.0 |
| Oils and perfumes | 0.6 | 1.1 | 1.0 | 0.9 | 0.6 |
| Glass products | 0.6 | 0.4 | 0.5 | 0.8 | 1.7 |
| Electronics | 18.7 | 3.8 | 1.1 | 0.4 | 0.7 |
| Furniture | 0.6 | 0.3 | 0.3 | 0.7 | 1.3 |
| Footwear | 0.2 | 0.4 | 0.3 | 0.6 | 1.5 |
| Other labor-intensive | 7.8 | 4.1 | 5.3 | 2.8 | 6.0 |
| Capital-intensive | 19.3 | 13.0 | 14.4 | 14.3 | 16.8 |
| Rubber tires | na | 0.3 | 0.4 | 0.6 | 0.8 |
| Fertilizers | 7.0 | 3.9 | 4.8 | 2.2 | 2.4 |
| Inorganic chemicals | na | 1.7 | 1.0 | 0.6 | 0.6 |
| Paper and products | 1.0 | 1.0 | 1.3 | 2.5 | 2.3 |
| Steel products | 1.6 | 1.4 | 2.2 | 3.5 | 4.9 |
| Other capital-intensive | na | 4.7 | 4.6 | 4.9 | 5.8 |

na = Not available.

[a]Following Hill (1990a), exports are classified by SITC section as follows:  agriculture = 0+1+2-27-28+4; oil, gas, and minerals = 27+28+3+68; manufacturing = 5+6-68+7 +8+9; resource-intensive = 61+63+66-664-665-666+671; plywood = 634; cement = 661; leather = 611; labor-intensive = 54+55+65+664+665+666+695+696+697+749 +776+778+793+81+82+83+84+85+89-896-897; garments=84; woven cloth=65-651; yarn = 651; oils and perfumes = 551; glass and products = 664+665; electronics = 749+776+778; furniture = 821; footwear = 851; capital-intensive = 5-54-55+62+64 +67-671+69-695-696-697+7-749-776-778-793+86+87+88+896+897; rubber tires = 625; fertilizers = 562; inorganic chemicals = 522; paper and products = 641; steel products = 672+673.

Source:  Biro Pusat Statistik (various years a).

Table 3.3 Debt Service Ratios, Capital Flows, and Net Board of Investment Approvals in Indonesia, 1967-1988 (annual averages, US$ millions except as noted)

| Period | Debt Service Ratio[b] (percent) | Balance of Payments | | | Net Nonoil Investment Approvals[a] | | | |
|---|---|---|---|---|---|---|---|---|
| | | Current Account Balance | Total Long-term Capital[c] | Direct Investment | Total[a] | | Manufacturing | |
| | | | | | Foreign | Domestic | Foreign | Domestic |
| 1967-1972 | na | -305 | 318 | 75 | 388 | 348 | 127 | 209 |
| 1973-1981 | na | -9 | 1,417 | 205 | 925 | 1,377 | 713 | 825 |
| 1982-1988 | na | -3,234 | 3,222 | 328 | 1,873 | 4,668 | 1,520 | 2,484 |
| 1967 | na | -254 | 247 | -10 | 125 | 0 | 28 | 0 |
| 1968 | na | -225 | 229 | -2 | 230 | 13 | 50 | 13 |
| 1969 | na | -336 | 267 | 32 | 682 | 101 | 75 | 58 |
| 1970 | na | -310 | 290 | 83 | 345 | 319 | 143 | 234 |
| 1971 | na | -372 | 377 | 139 | 426 | 939 | 249 | 483 |
| 1972 | na | -334 | 500 | 207 | 522 | 718 | 216 | 463 |
| 1973 | 6.3 | -476 | 520 | 15 | 655 | 1,465 | 472 | 829 |
| 1974 | 3.9 | 598 | 492 | -49 | 1,417 | 554 | 1,069 | 410 |
| 1975 | 7.5 | -1,109 | 1,043 | 476 | 1,757 | 593 | 1,160 | 470 |

| | | | | | | | | |
|---|---|---|---|---|---|---|---|---|
| 1976 | 8.7 | -907 | 1,982 | 344 | 449 | 672 | 348 | 431 |
| 1977 | 11.5 | -51 | 1,491 | 235 | 328 | 1,386 | 327 | 945 |
| 1978 | 18.2 | -1,413 | 1,596 | 279 | 397 | 1,715 | 275 | 1,181 |
| 1979 | 13.5 | 980 | 1,320 | 226 | 1,320 | 1,242 | 1,158 | 931 |
| 1980 | 13.9 | 2,864 | 2,156 | 183 | 914 | 2,086 | 773 | 1,743 |
| 1981 | 14.1 | -566 | 2,151 | 133 | 1,092 | 2,676 | 835 | 484 |
| 1982 | 18.2 | -5,324 | 5,096 | 225 | 1,800 | 2,949 | 1,120 | 2,147 |
| 1983 | 20.2 | -6,338 | 5,323 | 292 | 2,882 | 7,707 | 2,615 | 4,172 |
| 1984 | 21.4 | -1,856 | 2,981 | 222 | 1,121 | 1,873 | 1,002 | 1,277 |
| 1985 | 29.6 | -1,923 | 1,880 | 310 | 859 | 2,833 | 687 | 1,124 |
| 1986 | 35.7 | -3,911 | 2,882 | 258 | 826 | 3,261 | 537 | 1,331 |
| 1987 | 37.8 | -2,098 | 2,510 | 446 | 1,457 | 6,241 | 852 | 3,355 |
| 1988 | 43.7 | -1,189 | 1,883 | 542 | 4,166 | 7,813 | 3,828 | 3,985 |

na = Not available.

[a]Refers to new investments, expansions, mergers, and withdrawals; also excludes banking and insurance.

[b]Ratio of total debt service to total exports of goods and services.

[c]Includes direct investment, portfolio investment, and other long-term capital.

<u>Sources:</u> Board of Investment (various years); International Monetary Fund (1989); World Bank (various years).

Capital-intensive exports account for much lower shares of manufactured exports but paper and steel export shares have grown rapidly in recent years.

One last item that should be highlighted here is the movement of the debt service ratio (Table 3.3). Through the mid-1970s the debt service ratio was below 10 percent due to conservative borrowing practices; however this ratio shot up to 18 percent in 1978 largely as a result of the Pertamina crisis.[11] However through 1982 the ratio remained below 20 percent and it was not until 1986 (after the currency realignment and the plunge of oil prices) that the ratio broke 30 percent. The ratio subsequently increased to 44 percent in 1988 and the burden imposed by the need to repay foreign debts was one of the major reasons for the large economic reforms in recent years. However, despite the rise of the debt service ratio, the diversification of the Indonesian economy, as evidenced by a reduced reliance on primary products and the increased nonoil export capacity, leads one to believe that the debt problems will be manageable.

## Patterns of Direct Foreign Investment

It is difficult to find consistent, reliable, and comparable data on DFI in Indonesia (e.g., Hill 1988, Ch. 3). In this paper, three major data sets are used: (1) International Monetary Fund (IMF) figures on aggregate direct investment flows which are on a balance-of-payments basis; (2) Board of Investment data on DFI approvals, excluding oil and finance; and (3) Bank Indonesia data on planned and actual investments, excluding oil and finance. In using these data, there are several problems to take note of. First, the Board of Investment data include domestic equity contributions as well as foreign contributions and thereby inflate the figures. Second, the data all exclude large amounts of DFI in oil and finance.[12] Third, a large portion of the DFI entering through Overseas Chinese channels never gets reported as DFI but rather as domestic investment.

The IMF figures (Table 3.3) show that there has been a significant increase in long-term capital inflows. From an annual average of US$318 million in 1967–1972, long-term capital inflows increased to US$1,417 million in 1973–1981 and US$3,222 million in 1982–1988. In contrast, the current account deficit declined from US$305 million in 1967–1972 to only US$9 million in 1973–1981 before growing to US$3,234 million in 1982–1988. In short, before the period of the oil price decrease, long-term capital flows exceeded the total inflow on the capital and reserve accounts. Before 1972, DFI accounted for an average of 24 percent of all long-term capital inflows but this ratio fell to 14 percent in 1973–1981 and 10 percent in 1982–1988. Thus DFI has never been the major source of long-term foreign capital for Indonesia; rather foreign borrowing, mainly by the government, has been the main source. Of course there have been fluctuations in the share and the absolute level of DFI over time. DFI flows were notably high in 1970–1972 after the open-door policy took hold and in 1975–1976 due to large investments such as the Asahan Aluminum Project with the Japanese. There have also been high levels of DFI in 1987–1988 partially in response to the improved investment climate.

The Board of Investment data on net foreign investment approvals (Table 3.3) generally show a much higher level of investment, partly because the data include both domestic and foreign equity contributions. Another important reason is that many approved investments are never realized. However, the time trends exhibited from the approval data are similar to the trends in the balance-of-payments data. There does appear to be a lag between approval and realization of investment with large increases occuring slightly later in the balance-of-payments data. The decline in DFI in the late 1970s is related to the increasingly restrictive policies that were imposed in the oil boom period and the end of the easy phase of import substitution in final consumer goods. Restrictive government policies after the Pertamina crisis in 1976 also affected domestic demand growth during this period. Moreover the combination of high input costs resulting from protection and high administrative costs (due to regulation and abuses of the system) made export-oriented investments unattractive. Another factor in the declining investor interest during this period was the caution displayed by local Chinese businesses in the wake of increased emphasis on *pribumi* and indigenous participation in the post-1974 regulations. Indeed, Chinese businesses were also a target of the anti-Japanese riots of 1974 as they were often the joint venture partners of Japanese companies.

The gradual increase in approvals after 1978 was in part a lagged response to the improvements in the administration of investment applications in 1977. There were also new opportunities for import substitution in intermediate goods, raw material processing, and capital goods as the government employed several protectionist measures to encourage the creation of backward integration. The effects of the second oil boom also boosted domestic demand growth and there was a rush of DFI in 1983 to obtain approval under the old taxation regulations as most of the tax incentives for foreign investors were eliminated in the 1984 tax reforms.

In 1985 and 1986, investment approvals declined again as a result of a recession in Indonesia as well as in the world economy. These were transition years in which elements of the restructuring strategy were in place, but there was still a lack of clear direction. Furthermore there was speculation that a devaluation would be inevitable given the rapid decline in oil prices. Investment approvals, both foreign and domestic, picked up considerably after the devaluation in September 1986 as the government gave strong indications that it was serious about restructuring and reform, especially the promotion of exports.

From Table 3.4 it can be seen that Japan has been the largest single source of DFI accounting for 28 percent of net approvals and 41 percent of realized DFI through 1988. Japan has invested heavily in the Asahan Aluminum Project, textiles, nonmetallic minerals (mainly glass and cement), and metals. Asia's newly industrializing countries (NICs: Hong Kong, Korea, Singapore, and Taiwan), led by investments from Hong Kong in food, wood, and paper, also account for 10 percent of realized DFI (sectoral information from the sources of Table 3.4). Moreover gross DFI approvals from the NICs exceeded those from Japan as early as 1980–1984, and in 1985–1988 approvals from the NICs far outstripped approvals from Japan. Thus, although the realization rate for approvals from the NICs is relatively low, the NICs have become a major source of DFI for Indonesia and are likely to remain so in the future. The United States' share of realized DFI was only 3 percent and the other category accounted for a large 43 percent of all investment.[13] The other category includes European investments but primarily consists of investments not classified by country.

Table 3.4 Sources of Nonoil Foreign Investment[a] in Indonesia, 1967-1988 (US$ millions)

| Region/country | Gross Investment Approvals[b] | | | Net Investment Approvals[c], 1967-1988 | Planned Investment, 1967-1988 | | | Realized Investment, 1967-1988 | |
|---|---|---|---|---|---|---|---|---|---|
| | 1970-1979 | 1980-1984 | 1985-1988 | | Domestic Equity | Foreign Equity | Foreign Equity & Loans | Foreign Equity | Foreign Equity & Loans |
| Total | 8,321 | 7,346 | 7,563 | 21,512 | 2,487 | 4,679 | 20,468 | 2,050 | 6,687 |
| Japan | 3,540 | 1,471 | 1,239 | 6,020 | 857 | 1,296 | 5,393 | 615 | 2,762 |
| Asian NIEs | 1,203 | 1,515 | 2,050 | 4,612 | 364 | 548 | 3,026 | 230 | 700 |
| Hong Kong | 923 | 1,286 | 456 | 2,316 | 215 | 365 | 1,485 | 180 | 579 |
| Korea | 75 | 72 | 299 | 466 | 45 | 69 | 346 | 28 | 81 |
| Singapore | 102 | 122 | 356 | 753 | 53 | 69 | 902 | 12 | 19 |
| Taiwan | 104 | 35 | 938 | 1,077 | 52 | 45 | 293 | 10 | 22 |
| Other ASEAN | 76 | 16 | 36 | 105 | 15 | 34 | 80 | 10 | 17 |
| Malaysia | 42 | 1 | 24 | 46 | 7 | 16 | 43 | 5 | 12 |
| Philippines | 28 | 10 | 8 | 13 | 3 | 6 | 9 | 2 | 2 |
| Thailand | 6 | 5 | 4 | 46 | 5 | 12 | 28 | 4 | 4 |
| United States | 316 | 890 | 1,056 | 1,910 | 320 | 400 | 1,880 | 88 | 215 |
| Australia | 186 | 36 | 102 | 459 | 43 | 177 | 1,939 | 31 | 134 |
| Other | 3,001 | 3,418 | 3,080 | 8,406 | 887 | 2,224 | 1,712 | 1,076 | 2,858 |

[a]Excludes banking and insurance.
[b]Refers to new investments and expansion.
[c]Refers to new investments, expansions, mergers, and withdrawals.

Sources: Bank Indonesia (various years); Board of Investment (various years).

The data show that loans are the major source of DFI finance, accounting for almost 70 percent of planned investment. About 20 percent of the total planned investment is financed with foreign equity with the remaining 10 percent financed with domestic equity. A similar pattern emerges in data on realized foreign investments (the domestic equity portion is unavailable). Although these debt equity ratios are not high by international standards, Japanese investments have a much higher debt equity ratio compared with other countries. Among the NICs, Korea and Hong Kong also have relatively high debt equity ratios. In contrast, American investments display a lower debt equity ratio. Part of the reason for the high debt equity ratio of Japanese investments is the high leveraging involved in the Asahan project.

Most of the foreign investment that is outside of the oil and financial sectors is undertaken in the manufacturing sector (Table 3.5). This sector attracted 75 percent of net approvals and 65 percent of realized DFI in nonoil, nonfinance sectors. Within manufacturing, the main recipients of DFI are basic metals (much of it in the Asahan Project), chemicals, and textiles; these three industries alone account for 72 percent of all realized manufacturing DFI. The top five industries (the top three plus nonmetallic minerals and metal products and machinery) account for 93 percent of all realized manufacturing DFI. From the gross approval data, it can be seen that investments in textiles and basic metals have decreased over time while those in chemicals rose. Approved DFI in paper products has also risen dramatically in recent years.

The changing pattern of DFI reflects the changes in policies outlined above. In 1970–1979, relatively large shares of DFI were observed in consumer goods such as textiles, leather, and food products. Large investments in intermediate products such as basic metals also began in this period. In 1980–1984, foreign investments followed the next phase of import substitution into intermediate products as well as the increased processing of raw materials in industries such as metal products, paper products, and chemical and rubber products. In 1985–1988, there appears to have been a continued increase in investments in intermediate and resource-based products such as chemical and rubber, paper and paper products, and metal products. Note that several major projects in the petrochemical field were also undertaken in 1985–1988.

## Explaining the Patterns of Direct Foreign Investment

In past work (e.g., Pangestu 1987) I have used investment intensity indexes to identify the factors that can explain the pattern of bilateral foreign investment flows. The intensity index measures the extent to which the host country, Indonesia, is a relatively more important recipient of investment from the investor's viewpoint compared with investment flows from the source country to the control group, i.e., the less developing countries. Two broad sets of determinants that affect the intensity of bilateral investment flows can be hypothesized. First, factors such as relative factor endowments (including firm-specific advantages) and government policies that contribute to complementarity in the industry structure of direct investment determine the "expected" flow of investment and are summarized in a complementarity index. Second, country-bias factors such as geographical proximity and historical and

Table 3.5   Nonoil Foreign Investment in Indonesia by Industry[a], 1967-1988 (period totals, US$ millions)

| Industry | Gross Investment Approvals[b] | | | Net Investment Approvals[c] 1967-1988 | Planned Investment, 1967-1988 | | | Realized Investment, 1967-1988 | |
|---|---|---|---|---|---|---|---|---|---|
| | 1970-1979 | 1980-1984 | 1985-1988 | | Domestic Equity | Foreign Equity | Foreign Equity & Loans | Foreign Equity | Foreign Equity & Loans |
| All industries | 8,336 | 7,344 | 7,563 | 21,512 | 2,487 | 4,679 | 22,955 | 2,050 | 6,687 |
| Agriculture | 87 | 91 | 259 | 527 | 67 | 111 | 406 | 59 | 81 |
| Fisheries | 354 | 138 | 27 | 168 | 36 | 77 | 302 | 13 | 34 |
| Forestry | 113 | 48 | 197 | 386 | 111 | 152 | 1,003 | 54 | 144 |
| Mining | 1,505 | 43 | 0 | 1,821 | 32 | 855 | 4,126 | 662 | 1,567 |
| Manufacturing | 5,594 | 6,328 | 5,778 | 16,098 | 1,902 | 3,043 | 14,543 | 1,117 | 4,287 |
| Food | 276 | 220 | 204 | 911 | 84 | 184 | 601 | 67 | 167 |
| Textiles, garments, etc. | 1,197 | 253 | 349 | 1,409 | 131 | 371 | 1,450 | 186 | 618 |
| Wood and products | 47 | 153 | 169 | 451 | 37 | 44 | 280 | 23 | 57 |
| Paper and products | 122 | 773 | 1,688 | 2,161 | 105 | 106 | 690 | 34 | 52 |
| Chemicals and rubber | 772 | 1,109 | 2,390 | 3,871 | 419 | 827 | 3,808 | 230 | 648 |
| Pharmaceuticals | na | na | na | 286 | 0 | 0 | 0 | 0 | 0 |
| Other chemicals | na | na | na | 3,584 | 419 | 827 | 3,808 | 230 | 648 |
| Nonmetallic minerals | 621 | 349 | 284 | 1,249 | 126 | 149 | 1,035 | 110 | 511 |
| Basic metals | 2,070 | 1,533 | 174 | 3,362 | 603 | 802 | 4,135 | 316 | 1,839 |
| Metal prod. & machinery | 475 | 1,927 | 509 | 2,654 | 388 | 552 | 2,515 | 149 | 391 |
| Miscellaneous | 15 | 10 | 12 | 32 | 8 | 9 | 27 | 3 | 6 |
| Services | 683 | 696 | 1,302 | 2,513 | 338 | 441 | 2,575 | 145 | 575 |

[a]Excludes banking and insurance.
[b]Refers to new investments and expansion.
[c]Refers to new investments, expansions, mergers, and withdrawals.

Sources:  Bank Indonesia (various years); Board of Investment (various years).

institutional ties enhance or decrease the attractiveness of the host country as a location for the investment and can explain deviations of the intensity indexes from the complementarity indexes.

Complementarity between Indonesia and Japan in the primary sector (agriculture, forestry, fishery, and mining and petroleum) is due to the relative resource scarcity in Japan combined with strong Japanese government support for investment in this sector. Japanese investment abroad in raw material processing operations such as pulp, petrochemicals, nonferrous smelting, and steel has increased as a result of the high costs of installing antipollution devices in Japan. In addition, Indonesia (and other host countries) tightened measures to promote on-site processing of raw materials, and the import of bulky raw materials became inefficient relative to processing in Indonesia. Processed raw materials (for example, Asahan aluminium smelting, nickel matte manufactures, and wood products) are mostly exported back to Japan. The Japanese government supported investments in natural resources by assuming many of the financial risks involved in natural resource projects and more importantly by encouraging group investments by a number of Japanese firms to defray costs and minimize risks (Tsurumi 1976, 46–52). The Asahan Project with Sumitomo as the leader is one example.

For all source countries, complementarity in domestic market-oriented manufacturing investments generally arises from multinational firm-specific advantages combined with the inability to gain access to the Indonesian market through trade. Allen (1979) indicated that the motive of 51 percent of foreign investment in Indonesia was to secure, maintain, or develop an overseas market. As expected, securing, maintaining, and developing raw material supplies were also important motives given Indonesia's resource endowments; these motives accounted for 46 percent of investment. On the other hand, the product cycle model predicts that export-oriented investments will be undertaken to maintain the firm's competitive position by relocating production to lower-cost (mainly lower labor cost) bases with production being exported back to the home country or to third countries. Yet, in Allen's survey only 3 percent of investments were motivated by a low-cost labor base. Indeed this type of investment has only begun in the last two years in Indonesia and has been spurred by increasing costs and currency appreciation in Japan and the NICs combined with an improvement in Indonesia's investment climate.

U.S. DFI in manufacturing has been limited but strong technological advantages and marketing considerations has led several U.S. firms to establish themselves in capital-intensive and oligopolistic industries such as chemicals, machinery, transport equipment, and basic metals since the 1970s. However the United States has not been an important investor in manufacturing overall because Indonesia has not been a major recipient of investments which seek to utilize low-cost labor such as those in electronics. Two major U.S. electronic companies did enter Indonesia in the mid-1980s, Fairchild and National Semiconductor, and some exports of electronics did begin to take place. However due to the slump in world demand for components, low labor productivity in Indonesia, and ownership restrictions, the two companies closed down operations in 1985.

As for country biases, Japan's political, economic, and strategic interests in the region and its proximity to Indonesia enhance direct investment in a number of ways. Proximity eases coordination, communication, transportation, and the flow of information between subsidiaries and parents. In the Japanese case, bilateral aid has also facilitated investment flows. Anti-Japanese feelings in the mid-1970s did affect DFI but have since become unimportant. On the other hand, American interests in the region have mainly stemmed from strategic considerations related to Indochina. Bilateral aid flows from the United States are relatively low compared with U.S. flows to other regions and increasing restrictions on foreign ownership may have had an adverse effect on U.S. firms which prefer majority ownership to maintain control over their specialized technology. In this case, the lack of proximity is also a negative influence. Finally, although no formal analysis has been done, NIC investors appear to enjoy many of the same advantages stemming from proximity as do the Japanese.

## The Role of Foreign Firms
## in Manufacturing Production and Employment

As has been pointed out by many other studies in this and other volumes, the provision of capital through DFI is probably much less important than the supply of management skills, technology, market access, and access to finance. Although manufacturing is still a relatively small part of the Indonesian economy, it is clear that Indonesia views industrialization as an important aspect of overall economic development and that promotion of DFI has been an important part of the country's efforts to promote industrialization. Moreover there appears to be a clear correlation between levels and patterns of DFI and the policies employed.

Nonetheless, the role of foreign firms in Indonesian manufacturing has not been that large and over the 1974–1985 period this role has declined (Table 3.6). For example, if wholly foreign firms and all two-party foreign joint ventures (foreign-private, foreign-public) are combined, they accounted for only 11 percent of manufacturing employment in 1974 and 9 percent in 1985. Corresponding shares of value added were higher, 26 percent in 1974 and 19 percent in 1985. In 1985, three-party foreign joint ventures (foreign-public-private) also accounted for 15 percent of employment and 25 percent of value added. Yet private domestic firms form by far the largest single group of firms in Indonesian manufacturing followed by public firms (1974) or foreign-private-public joint ventures (1985). The large share of public-related firms reflects the control of strategic industries such as steel and cement by state enterprises.

These data also indicate that public-related and foreign firms tend to be much larger than private firms both in terms of value added and employment per firm. Another important characteristic is the relatively high level of average labor productivity in foreign firms. In 1974, indexes of value added per employee were 4 times the average for wholly foreign firms, 3 times the average in foreign-public firms, and almost 2 times the average in foreign-private firms. By 1985 labor productivity was actually below the average in wholly foreign firms but well above the average in all foreign-related joint ventures. If production is viewed as a function of labor and one nonlabor factor (call it capital for simplicity), the average product of labor can be decomposed into the product of the average product of capital and the capital-labor ratio. Thus, higher levels of labor productivity could reflect either greater capital intensity and/or greater efficiency of capital.

Table 3.6 Indicators of Industrial Firms in Indonesia by Ownership Category[a], 1974 and 1985

| Year/Firm Type | Firms (number & percent) | Employment (number & percent) | Value Added (in billions of rupiah & percent) | Employment per Firm (index) | Value Added per Firm (index) | Value Added per Employee (index) |
|---|---|---|---|---|---|---|
| All firms: 1974 | 7,091 | 655,824 | 478,446 | 100 | 100 | 100 |
| Wholly public | 6.8 | 19.3 | 25.9 | 285 | 398 | 129 |
| Wholly private | 87.9 | 68.9 | 47.2 | 78 | 54 | 68 |
| Wholly foreign | 1.4 | 2.6 | 10.8 | 181 | 756 | 418 |
| Public-private | 1.2 | 1.3 | 1.5 | 106 | 88 | 123 |
| Foreign-public | 0.2 | 0.7 | 2.2 | 346 | 1091 | 315 |
| Foreign-private | 2.5 | 7.3 | 13.3 | 292 | 534 | 183 |
| All firms: 1985 | 12,909 | 1,684,726 | 7,153,837 | 100 | 100 | 100 |
| Wholly public | 0.9 | 1.0 | 0.4 | 101 | 40 | 40 |
| Wholly private | 92.2 | 74.9 | 55.8 | 81 | 60 | 75 |
| Wholly foreign | 0.4 | 1.3 | 1.3 | 339 | 328 | 97 |
| Public-private | 0.6 | 0.4 | 0.4 | 61 | 64 | 105 |
| Foreign-public | 0.1 | 0.2 | 0.5 | 342 | 833 | 244 |
| Foreign-private | 2.7 | 7.4 | 17.1 | 279 | 641 | 230 |
| Foreign-public-private[b] | 3.1 | 14.9 | 24.7 | 480 | 794 | 165 |

[a]Includes firms employing 20 or more workers and exclude oil and gas processing.
[b]Foreign-public-private joint ventures are not identified in 1974; apparently these joint ventures were included in the wholly owned public category.

Source: Biro Pusat Statistik (various years c).

Table 3.7 Nonoil Manufacturing Value Added in Indonesia by Ownership Category[a], 1975 and 1985 (percentage shares of value added in each industry)

| ISIC Code, Industry | 1975 | | | | 1985 | | | |
|---|---|---|---|---|---|---|---|---|
| | Public[b] | Private[c] | Foreign[d] | Foreign-public Joint Venture[e] | Public[b] | Private[c] | Foreign[d] | Foreign-public Joint Venture[e] |
| Nonoil manufacturing | 26 | 51 | 21 | 2 | 1 | 58 | 17 | 24 |
| Food products (ISIC 311) | 64 | 28 | 8 | 0 | 2 | 61 | 7 | 30 |
| Food products (ISIC 312) | 8 | 71 | 10 | 11 | 1 | 69 | 18 | 11 |
| Beverages | ~ | 63 | 7 | 30 | 0 | 35 | 36 | 29 |
| Tobacco | 1 | 69 | 30 | 1 | ~ | 94 | 5 | 0 |
| Textiles | 14 | 66 | 18 | 2 | 1 | 61 | 29 | 10 |
| Garments | ~ | 100 | ~ | 0 | 0 | 98 | 1 | 1 |
| Leather products | 7 | 91 | 2 | 0 | 1 | 76 | 20 | 3 |
| Footwear | 0 | 15 | 85 | 0 | 0 | 59 | 41 | 0 |
| Wood products | 6 | 69 | 26 | 0 | 1 | 74 | 12 | 14 |
| Furniture | 6 | 91 | 2 | 0 | ~ | 98 | 2 | 0 |
| Paper products | 37 | 38 | 25 | 0 | 0 | 57 | 11 | 31 |
| Printing and publishing | 37 | 52 | 5 | 7 | 5 | 89 | 0 | 6 |
| Basic chemicals | 93 | 5 | 2 | 1 | 0 | 14 | 9 | 76 |
| Other chemicals | 4 | 45 | 50 | 0 | 0 | 59 | 29 | 12 |
| Rubber products | 34 | 15 | 51 | 0 | 2 | 83 | 7 | 8 |
| Plastic products | ~ | 86 | 14 | 0 | ~ | 43 | 57 | 0 |
| Pottery and china | 23 | 7 | 71 | 0 | 1 | 96 | 3 | 0 |
| Glass products | 22 | 44 | 35 | 0 | 0 | 15 | 81 | 4 |

| | | | | | | | | |
|---|---|---|---|---|---|---|---|---|
| Cement | 74 | 14 | 9 | 3 | 1 | 43 | 21 | 36 |
| Structural clay products | 3 | 97 | 1 | 0 | 1 | 93 | 4 | 2 |
| Other nonmet. minerals | 19 | 81 | 0 | 0 | 4 | 94 | 0 | 2 |
| Basic metals | 1 | 83 | 16 | 0 | 0 | 9 | 1 | 90 |
| Fabricated metal products | 15 | 42 | 38 | 6 | 0 | 67 | 21 | 12 |
| Nonelectric machinery | 57 | 26 | 10 | 8 | 0 | 29 | 19 | 52 |
| Electrical machinery | 6 | 51 | 35 | 8 | ~ | 45 | 40 | 15 |
| Transport machinery | 15 | 83 | 2 | 0 | ~ | 69 | 17 | 15 |
| Precision machinery | 0 | 100 | 0 | 0 | 0 | 77 | 23 | 0 |
| Miscellaneous | 50 | 48 | 2 | 0 | ~ | 78 | 21 | 2 |

~ = Negligible.

aIncludes firms with five or more employees and excludes oil and gas processing.

bWholly public and public-private joint ventures with 5-19 employees.

cWholly private and public-private joint ventures with 20 or more employees.

dWholly foreign and foreign-private joint ventures.

eForeign-public joint ventures in 1975; foreign-public and foreign-public-private joint ventures in 1985.

<u>Source:</u>  Biro Pusat Statistik (various years c).

Another reason for systematic differences in labor productivity in foreign-related firms overall is that they tend to be concentrated in more advanced, capital-intensive sectors which are generally characterized by higher labor productivity. Table 3.7 shows that foreign and foreign-private firms together accounted for only 21 percent of all nonoil manufacturing value added in 1975 and 17 percent in 1985. However these shares were 50 percent or greater in footwear, other chemicals, rubber products, and pottery and china in 1975, and in plastics and glass products in 1985. Industries with shares between 25 and 49 percent were tobacco, wood products, paper products, glass products, fabricated metals, and electrical machinery in 1975, and beverages, textiles, footwear, other chemicals, and electrical machinery in 1985. As above, in 1985 the public joint venture category also includes foreign-public-private joint ventures and these firms accounted for 24 percent of value added overall, over 50 percent of value added in basic chemicals, basic metals, and nonelectric machinery.[14]

Several of the industries that stand out as being foreign dominated (for example, plastics, glass, and electrical machinery) are capital and/or high-technology intensive. Foreign shares in these industries have also tended to increase since 1974. Brand name is another firm-specific advantage which leads to large foreign shares in consumer product industries such as beverages (mainly the brewery industry), footwear (mainly the large Bata plant), and other chemicals (mainly pharmaceuticals, detergents, and cosmetics). Brand name is also important for rubber products such as tires, but there has been a decline in the importance of foreign firms in tires because of divestment requirements and the fact that the growing demand for motorcycle and bicycle tires has reduced the importance of brand name and technological advantages.

Foreign-public joint ventures dominate basic chemicals (mainly fertilizers), basic metals (largely P.T. Indonesian Asahan Aluminum and more recently a cold rolling mill), and nonelectric machinery. These products are viewed as strategic inputs to production of many other manufactured goods with the result being government involvement. However they also require capital and technology that are not easily obtained in Indonesia; this leads to foreign involvement as well. The substantial increase in the importance of foreign-public joint ventures in some industries reflects (1) protection of intermediate and capital goods industries, (2) the allocation of government sector revenues for these strategic industries when oil revenues were high, and (3) the apparent reclassification of foreign-public-private joint ventures in 1985 which led to a corresponding decrease in public firm shares. Other relatively important foreign-public joint ventures (30–50 percent of value added) are in cement (1985), paper products (1985), food products (ISIC 311, 1985), and beverages (both years).

On the other hand, it is clear that the private sector dominates and is increasing that domination; the private sector's share of value added was 51 percent 1975 and 58 percent in 1985. In contrast with foreign joint ventures, private domestic firms are concentrated in consumer goods and labor-intensive industries such as *kretek* cigarettes, food products, textiles, garments, rubber products, and nonmetallic minerals. In textiles, weaving is dominated by the domestic private sector while spinning and synthetic fibers have a large foreign presence (mainly Japanese firms). The wood products industry, which requires a substantial amount of capital, is dominated by the domestic private sector because state banks subsidize credit to this industry in order to help it realize its substantial export potential. Technology and human capital were subsequently imported in this industry. Thus foreign firms have not been important in the major nonoil manufactured export industries such as textiles, garments, and plywood.

Table 3.8 shows that the high level of average labor productivity in public enterprises is due largely to oil industry activity. When only nonoil industries are considered, foreign firms (including foreign-private joint ventures) are characterized by the highest productivity followed by foreign-public joint ventures, and private firms (including private-public joint ventures). Moreover, foreign firm labor is the most productive in food, tobacco, textiles, leather, footwear, furniture, plastics, glass, cement, clay products, metal products, transport machinery, and professional equipment. Labor productivity is highest in foreign-public joint ventures in beverages, wood, paper, basic chemicals, other chemicals, oil and gas, basic metals, nonelectric machinery, electric machinery, and miscellaneous manufactures. In short, firms with foreign involvement are characterized by relatively high labor productivity in 23 of the 28 3-digit ISIC industries listed in the table. Unfortunately the lack of capital stock data precludes determining whether the relatively high labor productivity is due to relatively high capital-labor ratios or higher capital productivity. In addition, the industries in which foreign firms are dominant are often those in which foreign firms are likely to have firm-specific advantages in production technology, marketing, and management. This would suggest that measures like the ratio of skilled labor to total labor, the ratio of R&D to sales, and the ratio of advertising expenses to total expenses would also help illuminate why labor appears to be more productive in foreign-related firms.

Another important issue is the effect of foreign firms on technology development in local firms. On the one hand, one can envision a case where foreign firms with large technological advantages simply displace local firms in an industry eliminating the chance for any intraindustry spillovers. On the other hand, as Markusen (this volume) has described, there are several potential avenues for positive spillovers from foreign firms to local firms through the training of local employees and local suppliers of intermediate products. Moreover increased competition from foreign firms could also increase competitive pressures and spur local partners or other local firms to increase efficiency. Unfortunately there is little hard evidence to evaluate the effects of foreign firms on domestic technology in Indonesia; nevertheless, it is reasonable to expect that the positive spillovers were important in a number of Indonesian sectors, especially those which were heavily protected from import competition.

Of course even in industries closed to DFI or those dominated by public or private firms, there are instances in which foreign firms do play an important role in supplying technology. For instance, the state enterprise which assembles aircrafts under license, IPTN (Industri Pesawat Terbang Nusantara), has acquired much of its technology from foreign firms. Other examples are in the motor vehicle industry where foreign knockdown kits are assembled under license for a large number of foreign firms. Thus focusing on equity investments alone leaves out a substantial portion of foreign firms' involvement.

Finally, with regard to the role of foreign firms in structural change in Indonesia, Hill (1988) has observed that there is no consistent tendency for industries with

## Table 3.8 Indexes of Labor Productivity in Indonesia's Nonoil Manufacturing Sector by Ownership Category, 1985 (industry average = 100)[a]

| Industry | Private[b] | Public[c] | Foreign[d] | Foreign-public Joint Ventures[e] |
|---|---|---|---|---|
| Manufacturing | 47 | 832 | 133 | 237 |
| Nonoil manufacturing | 74 | 58 | 210 | 166 |
| Food products (ISIC 311) | 109 | 113 | 263 | 78 |
| Food products (ISIC 312) | 74 | 41 | 415 | 122 |
| Beverages | 43 | 16 | 198 | 414 |
| Tobacco | 98 | 10 | 373 | 13 |
| Textiles | 74 | 65 | 246 | 140 |
| Garments | 102 | 36 | 68 | 82 |
| Leather products | 67 | 23 | 2,574 | 196 |
| Footwear | 46 | ~ | 377 | ~ |
| Wood products | 84 | 85 | 108 | 595 |
| Furniture | 97 | 21 | 245 | 75 |
| Paper products | 73 | ~ | 142 | 187 |
| Printing and publishing | 102 | 158 | 79 | 69 |
| Basic chemicals | 37 | 21 | 93 | 148 |
| Other chemicals | 79 | 90 | 148 | 163 |
| Oil and gas processing | ~ | 87 | ~ | 113 |
| Rubber products | 136 | 70 | 59 | 33 |
| Plastic products | 43 | 18 | 1,674 | 15 |
| Pottery and china | 109 | 27 | 39 | ~ |
| Glass products | 22 | ~ | 301 | 66 |
| Cement | 56 | 73 | 498 | 121 |
| Structural clay products | 87 | 131 | 606 | 357 |
| Other nonmetallic minerals | 109 | 68 | ~ | 31 |
| Basic metals | 22 | ~ | 26 | 168 |
| Fabricated metal products | 83 | 17 | 168 | 145 |
| Nonelectric machinery | 41 | 18 | 186 | 213 |
| Electrical machinery | 66 | 13 | 153 | 271 |
| Transport machinery | 124 | 12 | 147 | 44 |
| Precision machinery | 75 | ~ | 502 | ~ |
| Miscellaneous | 71 | 2 | 278 | 797 |

~ = Negligible production and employment.
[a]Refers to firms with 20 or more employees.
[b]Wholly private firms and private-public joint ventures.
[c]Wholly public firms.
[d]Wholly foreign and foreign-private joint ventures.
[e]Foreign-public and foreign-public-private joint ventures.

Source: Biro Pusat Statistik (various years c).

substantial foreign investment to experience relatively high growth or to be large relative to total manufacturing value added. On the surface, this would seem to make the Indonesian experience somewhat different from others considered in this volume (e.g., Thailand, Korea, Taiwan). Nonetheless, part of the reason for the lack of foreign concentration in the high-growth sectors could be that the industries in which foreign firms are typically the dominant forces (e.g., chemicals, electric machinery, transport machinery) have yet to mature in Indonesia to the levels attained in the other countries studied. The implication here is that if Indonesian manufacturing experiences a transition from production of light-and resource-intensive manufactures to production of machinery and chemicals similar to that experienced elsewhere, the role of multinationals in future structural changes could be much more significant than it has been in the past. The potential for greater multinational involvement is also amplified by the recent policy changes which have served to open up the Indonesian economy to foreign influences, including multinationals.

## The Role of Foreign Firms in Exports

One area in which multinationals have played an important role is in exports. Although there are no Indonesian figures on actual foreign firm exports, according to U.S. data U.S. firms alone accounted for 41 percent of all Indonesian exports in 1977 and 29 percent in 1986 (Plummer and Ramstetter, this volume, Table 9.2). The vast majority of this was of course exports by U.S. oil firms in Indonesia and U.S. manufacturing firms only accounted for 8 percent of Indonesia's manufacturing exports in 1977 and 1 percent in 1986. However in the electric machinery sector U.S. firms accounted for 85 percent of all exports in 1982 and 68 percent in 1986 (Plummer and Ramstetter, this volume, Table 9.10).

Nonetheless, until recently most manufacturing DFI in Indonesia has been focused on the domestic market, not the export market. As pointed out above, the main cause of this phenomenon has been the desire to maintain market share in Indonesia's potentially large market combined with the need to jump import barriers imposed as part of the import substitution policy. Only in recent years, as Indonesia adopted measures to encourage exports of nonoil products, has export-oriented DFI increased.

An indication of the extent to which foreign firms in Indonesia have increased their export efforts can be garnished from figures on planned exports of BOI-approved firms. Projects defined by the Board of Investment as being export oriented constituted only 21 percent of the foreign projects approved in 1986 and 31 percent in 1987 but 78 percent in 1988 and 82 percent in 1989. For domestic projects these ratios were 50 percent, 63 percent, 72 percent, and 81 percent, respectively (Board of Investment, various years). Moreover planned exports rose from under US$500 million in 1986 and 1987 to US$2,498 million in 1988 and US$4,328 million in 1989 (Table 3.9). As a result, the ratio of planned exports to Indonesia's nonoil exports rose from 4 percent in 1986 to 6 percent in 1987 and 24 percent in 1988 (cf. Table 3.2). This indicates, as in many other Asian countries (e.g., Plummer and Ramstetter, this volume), that foreign firms in Indonesia play a larger role in exports than in investment, production, or employment.

Table 3.9  Planned Exports of Approved Nonoil Foreign Investment[a]
Projects in Indonesia by Country, 1986-1989
(total in US$ millions, shares in percent)

| Region/country | 1986 | 1987 | 1988 | 1989 | Total, 1986-1989 |
|---|---|---|---|---|---|
| All countries | 245 | 498 | 2,498 | 4,328 | 7,569 |
| Country shares |  |  |  |  |  |
| Japan | 8.0 | 25.9 | 6.8 | 31.1 | 22.0 |
| NIEs | 33.5 | 33.4 | 67.5 | 50.2 | 54.2 |
| Hong Kong | 4.0 | 16.9 | 10.6 | 9.7 | 10.3 |
| Korea | 7.7 | 9.8 | 15.9 | 21.6 | 18.5 |
| Singapore | 11.7 | 4.5 | 3.9 | 6.3 | 5.5 |
| Taiwan | 10.1 | 2.3 | 37.1 | 12.5 | 19.9 |
| Other Asia | 14.7 | 1.4 | 1.1 | 2.4 | 2.3 |
| Malaysia | 14.7 | 1.4 | 1.1 | 0.7 | 1.4 |
| Thailand | 0.0 | 0.0 | 0.0 | 0.9 | 0.5 |
| India | 0.0 | 0.0 | 0.0 | 0.8 | 0.4 |
| United States | 8.3 | 5.3 | 8.1 | 1.2 | 4.0 |
| Panama | 0.0 | 18.5 | 0.1 | 0.8 | 1.7 |
| Europe | 27.0 | 13.1 | 9.6 | 6.0 | 8.4 |
| Australia | 0.2 | 0.3 | 0.0 | 0.3 | 0.2 |
| Other | 8.4 | 2.0 | 6.7 | 8.0 | 7.2 |

[a]Excludes banking and insurance.

Source:  Board of Investment (various years).

Most of the export-oriented investments (76 percent in 1986–1989) are from Japan and the NICs. These investments are concentrated in wood products, textiles, leather, chemicals, and rubber products. More specifically, Japanese export-oriented investments have focused on fisheries (prawns), electrical machinery, precision equipment, and textiles. Hong Kong's investments in Indonesia's garments industry, which were motivated by the potential to use Indonesia's unfilled textile quotas, are dated. However because production costs have risen in Hong Kong, Hong Kong now has problems fulfilling its own quotas. As a result, there is a trend for unfinished garments to be exported to Hong Kong first and then re-exported to the final destination after finishing. Other than the textiles sector, there have also been Hong

Kong investments in wood products (furniture). Korean investments have been undertaken in wood products, footwear, and apparel with the latter two products being mainly exported to the United States. Taiwanese investments, on the other hand, have been concentrated in paper, textiles, and footwear, while Singaporean firms are concentrated in wood products, rubber products, and electric machinery (sectoral information from Board of Investment, various years).

Looking at the industry distribution of planned exports (Table 3.10), an increasingly large portion has been concentrated in manufacturing with manufacturing accounting for 93 percent of all planned exports in 1986–1989. Textiles and garments is by far the largest individual industry with a 27 percent share for the 4-year period. Nonpharmeceutical chemicals and rubber (15 percent), paper (13 percent), nonmetallic minerals (11 percent), and metal products and machinery (9 percent) follow. Thus planned exports of foreign firms have been concentrated in more or less the same sectors as Indonesia's exports overall.

Table 3.11 identifies some characteristics of the main export industries of Indonesia. Private firms account for over 60 percent of value added in the top three export industries (plywood, clothing, and woven fabrics) with foreign shares of value added at 21 percent in plywood, 3 percent in clothing, and 27 percent in woven fabrics. Since these industries alone accounted for 74 percent of all manufacturing exports, it is unlikely that foreign firms presently account for a large portion of Indonesia's manufactured exports. However, in view of the marked rise in planned exports noted above, the importance of foreign firms in Indonesia's manufacturing exports is likely to increase. Moreover the observed patterns of foreign involvement reflect in part the fact that Indonesia is just beginning the process of industrialization in many respects. Specifically, it seems likely that Indonesia's export structure may shift in favor of chemicals and machinery in the next decade as Indonesia develops a comparative advantage in the labor-intensive processes of these industries. Since foreign firms tend to be highly concentrated in these industries, foreign firms are likely to have a large role in such structural shifts.

Again the large policy changes in the previously highly protected Indonesian manufacturing sector should be stressed. Since Indonesia has always had a relatively large pool of cheap labor, the increased attractiveness of Indonesia as an export base owes much to the improved investment climate and the shift to export-oriented policies described above. One important policy in this regard is the improved import duty exemption scheme for inputs utilized in exports which was introduced in May 1986. Exporters are also allowed to import directly without going through the importers' approval system. In other words, exporters face no constraints in importing their inputs.

Of course the recent surge of export-oriented DFI cannot be explained without reference to the push factors which have been coincident in Japan and the NICs. In particular, currency appreciation (in Japan, Korea, and Taiwan in particular) and rising labor costs (all countries) have led many firms in these countries to look for new production locales. Moreover the marked shift in Indonesian policy has combined with the gradual shift to export orientation in Thailand (e.g., Tambunlertchai and Ramstetter, this volume) and the long-standing, export-promoting policies of Malaysia and Singapore to make Southeast Asia an extremely attractive production

Table 3.10  Planned Exports of Approved Nonoil Foreign Investment[a] Projects in Indonesia by Industry, 1986-1989 (percentage)

| Industry | 1986 | 1987 | 1988 | 1989 | Total, 1986-1989 |
|---|---|---|---|---|---|
| All industries (US$ millions) | 245 | 498 | 2,498 | 4,328 | 7,569 |
| Industry shares | | | | | |
| Agriculture | 8.2 | 1.0 | 0.9 | 1.7 | 1.6 |
| Food | 0.5 | 0.0 | 0.0 | 1.7 | 1.0 |
| Plantation | 7.1 | 1.0 | 0.8 | 0.0 | 0.6 |
| Livestock | 0.6 | 0.0 | 0.0 | 0.0 | 0.0 |
| Fisheries | 5.9 | 10.1 | 3.1 | 2.6 | 3.4 |
| Forestry | 0.0 | 3.6 | 1.9 | 0.5 | 1.1 |
| Manufacturing | 83.8 | 85.3 | 94.1 | 93.5 | 92.9 |
| Food and products | 13.6 | 7.1 | 4.7 | 6.8 | 6.4 |
| Textiles, garments, etc. | 2.0 | 31.7 | 23.0 | 30.1 | 27.0 |
| Wood and products | 22.3 | 16.4 | 6.1 | 6.4 | 7.5 |
| Paper and products | 10.1 | 1.4 | 36.4 | 1.7 | 13.4 |
| Chemicals and rubber | 31.1 | 13.6 | 10.1 | 16.5 | 14.7 |
| Pharmaceuticals | 0.2 | 0.6 | 0.2 | 0.2 | 0.2 |
| Other chemicals | 30.9 | 13.1 | 9.9 | 16.3 | 14.5 |
| Nonmetallic minerals | 0.0 | 5.1 | 1.3 | 17.1 | 10.6 |
| Basic metals | 0.0 | 3.4 | 6.9 | 2.1 | 3.7 |
| Metal prod. & machinery | 4.7 | 6.6 | 4.9 | 10.9 | 8.5 |
| Miscellaneous | 0.0 | 0.0 | 0.6 | 1.8 | 1.2 |
| Services | 2.0 | 0.0 | 0.0 | 1.7 | 1.0 |
| Trade | 0.0 | 0.0 | 0.0 | 0.6 | 0.3 |
| Other services | 2.0 | 0.0 | 0.0 | 1.1 | 0.7 |

[a]Excludes banking and insurance.

Source:  Board of Investment (various years).

locale for Japanese and NIC firms aiming to export to third markets. These forces have all combined to produce a boom in export-oriented investments in Southeast Asia in general, not just Indonesia.

It is difficult to evaluate the benefits of export-oriented investments in Indonesia, but to date there seems to have been little creation of domestic linkages and diffusion of technology and know-how. One reason for this is the existence of high foreign equity shares; this results in a dormant domestic partner and makes it more difficult to transfer technology. Another factor is the duty exemption scheme which allows export-oriented investors to import instead of immediately forging links with domestic input producers. High import content is to be expected because domestic inputs are more expensive, are not of the necessary quality, and there may be problems with timely delivery. This is perfectly normal and one can expect a high import content at the initial stages of investment projects. Increasing the utilization of domestic inputs will depend primarily on increasing the efficiency of domestic producers. Here again increasing competitive pressures through further deregulation and reduction of protection levels is likely to be important. Thus the main benefits from export-oriented investments at this stage are labor absorption, the training of labor, and to a limited extent, the transfer of managerial and marketing skills.

## Conclusions

Changes in policy, which have been closely related to oil price changes, have led to structural changes in the Indonesian manufacturing sector. DFI has in general responded to these policy changes as well as to specific changes in foreign investment policy and the usual resource endowment and domestic market size considerations. In response to the first phase of import substitution in final goods, most manufacturing DFI in 1970–1979 was in consumer goods such as textiles and food products. In 1980–1984 foreign investment followed the next phase of import substitution into intermediate goods such as chemicals and rubber, paper and paper products, metal products, and more recently, petrochemicals. DFI has also responded to the recent shift towards exports, though the majority of DFI in Indonesia is still by and large oriented towards the domestic market.

On average the overall contribution of foreign firms to industrialization and structural change has been relatively small in Indonesia thus far. DFI has been a small portion of long-term foreign capital and foreign shares of manufacturing value added are also minimal. Of course, foreign investment dominates some industries, especially those which are capital intensive and which employ nonstandardized technology. Nonetheless the evidence suggests that technology transfer from foreign firms in Indonesia has also been limited to date.

On the export side, it is clear that outside of the manufacturing sector, foreign firms have made large contributions to the growth of Indonesia's major exports, oil and gas. However, in manufacturing, their role has apparently been much smaller in most large exporting industries. Yet there is also a clear rationale to expect foreign firm shares of nonoil exports to increase as Indonesian manufacturing develops over the medium term. Moreover planned export figures indicate there may be a large increase in the short term as well.

Table 3.11 Characteristics of Indonesia's Major Manufacturing Export Industries, 1982-1987[a]

| Industry | Exports, 1987 (US$m) | Value Added per Employee, 1985 (index)[b] | Employment, 1985 ('000) | Index of Production, 1987 (1975=1) | Employment per Firm, 1985 (no.) | Effective Protection, 1985 (%)[c] | 4-firm Concentration Ratio, 1982 (%)[d] | Value Added Shares by Ownership Category, 1983 (%)[e] | | | |
|---|---|---|---|---|---|---|---|---|---|---|---|
| | | | | | | | | Private | Foreign | Public | Public Joint Venture |
| Manufacturing total | 3,895 | 100 | 1,684.7 | 2.90 | 130 | na | na | na | na | na | na |
| Plywood | 1,901 | 95 | 88.0 | 5.57 | 907 | 10 | 22 | 77.2 | 21.2 | 1.6 | 0.0 |
| Clothing | 596 | 39 | 69.7 | na | 108 | 26 | 46 | 97.2 | 2.6 | 0.2 | 0.0 |
| Woven fabrics | 385 | 50 | 156.3 | 1.54 | 152 | 61 | 35 | 62.2 | 27.4 | 9.2 | 1.2 |
| Steel products | 136 | 778 | 15.6 | 14.22 | 522 | 22 | 78 | 8.9 | 8.3 | 36.0 | 46.8 |
| Paper and products | 96 | 133 | 21.6 | 2.19 | 160 | 147 | 51 | 50.5 | 23.7 | 25.8 | 0.0 |
| Fertilizer | 86 | 499 | 16.8 | 9.27 | 1,200 | 74 | 68 | 0.0 | 0.0 | 100.0 | 0.0 |
| Yarn | 84 | 102 | 65.6 | 1.25 | 698 | 52 | 35 | 53.6 | 35.4 | 9.9 | 1.1 |
| Cement | 57 | 284 | 13.7 | 8.06 | 1,247 | 36 | 68 | 15.2 | 8.5 | 55.3 | 21.0 |
| Leather | 45 | 80 | 4.4 | na | 54 | 8 | 64 | 70.9 | 0.0 | 29.1 | 0.0 |
| Oils and perfumes | 34 | 114 | 6.5 | na | 112 | 34 | 63 | 35.4 | 64.6 | 0.0 | 0.0 |
| Glass and products | 31 | 241 | 10.5 | 3.48 | 263 | 65 | 78 | 26.0 | 70.2 | 3.8 | 0.0 |
| Musical instruments | 28 | 378 | 0.4 | na | 74 | 43 | 100 | 2.1 | 97.9 | 0.0 | 0.0 |
| Furniture | 27 | 37 | 12.6 | na | 44 | 67 | 25 | 87.1 | 12.4 | 0.5 | 0.0 |
| Inorganic chemicals | 25 | 130 | 12.1 | na | 105 | 4 | 48 | 25.5 | 28.0 | 28.7 | 17.8 |
| Rubber tires | 23 | 48 | 12.6 | 3.56 | 419 | 66 | 81 | 30.8 | 55.7 | 13.5 | 0.0 |
| Footwear | 22 | 89 | 8.9 | 1.76 | 77 | 79 | 71 | 17.9 | 75.6 | 6.6 | 0.0 |
| Electronics | 15 | 200 | 19.7 | 2.08 | 179 | 43 | 54 | 32.4 | 54.0 | 5.6 | 8.0 |

[a]Data on value added per employee, employment, employees per firm, and value added shares by ownership category refer to firms with at least 20 employees.

[b]Defined as $(V/E)i/(V/E)m*100$ where $Vi$=value added, $E$=employment, $i$=industry i, $m$=manufacturing total.

[c]Calculations employ an input-output classification that is not always consistent with those used for other data.

[d]Calculations based on value added.

[e]Private-foreign joint ventures are classified as foreign; all joint ventures involving the government are classified as public joint ventures.

<u>Sources:</u>  Biro Pusat Statistik (1986, various years a, various years b); Fane and Phillips (forthcoming); Hill (1990a).

However, even if DFI's role in Indonesian manufacturing grows, how should Indonesia try to maximize the benefits of this DFI? DFI is desirable to facilitate increased investment, production, exports, as well as higher levels of technology, management, and marketing know-how. The dilemma is that if one tries to "extract" the benefits from the foreign firms by using rigid performance requirements, this raises the cost of operations to the investor, sometimes to a level that discourages DFI altogether. In other words, another important role of policy is to encourage all investment, including DFI, by providing a healthy investment climate and some measure of certainty. In this context, the forced extraction of benefits is very difficult. However the government can enhance the potential for benefits to be realized by ensuring a competitive market environment and increasing the absorptive capacity of the local partners and employees through the provision of information and educational opportunities. Thus the successful extraction of benefits from DFI appears to depend more on general policies, such as those toward market structure and education, rather than on specific policies toward DFI.

## Notes

1. Foreign firms also play major roles in the petroleum and financial sectors but these investments are not dealt with in detail in this paper.

2. The weak sector is a term usually used to refer to *pribumi* (indigenous entrepreneurs), small-scale industries, and cooperatives, though this usage is less common since 1984.

3. Pangestu (1986) estimated that the effects of the devaluation eroded within two years.

4. The system functioned as a rebate scheme rather than a pure duty drawback scheme since the amount returned to exporters was based on the "average" rate of duty paid by exporters. This system was subject to abuses such as rebates for empty shipments.

5. This meant that licenses regarding land, environmental regulations, and labor regulations could all be processed through the Board of Investment rather than having to go through each responsible ministry.

6. The anti-Japanese feelings can be attributed to the high visibility of Japanese DFI. The high visibility was in turn partly due to the concentration of Japanese DFI in consumer products. On the other hand, U.S. investment was actually much higher overall due to large investments in the petroleum sector.

7. The tax reform aimed to increase revenues and rationalize the tax system. A value added tax was introduced, the income tax system was overhauled, and the tax holiday given to foreign investors was eliminated.

8. Specifically: (1) companies with a minimum of 75 percent Indonesian equity were allowed to distribute products domestically and get access to credit from state banks; (2) all sectors were opened to export-oriented joint ventures (joint ventures exporting 85 percent or more of their production); (3) a maximum foreign equity share of 95 percent was allowed for export-oriented joint ventures; and (4) export-oriented joint ventures were eligible to apply for the government-subsidized export credit scheme.

9. The presence of additional joint venture banks to serve their multinational clients should have a positive effect on foreign investment. This is especially true for Japanese investments. Prior to the banking deregulation, there was only one full Japanese branch and one Japanese joint venture in Indonesia's banking sector. By December 1989, ten joint venture banks had obtained licenses to operate, eight of which were Japanese.

10. Note that revised real GDP figures show higher GDP levels (1985 = 84,959 billion 1983 rupiah, 1986 = 90,014 billion 1983 rupiah, 1987 = 94,302 billion 1983 rupiah), GDP

growth rates (1986 = 6 percent, 1987 = 5 percent), and nonoil manufacturing shares (1985 = 11 percent, 1986 = 12 percent, and 1987 = 13 percent) than the older figures in Table 3.1. Note also that in 1988, growth was 6 percent and nonoil manufacturing's share of real GDP rose further to 14 percent (Biro Pusat Statistik, various years b). The new series differs mainly due to a more complete coverage of the industrial sector. However the new data are only available back to 1983 and are thus not used in Table 3.1.

11. Mismanagement led to a huge foreign debt being incurred by the state-owned oil company, Pertamina. The debt payments were rescheduled.

12. Investments in these two sectors are monitored by the Department of Mines and Energy and the Department of Finance, respectively, and are not reported as DFI to the IMF or other agencies. Furthermore, much of the capital flow into these sectors come in forms that are not usually defined as DFI (e.g., production sharing agreements).

13. Note that the United States is by far the largest investor in the oil sector and that if these investments were included, U.S. investment would probably exceed Japanese investment.

14. The exclusion of the oil sector understates the role of the public sector and thus overstates the role of foreign firms in all manufacturing. For example, in 1985 the inclusion of the oil and gas sector implies that the government sector accounts for 40 percent of value added compared with 24 percent when that sector is excluded. It should also be noted that industries closed to DFI (hence low foreign firm value added ratios) often engage in substantial licensing activity with foreign firms (e.g., motor vehicles and motorcycles).

# References

Allen, T. W. 1979. *The ASEAN Report*, Vol. 1. Hong Kong: Asian Wall Street Journal.

Balasubramayam, V. N. 1984. Factor Proportions and Productive Efficiency of Foreign Owned Firms in the Indonesian Manufacturing Sector. *Bulletin of Indonesian Economic Studies* 20(3): 70–94.

Bank Indonesia. Various years. Mimeos.

Biro Pusat Statistik. 1986. *Sensus Ekonomi* [Economic census]. Jakarta: Biro Pusat Statistik.

———. Various years a. *Exports*. Jakarta: Biro Pusat Statistik.

———. Various years b. *National Income of Indonesia*. Jakarta: Biro Pusat Statistik.

———. Various years c. Unpublished data based on Statistik Industri series. Jakarta: Biro Pusat Statistik.

Board of Investment. Various years. Mimeos.

Fane, George and Chris Phillips. forthcoming. Effective Protection in Indonesia. *Bulletin of Indonesian Economic Studies*.

Hill, Hal. 1988. *Foreign Investment and Industrialization in Indonesia*. New York: Oxford University Press.

———. 1990a. Indonesia: Export Promotion after the Oil Boom. In *Export Promotion: Theory and Evidence from Developing Countries*, edited by Chris Miner. New York: Harvester Wheatsheaf.

———. 1990b. Indonesia's Industrial Transformation. *Bulletin of Indonesian Economic Studies* 26(2).

International Monetary Fund (IMF). 1989. *International Financial Statistics Yearbook 1989*. Washington, D.C.: International Monetary Fund.

Pangestu, Mari. 1980. Japanese and Other Foreign Investment in the ASEAN Countries. Research Paper No. 73. Australia-Japan Research Centre, Australian National University, Canberra.

———. 1986. The Effect of Oil Shocks on a Small Oil Exporting Country: The Case of Indonesia. Ph.D. Dissertation, Department of Economics, University of California at Davis.

_____.1987. The Pattern of Direct Foreign Investment in ASEAN: the U.S. vs. Japan. *ASEAN Economic Bulletin* 3(3): 301–328.

Pangestu, Mari, and Boediono. 1986. Indonesia: The Structure and Causes of Manufacturing Sector Protection. In *The Political Economy of Manufacturing Protection: Experiences of ASEAN and Australia*, edited by C. Findlay and R. G. Garnaut. Sydney: Allen and Unwin.

Panglaykim, J., and Mari Pangestu. 1983. *Japanese Direct Investment in ASEAN: The Indonesian Experience.* Singapore: Maruzen Asia.

Thee Kian Wie. 1984a. Japanese Direct Investment in Indonesian Manufacturing. *Bulletin of Indonesian Economic Studies* 20(2): 90–106.

_____. 1984b. Japanese and American Direct Investment In Indonesian Manufacturing Compared. *Ekonomi dan Keuangan Indonesia* 32(1): 89–105.

_____. 1984c. Technology Transfer Through Transnational Corporations in Indonesia: Evaluation of TNCs Contribution to Technological Development-Twelve Case Studies. Draft report submitted to United Nations Economic and Social Commission for Asia and the Pacific, Bangkok.

Thee Kian Wie, and Kunio Yoshihara. 1987. Foreign and Domestic Capital in Indonesian Industrialization. *Southeast Asian Studies* 24(4): 327–49.

Tsurumi, Y. 1976. *The Japanese Are Coming: A Multinational Interaction of Firms and Politics.* Cambridge, Mass: Ballinger.

World Bank. Various years. *World Debt Tables*. Washington, D.C.: World Bank.

# 4

## Foreign Firms in Promoted Industries and Structural Change in Thailand

*Somsak Tambunlertchai and Eric D. Ramstetter*

### Structural Change and the Investment Environment

The Thai economy performed rather well over the last two decades with real GDP growing at an annual rate of 6.6 percent over the period 1970–1988 (NESDB, various years). This growth was accompanied by significant structural changes, the most significant being the gradual decline in agriculture's traditionally large share of economic activity in a country that is well endowed with fertile land. On the other hand, in nominal terms, the manufacturing sector's share of value added rose from 19 percent in 1974 to 23 percent in 1986 and 24 percent in 1988 (Table 4.1 and sources). Using SITC-ISIC (Standard International Trade Classification-International Standard Industrial Classification) converters developed by the Australian National University and the United Nations Industrial Development Organization (UNIDO) to calculate manufacturing exports, manufacturing exports as a share of total exports grew even more rapidly from 55 percent to 70 percent during this period.[1] On the other hand, manufacturing's share of employment declined, but there are statistical problems with the employment numbers which make their interpretation difficult.[2]

In addition, within the manufacturing sector, there were significant changes in terms of employment, value added, and exports. In particular, individual industry shares of total manufacturing declined in wood products and basic metals and increased in apparel, chemicals, electric machinery, and miscellaneous manufacturing. Other notable changes were general declines in textiles (employment and value added) and metal products (employment and value added) and increases in footwear and leather (value added and exports), nonmetallic minerals (employment and value added), nonelectric machinery (employment and exports), and transport machinery (employment and exports).

Since 1960 Thailand has generally welcomed direct foreign investment (DFI) and has offered a number of incentives for investment in promoted industries through the Board of Investment (BOI). Promoted industries are primarily concentrated in manufacturing since a long-standing goal of Thai policy has been to foster economic growth through industrialization. Both domestic and foreign firms are eligible to

Table 4.1  Structural Change in Thailand, 1974-1986

| Industry | Employment[a] (1,000) 1974 | 1986 | Value added (US$ millions) 1974 | 1986 | Exports[b] (US$ millions) 1974 | 1986 |
|---|---|---|---|---|---|---|
| All industries | 17,159 | 26,691 | 13,703 | 41,624 | 2,444 | 8,874 |
| Manufacturing | 1,239 | 1,384 | 2,625 | 9,697 | 1,342 | 6,213 |
| Manufacturing share (%) | 7.2 | 5.2 | 19.2 | 23.3 | 54.9 | 70.0 |
| As a share of manufacturing (%) | | | | | | |
| Food | 33.2 | 33.2 | 31.2 | 26.0 | 59.8 | 35.5 |
| Textiles | 18.9 | 12.2 | 11.8 | 10.7 | 8.2 | 8.5 |
| Apparel | 7.2 | 10.8 | 9.4 | 13.9 | 3.4 | 13.2 |
| Footwear, leather | 1.9 | 1.2 | 1.9 | 2.9 | 0.3 | 2.9 |
| Wood products | 6.1 | 3.7 | 7.2 | 3.6 | 3.9 | 2.7 |
| Paper products | 3.4 | 3.4 | 3.0 | 3.0 | 0.6 | 0.8 |
| Chemicals | 3.5 | 3.8 | 3.2 | 3.4 | 1.2 | 2.2 |
| Petroleum products | 0.2 | 0.2 | 5.4 | 10.1 | 1.3 | 0.2 |
| Rubber, plastics | 5.2 | 2.6 | 2.4 | 2.4 | 0.6 | 2.6 |
| Nonmetallic | 2.1 | 3.5 | 3.5 | 4.0 | 2.7 | 1.1 |
| Basic metals | 3.2 | 2.2 | 2.7 | 1.3 | 12.5 | 3.7 |
| Metal products | 2.7 | 2.1 | 3.1 | 2.6 | 0.9 | 1.3 |
| Nonelec. machinery | 3.1 | 3.7 | 2.6 | 2.4 | 0.2 | 3.0 |
| Electric machinery | 2.6 | 3.2 | 2.0 | 3.0 | 0.9 | 11.5 |
| Transport machinery | 4.0 | 5.0 | 8.1 | 4.9 | 0.1 | 0.6 |
| Miscellaneous[c] | 2.7 | 9.5 | 2.7 | 5.8 | 3.3 | 10.1 |

[a]Manufacturing and individual industry figures are based on industrial censuses.  Manufacturing figures from labor force surveys are higher, 1,694,000 in 1974 and 2,069,000 in 1986 or 9.9 and 7.8 percent of all employment in each year, respectively.
[b]Manufacturing and individual industry figures based on SITC-ISIC converters from UNIDO and Australian National University.
[c]Includes precision machinery.

Sources:  Asian Development Bank (various years); Australian National University (1989); International Monetary Fund (various years); NESDB (various years); UNIDO (1989).

receive BOI incentives according to generally the same criteria. However benefits of little meaning to domestic firms, such as the right to own land and create wholly owned ventures, may accompany BOI promotion of foreign firms. As this discussion implies, the BOI has been given substantial discretion in granting incentives and imposing restrictions on foreign firm activities. On the other hand, it is also true that the BOI has generally tended to act with restraint and its intervention in the marketplace has generally followed Thailand's overall industrial and trade policies. In this respect, the gradual shift in emphasis from import substitution in the 1960s and most of the 1970s to export promotion in the late 1970s and 1980s has increased promotion of export-oriented ventures and led to a general loosening of the BOI's restrictions on foreign firms.

This change in policy emphasis is also partly responsible for the changes in Thailand's industrial structure. In particular, the weakening of various protective policy measures promoted the movement of productive resources into sectors in which Thailand has a comparative advantage (for example, apparel, footwear and leather, electric machinery, and miscellaneous manufacturing). This paper explores further the extent to which foreign firms have been involved in and have contributed to changes in Thailand's industrial structure. To this end, detailed surveys that have been conducted by the BOI for a number of years are used to compare employment, production, and trade activities of foreign and domestic firms that have been promoted. Where possible, comparisons with all firms in Thailand are also made. However, since DFI in promoted firms is only a portion of total DFI in Thailand, it is first helpful to examine the trends and patterns of total DFI in Thailand.

## DFI Trends and Patterns

DFI inflows in Thailand (Table 4.2) have increased over time. From a range of US$39-188 million over the period 1970-1979 (an annual average of US$80 million), DFI inflows increased to US$164-408 million during the period 1980-1987 (an annual average of US$277 million). Then an unprecedented investment boom began as DFI jumped to US$1.1 billion in 1988 and US$1.7 billion in 1989. To date, most of the inflow has come in the form of equity.

As in most countries both political and economic factors have affected the timing of DFI inflows. In the Thailand during the 1970s, (1) several coups and related domestic political instability, (2) problems related to communist insurgencies in the northeast and the south, and (3) the wars in Vietnam and Cambodia all adversely affected the investment climate. In contrast, in the 1980s there has been greater domestic political stability and marked democratization while the communist insurgencies have all but disappeared. Although the war continues in Cambodia, its intensity has diminished to the point that there has been a growing interest in expanding commercial activity in Cambodia and Vietnam in recent years. In addition to these political factors, the changes in economic policy mentioned above, notably the reduced emphasis on import substitution and the loosening of restrictions on foreign firms, have also contributed to the growth of DFI inflows. Moreover there has been an economic boom in the late 1980s with real GDP growth rates reaching 9.5 percent in 1987, 13.2 percent in 1988, and 12.2 percent in 1989 (NESDB,

Table 4.2 DFI Flows in Thailand, 1970-1989

| Year | Net Inward DFI (US$ millions) | | | Net Outward DFI[a] (US$ m) | Inward DFI as a % of Long-term Capital Flow[b] | Inward DFI as a % of Total Capital Flow[c] | Inward DFI as a % of Private Fixed Investment | Inward DFI as a % of Total Fixed Investment |
|------|-------|--------|-------|---|------|------|-----|-----|
|      | Total | Equity | Loans |   |      |      |     |     |
| 1970 | 43  | 32  | 11  | 0  | 38.9 | 25.5 | 3.6 | 2.5 |
| 1971 | 39  | 33  | 6   | 0  | 48.6 | 23.7 | 3.2 | 2.3 |
| 1972 | 69  | 56  | 13  | 0  | 44.0 | 27.8 | 5.2 | 3.7 |
| 1973 | 78  | 67  | 11  | 0  | 98.5 | 29.7 | 4.2 | 3.2 |
| 1974 | 188 | 134 | 54  | 0  | 48.4 | 32.9 | 7.0 | 5.9 |
| 1975 | 86  | 64  | 22  | 0  | 45.1 | 14.9 | 3.3 | 2.5 |
| 1976 | 79  | 65  | 14  | 0  | 24.9 | 15.2 | 2.9 | 2.0 |
| 1977 | 106 | 55  | 51  | 0  | 24.8 | 9.7  | 2.9 | 2.1 |
| 1978 | 56  | 40  | 16  | 6  | 8.6  | 4.9  | 1.3 | 0.9 |
| 1979 | 55  | 62  | -7  | 4  | 3.7  | 2.8  | 1.1 | 0.8 |
| 1980 | 189 | 174 | 15  | 3  | 9.0  | 10.2 | 3.6 | 2.3 |
| 1981 | 294 | 186 | 108 | 2  | 15.6 | 11.3 | 5.3 | 3.4 |
| 1982 | 188 | 147 | 41  | -0 | 15.2 | 24.4 | 3.4 | 2.3 |
| 1983 | 358 | 298 | 59  | 1  | 27.4 | 14.0 | 5.7 | 3.8 |
| 1984 | 408 | 302 | 106 | 1  | 22.7 | 15.5 | 6.2 | 4.0 |
| 1985 | 164 | 201 | -37 | 1  | 10.0 | 10.0 | 3.0 | 1.8 |

| | | | | | | | | |
|---|---|---|---|---|---|---|---|---|
| 1986 | 263 | 222 | 41 | 1 | 298.5 | 56.2 | 4.5 | 2.9 |
| 1987 | 352 | 398 | -47 | 168 | 58.6 | 26.8 | 4.2 | 3.1 |
| 1988 | 1,117 | 901 | 216 | 24 | 82.3 | 26.9 | 9.6 | 7.5 |
| 1989 | 1,741 | 1,418 | 322 | 50 | na | na | na | na |
| Cumulative Total | | | | | | | | |
| 1970-74 | 416 | 322 | 95 | 0 | 51.2 | 29.5 | 5.0 | 3.8 |
| 1970-79 | 798 | 607 | 192 | 10 | 20.6 | 11.9 | 3.0 | 2.2 |
| 1970-81 | 1,282 | 967 | 315 | 15 | 16.3 | 11.4 | 3.5 | 2.4 |
| 1970-86 | 2,662 | 2,136 | 525 | 19 | 19.1 | 13.8 | 4.0 | 2.7 |
| 1970-87 | 3,013 | 2,535 | 478 | 187 | 20.7 | 14.6 | 4.0 | 2.8 |
| 1970-88 | 4,130 | 3,436 | 694 | 212 | 26.0 | 16.7 | 4.9 | 3.4 |
| 1970-89 | 5,871 | 4,854 | 1,016 | 262 | na | na | na | na |

na = not available.
[a]Data were not available before 1978 and were thus assumed to be zero.
[b]Long-term capital = direct investment + portfolio investment + other long-term capital.
[c]Total capital = long-term capital + short-term capital + errors and omissions.

Sources: Bank of Thailand (various years); International Monetary Fund (various years); NESDB (various years).

Table 4.3 Cumulative DFI and Registered Capital in Thailand by Country, 1974-1989
(yearend stock, US$ millions)

| Group/country | Cumulative Inward DFI from 1970 | | | | Cumulative Registered Capital of Firms Granted Promotion Certificates from 1960[a] | | | |
|---|---|---|---|---|---|---|---|---|
| | 1974 | 1981 | 1986 | 1989 | 1974 | 1981 | 1986 | 1989 |
| World | 416 | 1,282 | 2,662 | 5,871 | 182 | 222 | 417 | 1,838 |
| Japan | 116 | 351 | 784 | 2,182 | 76 | 69 | 109 | 1,007 |
| United States | 160 | 434 | 821 | 1,216 | 27 | 25 | 71 | 129 |
| Other OECD | 49 | 179 | 419 | 773 | 18 | 30 | 71 | 166 |
| Europe-5 | 47 | 169 | 395 | 741 | 17 | 28 | 58 | 149 |
| United Kingdom | 23 | 73 | 141 | 196 | 7 | 13 | 28 | 58 |
| Germany, West | 3 | 41 | 73 | 146 | 3 | 5 | 7 | 11 |
| France | 7 | 13 | 28 | 70 | 3 | 3 | 4 | 9 |
| Netherlands | 12 | 21 | 106 | 184 | 2 | 4 | 12 | 21 |
| Switzerland | 2 | 20 | 47 | 144 | 2 | 4 | 7 | 50 |
| Australia | 2 | 10 | 25 | 32 | 1 | 2 | 12 | 16 |
| NIC-3 | 69 | 241 | 423 | 1,331 | 34 | 46 | 77 | 328 |
| Hong Kong | 46 | 134 | 273 | 649 | 9 | 13 | 21 | 66 |
| Singapore | 22 | 104 | 133 | 316 | 3 | 3 | 18 | 62 |

|  |  |  |  |  |  |  |  |  |
|---|---|---|---|---|---|---|---|---|
| Taiwan | 2 | 2 | 17 | 366 | 22 | 30 | 38 | 200 |
| Other ASEAN-4 | 7 | 15 | 23 | 27 | 6 | 8 | 16 | 21 |
| Malaysia | 5 | 13 | 22 | 26 | 5 | 8 | 10 | 14 |
| Philippines | 2 | 2 | 1 | 1 | 1 | 1 | 6 | 6 |
| Other | 15 | 62 | 191 | 343 | 23 | 43 | 74 | 188 |
| For BOI-promoted firms: |  |  |  |  |  |  |  |  |
| Thai contribution to registered capital |  |  |  |  | 450 | 769 | 986 | 2,971 |
| Total registered capital |  |  |  |  | 633 | 991 | 1,403 | 4,809 |

<sup>a</sup>Registered capital often differs greatly from actual investment. Total actual investment (domestic and foreign) of BOI-promoted firms in operation was US$725 million in 1987, US$746 million in 1988, and US$1,028 million in 1989 while corresponding increments of registered capital stocks were US$538 million, US$1,137 million, and US$1,635 million, respectively. Actual foreign investment in BOI-promoted firms in operation was US$497 million in 1987, US$586 million in 1988, and US$814 million in 1989 while corresponding increments of registered capital stocks were US$216 million, US$589 million, and US$616 million, respectively. Data on actual investment in BOI-promoted firms are not available prior to 1986.

Sources: Bank of Thailand (various years); Board of Investment (various years); International Monetary Fund (various years).

various years). This boom has been both a cause and a result of large increases in investment, both domestic and foreign, in recent years. Thus both political and economic changes have worked to improve the investment environment and contributed to the increases in DFI inflows in the 1980s.

DFI inflows have been an important component of overall capital inflows, accounting for 25 percent or more of long-term capital flows and 15 percent or more of total capital flows before 1976. However ratios of DFI to long-term capital flows and to total capital flows declined markedly in the late 1970s and early 1980s; this decline in DFI shares was largely a result of increases in foreign loans to finance fiscal deficits and rapid expansion of public enterprises, particularly firms in the public utility sector. Since 1986, the shares of DFI in long-term and total capital flows have rebounded.

The ratio of DFI to domestic fixed investment displays a similar trend. From 3–5 percent in 1965–1975, the share of DFI decreased to 1–3 percent in 1976–1982 and then increased to 2–4 percent in 1983–1987 and 8 percent in 1988. Ratios of inward DFI to private fixed investment were somewhat larger. However DFI never exceeded 4 percent of cumulative total fixed investment and 5 percent of cumulative private fixed investment through 1988. Thus, although DFI has increased rapidly in recent years accounting for a significant portion of capital inflows and foreign firms have dominated in some individual manufacturing industries (see below), DFI's direct contribution to the aggregate capital stock in Thailand has been limited.[3]

Japan and the United States have been and continue to be the two most important sources of DFI in Thailand. Together these two countries accounted for 66 percent of the cumulative DFI flow through 1974; this share gradually dropped to 58 percent by 1989 (Table 4.3). Through 1986, the United States was the largest source of cumulative DFI, but Japan has since assumed the top spot. Asia's NICs, especially Hong Kong, Singapore, and more recently Taiwan,[4] and other developed OECD (Organizaion for Economic Cooperation and Development) economies are the other major investors.

Japan has been the biggest source of the large increase in DFI flows in recent years, accounting for 44 percent of the US$3.2 billion increase in cumulative DFI between 1986 and 1989. The substantial increase in Japanese investment is to a large degree a result of the yen's rapid appreciation which exacerbated the trend of rising production costs in Japan. Taiwan, which also faced similar pressures for restructuring in recent years, increased its cumulative investment in Thailand rapidly from only US$17 million in 1986 to US$366 million in 1989. Taken together, Taiwan, Hong Kong, and Singapore accounted for 28 percent of the total increase in cumulative DFI between 1986 and 1989. Another characteristic of the recent boom is that it has been centered in BOI-promoted activities with the foreign contribution to registered capital increasing more than fourfold between 1986 and 1989. One of the reasons for this is that investors from Japan and Taiwan have tended to focus on BOI-promoted activities. For example, at the end of 1989, the ratio of registered capital in BOI-promoted firms to total DFI was 46 percent for Japan and 55 percent for Taiwan; these ratios are relatively high compared to a ratio of 31 percent for all firms combined, 20 percent for the listed European countries, and only 11 percent for the United States.

DFI has recently become increasingly concentrated in manufacturing with this industry's share of the total cumulative inflow rising from 29 percent in 1974, to 32–33 percent in 1979 and 1986, and then to 42 percent in 1989 (Table 4.4). Through 1974, manufacturing DFI was concentrated in textiles which accounted for 14 percent of all DFI, followed by food (4 percent), chemicals, and electric machinery (3 percent each). Since 1974 manufacturing DFI has been heavily concentrated in electric machinery; its share of total cumulative DFI grew to 9 percent in 1986 and 15 percent in 1989. Other manufacturing also saw its share climb from about 1 percent in 1974 and 1979, to 3 percent in 1986, and to 6 percent in 1989; the chemicals share of DFI also rose to 6 percent by 1989. On the other hand, the share of DFI in textiles fell to 5 percent in 1986 and 4 percent in 1989. For much of the 1970–1986 period, trade received more DFI than other nonmanufacturing industries, but by 1989 finance and services received more. DFI in agriculture and mining (primarily oil exploration) was also significant, especially in the mid-1970s and the mid-1980s, but it tapered off in the latter years of both decades. The share of construction DFI also peaked in 1986 and has declined somewhat since.

Japanese DFI in particular has tended to be concentrated in manufacturing. Japan accounted for 47–48 percent of all cumulative manufacturing DFI in Thailand in 1974 and 1979; this share dipped to 32 percent in 1986 but rose again to 45 percent in 1989 as a result of the investment boom. In contrast, the U.S. share of DFI in Thailand's manufacturing sector rose from 16 percent in 1974 to 25 percent in 1986 and declined to 15 percent in 1989. In the 1980s, Japan has generally been the largest source of trade DFI and has become the major source of DFI in construction and in finance and services in recent years. On the other hand, the United States has accounted for the vast majority of the investment in oil exploration; much of this DFI was undertaken in the early and mid-1980s when natural gas was discovered in the Gulf of Thailand.

Within manufacturing, Japan accounted for over one-half of cumulative DFI in textiles, food, and chemicals in the 1970s. However in recent years Japan's share in these industries has dropped significantly while U.S. investments in these industries have also been limited; this trend reflects the growth of NICs' investment, especially in food and textiles. In the important electric machinery sector, the United States accounted for more than one-half of cumulative DFI through 1986 but its share has since fallen rapidly as cumulative Japanese DFI in this sector increased ninefold in the period 1986–1989 to capture a 63 percent share in 1989. In addition, Japan's share has risen to exceed 60 percent in metals and nonmetallic mineral products and nonelectric machinery (including automobiles).

## Capital and Employment in Promoted Firms

Having examined some characteristics of DFI flows in Thailand, the performance of domestic and foreign firms is compared below. This task is very difficult in Thailand due to the lack of systematic and consistent collection of data on the operations of both foreign and domestic firms. To further explore the differences between foreign and domestic firms in Thailand, we employ in this and the following two sections (1) our own compilations of data from BOI survey questionnaires

Table 4.4  Cumulative DFI in Thailand since 1970 by Industry and
Country, 1974-1989 (yearend stock, US$ millions)

| Country/industry[a] | 1974 | 1979 | 1986 | 1989 |
|---|---|---|---|---|
| World (total) | 416 | 798 | 2,662 | 5,871 |
| Agriculture and mining | 73 | 95 | 468 | 562 |
| Oil exploration | 67 | 82 | 389 | 435 |
| Manufacturing | 122 | 263 | 859 | 2,483 |
| Food | 16 | 28 | 68 | 209 |
| Textiles | 56 | 100 | 142 | 251 |
| Chemicals | 14 | 32 | 118 | 327 |
| Petroleum products | 6 | 10 | 102 | 88 |
| Metals and nonmetallic | 7 | 12 | 69 | 258 |
| Electric machinery | 12 | 56 | 231 | 855 |
| Nonelectric machinery | 4 | 16 | 60 | 123 |
| Other manufacturing | 7 | 9 | 69 | 371 |
| Construction | 42 | 92 | 404 | 685 |
| Trade | 75 | 172 | 522 | 981 |
| Finance, services, etc. | 106 | 176 | 409 | 1,160 |
| | | | | |
| Japan (total) | 116 | 242 | 784 | 2,182 |
| Agriculture and mining | 2 | 1 | 11 | 28 |
| Oil exploration | 0 | 1 | 1 | 1 |
| Manufacturing | 59 | 123 | 278 | 1,114 |
| Food | 13 | 18 | 11 | 32 |
| Textiles | 29 | 66 | 96 | 109 |
| Chemicals | 8 | 16 | 30 | 94 |
| Petroleum products | 0 | 1 | 1 | 2 |
| Metals and nonmetallic | 2 | 3 | 41 | 172 |
| Electric machinery | 5 | 9 | 59 | 535 |
| Nonelectric machinery | 2 | 7 | 22 | 77 |
| Other manufacturing | 1 | 3 | 19 | 93 |
| Construction | 6 | 23 | 220 | 409 |
| Trade | 32 | 54 | 196 | 331 |
| Finance, services, etc. | 17 | 42 | 78 | 299 |

Table 4.4 (continued)

| Country/industry[a] | 1974 | 1979 | 1986 | 1989 |
|---|---|---|---|---|
| United States (total) | 160 | 288 | 821 | 1,216 |
| Agriculture and mining | 70 | 83 | 295 | 332 |
| Oil exploration | 66 | 77 | 282 | 310 |
| Manufacturing | 20 | 54 | 214 | 384 |
| Food | 1 | 3 | 22 | 47 |
| Textiles | 4 | 5 | 6 | 23 |
| Chemicals | 1 | 2 | 19 | 37 |
| Petroleum products | 5 | 9 | 29 | 29 |
| Metals and nonmetallic | 2 | 3 | 1 | 5 |
| Electric machinery | 6 | 31 | 120 | 178 |
| Nonelectric machinery | 0 | 6 | 10 | 12 |
| Other manufacturing | 1 | -4 | 8 | 53 |
| Construction | 21 | 24 | 60 | 69 |
| Trade | 20 | 57 | 115 | 210 |
| Finance, services, etc. | 29 | 70 | 137 | 221 |
| Other (total) | 140 | 268 | 1,057 | 2,473 |
| Agriculture and mining | 1 | 11 | 163 | 202 |
| Oil exploration | 1 | 5 | 106 | 124 |
| Manufacturing | 43 | 87 | 366 | 986 |
| Food | 2 | 7 | 34 | 130 |
| Textiles | 24 | 29 | 40 | 119 |
| Chemicals | 5 | 14 | 70 | 197 |
| Petroleum products | 1 | 1 | 72 | 57 |
| Metals and nonmetallic | 4 | 6 | 27 | 81 |
| Electric machinery | 1 | 16 | 52 | 142 |
| Nonelectric machinery | 2 | 3 | 29 | 34 |
| Other manufacturing | 5 | 10 | 42 | 225 |
| Construction | 14 | 45 | 124 | 206 |
| Trade | 23 | 61 | 211 | 439 |
| Finance, services, etc. | 59 | 64 | 194 | 640 |

[a]Nonelectric machinery includes transport machinery.

Sources: Bank of Thailand (various years); International Monetary Fund (various years).

Table 4.5  Registered Capital in Sample of Promoted Firms in Thailand, 1974 and 1986

| Industry[c] | Foreign Firms[a] | | | Domestic Firms[b] | | |
|---|---|---|---|---|---|---|
| | | Registered Capital | | | Registered Capital | |
| | Number | Amount (US$1,000) | Foreign Share (%) | Number | Amount (US$1,000) | Foreign Share (%) |
| **1974** | | | | | | |
| Manufacturing | 180 | 255,708 | 46.7 | 98 | 147,485 | 1.4 |
| Food | 22 | 15,434 | 52.1 | 20 | 16,829 | 0.0 |
| Textiles | 43 | 98,104 | 42.4 | 14 | 17,546 | 4.9 |
| Apparel | 7 | 4,663 | 36.3 | 3 | 1,129 | 0.0 |
| Footwear, leather | 0 | 0 | nc | 0 | 0 | nc |
| Wood products | 2 | 551 | 67.9 | 7 | 7,409 | 0.2 |
| Paper products | 4 | 3,779 | 60.1 | 8 | 16,344 | 6.5 |
| Chemicals | 29 | 52,640 | 53.7 | 3 | 37,350 | 0.0 |
| Rubber, plastics | 10 | 11,436 | 51.3 | 5 | 2,403 | 0.0 |
| Nonmetallic | 14 | 20,545 | 36.2 | 8 | 15,877 | 0.0 |
| Basic metals | 5 | 12,147 | 32.8 | 3 | 2,454 | 0.0 |
| Metal products | 17 | 20,147 | 49.1 | 14 | 24,402 | 0.6 |
| Nonelec. machinery | 1 | 1,078 | 49.0 | 2 | 491 | 0.0 |
| Electric machinery | 12 | 8,083 | 72.0 | 2 | 1,178 | 2.1 |

| | | | | | |
|---|---|---|---|---|---|
| Transport machinery | 11 | 6,462 | 52.4 | 7 | 3,730 | 0.0 |
| Miscellaneous | 3 | 638 | 48.3 | 2 | 344 | 0.0 |
| **1986** | | | | | | |
| Manufacturing | 202 | 507,014 | 44.4 | 117 | 314,422 | 1.3 |
| Food | 36 | 66,442 | 46.8 | 30 | 64,468 | 1.6 |
| Textiles | 17 | 137,037 | 25.6 | 13 | 92,353 | 2.2 |
| Apparel | 9 | 14,569 | 47.5 | 1 | 1,963 | 3.2 |
| Footwear, leather | 1 | 2,699 | 24.6 | 3 | 4,417 | 0.0 |
| Wood products | 5 | 8,980 | 35.5 | 2 | 2,699 | 0.0 |
| Paper products | 3 | 10,405 | 46.9 | 6 | 24,785 | 1.5 |
| Chemicals | 33 | 54,564 | 71.4 | 4 | 18,405 | 0.0 |
| Rubber, plastics | 17 | 12,787 | 44.8 | 12 | 15,632 | 0.0 |
| Nonmetallic | 9 | 58,822 | 34.0 | 13 | 35,313 | 1.3 |
| Basic metals | 5 | 26,856 | 30.9 | 5 | 23,886 | 0.1 |
| Metal products | 18 | 33,427 | 65.7 | 7 | 6,015 | 1.1 |
| Nonelec. machinery | 7 | 21,485 | 45.4 | 3 | 4,000 | 1.8 |
| Electric machinery | 14 | 23,224 | 75.5 | 5 | 4,908 | 0.0 |
| Transport machinery | 11 | 13,673 | 46.2 | 0 | 0 | nc |
| Miscellaneous | 17 | 22,042 | 65.8 | 13 | 15,577 | 0.3 |

nc = Not calculable.

[a] Firms with foreign shares of registered capital equal to or above 10 percent.

[b] Firms with foreign shares of registered capital below 10 percent.

[c] Manufacturing excludes petroleum products; miscellaneous manufacturing includes precision machinery.

Source: Authors' compilation of Board of Investment questionnaires; International Monetary Fund (various years).

which were collected from promoted firms, both domestic and foreign, (2) UNIDO compilations of Thai industrial surveys, and (3) estimates of ISIC-based exports from UNIDO and Australian National University. It should be stressed, however, that because the coverage of promoted firm surveys and Thai industrial surveys differs greatly from year to year, analyses over time (such as those attempted here) are very complicated. In addition, the commodity classification of total Thai exports does not correspond precisely with the enterprise classification of promoted firm exports, causing further difficulties.

As for the promoted firm data itself, the BOI has distributed questionnaires to all promoted firms for all years since 1970 but reply rates have generally been quite low (20–40 percent). In order to generate more complete samples for the years that were chosen for these analyses (1974 and 1986), we have added replies from the 1973 survey to the 1974 sample and replies from the 1985 survey to the 1986 sample for firms which did not provide replies in the sample years. We then dropped from this sample all firms which reported zero employment, zero fixed assets, and/or zero or negative value added (calculated as the difference between total sales and total input purchases). Foreign firms are defined as those firms with 10 percent or more of their registered capital coming from foreign investors while domestic firms are defined as those firms with under 10 percent of their registered capital coming from foreign sources.

The resulting 1974 sample consists of 180 foreign firms and 98 domestic firms while the 1986 sample consists of 202 foreign firms and 117 domestic firms, all of which were in the manufacturing sector (Table 4.5). The total registered capital of the firms in the 1974 sample amounts to US$403 million or 64 percent of the registered capital for all firms receiving promotion certificates by the end of that year (cf. Table 4.3). For 1986, corresponding figures were US$821 million and 59 percent, respectively. Also in 1974, the total foreign contribution to registered capital (in both domestic and foreign firms) amounted to US$122 million or 67 percent of the foreign contribution to registered capital for all firms receiving promotion certificates; in 1986 these figures were US$229 million and 55 percent, respectively. Considering that (1) some firms receiving promotion certificates never actually begin operation and (2) several promoted firms operate in sectors other than manufactur- ing, these samples cover approximately two-thirds to three-fourths of all the registered capital in BOI-promoted manufacturing firms. In addition, since several foreign manufacturing firms have set up operations without going through the BOI, even complete coverage of BOI-promoted manufacturing firms would understate the extent of foreign firm activity in Thai manufacturing.

Interestingly, there was little change in the share of foreign capital in total capital in this sample over time. Foreign capital accounted for 44–47 percent of all registered capital in foreign firms and 1 percent in domestic firms for both 1974 and 1986. However these ratios changed in the individual industries. For example, foreign capital shares in foreign firms fell over 10 percentage points in textiles, wood products, and paper products while increases of at least 10 percentage points occurred in apparel, chemicals, metal products, and miscellaneous manufactures. In domestic firms, declines of foreign capital shares over 2 percentage points were observed in textiles, paper products, and electric machinery with an increase of similar magnitude in apparel. Thus there was a weak tendency for foreign ownership shares to decline in industries employing relatively standardized technologies (e.g., textiles, wood products, and paper products) and to increase in industries using more sophisticated technologies (e.g., chemicals and metal products).

Nonetheless these figures hide the fact that wholly owned foreign ventures have become much more important among promoted firms in recent years as the BOI has relaxed its local participation requirements. For example, although wholly owned foreign ventures accounted for only 2 percent of all promoted firms receiving promotion certificates and 2 percent of all registered capital in these firms at yearend 1983, at yearend 1986 these ratios had risen to 4 percent and 8 percent, respectively, and at yearend 1989 these ratios were 5 percent and 11 percent, respectively (Board of Investment, various years). Thus while our sample reveals little change in the share of foreign capital, the ownership structure has been changing quite a bit in recent years.

Returning to our sample of promoted firms, the foreign firms in this sample employed 94,591 workers in 1974 but only 79,189 persons in 1986 (Table 4.6). The textiles industry accounted for the largest share of this employment in both years, 51 percent in 1974 and 20 percent in 1986. Other industries with high employment in 1974 include apparel, metal products, nonmetallic minerals, food, and chemicals, though none of these industries accounted for more than 8 percent of the total. By 1986, there was substantial diversification as textiles was followed closely by food (19 percent), apparel (14 percent), electric machinery (11 percent), miscellaneous manufacturing (7 percent), and rubber and plastics (6 percent). Foreign firms dominated the sample of promoted firms accounting for 74 percent of all promoted firm employment in 1974 and 62 percent in 1986. In 1974, foreign firm shares of employment in sample promoted firms exceeded 80 percent in textiles, apparel, chemicals, rubber and plastics, basic metals, and electric machinery. In 1986, this list consisted of apparel, chemicals, and the three machinery industries. On the other hand, the foreign share of total Thai employment was much smaller with foreign shares of Thai manufacturing employment at only 8 percent in 1974 and 6 percent in 1986. Moreover foreign firm shares reached double-digit levels in only a few industries, namely, nonmetallic minerals, metal products, textiles, and chemicals in 1974, and electric machinery, rubber and plastics, and metal products in 1986.

It should be noted, however, that these figures probably underestimate the extent of foreign firm employment, with the underestimation likely to be larger in the latter year. An indication of the extent of underestimation comes from a more complete survey of 600 foreign manufacturing firms in 1985 compiled from the BOI and several other sources by Sibunruang and Brimble (1988). They estimate foreign firm employment to be 182,655 in manufacturing or 2.3 times the 1986 figure given in Table 4.6. Despite this large difference in magnitude, Sibunruang and Brimble's figures on the industrial distribution of employment were similar to that in Table 4.6 with the figures varying between 1.1 and 2.5 times our estimates in all but five industries, namely, footwear and leather (11.5-fold differential), chemicals (5.4-fold differential), wood products (5.3-fold differential), transport machinery (4.2-fold differential), and paper products (3.9-fold differential).[5] They also use labor force survey data on total Thai employment which were one-and-a-half times as large as

Table 4.6 Employment in Sample of Promoted Firms in Thailand, 1974 and 1986

| Industry[a] | Employment in Foreign Firms | Foreign Share (%) | | Average Employment of a Promoted Firm | |
|---|---|---|---|---|---|
| | | Promoted Firms | All Thailand | Foreign Firms | Local Firms |
| **1974** | | | | | |
| Manufacturing | 94,591 | 74.3 | 7.7 | 526 | 333 |
| Food | 5,849 | 45.2 | 1.4 | 266 | 355 |
| Textiles | 48,647 | 86.8 | 20.7 | 1,131 | 528 |
| Apparel | 7,979 | 89.8 | 9.0 | 1,140 | 302 |
| Footwear, leather | 0 | nc | 0.0 | nc | nc |
| Wood products | 341 | 14.3 | 0.5 | 171 | 291 |
| Paper products | 837 | 24.2 | 2.0 | 209 | 327 |
| Chemicals | 5,474 | 85.0 | 12.6 | 189 | 323 |
| Rubber, plastics | 3,116 | 83.0 | 4.8 | 312 | 128 |
| Nonmetallic | 6,389 | 62.9 | 24.5 | 456 | 472 |
| Basic metals | 3,108 | 92.5 | 7.8 | 622 | 84 |
| Metal products | 7,354 | 63.4 | 22.2 | 433 | 303 |
| Nonelec. machinery | 147 | 33.6 | 0.4 | 147 | 145 |
| Electric machinery | 2,987 | 89.3 | 9.4 | 249 | 180 |

| | | | | |
|---|---|---|---|---|
| Transport machinery | 1,534 | 46.5 | 3.1 | 139 | 252 |
| Miscellaneous | 829 | 70.9 | 2.5 | 276 | 170 |

**1986**

| | | | | | |
|---|---|---|---|---|---|
| Manufacturing | 79,189 | 62.1 | 5.7 | 392 | 412 |
| Food | 15,331 | 54.0 | 3.3 | 426 | 435 |
| Textiles | 15,719 | 53.7 | 9.3 | 925 | 1,041 |
| Apparel | 11,060 | 97.0 | 7.4 | 1,229 | 340 |
| Footwear, leather | 473 | 16.4 | 2.9 | 473 | 804 |
| Wood products | 907 | 64.9 | 1.8 | 181 | 246 |
| Paper products | 803 | 31.7 | 1.7 | 268 | 289 |
| Chemicals | 3,197 | 89.8 | 6.1 | 97 | 91 |
| Rubber, plastics | 5,142 | 74.5 | 14.4 | 302 | 147 |
| Nonmetallic | 3,204 | 39.6 | 6.7 | 356 | 377 |
| Basic metals | 1,588 | 37.6 | 5.2 | 318 | 526 |
| Metal products | 3,465 | 79.1 | 12.2 | 193 | 131 |
| Nonelec. machinery | 1,773 | 81.6 | 3.5 | 253 | 133 |
| Electric machinery | 9,100 | 87.6 | 20.8 | 650 | 258 |
| Transport machinery | 2,088 | 100.0 | 3.0 | 190 | nc |
| Miscellaneous | 5,339 | 54.5 | 4.1 | 314 | 343 |

nc = Not calculable.

aManufacturing excludes petroleum products; miscellaneous manufacturing includes precision machinery.

Source: Authors' compilation of Board of Investment questionnaires; UNIDO (1989).

the UNIDO estimates used here in the manufacturing aggregate (cf. Table 4.1 and endnote 2). In individual industries the estimates based on the labor force survey were much larger in wood products (5.5-fold differential), transport equipment (2.6-fold differential), rubber and plastics (2.1-fold differential), footwear and leather (2.1-fold differential), and basic metals and metal products combined (2.0-fold differential), and were much smaller in nonelectric machinery (0.3-fold differential); in other industries the differential varied from 0.7-fold to 1.7-fold. As a result, Sibunruang and Brimble estimate significantly larger foreign firm shares of total Thai employment in a number of sectors (38 percent in nonelectric machinery, 31 percent in electric machinery, 23 percent in chemicals and petroleum products, 22 percent in rubber and rubber products, 18 percent in textiles, 16 percent in footwear and leather, 10 percent in metals and metal products combined, and 9 percent in the manufacturing aggregate). Since their data base is more complete for both foreign firms and all Thailand, it is likely that our data underestimate the scope of total foreign firm employment in 1986, though it is impossible to ascertain whether this also holds for 1974.

Taken together, these data suggest that foreign firms were large direct sources of employment in nonmetallic minerals, textiles, and metal products in 1974 but that the relative importance of foreign firms declined markedly in these industries over time; at the same time the relative importance of foreign firms has increased significantly in electric machinery and nonelectric machinery. The direct employment effects, however, are only part of the story as foreign firms can indirectly stimulate employment creation through input-output linkages. Sibunruang and Brimble (1988) estimated the ratio of indirectly created employment to direct employment in 1985 to be 2.2 in foreign manufacturing firms. This ratio was lowest (0.5–0.8) in apparel, wood products, nonmetallic minerals, and metals and metal products, and was highest (6.4–7.8) in food and nonelectric machinery. In all other industries, the ratio varied between 1.2 and 1.8. Thus, if indirect effects are included in the analysis, the contribution of foreign firms would be even larger with the indirect contributions being greatest in food and nonelectric machinery.

Returning to our sample of promoted firms (Table 4.6), we find that employment per foreign manufacturing firm declined from 526 to 392 while employment per domestic manufacturing firm grew from 333 to 412. That is, on average, foreign firms tended to be larger than domestic firms in 1974 while the reverse was true in 1986 (though the difference between local and foreign firms was very small in the latter year). Much of this shift is due to the fact that in textiles, the largest source of foreign firm employment in 1974, employment per foreign firm fell from 1,131 to 925 while employment per domestic firm rose from 528 to 1,041. On the other hand, even in 1986, promoted foreign firms had significantly more employees per firm than their local counterparts in apparel, rubber and plastics, metal products, nonelectric machinery, and electric machinery.

Despite the decrease in total foreign firm employment and employment per foreign firm, total fixed capital in foreign manufacturing firms and fixed capital per foreign manufacturing firm increased 2.0-fold and 1.8-fold, respectively, over the 1974–1986 period (Table 4.7). Because these figures on capital are expressed in historical book values, the absolute magnitude of the increases discussed have little meaning. However, if one assumes that the differences between historical, current, and constant price valuations are similar for domestic and foreign firms, then comparisons between domestic and foreign firms are meaningful. As shown in Table 4.7, total capital and capital per firm increased even more rapidly in domestic firms. This is reflected in the decline of the foreign firms' share of total promoted firm capital from 74 percent in 1974 to 67 percent in 1986. As with employment, textiles accounted for the largest share of foreign firm capital, 40 percent in 1974 and 34 percent in 1986.

Although textile's share of foreign firm capital was markedly below its corresponding share of foreign firm employment, this pattern was dramatically reversed by 1986. In other words, capital per employee increased dramatically (534 percent to be precise) in foreign textiles firms, while capital per employee increased much more slowly in domestic firms in this industry. In short, foreign firms in this industry went from being more labor intensive to being much more capital intensive than their domestic counterparts. Indeed, foreign firms went from being more labor intensive than domestic firms to more capital intensive in a variety of other industries including apparel, wood products, paper products, basic metals, and electric machinery. Partly as a result of this capital deepening, foreign firms in manufacturing as a whole were 26 percent more capital intensive than their local counterparts in 1986 but only 2 percent more capital intensive in 1974. A second factor that has led to the widening gap in capital intensity between foreign and local firms over time is that foreign capital has become more concentrated in relatively capital-intensive industries. More specifically, the ratio of fixed capital in foreign firms operating in industries with a capital intensity greater than the average capital intensity for all foreign manufacturing firms to fixed capital in all foreign firms was only 43 percent in 1974 but 67 percent in 1986. Thus, capital deepening within industries and the changing interindustry distribution of capital have both contributed to the increase of foreign firm capital intensity relative to domestic firms.

These data thus show substantial changes in size and factor intensities both in the aggregate and in individual industries. They also show a marked diversification in Thai manufacturing activity, both in foreign and domestic firms. In addition to the interindustry diversification revealed in the data, it is also important to note that there has been substantial diversification within individual industries and firms as product lines have been added and firms have upgraded their operations. Although the data do not show the precise extent of this intraindustry diversification, changes in factor intensity are thought to result in large part from the introduction of new equipment and technologies necessary to produce new products. The data also show that changes in size and factor intensities in foreign firms are similar to corresponding changes in the Thai manufacturing sector overall. Thus the data suggest that foreign firms have contributed to changes in the structure of employment and fixed capital stocks in Thai manufacturing.

## Value Added and Productivity in Promoted Firms

Turning to the production side (Table 4.8), we observe a more than threefold increase in nominal foreign firm value added (estimated as the difference between

Table 4.7  Fixed Capital and Capital Intensity in Sample of Promoted Firms in Thailand, 1974 and 1986

| Industry[a] | Fixed Capital of Promoted Foreign Firms (US$) | Foreign Share of All Promoted Firms (%) | Capital per Firm in Promoted Firms (US$) | | Capital per Employee in Promoted Firms (US$) | |
|---|---|---|---|---|---|---|
| | | | Foreign Firms | Local Firms | Foreign Firms | Local Firms |
| 1974 | | | | | | |
| Manufacturing | 628,588 | 74.0 | 3,492 | 2,259 | 6,645 | 6,777 |
| Food | 37,052 | 60.8 | 1,684 | 1,193 | 6,335 | 3,362 |
| Textiles | 251,137 | 82.8 | 5,840 | 3,735 | 5,162 | 7,074 |
| Apparel | 7,952 | 60.3 | 1,136 | 1,743 | 997 | 5,772 |
| Footwear, leather | 0 | nc | nc | nc | nc | nc |
| Wood products | 352 | 4.8 | 176 | 1,000 | 1,032 | 3,437 |
| Paper products | 9,538 | 18.7 | 2,385 | 5,193 | 11,396 | 15,880 |
| Chemicals | 146,346 | 91.5 | 5,046 | 4,560 | 26,735 | 14,117 |
| Rubber, plastics | 29,962 | 94.6 | 2,996 | 343 | 9,615 | 2,681 |
| Nonmetallic | 52,848 | 68.1 | 3,775 | 3,095 | 8,272 | 6,557 |
| Basic metals | 28,086 | 88.7 | 5,617 | 1,195 | 9,037 | 14,282 |
| Metal products | 39,585 | 50.4 | 2,329 | 2,778 | 5,383 | 9,167 |
| Nonelec. machinery | 1,271 | 53.6 | 1,271 | 551 | 8,648 | 3,800 |
| Electric machinery | 12,693 | 83.0 | 1,058 | 1,295 | 4,250 | 7,217 |

| | | | | | | |
|---|---|---|---|---|---|---|
| Transport machinery | 2,585 | 5,931 | 651 | 827 | 66.6 | 9,098 |
| Miscellaneous | 1,871 | 3,219 | 318 | 890 | 80.8 | 2,669 |
| **1986** | | | | | | |
| Manufacturing | 12,830 | 16,155 | 5,292 | 6,333 | 67.4 | 1,279,297 |
| Food | 8,609 | 9,159 | 3,744 | 3,900 | 55.6 | 140,412 |
| Textiles | 11,727 | 27,571 | 12,204 | 25,494 | 73.2 | 433,392 |
| Apparel | 1,136 | 2,166 | 386 | 2,662 | 98.4 | 23,961 |
| Footwear, leather | 2,590 | 8,583 | 2,081 | 4,060 | 39.4 | 4,060 |
| Wood products | 3,732 | 13,321 | 916 | 2,416 | 86.8 | 12,082 |
| Paper products | 34,323 | 47,125 | 9,919 | 12,614 | 38.9 | 37,842 |
| Chemicals | 115,516 | 23,771 | 10,512 | 2,303 | 64.4 | 75,996 |
| Rubber, plastics | 11,651 | 9,200 | 1,708 | 2,783 | 69.8 | 47,309 |
| Nonmetallic | 21,474 | 48,196 | 8,089 | 17,158 | 59.5 | 154,419 |
| Basic metals | 25,434 | 31,032 | 13,388 | 9,856 | 42.4 | 49,279 |
| Metal products | 8,917 | 18,603 | 1,164 | 3,581 | 88.8 | 64,459 |
| Nonelec. machinery | 13,849 | 25,882 | 1,847 | 6,556 | 89.2 | 45,890 |
| Electric machinery | 10,658 | 12,737 | 2,750 | 8,279 | 89.4 | 115,910 |
| Transport machinery | nc | 15,583 | nc | 2,958 | 100.0 | 32,537 |
| Miscellaneous | 4,083 | 7,820 | 1,399 | 2,456 | 69.7 | 41,752 |

nc = Not calculable.

aManufacturing excludes petroleum products; miscellaneous manufacturing includes precision machinery.

<u>Source</u>: Authors' compilation of Board of Investment questionnaires; International Monetary Fund (various years).

Table 4.8 Value Added and Productivity in Sample of Promoted Foreign Firms in Thailand, 1974 and 1986

| Industry[a] | Foreign Firm Value Added (US$1,000) | Foreign Share (%) | | Value Added per Worker (US$) | | | Ratio of Promoted Firm Value Added to Capital | |
|---|---|---|---|---|---|---|---|---|
| | | Promoted Firms | All Thailand | Promoted Foreign | Promoted Domestic | All Thailand | Foreign | Domestic |
| **1974** | | | | | | | | |
| Manufacturing | 403,902 | 72.8 | 16.3 | 4,270 | 4,626 | 2,008 | 0.64 | 0.68 |
| Food | 29,762 | 72.1 | 3.6 | 5,088 | 1,622 | 1,990 | 0.80 | 0.48 |
| Textiles | 137,654 | 74.7 | 44.5 | 2,830 | 6,322 | 1,319 | 0.55 | 0.89 |
| Apparel | 3,991 | 70.4 | 1.6 | 500 | 1,856 | 2,758 | 0.50 | 0.32 |
| Footwear, leather | 0 | nc | 0.0 | nc | nc | 2,058 | nc | nc |
| Wood products | 230 | 4.1 | 0.1 | 674 | 2,658 | 2,506 | 0.65 | 0.77 |
| Paper products | 7,509 | 33.5 | 9.6 | 8,971 | 5,696 | 1,875 | 0.79 | 0.36 |
| Chemicals | 60,505 | 81.9 | 72.6 | 11,053 | 13,809 | 1,920 | 0.41 | 0.98 |
| Rubber, plastics | 31,987 | 97.6 | 50.8 | 10,265 | 1,211 | 973 | 1.07 | 0.45 |
| Nonmetallic | 32,511 | 66.6 | 35.7 | 5,089 | 4,320 | 3,493 | 0.62 | 0.66 |
| Basic metals | 24,902 | 92.0 | 35.3 | 8,012 | 8,640 | 1,778 | 0.89 | 0.60 |
| Metal products | 25,633 | 51.4 | 31.6 | 3,486 | 5,722 | 2,457 | 0.65 | 0.62 |
| Nonelec. machinery | 1,054 | 68.0 | 1.5 | 7,167 | 1,706 | 1,766 | 0.83 | 0.45 |
| Electric machinery | 14,431 | 95.5 | 27.1 | 4,831 | 1,915 | 1,677 | 1.14 | 0.27 |
| Transport machinery | 30,016 | 70.8 | 14.2 | 19,567 | 7,024 | 4,278 | 3.30 | 2.72 |
| Miscellaneous | 3,720 | 89.5 | 5.3 | 4,488 | 1,279 | 2,096 | 1.39 | 0.68 |

## 1986

| | | | | | | | |
|---|---|---|---|---|---|---|---|
| Manufacturing | 1,260,093 | 71.8 | 14.4 | 15,912 | 10,258 | 6,315 | 0.98 | 0.80 |
| Food | 170,588 | 59.4 | 6.8 | 11,127 | 8,951 | 5,498 | 1.21 | 1.04 |
| Textiles | 205,940 | 61.8 | 19.8 | 13,101 | 9,415 | 6,163 | 0.48 | 0.80 |
| Apparel | 29,616 | 92.1 | 2.2 | 2,678 | 7,472 | 9,039 | 1.24 | 6.57 |
| Footwear, leather | 5,559 | 56.5 | 2.0 | 11,752 | 1,779 | 16,732 | 1.37 | 0.69 |
| Wood products | 8,643 | 71.5 | 2.5 | 9,530 | 7,001 | 6,820 | 0.72 | 1.88 |
| Paper products | 23,884 | 37.6 | 8.3 | 29,743 | 22,897 | 6,087 | 0.63 | 0.67 |
| Chemicals | 98,015 | 90.8 | 29.3 | 30,658 | 27,416 | 6,417 | 1.29 | 0.24 |
| Rubber, plastics | 43,346 | 73.6 | 18.5 | 8,430 | 8,840 | 6,583 | 0.92 | 0.76 |
| Nonmetallic | 80,029 | 48.7 | 20.5 | 24,978 | 17,234 | 8,169 | 0.52 | 0.80 |
| Basic metals | 92,084 | 62.2 | 75.6 | 57,988 | 21,255 | 4,024 | 1.87 | 0.84 |
| Metal products | 39,865 | 83.8 | 16.0 | 11,505 | 8,452 | 8,769 | 0.62 | 0.95 |
| Nonelec. machinery | 28,489 | 87.4 | 12.3 | 16,068 | 10,292 | 4,554 | 0.62 | 0.74 |
| Electric machinery | 303,899 | 98.8 | 104.4 | 33,395 | 2,796 | 6,662 | 2.62 | 0.26 |
| Transport machinery | 70,787 | 100.0 | 14.9 | 33,902 | nc | 6,890 | 2.18 | nc |
| Miscellaneous | 59,349 | 75.2 | 10.5 | 11,116 | 4,405 | 4,308 | 1.42 | 1.08 |

nc = Not calculable.

*Manufacturing excludes petroleum products; miscellaneous manufacturing includes precision machinery.

Source: Authors' compilation of Board of Investment questionnaires; International Monetary Fund (various years); NESDB (various years); UNIDO (1989).

total sales and input purchases) between 1974 and 1986. In this case, local firm value added increased at a roughly equal rate and conseqently the foreign share of value added in the sample of all promoted firms which was rather constant at 72–73 percent. In 1974, textiles had the largest share of foreign firm value added (34 percent), followed by chemicals (15 percent), and nonmetallic minerals, rubber and plastics, transport machinery, and food (shares of 7–8 percent each). By 1986, the distribution had diversified as electric machinery had the largest share (24 percent), followed by textiles (16 percent), food (14 percent), chemicals (8 percent), and basic metals (7 percent).

Furthermore foreign firms accounted for 16 percent of all manufacturing value added in Thailand in 1974 and 14 percent in 1986. In the individual industries in 1974, foreign firms accounted for over 50 percent of Thai value added in chemicals and rubber and plastics, and 27–45 percent in textiles, nonmetallic minerals, basic metals, metal products, and electric machinery. In 1986, foreign firm shares were over 50 percent in basic metals and electric machinery, 20–29 percent in chemicals, nonmetallic minerals, and textiles, and 15–19 percent in rubber and plastics, metal products, and transport machinery.[6]

The differences between the foreign shares of value added and the foreign shares of employment reflect the differences in average labor productivity among domestic and foreign firms. For example, in the manufacturing aggregate, value added per employee in promoted foreign firms was about two times higher than in all firms in Thailand in 1974 and two-and-one-half times higher in 1986. It should be noted that our estimates of the labor productivity differential between sample foreign firms and all other firms in Thailand is on the low side since the estimates of total Thai employment obtained from the industrial survey that we used are lower than the estimates from the more widely used labor force survey (cf. employment discussion above). Labor productivity was also higher in promoted foreign firms in all individual industries except apparel (both years), footwear and leather (1986), and wood products (1974). Moreover, the labor productivity differential between foreign and domestic firms was especially high (5–14 times) in paper, chemicals, basic metals, and transport machinery in both 1974 and 1986, in rubber and plastics in 1974, and in electric machinery in 1986. Thus compared to all firms in Thailand, promoted foreign firms are characterized by much higher labor productivity with these differences being quite large in a number of industries.

However when one compares promoted domestic and promoted foreign firms, the picture is much more mixed. For example, in the manufacturing aggregate, value added per employee in promoted foreign firms was slightly lower than value added per employee in promoted domestic firms in 1974; however value added per employee was 1.6 times larger in promoted foreign firms by 1986. Moreover, promoted domestic firms were characterized by higher labor productivity than promoted foreign firms in textiles, apparel, wood products, chemicals, basic metals, and metal products in 1974. Since labor productivity grew more rapidly in promoted foreign firms, promoted domestic firms had higher labor productivity in only two industries in 1986, apparel and rubber and plastics. Thus the productivity differential was much smaller between promoted foreign and promoted domestic firms than between promoted foreign and all Thai firms. Nevertheless labor productivity grew much faster in promoted foreign firms than in promoted domestic or all Thai firms. Of course, since the data on value added are in current prices, much of the increase observed is due to an increase in prices; however, if one assumes that prices increased at the same rate for promoted domestic firms, promoted foreign firms, and all firms in Thailand (and for all practical purposes one must assume this since separate deflators do not exist), the comparative analysis remains valid.

Since the average product of labor can be rewritten as the product of the capital-labor ratio and the average product of capital, it is convenient to decompose the average labor productivity differential into the product of the differential in capital intensity and the differential in capital productivity as follows:

$$(V_f /E_f )/(V_d /E_d ) = ((K_d /E_d )/(K_f /E_f ))$$
$$* ((V_f /K_f )/(V_d /K_d ))$$

(4.1)

where $V$ = value added, $K$ = capital, $E$ = employment, and $f$ and $d$ are subscripts indicating foreign and domestic promoted firms, respectively. For example, for promoted foreign and promoted domestic firms in the manufacturing aggregate in 1974, the labor productivity differential, $(V_f/E_f)/(V_d/E_d)$, was 0.923 while the capital intensity differential, $(K_f/E_f)/(K_d/E_d)$, was smaller at 0.981. The majority of the labor productivity differential was due to the capital productivity differential, $(V_f/K_f)/(V_d/K_d)$, of 0.941. Interestingly, by 1986 when the labor productivity differential grew to 1.551, the capital intensity and capital productivity differentials were very similar at 1.259 and 1.232, respectively. The largest capital productivity differentials, 4.284 in 1974 and 9.993 in 1986, are observed in electric machinery with a large differential also observed in chemicals in 1986 (5.434). In electric machinery in 1974 and in chemicals in 1986, the capital intensity differentials were 0.589 and 0.206, respectively, while the labor productivity differentials were 2.522 and 1.118, respectively. In other words, the greater labor productivity among foreign firms in these industries was due solely to greater capital productivity.

The differences between productivity in promoted foreign and local firms in machinery and electronics industries was studied by Khanthachai, Tanmavad, Boonsiri, Nisaisook, and Arttanuchit (1987). They estimated Cobb-Douglas production functions for both types of firms using firm-level, cross-section data from 1982 and 1983. Formal tests of coefficient equality (Chow tests) were also undertaken to see if the production function parameters (factor output elasticities and the technology coefficient) are significantly different in foreign and domestic firms. However they found that the hypothesis that the parameters are equal in domestic and foreign firms could not be rejected for any of their samples. In short, their results suggest that the differences in average factor productivity that are observed in Table 4.8 are not a result of systematically different production behavior between foreign and domestic firms.

We have also estimated similar Cobb-Douglas production functions using our sample data (Table 4.9). The functional form used is as follows:

$$ln(V_i ) = A_i + B_i * ln(K_i ) + C_i * ln(E_i )$$

(4.2)

Table 4.9 Cobb-Douglas Production Functions for Sample of Promoted Firms in Thailand, 1974 and 1986: Ordinary Least Squares Estimates by Firm-level Cross-section

| Year, industry, firm type ($i$) | Parameters[a] | | | Adjusted $R^2$ | $F$ | Sum of Squared Residuals | Number of Firms |
|---|---|---|---|---|---|---|---|
| | $A_i$ | $B_i$ | $C_i$ | | | | |
| **1974** | | | | | | | |
| Manufacturing, $i=t$ | 5.819* | 0.518* | 0.362* | 0.521 | 151.94* | 330.1854 | 278 |
| Manufacturing, $i=l$ | 3.899* | 0.639* | 0.282* | 0.637 | 86.10* | 95.00812 | 98 |
| Manufacturing, $i=f$ | 7.795* | 0.421* | 0.339* | 0.401 | 60.93* | 210.1648 | 180 |
| Test of $H_o$: $A_t=A_l=A_f$; $B_t=B_l=B_f$; $C_t=C_l=C_f$ | | | | | $F_{(3,272)}=7.43$* | | |
| Food, $i=t$ | 7.162* | 0.534* | 0.019 | 0.257 | 8.08* | 60.29798 | 42 |
| Food, $i=l$ | 8.085* | 0.435*** | 0.030 | 0.154 | 2.73*** | 32.04494 | 20 |
| Food, $i=f$ | 10.156* | 0.436* | -0.139 | 0.272 | 4.92** | 12.37023 | 22 |
| Test of $H_o$: $A_t=A_l=A_f$; $B_t=B_l=B_f$; $C_t=C_l=C_f$ | | | | | $F_{(3,36)}=4.29$** | | |
| Textiles, $i=t$ | 6.876* | 0.231* | 0.963* | 0.675 | 59.09* | 43.90692 | 57 |
| Textiles, $i=l$ | 0.882 | 0.747* | 0.438 | 0.824 | 31.42* | 5.812626 | 14 |
| Textiles, $i=f$ | 8.176* | 0.177** | 0.915* | 0.566 | 28.33* | 34.58797 | 43 |
| Test of $H_o$: $A_t=A_l=A_f$; $B_t=B_l=B_f$; $C_t=C_l=C_f$ | | | | | $F_{(3,51)}=1.48$ | | |
| Metal Products, $i=t$ | 3.602** | 0.644* | 0.389*** | 0.728 | 41.10* | 21.67412 | 31 |
| Metal Products, $i=l$ | 1.286 | 0.851** | 0.156 | 0.795 | 26.19* | 9.573139 | 14 |
| Metal Products, $i=f$ | 7.721** | 0.423** | 0.341 | 0.388 | 6.08* | 9.771537 | 17 |
| Test of $H_o$: $A_t=A_l=A_f$; $B_t=B_l=B_f$; $C_t=C_l=C_f$ | | | | | $F_{(3,25)}=1.00$ | | |

1986

| | $A_i$ | $B_i$ | $C_i$ | | | | N |
|---|---|---|---|---|---|---|---|
| Manufacturing, $i=t$ | 6.235* | 0.507* | 0.428* | 0.376 | 96.92* | 652.7158 | 319 |
| Manufacturing, $i=l$ | 5.091* | 0.517* | 0.569* | 0.490 | 56.73* | 182.7453 | 117 |
| Manufacturing, $i=f$ | 6.967* | 0.498* | 0.344* | 0.323 | 48.95* | 454.9102 | 202 |
| Test of $H_o$: $A_t=A_l=A_f$; $B_t=B_l=B_f$; $C_t=C_l=C_f$ | | | | | $F_{(3,313)}=2.46$*** | | |
| Food, $i=t$ | 5.099 | 0.649* | 0.144 | 0.185 | 8.15* | 213.8928 | 64 |
| Food, $i=l$ | 4.797 | 0.591** | 0.387 | 0.283 | 6.71* | 67.73198 | 30 |
| Food, $i=f$ | 4.610 | 0.716* | 0.010 | 0.098 | 2.79*** | 143.6107 | 34 |
| Test of $H_o$: $A_t=A_l=A_f$; $B_t=B_l=B_f$; $C_t=C_l=C_f$ | | | | | $F_{(3,58)}=0.23$ | | |
| Textiles, $i=t$ | 2.987*** | 0.549* | 0.794* | 0.824 | 68.83* | 12.86007 | 30 |
| Textiles, $i=l$ | 2.260 | 0.538** | 0.922** | 0.824 | 29.01* | 6.498566 | 13 |
| Textiles, $i=f$ | 4.690** | 0.583*** | 0.451*** | 0.802 | 33.47* | 4.576485 | 17 |
| Test of $H_o$: $A_t=A_l=A_f$; $B_t=B_l=B_f$; $C_t=C_l=C_f$ | | | | | $F_{(3,24)}=1.29$ | | |
| Rubber-Plastics, $i=t$ | 5.876 | 0.561* | 0.320 | 0.228 | 5.14* | 76.35995 | 29 |
| Rubber-Plastics, $i=l$ | 3.349 | 0.612** | 0.638** | 0.549 | 7.70* | 6.298074 | 12 |
| Rubber-Plastics, $i=f$ | 8.795 | 0.540** | -0.126 | 0.179 | 2.74* | 63.93194 | 17 |
| Test of $H_o$: $A_t=A_l=A_f$; $B_t=B_l=B_f$; $C_t=C_l=C_f$ | | | | | $F_{(3,23)}=0.67$ | | |
| Miscellaneous, $i=t$ | 5.974*** | 0.327 | 0.962* | 0.369 | 9.49* | 75.69078 | 30 |
| Miscellaneous, $i=l$ | 11.933 | -0.019 | 0.920 | 0.115 | 1.78 | 46.45002 | 13 |
| Miscellaneous, $i=f$ | 4.501* | 0.385** | 1.088* | 0.538 | 10.31* | 26.63984 | 17 |
| Test of $H_o$: $A_t=A_l=A_f$; $B_t=B_l=B_f$; $C_t=C_l=C_f$ | | | | | $F_{(3,24)}=0.28$ | | |

[a]$A_i$=technology coefficient for the ith type of firm; $B_i$=capital-output elasticity for ith type of firm; $C_i$=output-labor elasticity for ith type of firm; $i=t$ (all firms), $l$ (local firms), $f$ (foreign firms); *, **, ***=coefficient or statistic significant at 0.01, 0.05, and 0.10 levels, respectively (coefficient significance based on two-tailed t-tests).

where $V_i$ = value added in the $i$th type of firm, $K_i$ = fixed capital in the $i$th type of firm, $E_i$ = employment in the $i$th type of firm, and $A_i$, $B_i$, and $C_i$ are production function parameters for the $i$th type of firm.

Estimates for all manufacturing firms showed that differences between domestic and foreign firm production function parameters were significant at the 0.01 level in 1974 and at the 0.10 level in 1986. In 1974, the labor-output elasticity was larger in foreign firms, while the capital-output elasticity was smaller. By 1986, foreign firms were characterized by a lower labor-output elasticity and capital-output elasticities were roughly equal in both domestic and foreign firms. On the other hand, the technology coefficient was larger in foreign firms in both years, 1.9 times in 1974 and 1.4 times in 1986. This suggests that the greater efficiency of foreign firms, as indicated by the relatively high average products of capital and labor for foreign firms in Table 4.8, is probably due more to differences in technology than to differences in labor-output and capital-output elasticities per se.

On the other hand, when we estimate similar functions for the individual industries listed in Table 4.8 that have a reasonably large number of both foreign and local firms (at least 10 of each firm type), we can find statistically significant differences in production function parameters for only one case, that of the food industry in 1974. In this case, the differences between the output elasticities were small but the technology coefficient was again larger in foreign firms. In the other individual industries for which samples were reasonably large (food in 1986, textiles in both years, rubber and plastics in 1986, metal products in 1974, and miscellaneous manufactures in 1986), the differences observed were not statistically significant. Combined with the results of Khanthachai et al. (1987) discussed above, these results suggest two things. First, differences between the production behavior of promoted foreign and promoted domestic firms that may have existed in 1974 appear to have diminished over time. Second, the differences observed in the manufacturing aggregate may have been due more to differences in the interindustry distribution of activities than to differences in domestic and foreign firm behavior within industries. However, given that average labor productivity is much higher than the Thai average among even domestic promoted firms, we would caution against applying these results to Thailand as a whole. In other words, we would suggest that many promoted local firms are among the most efficient of Thai firms and they may indeed be as efficient as foreign firms in many respects. However, based on both empirical data (e.g., Table 4.8) and theoretical considerations (e.g., Markusen, this volume), we do not generally believe that local Thai firms are usually as efficient as foriegn firms. Thus foreign firms have probably stimulated productivity growth in several manufacturing industries in Thailand and thereby contributed to the changes observed in the structure of Thai value added.

## International Trade in Promoted Firms

The industrial distribution of exports from foreign firms differs from the distributions of employment, capital, and value added in that foreign firm exports have been more concentrated in relatively few industries (Table 4.10). For example, in 1974, textiles accounted for nearly one-half (47 percent) of total foreign firm exports, followed by food (18 percent), and apparel (14 percent); no other industry accounted for more than 6 percent of foreign firm exports. By 1986, the distribution of foreign firm exports had changed and diversified somewhat with electric machinery having the largest share (34 percent), followed by food (29 percent) and textiles and apparel (10 percent each); however, once again no other industry had a share over 5 percent. Not only has the interindustry distribution of exports shifted markedly as illustrated by the data, but firms in leading export industries (especially in food and textiles and apparel) have also increased the range of products they export in the 1980s.

Although foreign firm exports are relatively concentrated, the relative efficiency of foreign firms contributes to making the products of foreign firms relatively competitive on the world market and this is reflected in a relatively large share for foreign firms in Thai exports. In contrast to the cases of employment, capital, and value added, the foreign share of promoted firm exports rose from 61 percent in 1974 to 75 percent in 1986. Moreover, in both 1974 and 1986, foreign shares of promoted firm exports have been exceedingly high (over 90 percent) in apparel, chemicals, basic metals, and electric machinery. In 1974 this list also included nonmetallic minerals and miscellaneous manufactures while in 1986 nonelectric machinery and transport machinery were also on the list.

The foreign share of all Thai manufacturing exports also rose, increasing from 11 percent in 1974 to 15 percent in 1986 (Table 4.10).[7] In 1974, foreign shares were 75 percent in metal products and 64 percent in textiles, with foreign shares of 30–46 percent observed in apparel, chemicals, and paper products. By 1986 foreign shares exceeded 40 percent in only two industries, nonmetallic minerals and electric machinery, and shares of 22–24 percent were found in chemicals and rubber and plastics. However, despite the declines in foreign shares in several individual industries, foreign firm export growth was strong in a many of these industries.[8] In other words, strong export growth in foreign firms was generally outstripped by even stronger export growth in local firms not included in our sample. The major exception to this trend is in electric machinery where foreign firms have been a significant factor in the founding and growth of this increasingly important industry in Thailand. Yet, even in this industry, it would not be surprising to find local firm export growth exceeding that of foreign firms in the not-too-distant future.

Despite the generally decreasing foreign shares of total Thai exports, the export propensity of foreign firms, as measured by the ratio of exports to total sales, has increased very rapidly in the manufacturing aggregate from 15 percent in 1974 to 42 percent in 1986 (Table 4.10). The export-to-sales ratio for all firms in Thailand also increased significantly, but remained at a relatively low level (13 percent and 20 percent in 1974 and 1986, respectively). In contrast, the corresponding ratio for promoted local firms remained more or less constant at 29–30 percent.

Among foreign firms in 1974, export-to-sales ratios exceeded 50 percent in only one industry, apparel. However, by 1986 this list included food, wood products, apparel, and electric machinery with ratios exceeding 90 percent in the latter two industries. Moreover, even at the industry level, foreign firm export ratios were generally higher than the corresponding ratios for promoted local firms and all domestic firms by 1986.

The increasing export orientation of foreign firms is also reflected in the increasing number of foreign-invested export projects which the BOI has approved. In 1975–

Table 4.10  Exports and Export Propensities for Sample of Firms in Thailand, 1974 and 1986

| Industry[a] | Foreign Firm Exports (US$1,000) | Foreign Share (%) | | Ratio of Export to Sales (%) | | |
|---|---|---|---|---|---|---|
| | | Promoted Firms | All Thailand | Promoted Foreign Firms | Promoted Local Firms | All Thailand[b] |
| **1974** | | | | | | |
| Manufacturing | 151,439 | 60.5 | 11.4 | 15.1 | 30.4 | 12.9 |
| Food | 26,629 | 44.2 | 3.3 | 23.9 | 68.6 | 18.3 |
| Textiles | 70,601 | 62.2 | 64.3 | 21.8 | 54.7 | 8.2 |
| Apparel | 20,920 | 94.0 | 46.1 | 75.9 | 44.2 | 12.8 |
| Footwear, leather | 0 | nc | 0.0 | nc | nc | 4.4 |
| Wood products | 0 | 0.0 | 0.0 | 0.0 | 59.1 | 12.2 |
| Paper products | 2,319 | 31.8 | 29.9 | 16.7 | 11.7 | 2.2 |
| Chemicals | 7,296 | 100.0 | 43.7 | 5.6 | 0.0 | 4.2 |
| Rubber, plastics | 1,708 | 85.5 | 20.3 | 2.9 | 11.4 | 2.0 |
| Nonmetallic | 8,475 | 94.2 | 23.0 | 21.4 | 1.4 | 15.5 |
| Basic metals | 1,324 | 100.0 | 0.8 | 1.9 | 0.0 | 26.5 |
| Metal products | 8,774 | 76.1 | 75.4 | 9.5 | 5.4 | 4.3 |
| Nonelec. machinery | 0 | nc | 0.0 | 0.0 | 0.0 | 0.8 |
| Electric machinery | 1,318 | 100.0 | 10.8 | 3.4 | 0.0 | 5.5 |
| Transport machinery | 43 | 0.6 | 2.4 | 0.0 | 22.4 | 0.3 |
| Miscellaneous | 2,033 | 94.6 | 4.6 | 21.7 | 18.7 | 22.0 |

## 1986

| | | | | | |
|---|---|---|---|---|---|
| Manufacturing | 938,241 | 74.5 | 15.3 | 42.3 | 29.0 | 19.6 |
| Food | 273,964 | 66.3 | 12.4 | 54.4 | 32.1 | 21.1 |
| Textiles | 95,527 | 64.6 | 18.1 | 25.9 | 25.3 | 18.2 |
| Apparel | 95,371 | 99.2 | 11.6 | 96.9 | 20.5 | 33.4 |
| Footwear, leather | 4,675 | 26.7 | 2.6 | 35.8 | 76.7 | 79.6 |
| Wood products | 7,452 | 44.3 | 4.5 | 62.3 | 99.5 | 23.3 |
| Paper products | 3,387 | 67.3 | 7.0 | 8.8 | 2.1 | 3.6 |
| Chemicals | 30,349 | 99.8 | 21.9 | 18.8 | 0.6 | 7.0 |
| Rubber, plastics | 39,355 | 69.1 | 24.2 | 42.4 | 63.8 | 11.4 |
| Nonmetallic | 33,662 | 64.2 | 47.6 | 32.3 | 14.9 | 5.5 |
| Basic metals | 524 | 98.9 | 0.2 | 0.5 | 0.0 | 14.7 |
| Metal products | 9,783 | 74.0 | 12.5 | 11.7 | 19.0 | 12.9 |
| Nonelec. machinery | 1,205 | 96.3 | 0.7 | 1.9 | 0.4 | 25.5 |
| Electric machinery | 314,889 | 93.0 | 43.9 | 90.0 | 94.4 | 60.2 |
| Transport machinery | 2,969 | 100.0 | 7.7 | 2.5 | nc | 1.5 |
| Miscellaneous | 25,130 | 38.2 | 4.4 | 26.1 | 86.7 | 30.2 |

nc = Not calculable.

[a]Manufacturing excludes petroleum products; miscellaneous manufacturing includes precision machinery.
[b]Sales are proxied by gross output.

Sources: Authors' compilation of Board of Investment questionnaires; Australian National University (1989); International Monetary Fund (various years); UNIDO (1989).

Table 4.11  Imports, Import Propensities, and Ratio of Trade Balance to Value Added for Sample of Firms in Thailand, 1974 and 1986

| Industry[a] | Foreign Firm Imports (US$1,000) | Foreign Share of Promoted Firms (%) | Ratio of Imports to Purchases (%) | | Ratio of Trade Balance to Value Added (%) | |
|---|---|---|---|---|---|---|
| | | | Promoted Foreign Firms | Promoted Local Firms | Promoted Foreign Firms | Promoted Local Firms |
| 1974 | | | | | | |
| Manufacturing | 387,204 | 82.0 | 64.6 | 49.0 | -58.4 | 9.2 |
| Food | 34,882 | 96.8 | 42.6 | 3.1 | -27.7 | 282.4 |
| Textiles | 108,667 | 80.2 | 58.2 | 84.6 | -27.7 | 34.5 |
| Apparel | 17,069 | 100.0 | 72.5 | 0.0 | 96.5 | 78.8 |
| Footwear, leather | 0 | nc | nc | nc | nc | nc |
| Wood products | 276 | 34.5 | 71.5 | 14.9 | -120.1 | 87.9 |
| Paper products | 4,654 | 22.1 | 73.3 | 59.8 | -31.1 | -76.7 |
| Chemicals | 56,503 | 98.5 | 80.7 | 74.7 | -81.3 | -6.6 |
| Rubber, plastics | 18,704 | 95.8 | 71.7 | 47.2 | -53.1 | -69.5 |
| Nonmetallic | 4,907 | 37.6 | 68.4 | 39.8 | 11.0 | -46.8 |
| Basic metals | 29,980 | 98.7 | 68.4 | 38.0 | -115.1 | -18.5 |
| Metal products | 38,713 | 66.0 | 58.2 | 73.8 | -116.8 | -70.7 |
| Nonelec. machinery | 522 | 36.8 | 75.0 | 87.9 | -49.5 | -181.3 |
| Electric machinery | 18,124 | 98.2 | 73.3 | 82.3 | -116.5 | -49.5 |
| Transport machinery | 50,044 | 85.5 | 90.0 | 45.1 | -166.6 | -12.1 |

| | | | | | | |
|---|---|---|---|---|---|---|
| Miscellaneous | 4,160 | 97.5 | 73.8 | 55.2 | -57.2 | 2.7 |
| **1986** | | | | | | |
| Manufacturing | 469,707 | 76.9 | 48.9 | 23.1 | 37.2 | 36.2 |
| Food | 72,023 | 87.8 | 21.6 | 3.1 | 118.4 | 110.8 |
| Textiles | 106,775 | 74.6 | 65.7 | 45.8 | -5.5 | 12.5 |
| Apparel | 52,165 | 99.6 | 75.8 | 16.9 | 145.9 | 22.1 |
| Footwear, leather | 3,159 | 70.4 | 42.1 | 10.7 | 27.3 | 268.0 |
| Wood products | 530 | 29.4 | 16.0 | 21.3 | 80.1 | 235.5 |
| Paper products | 4,055 | 22.5 | 27.7 | 37.7 | -2.8 | -31.0 |
| Chemicals | 35,390 | 95.7 | 55.9 | 61.3 | -5.1 | -15.4 |
| Rubber, plastics | 29,907 | 79.6 | 60.6 | 63.5 | 21.8 | 64.0 |
| Nonmetallic | 15,891 | 45.0 | 66.0 | 46.6 | 22.2 | -0.8 |
| Basic metals | 5,925 | 28.3 | 27.1 | 43.4 | -5.9 | -26.8 |
| Metal products | 28,535 | 86.4 | 65.2 | 43.4 | -47.0 | -13.7 |
| Nonelec. machinery | 18,963 | 77.1 | 54.8 | 81.0 | -62.3 | -135.4 |
| Electric machinery | 39,270 | 94.1 | 85.3 | 11.4 | 90.7 | 590.4 |
| Transport machinery | 34,599 | 100.0 | 68.9 | nc | -44.7 | nc |
| Miscellaneous | 22,520 | 50.5 | 61.2 | 80.9 | 4.4 | 94.7 |

nc = Not calculable.

ªManufacturing excludes petroleum products; miscellaneous manufacturing includes precision machinery.

Sources: Authors' compilation of Board of Investment questionnaires; International Monetary Fund (various years); UNIDO (1989).

1980 there were only an average of 13 such projects annually. However, in 1981–1983 there were an average of 26 export projects each year with 65 export projects in 1984 and 78 export projects in 1985 (Sibunruang and Brimble 1987, 332). Moreover, Japan, the United States, Europe, Australia, Hong Kong, and Taiwan together accounted for 78 export projects in 1986, 329 export projects in 1987, and 170 export projects in the first five months of 1988. These 577 export projects approved over the period January 1986–May 1988 represented 74 percent of all projects approved in this period (Board of Investment, various years). The increasing export orientation of foreign firms is of course highly related to changes in Thai policy which removed some of the anti-export bias that was present from previous import substitution policies and thereby made the BOI's long-standing incentives for export-oriented investors more attractive.

While foreign firms have increased the proportion of sales exported, they have also decreased the ratio of imports to total input purchases (Table 4.11). Between 1974 and 1986, the share of imports to purchases of foreign firms declined from 64 percent to 49 percent in the manufacturing aggregate; in addition, overall import growth in nominal terms was relatively slow (in comparison to exports, value added, and capital), increasing only 1.2-fold over the 12-year period. Import-to-purchase ratios also fell in all individual industries except textiles, apparel, metal products, and electric machinery. Interestingly, electric machinery, apparel, and textiles were also major export industries in 1986 with exports growing particularly rapidly in the former two industries in the 1974–1986 period. One interpretation of this phenomenon is that foreign firms have been able to utilize their comparative advantages most effectively in industries where the import policy has been relatively permissive. In other words, a liberal import policy has allowed the foreign firms in these industries to choose the most efficient mix of inputs and the resulting increase in efficiency has in turn been reflected in a high and rapidly growing level of exports.

On the other hand, a high level of imports is often thought to be undesirable for two reasons. First, a high level of import content is often believed to signify a low level of linkages with local suppliers of parts and intermediate inputs. Of course, where local suppliers can provide inputs efficiently it is clearly desirable for government to ensure that economic policy does not result in a bias against such activity. Moreover, despite the fact that the BOI has generally loosened domestic content requirements somewhat in recent years, especially for exporting projects, import-to-purchase ratios have generally declined. To understand this phenomenon, it is helpful to identify the major causes of high import-to-purchase ratios. These include (1) lack of information in both foreign firms and potential local suppliers about potential business opportunities, (2) the inefficiency of local suppliers, and (3) the lack of local suppliers. It should be clear that these factors are less severe the higher the level of local industrial development and the longer period of time that a foreign firm has operated in a host country. Thus the growing experience of foreign firms and their suppliers in Thailand and increased levels of Thai industrial development will continue to contribute to declining import-to-purchase ratios in coming years. On the other hand, the influx of large number of new foreign firms in recent years may outweigh these factors and lead to an increase in these ratios in the medium term.

A second problem is that foreign firms often run large trade deficits, especially in years immediately following the investment; this is a period in which imports are generally high and exports have not developed. For example, in 1974 for all of the foreign manufacturing firms in our sample, the ratio of the trade balance to value added was -58 percent. Deficits were also much larger than value added in a number of individual industries, namely wood products, basic metals, metal products, electric machinery, and transport machinery; apparel and nonmetallic minerals were the only industries in which foreign firms generated trade surpluses. By 1986 this pattern had changed dramatically with the trade balance for all of the sample of foreign firms turning strongly positive. The trade balance-to-value added ratio was 37 percent for all manufacturing, and was even larger (over 80 percent) for a number of industries including apparel, food, electric machinery, and wood products. In contrast, deficits greater than 6 percent of value added occurred in only three industries, namely, metal products, transport machinery, and nonelectric machinery. It should also be noted that promoted domestic firms in these industries and basic metals also ran deficits greater than 10 percent of value added. One reason for the large deficits for both domestic and foreign firms in these three industries (and basic metals for domestic firms) is the high degree of protection which has fostered a high level of production. If this protection were removed, it is highly likely that many of these firms would cease to operate and that the remaining firms would be more efficient. In the long run (though not necessarily in the short run), this would likely reduce the trade deficits these firms run relative to their value added since the firms would generally be forced to reduce costs (purchases) and/or boost revenues (sales).

Consideration of indirect effects could significantly change the story told by these data. One important possibility in Thailand is that foreign firms with high import-to-purchase ratios may have produced a large amount of import substitutes thereby leading actual declines in Thailand's overall import bill. Moreover one should also note that it is entirely possible that a firm could operate efficiently even if it is importing a large portion of its inputs and selling the vast majority of its output domestically. These points indicate the inherent difficulties in using import-to-purchase ratios and trade balance figures (in absolute terms or relative to value added or total sales); lower import-to-purchase ratios and larger trade surpluses for an individual firm may not necessarily be correlated with economic efficiency or the firm's overall effects on a country's trade balance. Indeed the large variety of policies adopted by host-country agencies (such as the BOI) to promote lower import-to-purchase ratios and higher export levels can lead firms to be less efficient than they would otherwise be. For example, the production of some automotive parts and components is not efficient in Thailand due to the lack of scale economies. Consequently local content requirements contribute to the inefficiency of automobile assemblers and the need for high protection in automobile assembly, an industry which is now 2 decades old. However the BOI has generally avoided severe over-regulation of foreign firms, and as was indicated in earlier discussion, most of the major problems foreign (and local) firms face when operating in Thailand are more related to protectionist hangovers from previous import-substitution policies.

## Foreign Firms and Structural Change
## in Thailand: A Summary

The substantial problems we have encountered in compiling consistent time series data on (1) foreign firm activity in Thailand and (2) employment, capital, sales, and purchases for all firms in Thailand necessarily make any conclusions emerging from this study tentative in nature. However it is clear that Thailand has undergone some important structural changes in the last decade and a half. Perhaps the most important cause of these changes has been the gradual shift of policy emphasis from promotion of import substitution in the 1960s and early 1970s to promotion of export expansion in the 1980s. This shift has been an important element in the relatively rapid growth in large exporting industries, most notably electric machinery, apparel, and miscellaneous manufacturing.

Our data also indicate that in two of the three most rapidly growing manufacturing industries, foreign firms have played important roles in Thailand. More specifically, foreign firms have been important in electric machinery in the 1980s and apparel in the 1970s but of little importance in miscellaneous manufacturing. Moreover, foreign firms accounted for moderate shares in two other very important export industries, namely, textiles in both the 1970s and 1980s and food in the 1980s. In short, foreign firms appear to have made important contributions to the growth of Thailand's export industries and thereby helped facilitate structural changes in Thai manufacturing.

However we have not been able to clearly determine whether foreign firm activity was the cause or a result of these structural changes. As our discussion indicates, we tend to view changes in policies and the accompanying changes in prices as the more fundamental causes of structural changes. In addition to this, other long-term factors such as income growth, technological progress, and changes in factor supplies have undoubtably played important roles. Moreover, in view of the apparently marginal differences between production technology among promoted foreign firms and promoted domestic firms, we would caution against overestimating the importance of foreign firms; we do believe, however, that important differences exist between production technology in foreign firms and domestic firms if nonpromoted firms are included. The relative efficiency of foreign firms is in turn related to the relatively large role of foreign firms in Thai exports since it makes the products of foreign firms relatively competitive on the world market. The large role of foreign firms in Thai exports also suggests that foreign firms have played a crucial role in developing export markets for Thailand, both for foreign firms themselves and for the domestic firms with whom they cooperate and compete. Finally, the dramatic increase in DFI in recent years suggests that the behavior of foreign firms may be of even more consequence in the years to come.

## Notes

1. These estimates of manufacturing exports are significantly higher than those found in many Thai data sources. For example, the Bank of Thailand (1989, 52) shows manufacturing exports in 1986 to be only US$4.9 billion while Table 4.1 shows a figure of US$6.2 billion. The primary reason for this difference is that the SITC-ISIC converter that was used classifies

a large number of processed foods as manufactured goods although they have often been defined as agricultural exports in other classifications. On the other hand, the input-output based estimates of manufacturing exports by Sibunruang and Brimble (1987, 326) are even larger than those generated by the converter used here (e.g., US$2.3 billion versus US$1.1 billion in 1975 and US$6.5 billion versus US$4.9 billion in 1985; see Australian National University (1989) and UNIDO (1989) for the SITC-ISIC converter figures that were used).

2. The manufacturing employment data that are used are UNIDO estimates based on industrial surveys and are generally lower than the estimates based on labor force surveys (see Table 4.1). However both figures probably underestimate manufacturing sector employment to some extent because part-time work in manufacturing by workers based in agriculture is not accounted for.

3. However this ratio does not necessarily reflect the total net contribution to fixed investment since foreign firm investment may indirectly stimulate or reduce investment in domestic firms.

4. Cumulative DFI from Korea is comparatively small, totalling only US$27 million at yearend 1989; nevertheless this represents a large increase over the US$6 million total at yearend 1987 (Bank of Thailand, various years).

5. Sibunruang and Brimble (1988) used a slightly different industrial classification. Most notably they include petroleum products with chemicals; petroleum products are excluded here. However this alone probably does not account for the large differences observed in this industry. Another, though less significant, point is that Sibunruang and Brimble do not distinguish between basic metals and metal products. Hence we can only compare the sum of these two industries.

6. Since the total value added data are generally accurate, the only problems that arise are (1) underestimation stemming from our limited sample and (2) mismatches between our industrial classification and the classification that was used in the total Thai value added calculations. The latter problem is not inconsequential given that ratios of foreign firm value added to total Thai value added exceed 100 percent in nonmetallic minerals in 1974 and electric machinery in 1986. Hence we must again caution that these ratios cannot give precise measures of foreign participation but can only provide a rough estimate of that participation.

7. In comparison, Sibunruang and Brimble (1987, 335–336 and 338) estimated that 106 promoted foreign manufacturing firms accounted for US$192 million in exports or 17 percent of all Thai manufacturing exports in 1975. They also estimated that 107 promoted foreign firms in manufacturing accounted for US$329 million in exports or 7 percent of all Thai manufacturing exports in 1984. Thus, in the manufacturing aggregate, their figures indicate a higher level of exports in the 1970s but a much lower level in the 1980s.

8. Although these are nominal growth rates that include increases in both prices and volume, separate deflators for foreign and other firms are not available. Thus, given that our primary purpose is comparison of growth in foreign firms and growth in other firms, the difference between nominal and real growth is of little consequence here.

# References

Asian Development Bank. Various years. *Key Indicators of Developing Member Countries of ADB*. Manila: Asian Development Bank.
Australian National University. 1989. Mimeos from the International Economic Data Bank.
Bank of Thailand. 1989. *Quarterly Bulletin*, 29(4).
———. Various years. Mimeos.
Board of Investment. Various years. Mimeos.
International Monetary Fund (IMF). Various years. *International Financial Statistics*, 1989 Yearbook and August 1990 Monthly. Washington, D.C.: International Monetary Fund.

Khanthachai, Nathabhol, Kanchana Tanmavad, Tawatchai Boonsiri, Chantana Nisaisook, and Anucha Arttanuchit. 1987. *Technology and Skills in Thailand.* Singapore: Institute of Southeast Asian Studies.
National Economic and Social Development Board (NESDB). Various years. *National Income of Thailand*, 1970–1987, 1988, and 1989 issues. Bangkok: NESDB.
Sibunruang, Atchaka, and Peter Brimble. 1987. Foreign Investment and Export Orientation: A Thai Perspective. In *Direct Foreign Investment and Export Promotion: Policies and Experiences in Asia,* edited by Seiji Naya, Vinyu Vichit-Vadakan, and Udom Kerdpibule. Honolulu and Kuala Lumpur: East-West Center and Southeast Asian Central Banks Research and Training Centre.
_____. 1988. The Employment Effects of Manufacturing Multinational Enterprises in Thailand. Mimeo. Thammasat University, Bangkok.
United Nations Industrial Development Organization (UNIDO). 1989. Mimeos.

# PART THREE

# Inward Investment
# and Structural Change
# in Newly Industrializing Countries

# 5

## Direct Investment and Structural Change in Korean Manufacturing

*Chung H. Lee and Eric D. Ramstetter*

### Introduction

Korea's economic performance in the last two decades has been quite remarkable. Between 1965 and 1987, real gross national product (GNP) per capita grew more than 6 percent annually with nominal GNP per capita reaching US$2,690 in 1987. Real manufacturing value added grew rapidly at more than 19 percent annually in the period 1965–1980 and 11 percent in 1980–1987. In the same two periods, nominal exports expanded at 27 percent and 14 percent, respectively. These remarkably high rates of growth were far above the world and developing economy averages for these periods (World Bank 1989, 166–167). Moreover, Korea has maintained a relatively open trading regime compared to other developing economies (World Bank 1987, 83) and has come to exemplify the manufacturing-based, export-oriented pattern of economic development.

Korean manufacturing has not only grown remarkably, but has also undergone substantial structural changes with the nonelectric machinery, electric machinery, and transportation equipment industries expandingly especially rapidly in 1974–1986 (Table 5.1). These three machinery industries, which combined to account for only 18 percent of manufacturing employment in 1974, accounted for over 27 percent in 1986. In contrast, employment shares in the food, textiles and apparel, wood and paper, petroleum, and nonmetallic minerals industries declined somewhat over this period. In the nonpetroleum chemicals and metals industries, the shares have remained relatively constant. In short, the manufacturing boom during this period was primarily concentrated in the three machinery industries and to a lesser extent the metals and nonpetroleum chemicals industries.

Korea's encouragement of inward direct foreign investment (DFI) has been viewed as a contributing factor to economic growth overall and in particular, in the machinery industries. Some studies on DFI in Korea, in addition to providing general descriptions of investment patterns, have focused on how foreign firms make investment decisions, and their effects on employment, the balance of payments, growth, technology transfer, and other issues (Jo 1980; Koo 1985; Koo and Bark 1988). Other studies have compared the effects of foreign firms from Japan and the

Table 5.1  Structural Change in Korea, 1974-1986 (percentage)

| Industry | Nominal Value Added | | | Employment | | | Nominal Exports | | |
|---|---|---|---|---|---|---|---|---|---|
| | 1974 | 1978 | 1986 | 1974 | 1978 | 1986 | 1974 | 1978 | 1986 |
| All industries (US$m) | 18,867 | 50,088 | 98,145 | 11,421 | 13,412 | 15,505 | 4,460 | 12,711 | 34,715 |
| Manufacturing (US$m) | 4,616 | 16,928 | 37,304 | 1,275 | 2,081 | 2,691 | 4,127 | 11,677 | 33,085 |
| (% of all industries) | 24.5 | 33.8 | 38.0 | 11.2 | 15.5 | 17.4 | 92.5 | 91.9 | 95.3 |
| Shares of manufacturing (%) | | | | | | | | | |
| Food products | 16.6 | 18.0 | 12.7 | 11.8 | 8.2 | 7.6 | 2.9 | 2.2 | 0.9 |
| Textiles & apparel | 20.7 | 20.0 | 16.7 | 33.0 | 32.9 | 27.2 | 38.4 | 38.3 | 28.3 |
| Wood and paper products | 6.6 | 6.8 | 5.9 | 8.5 | 7.8 | 6.6 | 6.9 | 6.2 | 1.7 |
| Chemicals, except petroleum | 13.7 | 13.5 | 13.6 | 11.4 | 11.2 | 13.1 | 10.2 | 14.0 | 14.7 |
| Petroleum | 6.5 | 4.0 | 3.9 | 1.3 | 0.7 | 0.6 | 2.9 | 0.3 | 2.3 |
| Nonmetallic minerals | 5.4 | 5.0 | 4.7 | 4.6 | 4.4 | 4.2 | 2.1 | 2.4 | 1.4 |
| Metals | 12.3 | 10.3 | 11.6 | 7.7 | 8.5 | 9.2 | 14.3 | 9.9 | 11.0 |
| Nonelectric machinery | 2.7 | 4.9 | 6.5 | 3.7 | 5.9 | 7.0 | 2.7 | 3.3 | 7.4 |
| Electric machinery | 8.6 | 8.9 | 13.5 | 9.5 | 11.1 | 13.5 | 12.7 | 11.6 | 17.6 |
| Transportation equipment | 5.0 | 6.8 | 8.4 | 4.3 | 5.5 | 6.7 | 2.0 | 7.7 | 10.8 |
| Miscellaneous manufactures | 1.9 | 1.8 | 2.4 | 4.1 | 3.7 | 4.3 | 4.7 | 3.9 | 3.7 |

Sources:  Asian Development Bank (1988); Bank of Korea (1987, 1989); Economic Planning Board (1980, various years); Australian National University (1989).

United States on the Korean economy (Kojima 1985; Lee 1979, 1983, 1984; Ramstetter 1986, 1987). In most of these studies, Jo (1980) and Koo (1985) being the major exception, the primary focus has been on analyzing issues in a rather aggregate framework. Moreover, with the exception of Koo and Bark (1988), these studies focused on the 1970s or previous periods.

This study has two aims. First, we perform a disaggregated analysis that focuses on the manufacturing activities of the Korean economy over a longer period than has previously been possible. Specifically, the role of multinational firms in the manufacturing sector in the 1974-1986 period is considered. Second, explicit attention is given to the structural aspects of DFI's effects on the Korean economy. To this end, particular attention is paid to the effects of multinational activity on Korean value added, employment, and exports; technology-related issues are also touched upon. The study concludes with some observations about the recent growth of Korea's DFI abroad and the potential roles both inward and outward DFI may play in future structural changes in the Korean economy.

## Financial Dimensions and Determinants
## of Direct Investment

Before analyzing employment and export issues, it is helpful to first outline the financial aspects of DFI in Korea and look at some of the factors affecting the level of DFI. Unfortunately, this is more easily said than done since substantial data problems are encountered in trying to accurately determine the level of DFI in Korea. Three types of data on DFI inflows are available for the period 1962–1988: (1) balance-of-payments data on total net inflows, (2) data on gross arrivals by type of capital, and (3) data on approvals of inward DFI by country or by industry (Table 5.2 and sources). The data reveal that net inflows have consistently been less than gross arrivals, and approvals are generally larger than both these figures.[1] All of the data show large increases in inflows in the early 1970s and again in the mid-1980s. More precisely, net annual inflows averaged US$19 million in 1962–1971, US$86 million in 1970–1978, US$22 million in 1979–1980, US$87 million in 1981–1984, US$329 million in 1985–1986, and US$735 million in 1987–1988.

Two factors stand out in any attempt to describe the fluctuations in DFI inflows over time: (1) fluctuations in Korean economic activity, and (2) major changes in Korean economic policy. For example, in 1979–1980, there was a large downturn in DFI inflows. This period was characterized by a faltering economy and political turmoil following the death of former President Park Chung Hee. The influence of politics and policy on DFI flows is also seen in the two largest investment booms, the first in the early 1970s and the second in the mid-1980s. The first boom was related to a number of external factors, most notably the first steps toward liberalization of DFI abroad by the Japanese combined with growing Japanese confidence in the potential of Korean investments. However, the push into heavy and chemical industrialization that was initiated by the Park regime in 1972 and corresponding efforts to entice DFI, especially Japanese DFI, into these sectors were also important factors on the Korean side. The boom in the mid-1980s is also clearly related to the liberalization of DFI regulations that preceded it. Of course, a number of other

Table 5.2  DFI Flows and Approvals in Korea, 1962-1988

| | 1962-1971 | 1972-1981 | 1982 | 1983 | 1984 | 1985 | 1986 | 1987 | 1988 |
|---|---|---|---|---|---|---|---|---|---|
| Annual average amounts (US$ millions) | | | | | | | | | |
| Total net DFI in Korea[a] | 19 | 74 | 68 | 69 | 112 | 230 | 428 | 597 | 872 |
| Total gross DFI arrivals | 20 | 134 | 129 | 122 | 193 | 236 | 478 | 625 | 894 |
| Total DFI approvals | 38 | 160 | 189 | 269 | 422 | 532 | 354 | 1,060 | 1,283 |
| Share of gross arrivals (%) | | | | | | | | | |
| Capital goods | 42.0 | 29.0 | 24.7 | 23.0 | 31.4 | 41.1 | 25.4 | 29.1 | 30.9 |
| Cash | 57.9 | 70.9 | 75.3 | 77.0 | 68.6 | 58.9 | 74.5 | 70.9 | 69.1 |
| Technology | 0.1 | 0.1 | 0.0 | 0.0 | 0.0 | 0.0 | 0.1 | 0.0 | 0.0 |
| Share of approvals[b] (%) | | | | | | | | | |
| Japan | 36.8 | 57.9 | 21.3 | 62.4 | 39.0 | 68.4 | 38.9 | 46.6 | 57.7 |
| United States | 45.2 | 23.2 | 53.4 | 20.1 | 45.8 | 21.0 | 35.4 | 24.1 | 19.7 |
| Europe | 7.8 | 8.4 | 7.6 | 9.1 | 11.8 | 7.4 | 17.9 | 19.8 | 17.1 |
| Developing Asia | 2.3 | 3.8 | 14.6 | 2.6 | 1.0 | 2.7 | 4.6 | 6.9 | 1.3 |
| Other | 7.8 | 6.7 | 3.1 | 5.9 | 2.4 | 0.4 | 3.2 | 2.6 | 4.2 |

| | | | | | | | | | |
|---|---|---|---|---|---|---|---|---|---|
| Manufacturing (%) | 87.0 | 72.4 | 64.6 | 38.3 | 60.2 | 34.0 | 76.1 | 73.1 | 51.1 |
| Food products | 2.1 | 3.3 | 5.7 | 2.8 | 4.5 | 0.7 | 12.5 | 4.7 | 0.8 |
| Textiles & apparel | 8.5 | 10.8 | 2.0 | 0.8 | 0.5 | 0.1 | 2.2 | 1.2 | 0.9 |
| Wood and paper products | 0.7 | 0.7 | 4.0 | 0.7 | 0.4 | 0.4 | 0.1 | 1.4 | 0.4 |
| Chemicals, except petroleum | 19.7 | 22.0 | 30.3 | 9.7 | 2.9 | 10.2 | 12.3 | 17.6 | 19.0 |
| Petroleum | 16.1 | 2.6 | 0.1 | 0.0 | 1.2 | 0.0 | 0.0 | 5.2 | 0.0 |
| Nonmetallic minerals | 4.0 | 1.0 | 0.2 | 0.0 | 1.1 | 1.7 | 0.3 | 0.7 | 1.2 |
| Metals | 6.7 | 5.1 | 1.6 | 0.6 | 1.9 | 0.2 | 2.2 | 1.7 | 1.2 |
| Nonelectric machinery | 7.9 | 6.2 | 1.0 | 1.1 | 2.8 | 1.3 | 8.4 | 8.3 | 4.6 |
| Electric machinery | 17.0 | 14.3 | 10.6 | 15.7 | 16.3 | 10.4 | 18.8 | 19.6 | 18.0 |
| Transportation equipment | 1.6 | 4.9 | 8.2 | 6.0 | 27.9 | 8.4 | 17.3 | 11.3 | 3.7 |
| Miscellaneous manufactures | 2.8 | 1.5 | 0.8 | 0.9 | 0.7 | 0.4 | 1.9 | 1.5 | 1.2 |

na = Not available.

[a]1965-1971.

[b]Shares for 1988 based on January-September totals.

Sources: Economic Planning Board (1989); International Monetary Fund (1988, 1989); Ministry of Finance (1988).

factors—for example, changes in labor costs, capital costs, human capital costs, exchange rate fluctuations, and protection of the Korean market—are also relevant factors. Yet these two factors, the health of the Korean economy and Korean policy, have had undeniably large influences on the fluctuations of DFI over time.

Turning to structural characteristics, over two-thirds of gross arrivals were in the form of cash. Capital goods account for the vast majority of the remainder and technology is of minimal quantitative importance. Based on the approval data (Table 5.2), manufacturing has attracted the largest but declining share of DFI. Manufacturing shares were 87 percent in 1962–1971, 72 percent in 1972–1981, and 57 percent in January 1982–September 1988. Within manufacturing, the largest share of total DFI has historically been in nonpetroleum chemicals. However, this share has declined markedly in recent years from 20 percent in 1962–1971 and 22 percent in 1972–1981 to 15 percent in 1982–1988. Other industries with declining shares in recent years are textiles and apparel, petroleum, nonmetallic minerals, metals, nonelectric machinery, and miscellaneous manufacturing. In contrast, the share of DFI flowing to the electric machinery industry has been relatively constant at 17 percent in 1962–1971, 14 percent in 1972–1981, and 17 percent in 1982–1988; in 1982–1988, the electric machinery became the largest industry by a narrow margin. The share of DFI flowing to the wood and paper industry also remained relatively constant but at a very low level. On the other end of the spectrum, there has been substantial growth in transportation equipment shares from under 2 percent in 1962–1971 to 5 percent in 1972–1981 and more than 11 percent in 1982–1988 while food shares also grew rapidly. In short, DFI approvals have tended to be increasingly concentrated in the rapidly growing electric machinery and transportation equipment industries; there has also been a substantial presence in nonpetroleum chemicals.

Looking at the sources of approved investment, Japan is by far the largest investor overall, accounting for well over one-half of approved total investment since 1972 (Table 5.2). The United States was the largest investor prior to 1972 with a share of 45 percent but this share averaged only 23 percent in 1972–1981 and 26 percent in 1982–1988. Interestingly, however, through September 1987 (Koo and Bark 1988, 13), U.S. manufacturing DFI almost equaled Japanese manufacturing DFI (US$1,151 million versus US$1,167 million) and manufacturing accounted for a much larger share of total U.S. DFI than of total Japanese DFI (89 percent versus 53 percent).[2] Together, the United States and Japan accounted for 78 percent of all manufacturing DFI in Korea with electric machinery, nonpetroleum chemicals, and transportation equipment combining to account for 79 percent of U.S. manufacturing DFI and 55 percent of Japanese manufacturing DFI. Thus, notwithstanding differences noted previously (e.g., Lee 1979), investment from these two countries is similar in important respects.[3] These fast-growing industries also dominate Europe's DFI in manufacturing (49 percent) and manufacturing DFI from other countries (61 percent). Note too that investments in Korea from Europe and developing Asia, especially Hong Kong, have been growing in recent years.

Data on DFI approvals or balance-of-payments flows and/or position do not necessarily reflect actual capital formation. This becomes clear from close examination of capital expenditure data. In comparing data on total expenditures in Table

5.3 with data on investment in Table 5.2, we find that expenditures exceeded investment by a significant margin. This is not surprising since total expenditures include expenditures of Korean partners. Nevertheless, the foreign contribution to capital expenditures, which is defined as total expenditures weighted by the foreign equity share, does seem comparatively large at 355 percent of gross DFI arrivals in 1984–1986. One possible explanation for the relatively large share is that reinvested earnings, which are an important source of DFI for U.S. firms, are excluded from the DFI data.[4] Another possible explanation is that the capital expenditure shares differ from the equity shares which are used as weights to calculate foreign contributions. In any case, the capital expenditure data imply a markedly higher level of DFI in Korea for 1984–1986 than do the more commonly-used measures of foreign investment activity in Table 5.2. Moreover, the capital expenditures data also imply a very different industrial distribution, with manufacturing accounting for 91–95 percent of weighted capital expenditures in 1984–1986. Within manufacturing, the shares of electric machinery, transportation equipment, and petroleum in weighted expenditures are also markedly larger than corresponding shares of total approvals. On the other hand, the share of nonpetroleum chemicals is smaller.

Although the above discussion, which focuses on the weighted amount of foreign firm expenditures, allows for comparison with commonly-used DFI figures, a more helpful measure of the scale of foreign firm activity is the ratio of all foreign firm capital expenditures to total Korean capital expenditures (Table 5.3). It must be stressed that these ratios are not perfect measures of the net contribution of foreign firms to Korean capital formation since foreign firm expenditures may indirectly stimulate or reduce domestic firm expenditures through the creation or destruction of new business opportunities.[5] However, these ratios do provide a useful measure of the scale of activity, showing that foreign firms accounted for 5 percent of all capital expenditures in Korea in 1984, 7 percent in 1985, and 10 percent in 1986. In manufacturing, the ratio also increased steadily from 19 percent in 1984 to 31 percent in 1986. In individual industries, ratios above 45 percent are observed in petroleum (1984 and 1986), transportation equipment (1985 and 1986), and electric machinery (all three years). The ratios for textiles and apparel were close to the average for manufacturing as a whole in all years, and other industries tended to have ratios somewhat below the manufacturing average. Thus, in recent years, foreign firms have not been a major source of capital in the overall Korean economy, but they were very significant sources of capital in manufacturing as a whole and in the electric machinery and transportation equipment industries in particular.

## Multinationals and Changes in the Structure of Korean Value Added

Comparison of data on the production, employment, technology, and trade of multinationals from two surveys, one for 1974–1978 (Koo 1982, 1985) and one for 1984–1986 (Korea Credit Appraisal Inc. 1987; Koo and Bark 1988), with data of manufacturing firms in Korea from censuses and surveys (Economic Planning Board 1980, various years) allows us to ascertain the scale of foreign firm activity and to compare the performance of firms with foreign participation with the

Table 5.3  Capital Expenditures by Foreign Firms in Korea, 1984-1986

| Industry | Foreign Firm Capital Expenditures | | | | | | Foreign Firm Capital Expenditures Weighted by Foreign Equity Share (US$ millions) | | |
| --- | --- | --- | --- | --- | --- | --- | --- | --- | --- |
| | Amount (US$ millions) | | | As a Percentage of Total Korean Capital Expenditures | | | | | |
| | 1984 | 1985 | 1986 | 1984 | 1985 | 1986 | 1984 | 1985 | 1986 |
| All industries | 1,228 | 1,681 | 2,903 | 4.8 | 6.5 | 9.7 | 737 | 1,063 | 1,419 |
| Manufacturing | 1,174 | 1,582 | 2,757 | 18.6 | 26.4 | 31.3 | 700 | 986 | 1,289 |
| Food products | 27 | 28 | 33 | 4.3 | 5.3 | 4.4 | 22 | 17 | 23 |
| Textiles & apparel | 165 | 154 | 269 | 19.8 | 21.2 | 25.8 | 63 | 50 | 94 |
| Wood and paper products | 12 | 15 | 35 | 2.8 | 3.8 | 8.3 | 69 | 64 | 18 |
| Chemicals, except petroleum | 108 | 92 | 92 | 11.7 | 11.0 | 8.0 | 75 | 48 | 59 |
| Petroleum | 55 | 75 | 142 | 87.9 | 26.6 | 84.0 | 37 | 135 | 68 |
| Nonmetallic minerals | 55 | 39 | 67 | 13.9 | 7.2 | 13.1 | 22 | 12 | 39 |
| Metals | 46 | 69 | 156 | 6.3 | 11.4 | 14.7 | 52 | 65 | 88 |
| Nonelectric machinery | 16 | 24 | 37 | 4.3 | 6.0 | 5.7 | 11 | 16 | 24 |
| Electric machinery | 506 | 483 | 737 | 44.6 | 51.9 | 46.7 | 281 | 283 | 409 |
| Transportation equipment | 178 | 587 | 1,173 | 24.9 | 90.0 | 85.5 | 65 | 289 | 462 |
| Miscellaneous manufactures | 7 | 16 | 16 | 7.8 | 21.0 | 14.8 | 2 | 8 | 6 |

Sources:  Asian Development Bank (1988); Economic Planning Board (various years); Korea Credit Appraisal Inc. (1987).

performance of domestic firms. Because the surveys and censuses differ in a number of important respects and data on a number of foreign firm indicators for 1984–1986 are only available for six or seven manufacturing industries, this exercise is not problem-free.[6] Nevertheless, the analysis does yield some interesting insights into foreign investment activity.

As shown in Table 5.4, the direct contribution of foreign firms in terms of value added is relatively small in the aggregate ranging between 3 and 6 percent of total Korean value added in 1974–1978. The contribution of foreign firms is more significant in manufacturing, however, ranging between 10 and 16 percent in the period 1974–1978 and 10 and 11 percent in 1984–1986. Since foreign firm value added grew more slowly in 1974–1978, the decline in the foreign firm share of manufacturing between 1978 and 1984 was primarily a result of the rapid growth of domestic firms. In individual industries, foreign firm shares were largest in chemicals for 1974–1978 (29–33 percent), and machinery and fabricated metals for 1984–1986 (18–19 percent). The relatively high machinery and metals shares likely reflect the growth of electric machinery affiliates. More detailed data for 1974–1978 show that foreign firm shares of value added in the electric machinery sector exceeded those in nonpetroleum chemicals, the largest chemicals industry, as early as 1976–1977 (Table 5.4 and sources). Thus, the concentration of multinational activity in the rapidly growing sectors of the Korean economy is again observed from the value added data.

However note that, as in the capital expenditure case, these ratios do not measure the total net contribution of foreign firms to Korean value added since foreign firm activity can indirectly affect domestic firm activity. In order to further illuminate the effects of foreign firm activity in Korea, some simple simultaneous equation models of production and employment in domestic and foreign firms in 1978 were estimated using a twenty-two industry cross-section (see Appendix Table 5.A). In the base model, production is hypothesized to be a function of the number of employees, capital stocks, and the level of skill intensity (the percentage of nonoperative employees in total employment). A Cobb-Douglas functional form is assumed with the skill-intensity variable used in the same manner as the usual technology constant.[7] Note that this equation only describes static intraindustry variation in production, and ignores important dynamic and interindustry relationships. Nonetheless the model simulates what actually occurred rather well and helps to illuminate the relationship between foreign and domestic firm activity in a number of ways.

First, comparison of the base-case production function estimates for domestic and foreign firms (base model, Appendix Table 5.A) shows that the labor-output elasticity is 57 percent larger for domestic firms, while the capital-output elasticity is 53 percent larger in foreign firms. However, at the means, the marginal product of labor is only 2 percent larger in domestic firms while the marginal product of capital was over six times larger in foreign firms. The observation of higher capital productivity in foreign firms is generally consistent with previous time-series estimates of total production functions where capital has been disaggregated by source (Ramstetter 1986; Naya and Ramstetter 1988). Thus, the indication is that the intangible assets transferred by foreign firms make capital, not labor, more productive in foreign firms as compared to domestic firms.

Table 5.4 Value Added of Foreign Affiliates in Korea, 1974-1986

| Foreign Affiliate Value Added[a] | 1974 | 1975 | 1976 | 1977 | 1978 | 1984 | 1985 | 1986 |
|---|---|---|---|---|---|---|---|---|
| Total value (US$ millions) | | | | | | | | |
| All industries | 518 | 816 | 1,358 | 2,070 | 2,672 | na | na | na |
| Manufacturing | 468 | 755 | 1,288 | 1,887 | 2,414 | 2,959 | 3,277 | 4,014 |
| Manufacturing-Masan | 56 | 52 | 94 | 102 | 135 | na | na | na |
| Manufacturing-non-Masan | 412 | 703 | 1,194 | 1,786 | 2,280 | na | na | na |
| | | | | | | | | |
| Food products | 31 | 43 | 54 | 98 | 153 | 95 | 107 | 147 |
| Textiles & apparel | -180 | -68 | -52 | 127 | 174 | 338 | 371 | 427 |
| Wood and paper products | 11 | 13 | 17 | 43 | 61 | 74 | 73 | 100 |
| Chemicals | 272 | 406 | 575 | 691 | 970 | 519 | 581 | 622 |
| Nonmetallic minerals | 28 | 34 | 60 | 72 | 96 | 111 | 113 | 137 |
| Basic metals | 18 | 19 | 46 | 56 | 80 | 194 | 198 | 238 |
| Machinery & fabricated metals | 218 | 240 | 473 | 669 | 709 | 1,591 | 1,798 | 2,291 |
| Miscellaneous manufactures | 12 | 16 | 21 | 29 | 38 | 36 | 36 | 52 |

Percent of total Korean value added

| | | | | | | | | |
|---|---|---|---|---|---|---|---|---|
| All industries | 2.7 | 3.9 | 4.7 | 5.6 | 5.3 | na | na | na |
| Manufacturing | 10.1 | 12.9 | 15.3 | 16.3 | 14.3 | 9.7 | 10.7 | 10.8 |
| Manufacturing-Masan | 1.2 | 0.9 | 1.1 | 0.9 | 0.8 | na | na | na |
| Manufacturing-non-Masan | 8.9 | 12.0 | 14.2 | 15.4 | 13.5 | na | na | na |
| | | | | | | | | |
| Food products | 4.0 | 3.5 | 3.4 | 4.5 | 5.0 | 2.2 | 2.5 | 3.1 |
| Textiles & apparel | -18.8 | -5.3 | -2.7 | 5.6 | 5.1 | 6.6 | 7.3 | 6.9 |
| Wood and paper products | 3.7 | 3.5 | 3.4 | 5.6 | 5.3 | 3.9 | 3.9 | 4.5 |
| Chemicals | 29.2 | 31.9 | 33.0 | 32.6 | 32.7 | 9.4 | 10.2 | 9.5 |
| Nonmetallic minerals | 11.3 | 10.4 | 14.9 | 11.9 | 11.4 | 7.5 | 7.6 | 7.7 |
| Basic metals | 4.2 | 6.7 | 10.0 | 8.4 | 7.1 | 7.9 | 8.3 | 8.8 |
| Machinery & fabricated metals | 24.3 | 25.2 | 28.3 | 24.7 | 17.3 | 17.5 | 19.1 | 18.7 |
| Miscellaneous manufactures | 13.8 | 14.7 | 12.6 | 13.4 | 12.4 | 6.1 | 6.0 | 5.8 |

na = Not available.

ᵃFor 1974-1978, individual manufacturing industry figures refer only to affiliates outside the Masan EPZ; for 1984-1986, figures refer to all affiliates. For 1974-1978, foreign affiliate value added was calculated as the difference between sales and input purchases following Koo (1982).

Sources: Asian Development Bank (1988); Bank of Korea (1987, 1989); Economic Planning Board (1980, various years); Koo (1982); Korea Credit Appraisal Inc. (1987).

Table 5.5  Ratio of Value Added to Total Output for Foreign Affiliates and Domestic Firms in Korea, 1974-1986

| Value Added/Total Output (%) | 1974 | 1975 | 1976 | 1977 | 1978 | 1984 | 1985 | 1986 |
|---|---|---|---|---|---|---|---|---|
| Foreign affiliates[a] | | | | | | | | |
| All industries | 18.0 | 23.0 | 26.6 | 31.6 | 31.0 | na | na | na |
| Manufacturing | 16.6 | 21.8 | 25.7 | 29.9 | 29.0 | 20.2 | 21.7 | 21.4 |
| Manufacturing-Masan | 30.9 | 30.0 | 31.0 | 27.7 | 27.8 | 20.2 | 21.7 | 21.4 |
| Manufacturing-non-Masan | 15.6 | 21.4 | 25.4 | 30.1 | 29.1 | 20.2 | 21.7 | 21.4 |
| Food products | 34.6 | 41.5 | 38.3 | 42.5 | 36.5 | 31.9 | 31.1 | 35.2 |
| Textiles & apparel | -139.2 | -30.0 | -16.3 | 34.7 | 36.3 | 28.6 | 29.0 | 29.5 |
| Wood and paper products | 40.1 | 42.2 | 40.6 | 48.7 | 48.9 | 39.0 | 35.3 | 37.2 |
| Chemicals | 16.3 | 19.0 | 21.1 | 21.2 | 25.2 | 10.6 | 12.2 | 15.0 |
| Nonmetallic minerals | 77.0 | 79.5 | 84.1 | 83.3 | 84.1 | 50.5 | 53.0 | 51.2 |
| Basic metals | 24.6 | 24.8 | 35.8 | 35.0 | 29.3 | 26.8 | 26.9 | 26.3 |
| Machinery & fabricated metals | 36.8 | 37.3 | 38.2 | 39.6 | 28.5 | 25.9 | 27.8 | 24.0 |
| Miscellaneous manufactures | 55.9 | 57.9 | 46.6 | 44.1 | 43.5 | 3.6 | 3.3 | 2.9 |

| Domestic firms | | | | | | | |
|---|---|---|---|---|---|---|---|
| All industries | 44.9 | 45.3 | 46.1 | 46.4 | 46.6 | na | na | na |
| Manufacturing | 36.8 | 37.9 | 37.3 | 37.8 | 41.0 | 37.4 | 37.4 | 38.9 |
| Manufacturing-Masan | 32.8 | 34.7 | 34.9 | 36.4 | 38.8 | 37.4 | 37.4 | 38.9 |
| Manufacturing-non-Masan | 36.7 | 37.8 | 37.2 | 37.7 | 40.8 | 37.4 | 37.4 | 38.9 |
| | | | | | | | | |
| Food products | 31.4 | 41.5 | 41.2 | 44.0 | 47.4 | 40.0 | 39.6 | 39.6 |
| Textiles & apparel | 42.8 | 38.3 | 37.4 | 33.7 | 38.9 | 38.6 | 38.5 | 38.2 |
| Wood and paper products | 27.6 | 31.4 | 32.3 | 34.1 | 38.6 | 36.7 | 37.4 | 37.9 |
| Chemicals | 40.4 | 39.2 | 38.5 | 37.4 | 37.5 | 30.5 | 30.7 | 33.3 |
| Nonmetallic minerals | 42.8 | 46.1 | 42.4 | 44.4 | 47.4 | 40.3 | 40.5 | 41.0 |
| Basic metals | 33.4 | 26.2 | 25.5 | 26.9 | 33.3 | 30.0 | 30.0 | 30.3 |
| Machinery & fabricated metals | 36.6 | 36.4 | 37.2 | 41.2 | 41.9 | 42.0 | 41.3 | 43.2 |
| Miscellaneous manufactures | 41.7 | 46.0 | 44.0 | 43.0 | 48.4 | 137.8 | 176.0 | 246.9 |

na = Not available.

[a]For 1974-1978, individual manufacturing industry figures refer only to affiliates outside the Masan EPZ; for 1984-1986, figures refer to all affiliates. Output proxied with total sales for foreign affiliates in 1974-1978; see table 5.4 for notes on foreign affiliate value added.

Sources: Asian Development Bank (1988); Bank of Korea (1987, 1989); Economic Planning Board (1980, various years); Koo (1982); Korea Credit Appraisal Inc., (1987).

In addition to the base-case estimates, the effects of expanded foreign firm production on domestic firm production were estimated by adding (1) the level of foreign firm production in 1978, and/or (2) the sum of foreign firm production levels in 1974 through 1977 as arguments in the domestic firm production function (base model extensions, Appendix Table 5.A). These variables can be interpreted as proxies for the static and dynamic intraindustry externalities that expansion of foreign firm production imposes on domestic firm production. However, the coefficients on these foreign firm variables are found to be very small in absolute value and statistically insignificant. Hence the evidence is that the intraindustry spillovers from foreign firm production to domestic firm production in 1978, either past or present, are minimal at best.[8]

One criticism often heard in developing economies is that multinational firms in manufacturing have a tendency to create enclaves in which low-value added production is concentrated. In short, foreign firms are accused of being overly dependent on inputs, especially imported inputs, and of having weak linkages with the domestic economy; it is thus argued that multinationals have little effect on the structure of the domestic economy. Linkages-related issues are examined in the discussion of trade that follows, but here we note that the ratios of value added to total output are generally lower in foreign firms than in their domestic counterparts (Table 5.5). This is true for all industries, including total manufacturing, food products, textiles and apparel, chemicals, and machinery and fabricated metals for most of the years. On the other hand, foreign firm ratios were generally higher in nonmetallic minerals and no consistent differences are observed in other industries.[9] In the manufacturing aggregate, value added-to-total output ratios for foreign firms increased in 1974–1978 but declined substantially by 1984–1986, while domestic firm ratios remained relatively constant over this period.[10] Although policy makers tend to view low ratios as unfavorable, in the absence of further information about differences in distortions affecting domestic and foreign firms, low ratios imply nothing about the relative efficiency of foreign firms. Moreover, the preceding analysis of value added in foreign firms suggests that foreign firms have concentrated production in Korea's leading sectors. Hence foreign firms appear to have contributed to changes in Korea's production structure.

## Multinationals, Changes in Employment Structure, and Technology

In general, the contribution of foreign firms to employment in Korea (Table 5.6) is somewhat smaller than the contribution to value added. Shares of foreign firm employment in total Korean employment gradually increased from 1 percent to 3 percent over the period 1974–1986. However, in manufacturing, employment shares are comparatively large at 12–13 percent in 1974–1975, 18 percent in 1976, and 13–14 percent in 1977–1978 and 1984–1986. These ratios have been highest in the fast-growing electric machinery industry, 36–40 percent in 1974–1978 and 57–68 percent in 1984–1986. The electric machinery industry has been by far the most significant in terms of foreign firm employment and is one of the few industries in which foreign firm employment shares are higher than foreign firm capital expenditure shares for 1984–1986. Foreign firm employment shares have also been much higher than the manufacturing average in petroleum (1974–1978), transportation equipment (1984–1986), and miscellaneous manufacturing (1977–1978). Notably low ratios have consistently been observed in food, textiles and apparel, wood and paper, nonmetallic minerals, and metals. Thus, the tendency for foreign firms to be concentrated in Korea's rapidly growing machinery sectors is also observed in terms of employment.

Because ratios of foreign firm employment to total Korean activity do not necessarily measure the net contribution of foreign firms to Korean employment, an analysis of net intraindustry effects similar to the production analysis in the preceding section was done. In our base model of domestic firm production and employment in 1978 (base model, Appendix Table 5.A), employment is estimated as a function of domestic firm production, wage rates, and skill intensity. Although the model only measures intraindustry effects, it describes variation in employment rather well, both in domestic and foreign firms. In terms of employment, the employment-production elasticity was 63 percent higher in domestic firms than in foreign firms. This implies that, at the means, the marginal employment-production ratio was over two-and-a-half times higher for domestic firms. The marginal employment-production ratio can be further decomposed into the product of the incremental labor-capital ratio and the inverse of the marginal product of capital. It was estimated earlier that the marginal product of capital is six times larger in foreign firms; thus, the incremental labor-capital ratio is roughly 15 times higher in domestic firms. According to the limited information on factor intensities (Table 5.7), domestic incremental labor-capital ratios were actually only three times smaller than foreign ratios in the manufacturing aggregate by 1985–1986. This suggests that the 1978 data may have overestimated the incremental labor-capital ratio in foreign firms.[11] Nonetheless all evidence suggests domestic firms generate more employment per unit of output.

As in the case of production, an attempt was made to estimate the relationship between domestic firm employment and foreign firm employment by adding foreign firm employment in 1978 and/or the sum of foreign firm employment in 1974–1977 as independent variables to the base employment equation (base model extensions, Appendix Table 5.A). The rationale for adding these varibles is, as in the production case, to capture the externalities that increased foreign firm employment may impart on domestic firm employment activities. However, despite the evidence that employment determination is different in foreign and domestic firms, foreign firm employment is not found to have any significant direct impact on domestic firm employment. On the other hand, Jo (1980, 158–164) found that foreign manufacturing firms indirectly created 101,623 jobs through interindustry input-output linkages in 1973–1974 although they only employed 162,060 workers themselves. The ratio of indirectly created employment to direct employment was thus 61 percent. This ratio was even higher in petroleum (226 percent), food (87 percent), electric machinery (78 percent), and nonmetallic minerals (68 percent), but was significantly lower (under 36 percent) in all other manufacturing industries. Thus the omission of interindustry effects is likely to bias our estimates in the direction of finding no employment spillovers from foreign to domestic firms.

As the discussion indicates, one reason foreign firms have different employment effects is that they employ different technologies. Estimates of machinery and

Table 5.6  Employment of Foreign Affiliates in Korea[a], 1974-1986

| Foreign Affiliate Employment | 1974 | 1975 | 1976 | 1977 | 1978 | 1984 | 1985 | 1986 |
|---|---|---|---|---|---|---|---|---|
| Total employment (thousands) | | | | | | | | |
| All industries | 159 | 182 | 226 | 258 | 316 | 363 | 363 | 418 |
| Manufacturing | 153 | 175 | 298 | 246 | 289 | 319 | 321 | 373 |
| Manufacturing-Masan | 21 | 22 | 30 | 28 | 31 | na | na | na |
| Manufacturing-non-Masan | 133 | 152 | 189 | 217 | 258 | na | na | na |
| Food products | 11 | 11 | 9 | 11 | 14 | 9 | 9 | 10 |
| Textiles & apparel | 25 | 32 | 35 | 36 | 42 | 22 | 23 | 24 |
| Wood and paper products | 3 | 3 | 3 | 8 | 9 | 4 | 4 | 5 |
| Chemicals, except petroleum | 16 | 18 | 26 | 26 | 31 | 20 | 23 | 24 |
| Petroleum | 4 | 4 | 4 | 4 | 4 | 2 | 2 | 3 |
| Nonmetallic minerals | 4 | 5 | 6 | 7 | 7 | 10 | 11 | 11 |
| Metals | 6 | 8 | 10 | 12 | 16 | 17 | 18 | 20 |
| Nonelectric machinery | 6 | 9 | 11 | 13 | 20 | 13 | 13 | 15 |
| Electric machinery | 48 | 49 | 67 | 75 | 82 | 187 | 176 | 205 |
| Transportation equipment | 4 | 5 | 7 | 9 | 17 | 29 | 35 | 48 |
| Miscellaneous manufactures | 6 | 9 | 11 | 15 | 16 | 6 | 6 | 8 |

As a share of total Korean employment (%)

| | | | | | | | | |
|---|---|---|---|---|---|---|---|---|
| All industries | 1.4 | 1.6 | 1.8 | 2.0 | 2.4 | 2.5 | 2.4 | 2.7 |
| Manufacturing | 12.0 | 12.5 | 17.6 | 13.0 | 13.9 | 13.9 | 13.4 | 13.8 |
| Manufacturing-Masan | 1.6 | 1.6 | 1.8 | 1.5 | 1.5 | na | na | na |
| Manufacturing-non-Masan | 10.4 | 10.9 | 11.2 | 11.5 | 12.4 | na | na | na |
| | | | | | | | | |
| Food products | 7.0 | 7.6 | 6.1 | 6.7 | 7.9 | 4.6 | 4.9 | 5.0 |
| Textiles & apparel | 6.1 | 6.5 | 5.8 | 5.6 | 6.1 | 3.4 | 3.4 | 3.3 |
| Wood and paper products | 2.5 | 2.6 | 2.6 | 5.1 | 5.3 | 2.3 | 2.5 | 2.5 |
| Chemicals, except petroleum | 11.0 | 11.2 | 12.4 | 11.9 | 13.4 | 7.3 | 7.7 | 6.9 |
| Petroleum | 24.1 | 23.5 | 25.7 | 27.5 | 28.2 | 14.1 | 13.9 | 14.6 |
| Nonmetallic minerals | 6.2 | 7.9 | 9.6 | 8.6 | 7.5 | 9.9 | 10.1 | 9.7 |
| Metals | 6.3 | 8.3 | 9.1 | 8.1 | 9.1 | 7.7 | 8.0 | 8.2 |
| Nonelectric machinery | 12.6 | 13.8 | 12.8 | 13.0 | 16.4 | 8.8 | 8.6 | 8.1 |
| Electric machinery | 39.3 | 38.5 | 36.6 | 40.1 | 35.7 | 68.2 | 60.8 | 56.5 |
| Transportation equipment | 8.1 | 9.7 | 9.8 | 9.9 | 14.7 | 18.0 | 20.2 | 26.7 |
| Miscellaneous manufactures | 11.0 | 15.1 | 14.7 | 18.7 | 20.3 | 6.3 | 6.3 | 6.6 |

na = Not available.

ªFor 1974-1978, individual manufacturing industry figures refer only to affiliates outside the Masan EPZ; for 1984-1986, figures refer to all affiliates.

Sources: Asian Development Bank (1988); Economic Planning Board (1980, various years); Koo (1982); Korea Credit Appraisal Inc. (1987).

Table 5.7  Capital-Labor Ratios in Korea, 1984-1986 (US$ per
Employee)

Part A:  By industry

| Industry | Capital-Labor Ratio, Korea, 1984 | Incremental Capital-Ratio, Domestic Firms, 1985-1986 | Incremental Capital-Labor Ratio, Foreign Firms, 1985-1986 |
|---|---|---|---|
| All industries | na | 49,934 | 83,273 |
| Manufacturing | 12,958 | 31,281 | 80,760 |
| Food products | 16,481 | 82,414 | 39,060 |
| Textiles & apparel | 6,908 | 20,095 | 293,068 |
| Wood and paper products | 11,888 | 62,591 | 62,752 |
| Chemicals, except petroleum | 15,003 | 24,489 | 43,016 |
| Petroleum | 45,030 | 228,519 | 788,615 |
| Nonmetallic minerals | 19,526 | 153,600 | 267,126 |
| Metals | 26,168 | 52,420 | 63,604 |
| Nonelectric machinery | 10,569 | 24,822 | 24,377 |
| Electric machinery | 9,655 | 18,223 | 68,081 |
| Transportation equipment | 19,378 | 727,056 | 91,403 |
| Miscellaneous manufactures | 3,539 | 7,288 | 18,112 |

Part B:  By source in manufacturing[a]

| | | | |
|---|---|---|---|
| Domestic firms | 35,487 | 36,465 | 39,193 |
| Foreign firms | 38,274 | 38,954 | 43,337 |
| Japanese firms | 26,756 | 29,448 | 35,288 |
| U.S. firms | 50,246 | 49,564 | 54,446 |

na = Not available.
[a]The following data, which was based on data from the Ministry of Finance, imply far larger capital stocks and larger domestic employment than the mining and manufacturing survey data used in the industry data on the upper half of the table.

Sources:  Asian Development Bank (1988); Economic Planning Board (various years); Koo and Bark (1988, 43); Korea Credit Appraisal Inc. (1987).

equipment per worker for 1974 (Jo 1980, 148) showed that foreign firms use at least 50 percent more capital per worker than did domestic firms in the industries where foreign investment was concentrated, i.e., textiles and apparel, nonpetroleum chemicals, electric machinery, and transportation equipment. Consequently, foreign manufacturing firms were more than twice as capital-intensive in the manufacturing aggregate. More recent figures show that the aggregate manufacturing differential diminished dramatically by 1984–1986 (Koo and Bark 1988, 43 and Table 5.7, Part B). Among foreign firms, U.S. firms are very capital-intensive while Japanese firms are more labor-intensive, even more so than domestic firms. The total capital-labor ratios calculated in Table 5.7 are much lower than those in Koo and Bark,[12] but our calculations show that incremental capital-labor ratios for 1985–1986 were higher than capital stock-labor ratios for both domestic and foreign firms. Thus both domestic and foreign firms have contributed to capital deepening in all manufacturing industries of the Korean economy in recent years. Second, the incremental ratios indicate that in most industries, except for food and transportation equipment, foreign firms are increasing their capital intensity in larger absolute amounts than are domestic firms. On the other hand, the large increase in the capital intensity of domestic transportation equipment firms is quite interesting because it indicates that, although foreign firms dominated capital expenditures in this industry, domestic firms altered their factor proportions much more in absolute terms.

Another set of related issues surrounds the technology intensity of foreign firms. It is well known that multinationals tend to be technology intensive in general (Markusen, this volume) and that countries like Korea have sought to promote DFI to facilitate transfers of technology from the multinationals. Ratios of R&D expenditure to total sales for 1980 show that foreign firms tend to be more technology intensive in the economy as a whole and in manufacturing, especially in the food, chemicals including petroleum, nonmetallic minerals, basic metals, and transportation equipment industries (Koo and Bark 1988, 49). However, in the textiles and apparel, paper and printing, nonelectric machinery, and electric machinery industries, domestic firms were more R&D intensive. The 1984–1986 survey used here indicates that the R&D-to-sales ratio of foreign firms has fallen for manufacturing and for individual industries such as chemicals including petroleum, while it has increased somewhat in metals and machinery (Korea Credit Appraisal Inc. 1987). It is interesting to note that among foreign firms, R&D intensity, whether it is measured by the ratio of R&D expenditure to total sales or by the ratio of R&D employees to total employees, was highest in metals and machinery, transportation equipment,[13] and textiles and apparel. The high R&D intensity of textiles and apparel is particularly interesting because it indicates that foreign firms in this sector are using increasingly sophisticated techniques in Korea to cope with competition from developing countries with lower labor costs. In other words, not only do foreign firms affect the level and distribution of Korean employment among industries, but they also affect the composition of employment within industries.

## Multinationals and Korean Trade

Perhaps the most important aspect of multinational involvement in the Korean economy is its impact on trade. Although foreign firms have never accounted for

Table 5.8  Exports of Foreign Affiliates in Korea, 1974-1986[a]

| Foreign Affiliate Exports | 1974 | 1975 | 1976 | 1977 | 1978 | 1984 | 1985 | 1986 |
|---|---|---|---|---|---|---|---|---|
| Foreign affiliate exports (US$ thousands) | | | | | | | | |
| All industries | 1,028 | 1,135 | 1,962 | 2,332 | 2,899 | 6,757 | 7,402 | 10,060 |
| Manufacturing | 1,002 | 1,096 | 1,927 | 2,271 | 2,810 | 5,594 | 6,249 | 8,621 |
| Manufacturing-Masan | 178 | 169 | 286 | 347 | 416 | na | na | na |
| Manufacturing-non-Masan | 823 | 927 | 1,641 | 1,924 | 2,394 | na | na | na |
| | | | | | | | | |
| Food products | 21 | 29 | 25 | 39 | 155 | 26 | 33 | 56 |
| Textiles & apparel | 86 | 166 | 238 | 271 | 349 | 920 | 923 | 1,099 |
| Wood and paper products | 9 | 7 | 12 | 16 | 20 | 6 | 8 | 26 |
| Chemicals, except petroleum | 126 | 178 | 371 | 462 | 589 | 634 | 650 | 591 |
| Petroleum | 145 | 127 | 198 | 195 | 100 | 577 | 504 | 290 |
| Nonmetallic minerals | 14 | 15 | 22 | 26 | 26 | 64 | 65 | 98 |
| Metals | 30 | 25 | 48 | 44 | 73 | 288 | 280 | 347 |
| Nonelectric machinery | 30 | 29 | 51 | 61 | 75 | 146 | 161 | 224 |
| Electric machinery | 342 | 324 | 622 | 729 | 887 | 2,628 | 2,929 | 4,229 |
| Transportation equipment | 1 | 2 | 12 | 25 | 54 | 255 | 645 | 1,575 |
| Miscellaneous manufactures | 20 | 25 | 41 | 57 | 66 | 50 | 51 | 86 |

As a share of total Korean exports (%)

| | | | | | | | | |
|---|---|---|---|---|---|---|---|---|
| All industries | 23.0 | 22.3 | 25.4 | 23.2 | 22.8 | 23.1 | 24.4 | 29.0 |
| Manufacturing | 24.3 | 24.2 | 27.0 | 25.3 | 24.1 | 19.9 | 21.5 | 26.1 |
| Manufacturing-Masan | 4.3 | 3.7 | 4.0 | 3.9 | 3.6 | na | na | na |
| Manufacturing-non-Masan | 20.0 | 20.4 | 23.0 | 21.4 | 20.5 | na | na | na |
| | | | | | | | | |
| Food products | 17.7 | 13.3 | 14.6 | 15.7 | 59.2 | 10.6 | 13.2 | 19.0 |
| Textiles & apparel | 5.4 | 8.5 | 8.1 | 8.0 | 7.8 | 12.2 | 12.4 | 11.7 |
| Wood and paper products | 3.1 | 2.1 | 2.5 | 2.7 | 2.8 | 1.4 | 2.1 | 4.5 |
| Chemicals, except petroleum | 30.0 | 38.3 | 43.5 | 39.8 | 36.1 | 14.3 | 13.0 | 12.2 |
| Petroleum | 122.1 | 120.1 | 132.0 | 169.1 | 259.6 | 63.6 | 49.3 | 38.4 |
| Nonmetallic minerals | 17.0 | 14.4 | 12.4 | 9.9 | 9.4 | 17.7 | 18.9 | 21.3 |
| Metals | 5.0 | 6.8 | 8.1 | 4.5 | 6.3 | 7.9 | 7.9 | 9.5 |
| Nonelectric machinery | 26.6 | 21.8 | 20.2 | 21.7 | 19.1 | 11.1 | 10.6 | 9.2 |
| Electric machinery | 65.2 | 64.5 | 68.2 | 71.2 | 65.6 | 67.0 | 76.1 | 72.6 |
| Transportation equipment | 1.5 | 1.3 | 5.3 | 4.9 | 6.0 | 5.9 | 13.4 | 44.1 |
| Miscellaneous manufactures | 10.3 | 11.7 | 12.9 | 14.7 | 14.5 | 5.9 | 6.0 | 7.1 |

na = Not available.

[a]For 1974-1978, individual manufacturing industry figures refer only to affiliates outside the Masan EPZ; 1984-1986 figures refer to all affiliates.

Sources: Asian Development Bank (1988); Australian National University (1989); Economic Planning Board (1980, various years); Koo (1982, 98-102); Korea Credit Appraisal Inc. (1987).

over 10 percent of total capital expenditure, value added, or employment, foreign firms accounted for 20–34 percent of total imports and 20–29 percent of total exports (Table 5.8 and sources). Interestingly, foreign firm shares of total Korean imports have declined over time from 28–34 percent in 1974–1978 to 20–24 percent in 1984–1986, while foreign firm shares of exports have increased from 20–25 percent in 1974–1978 to 23–29 percent in 1984–1986. Since it is impossible to evaluate the relationship between domestic and foreign firm import structures,[14] attention is focused on the structure of exports to discern sectoral patterns.

An interesting pattern that can be seen from the disaggregated export data (Table 5.8) is that the foreign firm share of manufactured exports exceeded the foreign firm share of total exports in 1974–1978, while the opposite was true in 1984–1986. Within manufacturing, foreign firm shares of exports were largest in electric machinery with foreign firms accounting for two-thirds to three-fourths of Korean exports in this growing industry. Foreign firm shares of exports have also taken off in transportation equipment in recent years rising from 6 percent before 1984 to 44 percent in 1986. This increase in foreign firm shares clearly reflects the growing exports of Korean automobiles manufactured in joint ventures with foreign firms.[15] Foreign firm shares of petroleum exports are also quite large,[16] although they have fallen in recent years. The decline in nonpetroleum chemical and nonelectric machinery shares are significant and are similar in scope to the decreases in foreign firm shares of employment and value added in these industries. On the other hand, there have been increases in textiles and apparel, and nonmetallic minerals, which is in contrast to the decline of foreign firm shares of textiles and apparel employment and nonmetallic minerals value added.

Although these ratios do not measure the total effects of foreign firms on Korean exports, the paucity of data prevents construction of a model that is comparable to those employed earlier in analyzing the full impact of foreign firms on production and employment. Some reduced-form, time-series estimates of the effects of foreign capital stocks on Korean trade flows have been made by Ramstetter (1986) and Naya and Ramstetter (1988). The results show that foreign capital had no net effect on imports, and Japanese capital stimulated Korean exports while U.S. capital had the opposite effect. Unfortunately, these estimates are very sensitive to specification and are plagued with statistical problems that make interpretation difficult. However, as discussed in Lee (1983), Koo and Bark (1988), and Naya and Ramstetter (1988), ratios of exports to total sales have been higher for Japanese firms than for other foreign firms; thus, there is strong evidence that Japanese firms are among the most export-oriented in Korea.[17]

It is also clear that foreign firms in general have higher ratios of exports to total output or total sales than do domestic firms (Table 5.9 and sources). Indeed for the total economy, these ratios were over 30 percent for foreign firms, but only 9–10 percent for domestic firms in 1974–1978. This reflects the heavy concentration of foreign firms in manufacturing where ratios are higher and the differential between foreign firms and domestic firms is smaller. In 1974–1978, the ratio of exports to total output in manufacturing was 32–39 percent for foreign firms versus 25–28 percent for domestic firms. In 1984–1986, the ratios were 38–46 percent versus 29–31 percent, respectively. Foreign firm ratios are very high in metals and machinery, ranging from 46–69 percent or two to three times domestic firm levels. Electric machinery dominates metal and machinery exports (Table 5.8) and thus accounts for much of the large differential between domestic and foreign firms in this industry. In contrast, over the 1974–1978 period, domestic firm ratios sometimes exceeded the foreign firm ratios in basic and fabricated metals and transportation equipment (Table 5.9 and sources), although the large increases in foreign firm transportation equipment exports in 1984–1986 (Table 5.8) would suggest this is no longer the case in the latter industry. Foreign firm ratios were also generally higher in food, textiles and apparel, and nonmetallic minerals. Moreover foreign firms in textiles and apparel have generally had the highest ratios, suggesting that these have been among the most export-oriented firms in Korea.

Although the preceding analysis indicates that foreign firms have clearly contributed to the growth of Korean exports, multinationals in Korea and elsewhere are still criticized for an excessively high dependence on imported inputs. There are two separate issues here: (1) high import dependence is thought to be undesirable because weak linkages between foreign firms and the domestic economy contribute to enclave creation; and (2) high import dependence contributes to balance-of-trade difficulties. In the Korean case, import-content ratios (ratios of imported intermediate inputs to total intermediate inputs) for all industries and manufacturing were over 70 percent but fell gradually over the 1974–1978 period (Table 5.10). By 1984–1986, these ratios had declined to 48–52 percent for manufacturing. For 1974–1978, import-content ratios were lower in the Masan EPZ, a policy-enforced enclave, than outside the EPZ, and the ratios were substantially higher than the manufacturing aggregate in only one industry, petroleum. Because petroleum alone accounted for over one-half of imported inputs, the decline of the aggregate manufacturing ratio in the 1984–1986 period is largely due to the decline of petroleum imports. In food, textiles and apparel, metals and machinery, and miscellaneous manufactures, import-content ratios declined in 1974–1978 but increased during the investment boom of 1984–1986.

Two important points must be emphasized. First, although it may be reasonable to have a policy goal of decreasing import content during the process of industrialization, the decreases must be due to improved efficiency of domestic industry relative to imports in order for the reduction in import content to be welfare increasing. Decreases in import content that are strictly policy-induced (i.e., are not accompanied by an increase in the relative efficiency of domestic industry) are not necessarily beneficial for the host economy. Note that in Korea policy constraints on foreign firm trading activity were rather strict in 1974–1978 but significantly loosened in the early 1980s. Second, there is a problem with timing. When a foreign firm is new, it may know little about domestic sources of intermediate inputs; in addition, the inputs required are often not available from domestic firms in the quantity and quality required. Hence it is more efficient for the foreign firm to import the necessary inputs. However, with the passage of time, the foreign firm increases its knowledge of domestic sources, and the ability of the domestic economy to supply needed inputs increases as domestic entrepreneurs seize new business opportunities. Indeed our conversations with textiles and apparel and electronics firms in Korea (as well as Taiwan) indicate it is common for former employees of foreign firms to start

Table 5.9  Ratios of Export to Total Output for Foreign Affiliates and Domestic Firms in Korea, 1974-1986[a]

|  | 1974 | 1975 | 1976 | 1977 | 1978 | 1984 | 1985 | 1986 |
|---|---|---|---|---|---|---|---|---|
| Foreign affiliates |  |  |  |  |  |  |  |  |
| All industries | 35.6 | 32.0 | 38.4 | 35.7 | 33.6 | na | na | na |
| Manufacturing | 35.5 | 31.7 | 38.5 | 36.0 | 33.8 | 38.2 | 41.4 | 45.9 |
| Manufacturing-Masan | 97.9 | 96.9 | 94.3 | 94.3 | 85.9 | na | na | na |
| Manufacturing-non-Masan | 31.2 | 28.2 | 34.9 | 32.4 | 30.6 | na | na | na |
|  |  |  |  |  |  |  |  |  |
| Food products | 23.5 | 28.1 | 17.6 | 16.9 | 37.0 | 8.7 | 9.6 | 13.4 |
| Textiles & apparel | 66.4 | 73.4 | 74.9 | 74.1 | 72.7 | 77.8 | 72.2 | 76.0 |
| Wood and paper products | 31.6 | 20.8 | 29.0 | 18.5 | 16.3 | 3.2 | 3.8 | 9.7 |
| Chemicals | 16.2 | 14.3 | 20.9 | 20.2 | 17.9 | 24.8 | 24.3 | 21.2 |
| Nonmetallic minerals | 39.2 | 35.9 | 31.6 | 30.7 | 23.1 | 29.0 | 30.6 | 36.7 |
| Metals and machinery | 68.5 | 61.4 | 61.0 | 54.3 | 46.4 | 48.3 | 55.7 | 61.0 |
| Miscellaneous manufactures | 90.1 | 88.9 | 90.8 | 85.7 | 76.6 | 5.0 | 4.7 | 4.8 |

| Domestic firms | | | | | | | |
|---|---|---|---|---|---|---|---|
| All industries | 8.4 | 8.8 | 9.6 | 10.2 | 9.6 | na | na | na |
| Manufacturing | 27.7 | 25.6 | 27.2 | 26.2 | 25.0 | 30.4 | 31.1 | 28.6 |
| | | | | | | | | |
| Food products | 4.2 | 6.6 | 4.0 | 4.4 | 1.7 | 2.0 | 2.1 | 2.0 |
| Textiles & apparel | 56.5 | 50.6 | 52.2 | 49.1 | 49.8 | 53.7 | 53.5 | 54.5 |
| Wood and paper products | 25.8 | 26.1 | 31.2 | 28.0 | 24.8 | 8.7 | 7.9 | 9.9 |
| Chemicals | 16.4 | 12.0 | 14.3 | 16.1 | 18.4 | 25.1 | 29.3 | 26.6 |
| Nonmetallic minerals | 13.6 | 14.3 | 19.7 | 20.2 | 16.1 | 8.7 | 8.2 | 9.1 |
| Metals and machinery | 25.7 | 22.0 | 21.8 | 23.2 | 21.5 | 39.1 | 38.1 | 29.5 |
| Miscellaneous manufactures | 93.6 | 92.2 | 82.7 | 75.0 | 71.5 | 200.2 | 252.1 | 329.3 |

na = Not available.

[a] For 1974-1978, individual manufacturing industry figures refer only to affiliates outside the Masan EPZ; 1984-1986 figures refer to all affiliates; total output proxied with total sales for foreign firms in 1974-1978.

Sources: Asian Development Bank (1988); Australian National University (1989); Bank of Korea (1987, 1989); Economic Planning Board (1980, various years); Koo (1982, 98-102); Korea Credit Appraisal Inc. (1987).

Table 5.10 Ratios of Import Content and Trade Balance/Value Added for Foreign Affiliates in Korea, 1974-1986[a]

| | 1974 | 1975 | 1976 | 1977 | 1978 | 1984 | 1985 | 1986 |
|---|---|---|---|---|---|---|---|---|
| Import content ratio (imports/total inputs) | | | | | | | | |
| All industries | 81.9 | 82.7 | 78.8 | 77.7 | 70.0 | na | na | na |
| Manufacturing | 80.2 | 83.2 | 79.4 | 78.5 | 70.5 | 50.9 | 51.9 | 47.7 |
| Manufacturing-Masan | 78.0 | 75.2 | 69.5 | 66.6 | 68.9 | na | na | na |
| Manufacturing-non-Masan | 82.6 | 83.5 | 80.0 | 79.2 | 70.6 | na | na | na |
| Food products | 32.1 | 24.1 | 27.6 | 26.3 | 18.5 | 19.1 | 23.7 | 37.0 |
| Textiles & apparel | 58.3 | 65.8 | 57.0 | 63.4 | 57.8 | 51.4 | 54.6 | 58.9 |
| Wood and paper products | 52.5 | 54.0 | 56.5 | 64.6 | 60.4 | 77.7 | 64.0 | 76.4 |
| Chemicals | 92.7 | 92.0 | 91.2 | 91.9 | 91.4 | 67.2 | 63.9 | 51.5 |
| Nonmetallic minerals | 30.1 | 38.4 | 34.5 | 29.6 | 33.3 | 15.6 | 19.0 | 24.6 |
| Metals and machinery | 67.8 | 73.7 | 68.8 | 62.9 | 53.3 | 47.4 | 53.6 | 54.6 |
| Miscellaneous manufactures | 71.0 | 68.3 | 67.1 | 57.4 | 49.6 | 2.4 | 2.1 | 1.8 |

Trade balance/value added

| | | | | | | | | |
|---|---|---|---|---|---|---|---|---|
| All industries | -175.9 | -137.1 | -73.2 | -55.3 | -47.7 | na | na | na |
| Manufacturing | -189.5 | -152.9 | -79.7 | -63.5 | -55.9 | -12.0 | 3.4 | 39.5 |
| Manufacturing-Masan | 142.5 | 147.5 | 149.4 | 166.9 | 130.0 | na | na | na |
| Manufacturing-non-Masan | -246.9 | -175.3 | -97.7 | -76.6 | -66.8 | na | na | na |
| Food products | 7.2 | 33.8 | 1.4 | 4.1 | 69.2 | -13.6 | -21.6 | -30.0 |
| Textiles & apparel | 52.4 | 40.3 | -53.0 | 94.3 | 99.0 | 143.7 | 115.4 | 116.8 |
| Wood and paper products | 0.3 | -24.8 | -11.2 | -30.1 | -29.9 | -113.4 | -106.2 | -103.1 |
| Chemicals | -375.8 | -317.2 | -241.5 | -245.7 | -199.9 | -332.1 | -260.1 | -150.4 |
| Nonmetallic minerals | 41.9 | 35.2 | 31.1 | 31.0 | 21.1 | 42.2 | 40.8 | 48.3 |
| Metals and machinery | 69.9 | 38.5 | 47.5 | 39.9 | 29.0 | 50.8 | 61.3 | 81.0 |
| Miscellaneous manufactures | 105.1 | 103.7 | 118.0 | 121.5 | 111.5 | 75.6 | 80.9 | 106.3 |

na = Not available.

[a]For 1974-1978, individual manufacturing industry figures refer only to affiliates outside the Masan EPZ; 1984-1986 figures refer to all affiliates.

Sources: Asian Development Bank (1988); Bank of Korea (1987, 1989); Economic Planning Board (1980, various years); Koo (1982, 98-102); Korea Credit Appraisal Inc. (1987).

businesses which produce intermediate goods used by the foreign firms. Thus there is every reason to expect these ratios to decline over time in many industries. However, and this brings us back to the first point, this is not possible if factor endowments, technology levels, and/or demand conditions are not consistent with the development of a comparative advantage in domestic firms.

Ratios of trade balance to value added for foreign firms (Table 5.10 and sources) give us an idea of the scope of foreign firm trade deficits in Korea. Foreign firm trade deficits were quite large relative to the value added for all industry and manufacturing aggregates in 1974–1978. Note, however, that these ratios declined steadily over the period and by 1985, foreign manufacturing firms in Korea were generating trade surpluses (largely due to declining deficits in petroleum). Moreover, foreign firms in textiles and apparel, nonmetallic minerals, and metals and machinery (especially fabricated metals and electric machinery) have run surpluses for almost the entire 1974–1978 and 1984–1986 periods. Foreign firms in chemicals and nonelectric machinery have also been able to turn deficits into surpluses.

As impressive as this performance may seem, the important point is not whether foreign firms run surpluses or deficits. As stressed by Markusen (this volume), foreign firms can contribute to increased welfare regardless of their impacts on trade flows. To be sure, by contributing to a reduction of trade deficits and an expansion of trade surpluses, foreign firms have simplified the political tasks of Korea's policy makers. Yet their primary economic task, that of maximizing the economic welfare of Koreans, was by no means dependent on the export expansion of foreign firms. In other words, it is perfectly plausible that increased foreign borrowing could have financed any trade deficit that lower foreign firm exports might have led to.

## Inward and Outward DFI and Structural Change in Korea

Korea's economic structure has changed rapidly over the last few decades with the manufacturing sector, and especially the metals and machinery industries, growing extremely fast. This paper has shown that foreign firms are an important source of investment, value added, employment, and exports in the electric machinery industry and more recently, the transportation equipment industry. The involvement of foreign firms has been somewhat limited in metals and in the slower-growing of Korea's manufacturing industries. This paper has also shown than export-oriented foreign firms, which are concentrated in electric machinery, have expanded employment opportunities in Korea rapidly and that the technology-related activities of foreign firms are also concentrated in the electric machinery industry. Thus there is strong evidence of correlation across industries between the level foreign firm activity and economic growth in Korea. This in turn implies foreign firms have been an important force in the evolution of Korea's economic structure in the 1974–1986 period.

However this correlation does not necessarily imply causation. Of course, as Markusen (this volume) emphasizes, there are important technological reasons for us to believe that foreign firms will be concentrated in industries like electric machinery and transportation equipment where substantial multiplant economies of scale exist. In this sense, the concentration of foreign firms in these Korean industries may be exogenously determined, implying that causation runs from foreign firm activity to Korean economic performance. However, as was discussed, foreign firm investment decisions are also affected by Korean economic performance and policy. Thus it is highly unlikely that causation is unidirectional. In any case, the importance of foreign firms in Korea's leading industries is undeniable and the continuing boom in inward direct investment suggests that foreign firm influence will continue into the 1990s.

However, Korea is now undergoing large changes which will likely alter the way in which multinationals affect the economy. First, Korea incurred large current account surpluses in 1986–1988 which have resulted in the won's appreciation and increased external pressure to further liberalize imports and inward investments. Much of this pressure is oriented toward liberalization in the services sector, since trade and investment in manufacturing is already liberalized to a great extent. Thus, in the next decade, the influence of foreign firms will likely increase in the services sector, perhaps more than in manufacturing. On the other hand, Japanese manufacturing investment is likely to continue at a rapid pace as Japan continues to adjust to an expensive yen and increasing domestic costs of production.

A second factor which will make the role of multinational firms in Korea quite different in the coming decade is the fact that many of the Korean firms that have been referred to as "domestic" in this paper are in the process of becoming or have already become multinationals in their own right. Korea's cumulative outward DFI increased almost 4 times in the aggregate between 1982 and 1988 and almost 12 times in manufacturing (Table 5.11). As a result, manufacturing's share of cumulative outward DFI rose from only 12 percent in 1982 to 35 percent in 1988. The vast majority of the rapid increase in DFI has gone to North America with this region increasing its share of the total from 27 percent to 44 percent. Asia also increased its share from 23 percent to 26 percent, overtaking the Middle East as the second most important destination in 1988. North America has also accounted for the majority of investment in manufacturing, 65 percent in 1988, followed again by Asia with a 12 percent share. Although the scale of this DFI is still small, the rapid growth of manufacturing DFI is a harbinger of new changes Korea's economy will have to undergo as it internationalizes further, both as a host and as a source of direct investment. In this respect, it is interesting that textiles and apparel, footwear, and wood and paper products, three of the slower-growing industries in Korea, accounted for 49 percent of outward manufacturing DFI approvals in 1987–1988 (Koo and Bark 1989, 41). Thus not only is inward DFI likely to continue as an important factor in the upgrading of Korean industrial structure, but outward DFI will also become an important element in the rationalization of Korean industrial structure as well.

## Notes

The authors would like to thank Shigeyuki Abe, Trent Bertrand, Robert McCleery, Michael Plummer, and Janis Togashi for comments and suggestions. However, the authors remain solely responsible for all errors of omission or commission.

1. This is what one would expect since net inflows will be smaller than gross arrivals by the amount of investment withdrawals and repatriated profits which are not reinvested.

Table 5.11   Net Flow of Korean Direct Investment Abroad, 1968-1987

| Region | Year | BOP Data[a] Total Amount (US$m) | MOF Data[b] Total Amount (US$m) | MOF Data[b] Manufac- turing Amount (US$m) | MOF Data[b] Manufac- turing Share (%) |
|---|---|---|---|---|---|
| Average annual flows | | | | | |
| World | 1968-1982 | 20 | 19 | 2 | 11.6 |
| | 1983 | 126 | 97 | 26 | 26.4 |
| | 1984 | 37 | 58 | 13 | 22.8 |
| | 1985 | 34 | 31 | 19 | 61.9 |
| | 1986 | 109 | 157 | 69 | 43.7 |
| | 1987 | 185 | 105 | 86 | 81.6 |
| Cumulative flows | | | | | |
| World | 1968-1982 | 304 | 290 | 33 | 11.6 |
| | 1968-1987 | 794 | 739 | 246 | 33.4 |
| Africa | 1968-1982 | na | 18 | na | na |
| | 1968-1987 | na | 11 | 8 | 70.8 |
| Asia | 1968-1982 | na | 66 | na | na |
| | 1968-1987 | na | 120 | 50 | 41.6 |
| Europe | 1968-1982 | na | 7 | na | na |
| | 1968-1987 | na | 18 | 6 | 32.2 |
| Latin America | 1968-1982 | na | 39 | na | na |
| | 1968-1987 | na | 63 | 4 | 6.2 |
| Middle East | 1968-1982 | na | 26 | na | na |
| | 1968-1987 | na | 130 | 16 | 12.5 |
| North America | 1968-1982 | na | 79 | na | na |
| | 1968-1987 | na | 315 | 160 | 50.6 |
| Oceania | 1968-1982 | na | 54 | na | na |
| | 1968-1987 | na | 81 | 3 | 3.5 |

na = Not available.
[a]IMF balance-of-payments data.
[b]From Korean Ministry of Finance data; 1987 and 1968-1987 figures refer to the period through March 1987.

Sources:  International Monetary Fund (1988, 1989); Ministry of Finance (1987a).

Moreover, there is a clear motive to obtain approvals that are larger than actually necessary to minimize bureaucratic transactions costs.

2. Investing country data on cumulative Japanese approvals (Japan, Ministry of Finance 1989) and actual U.S. DFI position (United States, Department of Commerce, Bureau of Economic Analysis, various years) suggest higher DFI levels for Japan and lower DFI levels for the United States than do the Korean approval data (Koo and Bark 1988, 13), with the difference being especially large for U.S. manufacturing DFI. Since Japanese and Korean DFI data are on an approval basis, these data tend to be biased upwards in comparison to the U.S. data; nevertheless, the differences observed in the data sets are difficult to explain in these terms alone and more fundamental differences in definitions and coverage are probably involved. For example, Korean approvals of Japanese DFI totalled US$2,203 million through September 1987, US$1,167 of which was in manufacturing; corresponding figures for U.S. DFI approvals were US$1,298 million and US$1,151 million in the respective years. On the other hand, Japan's approvals of DFI in Korea summed to US$2,765 million through March 1988, US$1,335 million of which was in manufacturing and the U.S. DFI position at yearend 1987 was US$1,018 million, of which only US$339 million was in manufacturing.

3. It has been argued by Kojima (1978, 1985) that Japanese DFI is more heavily concentrated in industries in which Japan is losing a comparative advantage, while U.S. and European DFI is more highly concentrated in industries in which the investing economies are comparatively advantaged. Lee (1979) provides supporting evidence for this assertion. The fact that textiles and apparel accounted for 17 percent of Japan's cumulative manufacturing DFI approvals by September 1987 but only 1 percent for the United States and Europe indicates that important differences in investment patterns between Japan and other developed countries still remain. Yet, even for Japan, the vast majority of DFI is concentrated in technologically sophisticated industries such as machinery and chemicals as conventional theory would suggest (Markusen, this volume).

4. Korean balance-of-payments data clearly exclude reinvested earnings. It is believed that approval and arrival data also exclude such DFI. Between 1977 and 1987, reinvested earnings accounted for 68 percent of the total US$467 in U.S. DFI capital flows to Korea (United States, Department of Commerce, Bureau of Economic Analysis 1986, various years).

5. Another way of looking at this problem comes from the two-gap literature (see, for example, Areskoug 1976; Lee and Go 1988) which assumes that foreign capital inflows may reduce or stimulate domestic saving and thus affect domestic investment.

6. First, it is not clear whether the 1984–1986 survey includes data for firms in the Masan EPZ (export processing zone). Hence for individual industries, the growth of multinational activity between 1974–1978 and 1984–1986 will tend to be overstated to the extent that firms in the Masan EPZ which were not included in the 1974–1978 survey are included in the 1984–1986 data. No mention of the EPZ is made in the report summarizing this survey (Korea Credit Appraisal Inc. 1987). Second, the 1974–1978 data are extrapolations made by Koo (1982, 1985) from sample data, while similar extrapolations have not been made for the 1984–1986 data. Thus the growth of multinational activity from 1974–1978 to 1984–1986 tends to be understated. On the other hand, the two samples are sufficiently large to have reasonable confidence in analysis of characteristics within each sample. The 1974–1978 survey is based on 468 survey replies for non-Masan EPZ firms (a reply rate of 68 percent) though not all replies were complete, reducing the sample used for estimating individual variables. Separate information on the 114 firms in the Masan EPZ was also used. The 1984–1986 survey is based on a sample of 573 firms (a 63 percent reply rate), 457 of which were in manufacturing (a 61 percent reply rate). A third problem arises because the industrial classifications in the foreign firm surveys are made on an enterprise (firm) basis but those in the surveys/censuses of all manufacturing firms in Korea are made on an establishment basis. Thus industry-level comparisons between domestic and foreign firms are only first approximations.

7. Because the usual technology constant becomes insignificant when the skill-intensity variable is included, it is dropped from the estimated production function.

8. On the other hand, Jo's (1980, 158–164) finding that foreign firms created substantial indirect employment through interindustry, input-output linkages suggests that the omission of interindustry effects biases our estimates in the direction of finding no spillover effects.

9. There is an apparent inconsistency in the data for miscellaneous manufacturing where value added as calculated is larger than total sales for domestic firms for 1984–1986. The problem arises because estimates of foreign firm value added are very low while estimates of total sales (proxied by total production) are very high. Since these figures are biased, they are not discussed further in the text.

10. Since similar declines are also observed for foreign firms in individual industries, differences in the 1974–1978 and 1984–1986 surveys are probably the major cause of these declines. However the declines are marked enough to suggest differences in surveys are not the only factors involved.

11. The major cause of the overestimation in the 1978 data is our apparent underestimation of foreign firm capital stocks. Foreign firm capital stocks were estimated as the sum of gross arrivals, which are apparently far below actual capital expenditures that are the basis of the factor-intensity calculations in Table 5.7.

12. These are calculated as $[(I_{85} + I_{86})/(E_{86} - E_{84})]$ where $I$ is investment, $E$ is employment and 84, 85, and 86 are subscripts referring to 1984, 1985, and 1986, respectively.

13. Only the R&D employment-to-total employment ratio is available for this sector.

14. The problem arises because a firm in industry A can easily import a product of industry B; on the other hand, it is plausible to assume that a firm in industry A exports products of industry A. Note that the total trade data used here and elsewhere in this paper are converted to be compatible with the ISIC-based data by the International Economic Data Bank of Australian National University.

15. Referring to firms such as Hyundai and Daewoo as foreign firms is a bit confusing because foreign influences over management decisions may be minimal. In this sense, these firms, as well as many others in our sample, do not fit the textbook definition of a foreign affiliate. Yet foreign participation in these firms has not been negligible, especially in terms of technology development. Hence the definition of a foreign firm that is used in the Korean surveys, i.e., a firm with foreign equity participation, was employed in this analysis.

16. In the period 1974–1978, the shares exceeded 100 percent. The most likely cause of this apparent discrepancy is the inclusion of certain nonmanufacturing exports in the figures for foreign petroleum firms.

17. Yoo (1981) disputes this contention on the grounds that indirect effects are not accounted for. He provides evidence that U.S. DFI indirectly promotes Korean exports by reducing the price of intermediate inputs.

# References

Areskoug, Kaj. 1976. Private Foreign Investment and Capital Formation in Developing Countries. *Economic Development and Cultural Change* 24(3): 539–47.

Asian Development Bank. 1988. *Key Indicators of Developing Member Countries of ADB,* July 1988 issue. Manila: Asian Development Bank.

Australian National University. 1989. Mimeos from the International Economic Data Bank.

Bank of Korea. 1987. *National Accounts 1987.* Seoul: Bank of Korea.

———. 1989. *Economic Statistics Yearbook 1989.* Seoul: Bank of Korea.

Economic Planning Board. 1980. *Census of Mining and Manufacturing Industries 1978.* Seoul: Economic Planning Board

————. 1989. *Major Statistics of the Korean Economy 1989.* Seoul: Economic Planning Board.

————. Various years. *Report on the Survey of Mining and Manufacturing Industries,* 1974–1977, 1984–1986 issues. Seoul: Economic Planning Board.

International Monetary Fund (IMF). 1988. *Balance of Payments Statistics,* computer tape (July).

————. 1989. *Balance of Payments Statistics Yearbook 1989.* Washington, D.C.: International Monetary Fund.

Japan, Ministry of Finance. 1989. Mimeos.

Jo, Sung-Hwan. 1980. Direct Foreign Private Investment. In *Macroeconomic and Industrial Development in Korea,* edited by Park Chong Kee. Seoul: Korea Development Institute.

Kojima, Kiyoshi. 1978. *Japanese Direct Foreign Investment: A Model of Multinational Business Operations.* Tokyo: Tuttle.

————. 1985. Japanese and American Direct Investment in Asia: A Comparative Analysis. *Hitotsubashi Journal of Economics* 26(1): 1–35.

Koo, Bohn-Ho, and Taeho Bark. 1988. The Role of Direct Foreign Investment in Korea's Recent Growth. Paper presented at the First Conference on Asia-Pacific Relations, sponsored by the Foundation for Advanced Information and Reseach (FAIR), 20–22 April, Tokyo, Japan.

————. 1989. Recent Macroeconomic Performance and Industrial Structural Adjustment in Korea. Paper presented at the FAIR conference, 18–19 August, Fukuoka, Japan.

Koo, Bohn Young. 1982. Status and Changing Forms of Foreign Investment in Korea. Paper presented at the Conference on "New Forms" of Investment in Developing Countries, sponsored by the Organisation for Economic Co-operation and Development, 15–19 March, Paris, France.

————. 1985. The Role of Direct Foreign Investment in Korea's Recent Economic Growth. In *Foreign Trade and Investment: Economic Development in the Newly Industrializing Asian Countries,* edited by Walter Galenson. Madison: University of Wisconsin Press.

Korea Credit Appraisal Inc. 1987. *A Survey on the Economic Effects and Financial Analysis of Foreign Affiliates in Korea.* (In Korean). Seoul: Korea Credit Appraisal Inc.

Lee, Chung H. 1979. United States and Japanese Direct Investment in Korea: A Comparative Study. *Journal of Economic Development* 4(2): 89–113.

————. 1983. International Production of United States and Japan in Korean Manufacturing Industries: A Comparative Study. *Weltwirtschaftliches Archiv* 119(4): 744–53.

————. 1984. Transfer of Technology from Japan and the United States to Korean Manufacturing Industries: A Comparative Study. *Hitotsubashi Journal of Economics* 25(2): 125–36.

Lee, J., and Evelyn M. Go. 1988. Foreign Capital, Balance of Payments and External Debt in Developing Asia. In *Challenge of Asian Developing Countries,* edited by Shinichi Ichimura. Tokyo: Asian Productivity Organization.

Ministry of Finance. 1987. *Overseas Investment System of Korea.* Seoul: Ministry of Finance.

————. 1988. Mimeos.

Naya, Seiji, and Eric D. Ramstetter. 1988. Direct Foreign Investment in Asia's Developing Economies and Trade in the Asia-Pacific Region. Paper presented at the Conference on Economic Cooperation through Foreign Investment in the ESCAP Region, 20–23 September, Beijing, China.

Ramstetter, Eric D. 1986. The Effects of Direct Foreign Investment on Korean Output, Investment, and Trade: A Macroeconometric Approach. In *ELSA Annual Report 1986.* Tokyo: Institute of Developing Economies.

————. 1987. The Impacts of Direct Foreign Investment on Host Country Trade and Output: A Study of Japanese and U.S. Direct Foreign Invesment in Korea, Taiwan, and

Thailand. In *Direct Foreign Investment and Export Promotion: Policies and Experiences in Asia*, edited by Seiji Naya, Vinyu Vichit-Vadakan, and Udom Kerdpibule. Honolulu and Kuala Lumpur: East-West Center and Southeast Asian Central Banks Research and Training Centre.

United States, Department of Commerce, Bureau of Economic Analysis. 1986. Mimeos, 21 November.

_____ . Various years. *Survey of Current Business*, August issues, 1986–1988. Washington, D.C.: Department of Commerce.

World Bank. 1987. *World Development Report 1987*. Washington, D.C.: Oxford University Press.

_____ . 1989. *World Development Report 1989*. Washington, D.C.: Oxford University Press.

Yoo, J. H. 1981. American Investment in Korea: Is it Market-Oriented or Export Promoting? Mimeo, Virginia Commonwealth University.

Appendix Table 5.A  A Simultaneous Equation Model of Production and Employment in Korea, 1978:  Weighted Two-Stage Least Squares Estimates, Twenty-two Industry Cross Section

Notes and definitions:

Figures in parentheses are absolute values of t-values

| | | |
|---|---|---|
| $\bullet$ | = | significant at the 0.10 level (two-tailed tests for t-values) |
| $\bullet\bullet$ | = | significant at the 0.05 level (two-tailed tests for t-values) |
| $\bullet\bullet\bullet$ | = | significant at the 0.001 level (two-tailed tests for t-values) |
| ED | = | employment in domestic firms (*ET-EF*) (number of employees), endogenous |
| EF | = | employment in foreign firms (number of employees), endogenous |
| ET | = | employment in all firms (number of employees), endogenous |
| LED | = | Log(*ED*), endogenous |
| LEF | = | Log(*EF*), endogenous |
| LKD | = | Log(capital stocks in domestic firms, in US\$ millions), exogenous |
| LKF | = | Log(captial stocks of foreign firms, cumulative gross inflows of DFI in US\$ millions), exogenous |
| LYD | = | Log(*YD*), endogenous |
| LYF | = | Log(*YF*), endogenous |
| SK | = | ratio of nonoperatives to total employees (percent), exogenous |
| YD | = | total production of domestic firms (*YT-YF*; US\$ millions), endogenous |
| YF | = | total production of foreign firms (proxied with total sales; US\$ millions), endogenous |
| YT | = | total production of all firms (US\$ millions), endogenous |
| WT | = | total compensation per employee for all firms (US\$), exogenous |
| 78 | = | subscript indicating an observation for 1978 |
| 7477 | = | subscript indicating sum of 1974, 1975, 1976, and 1977 observations |

Base model:  A simultaneous equation model of output and employment

$$LYD_{78} = 0.3609861(LED_{78}) + 0.4799459(LKD_{78}) + 0.0134402(SK_{78})$$
$$\quad\quad\quad (5.50)^{\bullet\bullet\bullet} \quad\quad\quad\quad (4.16)^{\bullet\bullet\bullet} \quad\quad\quad\quad (2.86)^{\bullet\bullet\bullet}$$

Adjusted $R^2$ = 0.960340    F-statistic = 255.2515$^{\bullet\bullet\bullet}$

$$LYF_{78} = 0.2298650(LEF_{78}) + 0.7340477(LKF_{78}) + 0.0414571(SK_{78})$$
$$\quad\quad\quad (4.15)^{\bullet\bullet\bullet} \quad\quad\quad\quad (5.48)^{\bullet\bullet\bullet} \quad\quad\quad\quad (5.53)^{\bullet\bullet\bullet}$$

Adjusted $R^2$ = 0.978088    F-statistic = 469.6886$^{\bullet\bullet\bullet}$

$$YT_{78} = \text{Exp}(LYD) + \text{Exp}(LYF)$$

$$LED_{78} = 15.216957 + 1.0106755(LYD_{78}) - 1.4375195(LWT_{78}) - 0.0139389(SK_{78})$$
$$\quad\quad\quad (4.59)^{\bullet\bullet\bullet} \quad (7.12)^{\bullet\bullet\bullet} \quad\quad\quad (3.36)^{\bullet\bullet\bullet} \quad\quad\quad (1.99)^{\bullet}$$

Adjusted $R^2$ = 0.951602    F-statistic = 138.6355$^{\bullet\bullet\bullet}$

## Appendix Table 5.A (continued)

$$LEF_{78} = 17.400293 + 0.6040276(LYF_{78}) - 1.3898561(LWT_{78}) - 0.0278711(SK_{78})$$
$$(3.68)^{***} \quad\quad (4.83)^{***} \quad\quad\quad (2.13)^{**} \quad\quad\quad\quad (2.84)^{**}$$

Adjusted $R^2 = 0.972998$     $F$-statistic $= 253.2367^{***}$

$$ET_{78} = \text{Exp}(LED) + \text{Exp}(LEF)$$

Base model: Root mean square percentage errors for simulation

$YD_{78} = 3.4\%;\ YF_{78} = 9.7\%;\ YT_{78} = 3.3\%$
$ED_{78} = 4.8\%;\ EF_{78} = 20.7\%;\ ET_{78} = 3.3\%$

Base model extensions: estimation of the foreign output and employment spillover effects on domestic output and employment

$$LYD_{78} = 0.3795734(LED_{78}) + 0.4373466(LKD_{78}) + 0.0133833(SK_{78}) + 0.0006478(YF_{78})$$
$$(5.56)^{***} \quad\quad\quad (3.62)^{***} \quad\quad\quad (2.48)^{**} \quad\quad\quad (0.88)$$

$$- 0.0002329(YF_{7477})$$
$$(0.77)$$

Adjusted $R^2 = 0.958311$     $F$-statistic $= 121.6838^{***}$

$$LYD_{78} = 0.3731743(LED) + 0.4571784(LKDG_{78}) + 0.0122568(SK_{78}) + 0.0000917(YF_{78})$$
$$(5.46)^{***} \quad\quad\quad (3.79)^{***} \quad\quad\quad (2.41)^{**} \quad\quad\quad (0.65)$$

Adjusted $R^2 = 0.959224$     $F$-statistic $= 165.6705^{***}$

$$LYD_{78} = 0.3657166(LED_{78}) + 0.4715945(LKD_{78}) + 0.0124927(SK_{78}) + 0.0000274(YF_{7477})$$
$$(5.32)^{***} \quad\quad\quad (3.91)^{***} \quad\quad\quad (2.39)^{**} \quad\quad\quad (0.46)$$

Adjusted $R^2 = 0.958711$     $F$-statistic $= 163.5384^{***}$

$$LED_{78} = 17.595981 + 1.0601890(LYD_{78}) - 1.8104406(LWT_{78}) - 0.0093244(SK_{78})$$
$$(4.33)^{***} \quad\quad (6.61)^{***} \quad\quad\quad (3.27)^{***} \quad\quad\quad (1.12)$$

$$+ 0.0000545(EF_{78}) - 0.0000186(EF_{7477})$$
$$(1.17) \quad\quad\quad (1.16)$$

Adjusted $R^2 = 0.947183$     $F$-statistic $= 76.31956^{***}$

$$LED_{78} = 15.188037 + 1.0073764(LYD_{78}) - 1.4315656(LWT_{78}) - 0.0138880(SK_{78})$$
$$(4.45)^{***} \quad\quad (6.49)^{***} \quad\quad\quad (3.21)^{***} \quad\quad\quad (1.93)^{**}$$

$$+ 0.0000001601(EF_{7477})$$
$$(0.08)$$

Adjusted $R^2 = 0.948941$     $F$-statistic $= 98.57186^{***}$

## Appendix Table 5.A (continued)

$$LED_{78} = 15.193559 + 1.0035298(LYD_{78}) - 1.4304838(LWT_{78}) - 0.0137046(SK_{78})$$
$$(4.48)^{***} \quad (6.55)^{***} \quad\quad (3.26)^{***} \quad\quad (1.89)^{*}$$

$$+ \ 0.000001209(EF_{78})$$
$$(0.22)$$

Adjusted $R^2$ = 0.949261    $F$-statistic = 99.21995$^{***}$

# 6

## Foreign Firms and Structural Change in Taiwan

*Chi Schive and Jenn-Hwa Tu*

### Introduction

Inward direct foreign investment (DFI) has played a subtle but important role in Taiwan's rapid economic development, especially in some of the rapidly growing sectors of the economy. However, because the important impacts of DFI are not easily quantified, it is important to examine the more subtle aspects of DFI's role in Taiwan. In examining DFI's role in the Taiwanese economy, including the structural changes in Taiwanese manufacturing since the mid-1970s, this paper explores the trends and patterns of DFI in Taiwan since the early 1960s.

Some of the structural changes that took place in Taiwan between 1976 and 1986 are summarized in Table 6.1. During this period, the manufacturing sector's share of value added, employment, and exports increased so that by 1986, manufacturing accounted for 30 percent of employment, 39 percent of GDP, and 98 percent of merchandise exports. Taiwan's manufacturing sector has been rather evenly distributed across many activities with food, textiles, apparel, rubber and plastics, chemicals and petroleum products, metals, nonelectric machinery (including transportation equipment), and electronic machinery all accounting for 10 percent or more of manufacturing employment, output, or exports at one time or another. In the last ten years, the relatively slow growth of the food, textiles, and wood industries, and the relatively rapid growth of the leather, rubber and plastics, metals, and electric and electronic machinery industries have been most outstanding. In short, the technology-and capital-intensive industries such as the chemicals, metals, nonelectric machinery, and electric and electronic machinery sectors have come to dominate Taiwan's economy in general and exports in particular.

The major concern of this paper is to examine the role of DFI in these structural changes. To this end, the following section summarizes DFI trends and patterns. The contribution of DFI to capital formation, employment, and exports is then examined and the relationships among technology, exports, and job creation in foreign firms are analyzed in detail. A four-equation macroeconometric model is used to further analyze the effects of DFI on investment, consumption, exports, and imports in Taiwan. Finally, policy implications arising from the Taiwanese

## Table 6.1   Structural Change in Taiwan, 1976-1986

| | GDP (current US$) | | Employment (thousands) | | Exports[b] (current US$) | |
|---|---|---|---|---|---|---|
| | 1976 | 1986 | 1976 | 1986 | 1976 | 1986 |
| **Totals (annual averages) and manufacturing share of totals** | | | | | | |
| All industries | 18,624 | 72,513 | 5,669 | 7,733 | 5,302 | 39,758 |
| Manufacturing | 6,289 | 28,472 | 1,577 | 2,291 | 5,021 | 39,002 |
| As a percentage of all industries | 33.8 | 39.3 | 27.8 | 29.6 | 94.7 | 98.1 |
| **Shares of manufacturing subtotals[a]** | | | | | | |
| Food & beverages | 17.6 | 10.8 | 7.0 | 5.6 | 11.8 | 5.0 |
| Textiles | 11.1 | 8.8 | 19.4 | 13.1 | 12.1 | 6.8 |
| Apparel | 5.0 | 6.5 | 5.9 | 6.9 | 17.3 | 12.0 |
| Wood, bamboo & rattan | 3.1 | 2.4 | 5.7 | 4.1 | 6.6 | 4.5 |
| Paper & paper products | 3.9 | 4.4 | 3.7 | 3.7 | 0.8 | 0.6 |
| Leather & leather products | 1.0 | 2.1 | 1.7 | 2.3 | 2.8 | 3.3 |
| Chemicals, rubber, plastics, etc. | 19.8 | 22.2 | 16.5 | 19.4 | 11.0 | 13.0 |
| Rubber & plastics | na | 7.4 | 11.1 | 13.9 | 7.8 | 10.1 |
| Chemicals & petroleum products | na | 14.8 | 5.4 | 5.4 | 3.2 | 2.9 |
| Nonmetallic products | 4.7 | 3.1 | 4.6 | 4.3 | 1.0 | 2.0 |
| Basic metals & products | 7.3 | 9.6 | 8.1 | 9.7 | 5.1 | 7.8 |
| Nonelec. machinery & trans. eq. | 8.6 | 9.8 | 9.2 | 9.6 | 7.9 | 6.0 |
| Electric & electronic machinery | 10.6 | 12.9 | 13.5 | 15.9 | 15.5 | 22.8 |
| Miscellaneous manufacturing | 7.4 | 7.4 | 4.7 | 5.4 | 7.9 | 16.3 |

na = Not available.

[a]Precision machinery included in miscellaneous manufacturing for value added, in nonelectric machinery and transportation equipment for others.

[b]Miscellaneous manufacturing calculated as difference between total manufacturing given in Directorate-General of Budget, Accounting and Statistics (1988b) and the sum of manufacturing industries covered in the foreign investment surveys.

Sources: Central Bank of China (various years b); Directorate-General of Budget, Accounting and Statistics (1988a, 1988b); Ministry of Economic Affairs, Investment Commission (various years a).

experience are summarized in light of Taiwan's transition to a capital-surplus economy in recent years.

## Trends and Patterns of DFI in Taiwan

Table 6.2 shows the time trends of inward and outward DFI in Taiwan since 1952.[1] Three important trends are observed. First, DFI rose quickly and rather continuously after 1966. The initial increase was largely a response to the establish-

Table 6.2  Inward and Outward Flows of DFI in Taiwan, 1952-1988
(annual averages, US$ millions)

| Period | Inward-DFI Approvals | Gross Inward-DFI Arrivals[a] | Withdrawals of Inward DFI | Outward DFI[b] |
|---|---|---|---|---|
| 1952-1959 | 2.52 | 3.96 | na | na |
| 1960-1964 | 14.59 | 11.00 | na | na |
| 1965 | 41.61 | 10.51 | na | 0.47 |
| 1966 | 29.28 | 9.59 | na | 1.16 |
| 1967 | 57.01 | 27.87 | na | 1.29 |
| 1968 | 89.89 | 27.89 | na | 0.60 |
| 1969 | 109.44 | 51.52 | na | 0.00 |
| 1970 | 138.90 | 61.93 | na | 0.53 |
| 1971 | 162.96 | 52.63 | na | 1.21 |
| 1972 | 126.66 | 36.37 | 9.28 | 3.40 |
| 1973 | 248.85 | 67.79 | 6.21 | 0.85 |
| 1974 | 189.38 | 104.05 | 21.89 | 0.86 |
| 1975 | 118.17 | 70.57 | 36.36 | 0.87 |
| 1976 | 141.52 | 90.71 | 20.19 | 3.89 |
| 1977 | 163.91 | 76.50 | 24.19 | 6.69 |
| 1978 | 212.93 | 129.74 | 15.88 | 4.16 |
| 1979 | 328.83 | 120.86 | 18.88 | 2.73 |
| 1980 | 465.96 | 190.83 | 29.52 | 45.36 |
| 1981 | 395.76 | 156.50 | 21.01 | 58.08 |
| 1982 | 380.01 | 149.18 | 50.43 | 21.84 |
| 1983 | 404.47 | 175.40 | 39.33 | 16.49 |
| 1984 | 558.74 | 231.59 | 80.99 | 70.32 |
| 1985 | 702.46 | 343.68 | 55.37 | 82.65 |
| 1986 | 770.38 | 350.22 | 69.22 | 68.50 |
| 1987 | 1418.80 | 847.92 | 226.08 | 709.58 |
| 1988 | 1182.54 | 1231.36 | 294.94 | 4119.64 |

na = Not available.
[a]Equivalent to the net inflow of DFI plus DFI withdrawals.
[b]1989 figures were estimated by the authors using balance-of-payments data.

Sources:  Central Bank of China (various years a, various years c);
Ministry of Economic Affairs, Investment Commission (various
years b).

ment of two export processing zones (EPZs) in the vicinity of Kaohsiung, Taiwan's largest port. Between 1966 and 1979, these two EPZs attracted a total of US$33 million in DFI, constituting 80 percent of total capital arrivals in the EPZs and 23 percent of total arrived DFI for this period. The establishment of bonded factories was another policy which stimulated export-oriented DFI.[2]

Second, the post-1966 trend faltered somewhat in 1972, 1975, and 1982. The first drop was largely due to unfavorable international political events, most notably the loss of Taiwan's seat in the United Nations. The DFI declines in 1975 and 1982 were the result of decreases in economic growth rates which dropped to 4 percent and 3 percent, respectively. In addition to these declines, there was also a slowdown in DFI inflows in 1979, a year after the break of formal diplomatic relations between the Republic of China and the United States. Therefore, both political stability and domestic economic conditions have had a great bearing on the timing of DFI

Third, both inward and outward DFI increased sharply in 1987–1989, with outward DFI surpassing inward DFI by a wide margin in 1988. This recent trend reflects several fundamental changes in the Taiwanese economy including: (1) the substantial and stable appreciation of the new Taiwanese dollar (NT$); (2) the liberalization of controls on capital movements (relaxation of restrictions on outward flows was particularly significant in this regard); (3) the reduction of tariffs and other import controls; and (4) the unprecedented expansion of the domestic market, especially in the services sector. In short, the Taiwanese economy opened up dramatically and capital flows grew commensurately. However, despite the undeniably large increases in inward and outward DFI flows, we should also caution that these figures may be misleading in some respects. For example, some of the increase in inward DFI that is recorded in the balance of payments is actually investment by foreign companies that are in fact controlled by Taiwanese conglomerates.

To get more detail on the sources of DFI and the sectors of investment, we must turn to data on DFI approvals or data on paid-up capital gathered in surveys of foreign firms (Table 6.3).[3] According to the approval data, Overseas Chinese accounted for 29 percent of the DFI stock in 1976 but this share fell to 20 percent by 1987; according to the paid-up capital data, the share of Overseas Chinese was somewhat lower in 1976 at 24 percent and declined more rapidly to 11 percent in 1987. Among non-Chinese approvals, the United States was the largest source accounting for 32 percent of the total in 1976 and 31 percent in 1987.[4] Japan's share was rather small in 1976 at 16 percent, but grew rapidly to 24 percent in 1987. In recent years, these trends have accelerated with the investment boom; the Overseas Chinese share of approvals fell to 16 percent, the U.S. share increased to 25 percent, and Japan's share rose to 26 percent by 1989 (Ministry of Economic Affairs, Investment Commission, various years b).

In contrast to their relatively small capital stocks, Overseas Chinese accounted for 2,102 of the 5,312 investment applications approved by yearend 1989. The share of applications by Japanese investors was also relatively large at 31 percent, while that of U.S. investors was relatively small at only 14 percent. As a result, investment per project was very small for Overseas Chinese, averaging only US$0.82 million per project through 1989. Investment per project was also relatively small for Japanese investments, US$1.74 million per project, as compared to US$3.66 million per

Table 6.3  Stock of Inward DFI in Taiwan, 1976 and 1987

| Industry | Total Approvals 1976 | Total Approvals 1987 | Total Arrivals[a] 1976 | Total Arrivals[a] 1987 | Overseas Chinese Approvals 1976 | Overseas Chinese Approvals 1987 | Overseas Chinese Arrivals[a] 1976 | Overseas Chinese Arrivals[a] 1987 | Non-Overseas Chinese Approvals 1976 | Non-Overseas Chinese Approvals 1987 | Non-Overseas Chinese Arrivals[a] 1976 | Non-Overseas Chinese Arrivals[a] 1987 | Japanese Approvals[b] 1976 | Japanese Approvals[b] 1987 | U.S. Approvals[b] 1976 | U.S. Approvals[b] 1987 |
|---|---|---|---|---|---|---|---|---|---|---|---|---|---|---|---|---|
| Total inward DFI (US$m) | 1,547 | 7,349 | 454 | 2,422 | 450 | 1,435 | 111 | 259 | 1,097 | 5,914 | 343 | 2,163 | 247 | 1,783 | 492 | 2,269 |
| **Total inward DFI (%)** | | | | | | | | | | | | | | | | |
| Primary | 0.7 | 0.6 | na | na | 2.0 | 2.1 | na | na | 0.2 | 0.2 | na | na | 0.1 | 0.1 | 0.1 | 0.3 |
| Manufacturing | 82.1 | 77.6 | 87.0 | 87.5 | 55.4 | 53.6 | 73.7 | 78.5 | 93.4 | 82.8 | 96.7 | 91.3 | 95.8 | 87.1 | 85.1 | 86.2 |
| Food & beverages | 2.1 | 3.0 | 2.5 | 2.2 | 4.6 | 3.9 | 5.6 | 9.3 | 1.1 | 2.8 | 1.7 | 1.3 | 2.1 | 1.2 | 1.0 | 4.0 |
| Textiles | 4.5 | 1.9 | 12.0 | 3.9 | 9.0 | 6.2 | 23.1 | 15.5 | 2.7 | 0.8 | 9.1 | 1.2 | 10.0 | 2.3 | 0.4 | 0.1 |
| Apparel | 2.1 | 0.8 | 2.9 | 1.6 | 4.0 | 2.0 | 8.9 | 3.5 | 1.2 | 0.5 | 1.2 | 1.4 | 2.1 | 0.5 | 0.5 | 0.2 |
| Wood, bamboo & rattan | 0.8 | 0.5 | 1.8 | 0.5 | 2.0 | 1.6 | 5.9 | 3.2 | 0.3 | 0.3 | 0.7 | 0.1 | 1.2 | 0.3 | 0.1 | 0.0 |
| Paper & paper products | 0.9 | 0.6 | 0.6 | 1.1 | 2.3 | 1.6 | 1.0 | 4.6 | 0.3 | 0.3 | 0.5 | 0.6 | 0.6 | 0.1 | 0.4 | 0.6 |
| Leather & leather products | 0.6 | 0.3 | 1.1 | 0.1 | 1.6 | 0.6 | 3.7 | 0.1 | 0.3 | 0.2 | 0.4 | 0.1 | 0.3 | 0.1 | 0.2 | 0.1 |
| Rubber & plastics | 2.5 | 3.1 | 3.6 | 3.9 | 3.7 | 2.7 | 5.4 | 3.0 | 1.9 | 3.2 | 3.2 | 4.0 | 4.4 | 5.7 | 1.9 | 1.2 |
| Chemicals & petrol. prod. | 11.7 | 14.8 | 11.6 | 17.5 | 3.7 | 4.1 | 4.6 | 17.4 | 15.0 | 17.4 | 14.5 | 17.5 | 12.6 | 8.0 | 18.9 | 23.4 |
| Nonmetallic products | 5.9 | 5.7 | 2.3 | 0.7 | 13.3 | 20.2 | 1.8 | 1.2 | 2.9 | 2.2 | 2.5 | 0.7 | 2.3 | 2.7 | 1.0 | 1.2 |
| Basic metals & products | 7.4 | 7.0 | 4.5 | 8.2 | 2.5 | 2.7 | 2.6 | 7.2 | 9.4 | 8.1 | 5.3 | 8.4 | 9.2 | 9.9 | 2.4 | 5.1 |
| Nonelec. mach. & trans. eq. | 8.0 | 9.4 | 6.0 | 9.3 | 1.7 | 2.3 | 1.2 | 5.2 | 10.5 | 11.1 | 8.0 | 10.2 | 9.1 | 23.8 | 1.8 | 4.7 |
| Electric & electronic mech. | 33.4 | 28.8 | 34.1 | 36.6 | 3.6 | 3.4 | 4.5 | 5.8 | 46.0 | 35.2 | 45.9 | 43.7 | 41.8 | 32.6 | 56.6 | 45.5 |
| Miscellaneous manuf. | 2.3 | 1.6 | 4.0 | 2.0 | 3.4 | 2.4 | 5.5 | 2.5 | 1.7 | 1.4 | 3.7 | 1.9 | na | na | na | na |

| | | | | | | | | | | | | | | | | |
|---|---|---|---|---|---|---|---|---|---|---|---|---|---|---|---|---|
| Services | 17.2 | 21.9 | 13.0 | 12.6 | 42.6 | 46.4 | 26.3 | 21.5 | 6.5 | 16.4 | 3.3 | 8.7 | 1.5 | 10.3 | 12.7 | 12.8 |
| Construction | 5.3 | 1.5 | 0.7 | 0.1 | 16.1 | 6.6 | 1.9 | 1.4 | 0.9 | 0.3 | 0.0 | 0.0 | 0.4 | 0.3 | 1.7 | 0.4 |
| Trade | 0.5 | 0.9 | 0.6 | 0.3 | 1.1 | 1.9 | 1.0 | 1.9 | 0.2 | 0.7 | 0.5 | 0.1 | 0.0 | 0.7 | 0.3 | 0.1 |
| Finance | 4.2 | 4.5 | na | na | 6.3 | 7.0 | na | na | 3.3 | 3.9 | na | na | 0.1 | 0.1 | 6.0 | 3.0 |
| Transportation | 2.1 | 2.0 | 6.2 | 4.1 | 5.8 | 4.0 | 6.3 | 6.5 | 0.3 | 1.6 | 0.6 | 3.8 | 0.1 | 0.1 | 1.5 | 0.3 |
| Other services | 5.2 | 12.9 | 5.6 | 8.0 | 13.2 | 26.9 | 17.0 | 11.6 | 1.8 | 10.1 | 2.2 | 4.8 | 0.8 | 9.2 | 3.3 | 9.0 |

na = Not available.

[a]Foreign contribution to paid-up capital stocks. Note that this definition generates much smaller estimates of arrivals than do the balance-of-payments data (cf. Table 6.2).

[b]Manufacturing subtotal excludes miscellaneous manufacturing.

Sources: Central Bank of China (various years b); Ministry of Economic Affairs, Investment Commission (various years a, various years b).

project for U.S. investors and US$2.87 million per project for all non-Chinese investors (Ministry of Economic Affairs, Investment Commission, various years b). It is also worthy to note that the small size of investment tends to be correlated with a preference for joint ventures.[5] For example, in 1985, 72 percent of Overseas Chinese firms and 77 percent of Japanese firms that invested in Taiwan were involved in joint ventures; in contrast, only 49 percent of U.S. investors and 66 percent of all non-Chinese investors investing in Taiwan invested through joint ventures (Ministry of Economic Affairs, Investment Commission, various years a).

Overseas Chinese investors, who are not actually foreigners and are not treated as such, are more familiar with Taiwan's economy and often have better local connections than other investors. These factors tend to make small investments by Overseas Chinese profitable, even when similar small investments might not profitable for other foreign investors. Another reason that investments by Overseas Chinese tend to be small is that most of these investors are from Hong Kong or Southeast Asia, countries where average firm size tends to be smaller than in developed economies. Japanese investors have a number of characteristics in common with the Overseas Chinese. During the fifty years of Taiwan's colonization by Japan, the Japanese not only learned a great deal about Taiwan's economy, language, and culture, but also built up cordial relationships with numerous Taiwanese businessmen. This unique relationship, based largely on personal contacts, helps to reduce the risks for small investors and the necessity for large investments.

According to both approval and survey data, DFI has been concentrated heavily in the manufacturing sector which accounted for 78 percent of all approvals and 88 percent of paid-up capital by 1987 (Table 6.3). The arrival data indicate little change in the manufacturing sector's share from 1976 to 1987, but the approval data show that the manufacturing share declined while the service sector share increased. According to both sets of data, electric and electronic machinery attracted the lion's share of investment, accounting for a little over one-third of all paid-up capital in both 1976 and 1987. By 1987, chemicals was the second largest industry attracting inward DFI, accounting for 18 percent of paid-up capital; other industries that also attracted significant shares of inward DFI were nonelectric machinery (9 percent) and metals (8 percent). All of these shares represent substantial increases over 1976 when textiles was the second largest sector followed by chemicals, nonelectric machinery, and metals. Most of the sectors that attracted relatively small shares of inward DFI in 1976 (for example, food, apparel, wood, leather, nonmetallic minerals, and miscellaneous manufacturing) also saw their shares fall; paper and paper products, and rubber and plastics were the only exceptions. In short, DFI has become increasingly concentrated in the fast-growing metals, nonelectric machinery, and electric and electronic machinery industries as well as the slower-growing chemicals industry.

This process is accentuated in non-Chinese DFI which is more heavily concentrated in the manufacturing sector overall and especially in the electrical and electronic machinery, chemicals, nonelectric machinery, and metals industries. The combined share of these four manufacturing industries in all non-Chinese paid-up capital grew from 76 percent in 1976 to 80 percent in 1987. In contrast, Overseas Chinese DFI has been more heavily concentrated in textiles, food, and services with the shares of the latter two industries and chemicals growing significantly. Finally, although only approval data are available for comparisons between these two years, the structure of Japanese DFI has apparently undergone some of the most significant changes in the last ten years with large declines in the shares of textiles and electric and electronic machinery, and large increases in the shares of nonelectric machinery and services. Within manufacturing, the distribution of U.S. approvals has changed in a similar direction but in much smaller magnitude, and it remains heavily concentrated in two industries, chemicals and electric and electronic machinery.

The differences in the industrial structures of Overseas Chinese and foreigners' investments in Taiwan are attributable to the different natures of the investors. First, since most Overseas Chinese investors were from Hong Kong and Southeast Asia, i.e., countries in which technology levels did not exceed those in Taiwan by much if at all, these investments were concentrated in the mature or light industries such as textiles and nonmetallic minerals. Second, Overseas Chinese also showed greater interest in the service sector, particularly in the construction and hotel industries. These two industries were generally not open to investment by foreigners, but many Overseas Chinese were allowed to invest in them after they abandoned their claim to exchange settlement. In short, Overseas Chinese DFI represents a neighboring investment which differs from the more traditional and more distant non-Chinese DFI.

## The Contribution of DFI to Taiwan's Investment, GDP, Employment, and Exports

Since DFI facilitates the transfer of capital, technology, and other intangible assets to the host country, it is important to analyze DFI's contributions to local economic activities. This section looks closely at the direct contributions of DFI in terms of investment, GDP, employment, and exports.[6] As shown in Table 6.4, the contribution of DFI to investment has generally been quite small. In all industries, the ratio of DFI to total fixed capital formation rose from 3 percent in 1965–1968 to over 4 percent in 1969–1972 and fell back to 1–2 percent in 1973–1986 before rising to 3 percent again in 1987–1988. The share of DFI in private capital formation was somewhat higher at 3–6 percent, as was the share of manufacturing DFI in manufacturing private capital formation (5–11 percent). Yet these figures show that DFI's contribution to Taiwan's aggregate capital formation has been modest at best.

Although DFI has not been a major source of Taiwan's capital formation, the foreign firm surveys indicate that foreign firms (defined as companies with any amount of foreign capital) accounted for larger shares of GDP. For all industries, foreign firm value added represented 6–8 percent of GDP and 16–20 percent of manufacturing value added (Table 6.5). Since many foreign firms are involved in joint ventures, these figures tend to overestimate the foreign contribution to the economy. To compensate for this, it is helpful to weight the foreign firm value added figures by foreign ownership shares. As would be expected, this significantly reduces the foreign firms' contribution to GDP; the shares fall to 3–4 percent overall and 8–10 percent in manufacturing. Thus, as was the case for investment, the foreign contribution to GDP is rather modest in manufacturing and small in the economy as a whole.

Table 6.4  Arrived DFI to Fixed Investment in Taiwan, 1965-1988

| Period | Amount of Cumulative Arrived DFI (US$m) | Total DFI as a % of Total Fixed Investment | Total DFI as a % of Private Fixed Investment | Manufacturing DFI as a % of Manufacturing Fixed Investment[a] |
|---|---|---|---|---|
| 1965-1968 | 75.86 | 2.7 | 4.4 | 8.6 |
| 1969-1972 | 202.45 | 3.5 | 6.3 | 10.7 |
| 1973-1976 | 333.12 | 2.0 | 3.9 | 5.3 |
| 1977-1980 | 517.93 | 1.5 | 2.9 | 5.4 |
| 1981-1983 | 481.08 | 1.3 | 2.5 | 4.8 |
| 1984-1986 | 925.49 | 1.9 | 3.5 | 4.7 |
| 1987-1988 | 2,079.28 | 2.5 | 4.1 | 6.0 |

[a]Manufacturing DFI is assumed to be 80 percent of total arrived DFI.

Sources:  Central Bank of China (various years b);
Directorate-General of Budget, Accounting and Statistics (1988a);
sources of Table 6.2.

The contribution to total Taiwanese employment (Table 6.6) is slightly smaller; using the weighted figures, the share is only 2–3 percent. The foreign firm employment share was rather high in manufacturing at 11 percent in 1976, but declined to 7 percent in 1986. Japanese and U.S. firms in the electric and electronic machinery industry accounted for a very large share of all foreign firm employment (39–42 percent using unweighted figures). Moreover these firms accounted for 40 percent of all Taiwanese employment in this sector in 1976 even if weighted figures are used. By 1986, this combined share fell to 19 percent as declines in U.S. firm employment offset increases in Japanese firm employment. Nonetheless these figures show that foreign firms still play a very significant role in this crucial industry. Weighted foreign firm employment as a share of total employment also reached double-digit levels in apparel and leather in 1976, with Overseas Chinese firms being the most important sources of employment in both sectors.

Thus, in these three sectors—electric and electronic machinery, apparel, and leather products—foreign firms have generated relatively large levels of employment. However it is also important to note that foreign firm shares of employment have declined markedly over time. Indeed declining foreign firm shares are observed in virtually all sectors (paper, an industry with limited foreign activity, is the only exception). At the same time however, the level of foreign firm employment did not

Table 6.5  Foreign Firm Value Added in Taiwan, 1974-1987

| Period | Industry | Foreign Firm Value Added | |
|--------|----------|--------------------------|---|
| | | Total Amount (Annual Averages, US$m) | As a % of Total GDP or GDP in Manufacturing |
| Unweighted foreign firm value added | | | |
| 1974-1976 | Total | 1,029 | 6.4 |
| 1977-1980 | Total | 2,323 | 7.5 |
| 1981-1983 | Total | 3,088 | 6.3 |
| 1984-1986 | Total | 4,678 | 7.4 |
| 1987 | Total | 8,069 | 8.3 |
| 1974-1976 | Manufacturing | 965 | 18.3 |
| 1977-1980 | Manufacturing | 2,190 | 20.0 |
| 1981-1983 | Manufacturing | 2,780 | 15.9 |
| 1984-1986 | Manufacturing | 4,206 | 17.5 |
| 1987 | Manufacturing | 6,685 | 17.3 |
| Weighted foreign firm value added[a] | | | |
| 1979-1980 | Total | 1,377 | 3.7 |
| 1981-1983 | Total | 1,511 | 3.1 |
| 1984-1985 | Total | 1,788 | 3.0 |
| 1979-1980 | Manufacturing | 1,308 | 9.8 |
| 1981-1983 | Manufacturing | 1,382 | 7.9 |
| 1984-1985 | Manufacturing | 1,658 | 7.6 |

[a]Data were weighted by foreign ownership shares to approximate the purely foreign contribution. Weighted figures were not available before 1979 or after 1985.

Sources:  Central Bank of China (various years b); Directorate-General of Budget, Accounting and Statistics (1988b); Ministry of Economic Affairs, Investment Commission (various years a).

Table 6.6 Foreign Firm Employment in Taiwan, 1976 and 1986

| Industry | Total | | Overseas Chinese | | Non-Overseas Chinese | | Japan | | United States | |
|---|---|---|---|---|---|---|---|---|---|---|
| | 1976 | 1986 | 1976 | 1986 | 1976 | 1986 | 1976 | 1986 | 1976 | 1986 |
| **Unweighted foreign firm employment (thousands)** | | | | | | | | | | |
| All industries | 290.1 | 263.7 | 71.7 | 48.3 | 218.4 | 215.4 | 125.6 | 133.8 | 69.8 | 53.1 |
| Manufacturing[a] | 269.3 | 246.3 | 67.7 | 41.0 | 201.6 | 205.3 | 118.0 | 129.2 | 62.8 | 48.5 |
| Food & beverages | 12.3 | 3.5 | 9.6 | 1.4 | 2.7 | 2.1 | 1.8 | 1.0 | 0.8 | 0.9 |
| Textiles | 26.9 | 15.6 | 13.9 | 1.8 | 13.0 | 13.8 | 11.3 | 3.6 | 1.7 | 10.1 |
| Apparel | 20.6 | 12.2 | 10.6 | 6.2 | 10.0 | 6.0 | 5.6 | 1.9 | 2.2 | 2.3 |
| Wood, bamboo & rattan | 5.0 | 3.3 | 2.4 | 2.7 | 2.6 | 0.6 | 2.1 | 0.4 | 0.0 | 0.1 |
| Paper & paper products | 1.7 | 3.2 | 0.9 | 1.8 | 0.8 | 1.5 | 0.4 | 0.1 | 0.4 | 0.9 |
| Leather & leather products | 5.5 | 1.5 | 3.0 | 0.4 | 2.5 | 1.1 | 0.7 | 0.5 | 1.1 | 0.5 |
| Rubber & plastics | 16.1 | 11.3 | 5.0 | 5.5 | 11.1 | 5.7 | 8.2 | 3.4 | 2.2 | 0.0 |
| Chemicals & petrol. products | 18.5 | 16.8 | 9.1 | 8.9 | 9.4 | 7.9 | 4.4 | 2.6 | 2.6 | 1.8 |
| Nonmetallic products | 8.5 | 8.4 | 4.1 | 2.7 | 4.3 | 5.7 | 2.6 | 2.0 | 0.0 | 1.5 |
| Basic metals & products | 11.1 | 10.0 | 2.5 | 0.6 | 8.6 | 9.3 | 6.5 | 6.7 | 1.9 | 1.6 |
| Nonelec. mach. & trans. eq. | 15.9 | 26.3 | 1.0 | 1.4 | 14.9 | 24.9 | 5.9 | 20.3 | 4.8 | 4.3 |
| Electric & electronic mach. | 127.1 | 134.1 | 5.5 | 7.5 | 121.6 | 126.6 | 68.5 | 86.6 | 45.2 | 24.6 |
| **Unweighted foreign firm employment as a share of total Taiwanese employment (percent)** | | | | | | | | | | |
| All industries | 5.1 | 3.4 | 1.3 | 0.6 | 3.9 | 2.8 | 2.2 | 1.7 | 1.2 | 0.7 |
| Manufacturing[a] | 17.9 | 11.4 | 4.5 | 1.9 | 13.4 | 9.5 | 7.8 | 6.0 | 4.2 | 2.2 |
| Food & beverages | 11.1 | 2.7 | 8.7 | 1.1 | 2.5 | 1.7 | 1.6 | 0.8 | 0.7 | 0.7 |
| Textiles | 8.8 | 5.2 | 4.5 | 0.6 | 4.3 | 4.6 | 3.7 | 1.2 | 0.6 | 3.4 |
| Apparel | 22.1 | 7.7 | 11.4 | 3.9 | 10.7 | 3.8 | 6.0 | 1.2 | 2.3 | 1.4 |

| Wood, bamboo & rattan | 5.6 | 3.5 | 2.7 | 2.8 | 2.9 | 0.7 | 2.4 | 0.5 | 0.0 | 0.1 |
| Paper & paper products | 2.9 | 3.8 | 1.5 | 2.1 | 1.4 | 1.7 | 0.6 | 0.1 | 0.7 | 1.0 |
| Leather & leather products | 20.8 | 3.0 | 11.2 | 0.9 | 9.5 | 2.1 | 2.5 | 0.9 | 4.2 | 1.0 |
| Rubber & plastics | 9.2 | 3.5 | 2.9 | 1.7 | 6.3 | 1.8 | 4.7 | 1.1 | 1.2 | 0.0 |
| Chemicals & petrol. products | 21.5 | 13.5 | 10.6 | 7.1 | 11.0 | 6.3 | 5.2 | 2.1 | 3.0 | 1.5 |
| Nonmetallic products | 11.5 | 8.5 | 5.6 | 2.8 | 5.9 | 5.8 | 3.5 | 2.0 | 0.0 | 1.5 |
| Basic metals & products | 8.8 | 4.5 | 2.0 | 0.3 | 6.8 | 4.2 | 5.1 | 3.0 | 1.5 | 0.7 |
| Nonelec. mach. & trans. eq. | 10.9 | 11.9 | 0.7 | 0.7 | 10.2 | 11.3 | 4.1 | 9.2 | 3.3 | 1.9 |
| Electric & electronic mach. | 59.8 | 36.8 | 2.6 | 2.0 | 57.2 | 34.7 | 32.2 | 23.8 | 21.3 | 6.8 |

Weighted foreign firm employment as a share of total Taiwanese employment[b] (percent)

| All Industries | 3.2 | 2.0 | 0.7 | 0.3 | 2.6 | 1.7 | 1.3 | 0.9 | 1.0 | 0.5 |
| Manufacturing[a] | 11.1 | 6.5 | 2.1 | 0.9 | 9.0 | 5.6 | 4.4 | 3.1 | 3.4 | 1.5 |
| Food & beverages | 2.4 | 1.9 | 1.0 | 0.9 | 1.4 | 1.0 | 0.8 | 0.4 | 0.5 | 0.4 |
| Textiles | 3.2 | 1.5 | 1.9 | 0.2 | 1.4 | 1.3 | 1.3 | 0.7 | 0.0 | 0.6 |
| Apparel | 16.7 | 6.2 | 10.2 | 3.6 | 6.5 | 2.6 | 3.7 | 0.8 | 0.4 | 0.8 |
| Wood, bamboo & rattan | 4.4 | 3.0 | 2.5 | 2.4 | 1.9 | 0.5 | 1.6 | 0.4 | 0.0 | 0.1 |
| Paper & paper products | 1.3 | 1.5 | 0.5 | 0.6 | 0.8 | 1.0 | 0.4 | 0.1 | 0.4 | 0.7 |
| Leather & leather products | 13.8 | 1.4 | 7.0 | 0.2 | 6.8 | 1.2 | 0.7 | 0.3 | 4.2 | 0.7 |
| Rubber & plastics | 6.1 | 1.6 | 2.2 | 0.7 | 3.9 | 0.9 | 3.2 | 0.7 | 0.3 | 0.0 |
| Chemicals & petrol. products | 6.4 | 5.4 | 1.2 | 1.1 | 5.2 | 4.2 | 1.8 | 1.4 | 1.6 | 0.9 |
| Nonmetallic products | 3.1 | 1.5 | 0.7 | 0.3 | 2.4 | 1.2 | 1.5 | 0.5 | 0.0 | 0.3 |
| Basic metals & products | 5.7 | 2.5 | 1.7 | 0.2 | 4.0 | 2.3 | 2.8 | 1.4 | 1.2 | 0.4 |
| Nonelec. mach. & trans. eq. | 7.1 | 6.7 | 0.7 | 0.5 | 6.4 | 6.2 | 3.0 | 5.4 | 0.5 | 0.8 |
| Electric & electronic mach. | 44.4 | 23.6 | 1.3 | 1.2 | 43.1 | 22.4 | 18.9 | 12.1 | 20.7 | 6.5 |

[a]Data refer to the sum of individual industries listed below, i.e., it excludes miscellaneous manufacturing.
[b]Foreign firm ownership shares are used to approximate the purely foreign contribution to foreign firm employment.

Sources: Directorate-General of Budget, Accounting, and Statistics (1988); Ministry of Economic Affairs, Investment Commission (various years a).

Table 6.7 Exports and Market Orientation of Foreign Firms in Taiwan, 1976 and 1986

| Industry | Total | | Overseas Chinese | | Non-Overseas Chinese | | Japan | | United States | |
|---|---|---|---|---|---|---|---|---|---|---|
| | 1976 | 1986 | 1976 | 1986 | 1976 | 1986 | 1976 | 1986 | 1976 | 1986 |
| Unweighted total foreign firm exports[a] (US$m) | | | | | | | | | | |
| All industries | 2,334 | 6,166 | 513 | 790 | 1,821 | 5,376 | 998 | 2,839 | 620 | 1,145 |
| Manufacturing[b] | 2,214 | 5,817 | 484 | 713 | 1,730 | 5,213 | 962 | 2,705 | 573 | 1,050 |
| Food & beverages | 43 | 39 | 23 | 2 | 21 | 38 | 19 | 25 | 0 | 11 |
| Textiles | 344 | 304 | 125 | 25 | 219 | 281 | 163 | 50 | 56 | 220 |
| Apparel | 156 | 207 | 85 | 101 | 71 | 107 | 39 | 10 | 22 | 26 |
| Wood, bamboo & rattan | 37 | 37 | 19 | 25 | 18 | 12 | 13 | 10 | 0 | 0 |
| Paper & paper products | 4 | 32 | 1 | 23 | 2 | 9 | 1 | 1 | 2 | 8 |
| Leather & leather products | 29 | 27 | 13 | 11 | 16 | 16 | 7 | 6 | 2 | 9 |
| Rubber & plastics | 106 | 256 | 25 | 115 | 82 | 167 | 62 | 71 | 16 | 0 |
| Chemicals & petrol. products | 261 | 326 | 145 | 218 | 117 | 191 | 45 | 35 | 34 | 49 |
| Nonmetallic products | 23 | 119 | 9 | 23 | 15 | 96 | 7 | 22 | 0 | 33 |
| Basic metals & products | 58 | 200 | 8 | 9 | 51 | 191 | 39 | 152 | 11 | 8 |
| Nonelec. mach. & trans. eq. | 96 | 587 | 5 | 24 | 91 | 562 | 57 | 494 | 23 | 62 |
| Electric & electronic mach. | 1,057 | 3,680 | 28 | 138 | 1,029 | 3,543 | 510 | 1,828 | 406 | 625 |
| Unweighted total foreign firm exports as a share of Taiwan exports[a] (percent) | | | | | | | | | | |
| All industries | 28.6 | 16.3 | 6.3 | 2.1 | 22.3 | 14.2 | 12.2 | 7.5 | 7.6 | 3.0 |
| Manufacturing[b] | 31.3 | 18.8 | 6.9 | 2.3 | 24.5 | 16.8 | 13.6 | 8.7 | 8.1 | 3.4 |
| Food & beverages | 6.4 | 2.1 | 3.4 | 0.1 | 3.0 | 2.1 | 2.8 | 1.3 | 0.0 | 0.6 |
| Textiles | 37.8 | 12.2 | 13.8 | 1.0 | 24.0 | 11.2 | 17.9 | 2.0 | 6.1 | 8.8 |
| Apparel | 11.7 | 4.7 | 6.3 | 2.3 | 5.3 | 2.4 | 2.9 | 0.2 | 1.7 | 0.6 |

| | | | | | | | | | | |
|---|---|---|---|---|---|---|---|---|---|---|
| Wood, bamboo & rattan | 6.7 | 2.2 | 3.5 | 1.5 | 3.2 | 0.7 | 2.4 | 0.6 | 0.0 | 0.0 |
| Paper & paper products | 6.7 | 13.6 | 2.2 | 9.9 | 4.5 | 3.7 | 1.3 | 0.4 | 3.2 | 3.3 |
| Leather & leather products | 11.1 | 2.2 | 5.1 | 0.9 | 6.0 | 1.3 | 2.7 | 0.5 | 0.8 | 0.8 |
| Rubber & plastics | 17.5 | 6.9 | 4.0 | 3.1 | 13.4 | 4.5 | 10.3 | 1.9 | 2.7 | 0.0 |
| Chemicals & petrol. products | 93.9 | 30.8 | 52.0 | 20.6 | 41.9 | 18.0 | 16.3 | 3.3 | 12.3 | 4.6 |
| Nonmetallic products | 23.6 | 15.9 | 8.9 | 3.0 | 14.7 | 12.9 | 7.3 | 2.9 | 0.0 | 4.3 |
| Basic metals & products | 15.4 | 6.9 | 2.0 | 0.3 | 13.4 | 6.6 | 10.3 | 5.2 | 3.0 | 0.3 |
| Nonelec. mach. & trans. eq. | 14.8 | 26.5 | 0.7 | 1.1 | 14.1 | 25.4 | 8.9 | 22.3 | 3.5 | 2.8 |
| Electric & electronic mach. | 82.9 | 43.6 | 2.2 | 1.6 | 80.7 | 42.0 | 40.0 | 21.7 | 31.9 | 7.4 |

Weighted total foreign firm exports as a share of Taiwan exports[a,c] (percent)

| | | | | | | | | | | |
|---|---|---|---|---|---|---|---|---|---|---|
| All industries | 18.8 | 11.4 | 2.8 | 1.1 | 16.0 | 10.3 | 8.0 | 4.9 | 6.0 | 2.2 |
| Manufacturing[b] | 20.5 | 13.5 | 2.9 | 1.1 | 17.6 | 12.4 | 8.8 | 5.8 | 6.4 | 2.5 |
| Food & beverages | 2.3 | 1.2 | 0.6 | 0.1 | 1.7 | 1.1 | 1.5 | 0.7 | 0.0 | 0.3 |
| Textiles | 12.5 | 3.2 | 5.6 | 0.5 | 6.9 | 2.6 | 6.3 | 1.0 | 0.6 | 1.7 |
| Apparel | 8.0 | 3.1 | 5.2 | 2.0 | 2.7 | 1.0 | 1.7 | 0.4 | 0.3 | 0.3 |
| Wood, bamboo & rattan | 5.0 | 1.8 | 3.2 | 1.2 | 1.8 | 0.6 | 1.3 | 0.6 | 0.0 | 0.0 |
| Paper & paper products | 2.6 | 4.9 | 0.2 | 2.4 | 2.6 | 2.5 | 1.0 | 0.3 | 1.6 | 2.2 |
| Leather & leather products | 6.4 | 1.2 | 2.8 | 0.2 | 3.5 | 1.0 | 1.2 | 0.2 | 0.8 | 0.7 |
| Rubber & plastics | 11.0 | 3.1 | 2.9 | 1.4 | 8.2 | 1.7 | 7.0 | 1.1 | 0.6 | 0.0 |
| Chemicals & petrol. products | 21.8 | 21.6 | 3.1 | 3.6 | 18.7 | 18.0 | 3.4 | 2.0 | 7.2 | 2.9 |
| Nonmetallic products | 5.7 | 3.2 | 0.7 | 0.0 | 5.0 | 3.2 | 3.2 | 0.6 | 0.0 | 0.8 |
| Basic metals & products | 10.8 | 4.3 | 1.7 | 0.3 | 9.2 | 4.0 | 6.6 | 2.9 | 2.5 | 0.2 |
| Nonelec. mach. & trans. eq. | 11.4 | 18.5 | 0.7 | 0.7 | 10.7 | 17.8 | 8.0 | 15.5 | 1.1 | 2.1 |
| Electric & electronic mach. | 72.0 | 35.5 | 1.3 | 1.2 | 70.7 | 34.3 | 30.7 | 14.6 | 31.4 | 7.3 |

Table 6.7 (continued)

| Industry | Total 1976 | Total 1986 | Overseas Chinese 1976 | Overseas Chinese 1986 | Non-Overseas Chinese 1976 | Non-Overseas Chinese 1986 | Japan 1979 | United States 1976 | United States 1986 |
|---|---|---|---|---|---|---|---|---|---|
| **Total exports as a share of foreign firm sales[a,d] (percent)** | | | | | | | | | |
| All industries | 61.4 | 46.4 | 58.6 | 33.5 | 62.3 | 49.2 | na | na | na |
| Manufacturing[b] | 62.3 | 47.8 | 61.1 | 34.1 | 62.6 | 51.7 | 57.5 | 68.0 | na |
| Food & beverages | 26.0 | 10.5 | 40.8 | 1.0 | 18.5 | 17.4 | 47.2 | 3.5 | na |
| Textiles | 85.3 | 43.4 | 85.1 | 33.8 | 85.4 | 44.8 | 81.1 | 88.2 | na |
| Apparel | 96.9 | 59.7 | 98.4 | 93.6 | 95.2 | 44.5 | 97.4 | 99.8 | na |
| Wood, bamboo & rattan | 90.3 | 94.8 | 88.9 | 95.5 | 91.8 | 93.6 | 100.0 | na | na |
| Paper & paper products | 12.1 | 15.6 | 6.4 | 20.7 | 17.6 | 9.4 | 21.8 | 17.5 | na |
| Leather & leather products | 100.0 | 60.1 | 100.0 | 96.3 | 100.0 | 54.3 | 99.0 | 100.0 | na |
| Rubber & plastics | 89.5 | 50.9 | 97.4 | 72.0 | 87.3 | 48.5 | 90.4 | 60.5 | na |
| Chemicals & petrol. products | 50.3 | 16.3 | 79.4 | 24.5 | 34.6 | 17.1 | 39.3 | 22.4 | 35.5 |
| Nonmetallic products | 8.0 | 21.1 | 4.8 | 10.3 | 13.6 | 28.0 | 62.4 | 100.0 | na |
| Basic metals & products | 58.2 | 39.9 | 75.2 | 23.8 | 56.3 | 41.3 | 44.5 | 82.1 | 43.9 |
| Nonelec. mach. & trans. eq. | 49.0 | 32.7 | 79.1 | 22.2 | 48.1 | 33.4 | 69.6 | 37.6 | 73.3 |
| Electric & electronic mach. | 70.6 | 72.3 | 66.4 | 76.1 | 70.7 | 72.1 | 51.1 | 98.4 | 94.0 |
| **Direct exports as a share of total foreign firm exports[a,d] (percent)** | | | | | | | | | |
| All industries | 74.7 | 86.7 | 64.8 | 91.3 | 77.4 | 86.0 | na | na | na |
| Manufacturing[b] | 73.9 | 88.1 | 63.0 | 90.7 | 76.9 | 85.9 | na | na | na |
| Food & beverages | 96.2 | 97.8 | 93.4 | 80.7 | 95.5 | 98.5 | na | na | na |
| Textiles | 40.4 | 99.8 | 53.5 | 99.5 | 32.9 | 99.3 | na | na | na |
| Apparel | 86.4 | 92.7 | 93.5 | 89.4 | 78.3 | 95.8 | na | na | na |

| | | | | | | | | | | |
|---|---|---|---|---|---|---|---|---|---|---|
| Wood, bamboo & rattan | 76.5 | 88.5 | 69.4 | 100.0 | 84.1 | 64.7 | na | na | na | na |
| Paper & paper products | 86.3 | 70.0 | 89.0 | 68.4 | 84.9 | 74.6 | na | na | na | na |
| Leather & leather products | 63.6 | 47.3 | 72.2 | 22.7 | 61.4 | 63.4 | na | na | na | na |
| Rubber & plastics | 84.7 | 99.0 | 77.9 | 89.1 | 86.8 | 90.9 | na | na | na | na |
| Chemicals & petrol. products | 40.7 | 93.2 | 35.1 | 96.9 | 47.6 | 48.8 | na | na | na | na |
| Nonmetallic products | 93.0 | 83.4 | 95.5 | 100.0 | 91.5 | 79.5 | na | na | na | na |
| Basic metals & products | 73.3 | 74.5 | 80.2 | 98.0 | 72.3 | 73.3 | na | na | na | na |
| Nonelec. mach. & trans. eq. | 97.0 | 84.0 | 78.1 | 99.1 | 98.0 | 83.4 | na | na | na | na |
| Electric & electronic mach. | 86.8 | 87.6 | 91.9 | 85.3 | 86.6 | 87.6 | na | na | na | na |

na = Not available.

[a]Total exports include direct and indirect exports. Indirect exports are sales of intermediate goods, parts, and materials to other firms which are subsequently exported by the purchaser.

[b]Data refer to the sum of the individual industries listed below, i.e., it excludes miscellaneous manufacturing.

[c]Foreign firm ownership shares were used to approximate the purely foreign contribution to foreign firm employment.

[d]Figures are not weighted by ownership shares.

Sources: Central Bank of China (various years b); Liu et al. (1983, 111); Ministry of Economic Affairs, Investment Commission (various years a); Wu (1987, 189); Wu et al. (1980, 124).

decline significantly in several of the major sectors of foreign firm activity—for example, chemicals, metals, nonelectric machinery, and electric and electronic machinery. That is, decreases in foreign firm employment shares have more often resulted from increases in domestic activity than from declines in foreign firm activity.

A larger foreign firm role is observed in Taiwan's exports (Table 6.7). Here again foreign firm activity is heavily concentrated in electric and electronic machinery with weighted foreign firm exports accounting for 72 percent of Taiwan's exports in the industry in 1976 and 36 percent in 1986. Moreover, weighted foreign firm shares of Taiwan's exports reached double-digit figures in a wide range of other industries including textiles, rubber and plastics, chemicals, basic metals, and nonelectric machinery. As with employment, there was a tendency for foreign shares to decline over time (the exceptions to this were the paper and nonelectric machinery industries). These relative declines are especially conspicuous in view of the rapid growth in the level of foreign firm exports in many sectors and in all industries overall. For example, unweighted foreign firm exports increased more than twofold in all industries and in manufacturing, but ratios of unweighted foreign firm exports to fell from 29 percent in 1976 to 16 percent in 1986 in all industries and from 31 percent to 19 percent in manufacturing. Ratios of weighted foreign firm exports to total Taiwanese exports fell from 19 percent to 11 percent in all industries and from 21 percent to 14 percent in manufacturing. Thus these data suggest that the foreign contribution to exports was much greater than the foreign contribution to investment, GDP, and employment, both in all industries overall and in individual industries, but that this contribution has declined rapidly over time.

One reason that foreign firms have had a relatively large impact on exports is because they tend to export a large proportion of their output (Table 6.7). Direct and indirect exports combined accounted for over 61 percent of all sales by foreign firms in 1976 and over 46 percent in 1986. In the important electric and electronic machinery sector, this ratio was over 70 percent in both years. In most other sectors, the share of total exports to foreign sales tended to fall over time (wood and nonmetallic products were the exceptions). Nonetheless, in addition to electric and electronic machinery, in 1986 exports still accounted for over one-half of all sales in the apparel, wood, leather, and rubber and plastic industries.

Thus foreign firms have generally been very export oriented and have used Taiwan as an export platform in their worldwide networks.[7] One reason for this orientation in the past was the ability to exploit Taiwan's endowment of abundant labor. Indeed, as was confirmed by Riedel (1975), low wages in Taiwan provided a strong incentive for labor-intensive and export-oriented DFI throughout the 1970s. However, not all DFI in Taiwan has been export oriented and Taiwan's expanding local market has been an increasingly important element in attracting DFI, as emphasized by the industrial organization approach (Hymer 1960).

It should also be pointed out that the foreign firm export figures tend to be inflated because indirect exports are included while similar indirect effects on other activities are not accounted for. Moreover, the share of indirect exports in all exports has generally fallen over time, which suggests that the decline of export shares is also overstated (Table 6.7). Yet these biases are not large enough to reverse any of the major patterns observed. Namely, these data show that: (1) foreign firms have been very export oriented and made relatively large contributions to Taiwanese exports; (2) foreign firm contributions have been concentrated in a few sectors with the contribution being especially significant in the electric and electronic machinery industry; and (3) the relative size of foreign firm activity has declined over time despite increases or little change in the absolute level of activity. We now turn to an analysis of why these patterns emerged.

### Foreign Firms' Technology, Employment, and Exports

There are two alternative hypotheses regarding the effects of foreign firm technology on resource allocation in host developing economies. According to the first hypothesis, if foreign firms apply the same, presumably capital-intensive, technology as do their parent companies and if capital costs are relatively high and wages relatively low in the host country, then foreign firm activity will decrease the efficiency of resource allocation in the host country. According to the second hypothesis, because foreign firms have superior intangible assets (e.g., technology, information, and/or experience), they have greater flexibility in choosing technologies or in adapting technology to the host countries' needs. Thus foreign firms will improve resource allocation in their host countries by applying more suitable technologies than their domestic counterparts. Our empirical analysis seeks to determine which of these conflicting hypotheses is correct; in other words, we wish to answer the question of whether foreign firm technology faciliates or hinders the efficient allocation of resources.

As shown in Table 6.8, in 1976 foreign firms on the whole used an average of US$6,490 in fixed assets per employee, a figure that is very close to the average for national firms of US$7,150. Moreover, foreign firms used more labor-intensive technologies than national firms in most industries including foods and beverages, apparel, wood, leather, rubber and plastics, chemicals, and electric and electronic machinery. However, in textiles, paper, nonmetallic minerals, and nonelectric machinery, foreign firms were more capital intensive than their local counterparts. Among these, the nonmetallic products industry is an extreme case in which foreign firms had a very high capital-labor ratio as compared to national firms in the same industry and foreign firms in other industries. A closer look at the data reveals that a few large minority-owned foreign cement factories accounted for this high capital-labor ratio. In short, foreign firms were generally more labor intensive than foreign firms overall and in most industries. However, in view of the variation across industries, it is difficult to establish any consistent relationship between factor intensities in local and foreign firms within industries.

By 1986, this picture had changed considerably. Foreign firms became more capital intensive than their national counterparts as a whole; this is shown by the foreign firms' average of US$19,680 in fixed assets per employee which is 35 percent more than their national counterparts. Moreover foreign firms were more capital intensive in all individual industries, with the exception of the wood industry. Note, however, that capital-labor ratios were remarkably similar in rubber and plastics and in metals. On the other hand, in both foreign and national firms, capital-labor ratios

Table 6.8  Fixed Assets per Employee in Taiwan, 1976 and 1986 (US$1,000)

| Industry | Foreign Firms | | | National Firms |
|---|---|---|---|---|
| | Overseas Chinese | Non-Chinese | Total | |
| **1976** | | | | |
| Manufacturing | 8.20 | 5.77 | 6.49 | 7.15 |
| Food & beverages | 4.32 | 6.13 | 5.40 | 11.68 |
| Textiles | 10.29 | 25.66 | 17.74 | 7.61 |
| Apparel | 1.32 | 1.13 | 1.24 | 1.53 |
| Wood, bamboo & rattan | 3.79 | 1.87 | 2.79 | 3.87 |
| Paper & paper products | 12.13 | 9.58 | 10.92 | 6.89 |
| Leather & leather products | 1.63 | 0.97 | 1.32 | 1.74 |
| Rubber & plastics | 2.29 | 2.05 | 2.13 | 3.58 |
| Chemicals & petrol. products | 15.05 | 11.66 | 13.32 | 21.84 |
| Nonmetallic products | 33.13 | 22.21 | 27.53 | 7.39 |
| Basic metals & products | 1.74 | 4.42 | 3.79 | 9.42 |
| Nonelec. mach. & trans. eq. | 1.74 | 17.32 | 16.32 | 6.87 |
| Electric & electronic mach. | 2.58 | 2.60 | 2.60 | 4.55 |
| **1986** | | | | |
| Manufacturing | 26.96 | 18.27 | 19.68 | 14.61 |
| Food & beverages | 61.92 | 21.52 | 37.55 | 23.73 |
| Textiles | 22.82 | 33.89 | 32.60 | 14.30 |
| Apparel | 2.96 | 9.44 | 6.14 | 4.08 |
| Wood, bamboo & rattan | 5.21 | 6.76 | 5.50 | 8.56 |
| Paper & paper products | 54.70 | 0.26 | 41.55 | 16.23 |
| Leather & leather products | 14.00 | 6.06 | 7.77 | 5.16 |
| Rubber & plastics | 12.76 | 36.56 | 24.87 | 24.19 |
| Chemicals & petrol. products | 45.01 | 60.82 | 52.45 | 32.31 |
| Nonmetallic products | 86.96 | 50.08 | 62.11 | 17.91 |
| Basic metals & products | 39.55 | 22.45 | 23.52 | 21.27 |
| Nonelec. mach. & trans. eq. | 32.20 | 1.80 | 18.76 | 13.10 |
| Electric & electronic mach. | 9.46 | 12.25 | 12.08 | 7.39 |

<u>Sources:</u>  Central Bank of China (various years b); Committee on Industrial and Commercial Censuses of the Taiwan-Fukien District (1978, 1989); Ministry of Economic Affairs, Investment Commission (various years a).

grew more rapidly in several industries than in manufacturing overall; these industries which include apparel, leather, and rubber and plastics, were characterized by relatively low capital-labor ratios in 1976. Growth in capital intensity was also particularly conspicuous in foreign firms in food and metals, two other industries which were labor intensive relative to the foreign average in 1976. In sum, the data indicate that foreign firms are now generally more capital intensive than their national counterparts.

To more fully explain the difference in aggregate factor intensities between national and foreign firms, the industrial structures of national and foreign firms' investment should be taken into account. Since the average capital-labor ratio in the aggregate is an average of each individual industry's capital-labor ratio weighted by each industry's employment, the differences in aggregate capital intensity between foreign and domestic firms can be decomposed into (1) differences in capital intensity between foreign and national firms at the industry level, and (2) differences in employment structures between foreign and national firms.

Table 6.9 indicates that, after accounting for differences in employment structures between national and foreign firms, foreign firms in fact used more capital-intensive technology than did national firms in both 1976 and 1986. That is, foreign firms were more labor intensive in the aggregate in 1976 primarily because DFI was heavily concentrated in labor-intensive industries. By 1986, foreign firms were still concentrated in labor-intensive industries but not to as great an extent as in 1976. Thus the increase in capltal intensity among foreign firms was due more to capital deepening than to changes in industrial structure. Moreover, this capital deepening occurred much more rapidly in foreign firms than in national firms.

Another factor which may affect the capital intensities of national and foreign firms is market orientation. Specifically, export-oriented firms may have systematically different factor intensities. To investigate this hypothesis, each foreign firm's capital-labor ratio was weighted by its exports and by its domestic sales in two separate calculations to account for the effects of market orientation on technology. This procedure assumes that identical technology is used in production for export and the domestic market at the firm level and was used to calculate two measures of capital intensity, machinery and equipment per unit of direct labor and fixed assets per employee (Table 6.10).

On average, foreign manufacturing firms used US$7,550 worth of machinery and equipment per unit of labor in export activities, but used US$15,470 worth of machinery and equipment per unit of labor in production for the domestic market. The 1986 figures show an even larger gap—US$19,250 worth of machinery and equipment per unit of labor for exports and US$62,300 for domestic sales. Moreover, similar differences are seen in figures on fixed assets per employee with foreign firms using one-half as much capital per unit of labor in export-oriented production as they did in production for the local market in 1975; in 1986, this ratio was about one to three. This suggests that, in the aggregate, foreign firms used different technologies for export production than for domestic production.

More specifically, both measures indicate that foreign firms used more capital-intensive technology in production for domestic sales than for exports in both 1975 and 1986 in food, apparel, plastics, nonmetallic products, and nonelectric machinery.

Table 6.9  Differences in Factor Intensity Between National and Foreign Firms in Taiwan Due to Intra- and Interindustry Differences[a], 1976 and 1986 (US$1,000 per employee)

|  |  | Difference in Fixed Assets per Employee (National Firms' less Foreign Firms') | Intraindustry Difference[b] | Interindustry Difference[b] |
|---|---|---|---|---|
| Based on national firms' | 1976 | 0.66 | -2.41 (-365.15) | 3.07 (465.15) |
| employment structure | 1986 | -5.07 | -9.50 (-187.34) | 4.43 (87.34) |
| Based on foreign firms' | 1976 | 0.66 | -0.16 (-24.24) | 0.82 (124.24) |
| employment structure | 1986 | -5.07 | -8.62 (-162.99) | 3.19 (62.99) |

[a]Decomposition formula is as follows:

$$k^N - k^f = \Sigma k_i^N w_i^N - \Sigma k_i^f w_i^f$$

$$= \Sigma(k_i^N - k_i^f)w_i^N + \Sigma(w_i^N - w_i^f)k_i^f$$

$$= \Sigma(k_i^N - k_i^f)w_i^f + \Sigma(w_i^N - w_i^f)k_i^N$$

Where  N = National firm
       f = foreign firm
       k = fixed assets per employee
       w = employment share
       i = ith industry.

[b]The values in parentheses is the intra- or interindustry difference as a percentage of the total difference.

Sources:  Central Bank of China (various years b); Committee on Industrial and Commercial Censuses of the Taiwan-Fukien District (1978, 1989); Ministry of Economic Affairs, Investment Commission (various years a).

Firms in the wood, paper, and chemicals industries applied similar technology in both types of production. The textile industry in 1975 was the only case in which foreign firms used unambiguously more capital-intensive technology for exports than for domestic production.[8]

The figures on machinery and equipment per unit of direct labor for electric and electronic machinery also suggest that foreign firms used slightly more capital-intensive technology for export production than production for the local market; the situation is reversed when we measure the capital-labor ratio in terms of fixed assets per employee. This disparity may stem from two factors. First, this industry includes

Table 6.10 Capital-Labor Ratios of Foreign Firms in Taiwan Weighted by Exports and Domestic Sales, 1975 and 1986

| Industry | Machinery and Equipment per Unit of Labor (US$1,000) | | | | Fixed Assets per Employee (US$1,000) | | | | Export/Sales (%) | |
| --- | --- | --- | --- | --- | --- | --- | --- | --- | --- | --- |
| | 1975 | | 1986 | | 1975 | | 1986 | | 1975 | 1986 |
| | Exports | Domestic Sales | Exports | Domestic Sales | Exports | Domestic Sales | Exports | Domestic Sales | | |
| Total | 7.55 | 15.47 | 19.25 | 62.30 | 9.00 | 18.18 | 16.71 | 45.38 | 57.96 | 49.07 |
| Food & beverages | 1.92 | 8.45 | 26.24 | 52.00 | 3.11 | 12.26 | 22.74 | 38.44 | 20.77 | 12.48 |
| Textiles | 21.24 | 14.34 | 58.70 | 64.11 | 26.84 | 19.95 | 45.44 | 49.33 | 77.61 | 46.43 |
| Apparel | 0.63 | 1.47 | 4.32 | 8.16 | 1.26 | 2.34 | 4.60 | 8.40 | 96.84 | 87.47 |
| Wood, bamboo & rattan | 1.18 | 1.37 | 8.30 | 17.88 | 1.92 | 2.74 | 7.66 | 18.06 | 93.89 | 97.37 |
| Paper & paper products | 8.74 | 8.87 | 48.12 | 62.01 | 12.00 | 11.42 | 32.38 | 39.89 | 16.69 | 15.86 |
| Leather & leather products | 0.66 | 1.63 | 4.76 | 25.08 | 1.61 | 2.76 | 5.24 | 23.30 | 99.96 | 59.36 |
| Rubber & plastics | 1.42 | 13.03 | 19.49 | 59.54 | 2.29 | 10.76 | 19.72 | 53.26 | 85.29 | 56.44 |
| Chemicals & petrol. products | 17.55 | 19.61 | 102.76 | 126.16 | 16.24 | 17.61 | 78.55 | 78.24 | 43.17 | 20.52 |
| Nonmetallic products | 28.71 | 42.97 | 44.06 | 136.29 | 25.58 | 50.79 | 40.93 | 108.03 | 8.58 | 19.39 |
| Basic metals & products | 2.42 | 4.08 | 23.69 | 48.70 | 3.89 | 5.24 | 20.53 | 36.75 | 50.13 | 44.08 |
| Nonelec. mach. & trans. eq. | 2.08 | 9.45 | 12.38 | 50.64 | 3.32 | 10.47 | 12.92 | 40.16 | 35.67 | 32.49 |
| Electric & electronic mach. | 2.05 | 1.95 | 15.87 | 26.62 | 2.89 | 3.95 | 13.08 | 21.55 | 63.56 | 75.02 |

Source: Central Bank of China (various years b); Ministry of Economic Affairs, Investment Commission (various years c).

a wide range of products, with the manufacture of some products (e.g., electrical equipment and electronic parts) requiring large capital inputs. Thus some of the exports in this industry may indeed be capital intensive. Second, our assumption that technologies for the export and domestic markets are identical at the firm level may not hold in reality; however the problem with this assumption may not be apparent in this analysis since technological differences tend to cancel each other out at this level of aggregation. Nevertheless, by 1986, production of electric and electronic machinery for the domestic market was substantially more capital intensive by either measure used, as was the case in many other industries.

Returning to the issue of resource allocation, foreign firms using labor-intensive technology in export production had significant effects on local employment. Assuming identical employment per dollar of sales, employment can be decomposed into two parts, employment due to export production and employment arising from local sales. By summing employment due to export production over firms for each industry and dividing the resulting figure by the industry's total employment, we obtain the industry-level employment effects attributable to exports. If this calculation reveals that the total percentage of employment due to exports is larger than the average export ratio, we can then conclude that production for export tends to create more jobs than does production for domestic sales. This pattern, in fact, is evident in Table 6.11. Exports accounted for 49–56 percent of total sales in 1975 and 1986, but employment due to exports accounted for 65–76 percent of total foreign firm employment with a similar pattern observed in most individual industries.[9]

### A Macroeconomic Analysis of DFI in Taiwan

Thus far this study has analyzed the characteristics and performances of foreign firms in Taiwan. The analyses, while illuminating, primarily describe the direct effects of foreign firms and ignore a large number of important indirect effects. For instance, by introducing relatively sophisticated technology, a foreign firm may impart demonstration effects on local competitors or imitators. Furthermore, foreign firms can create forward and/or backward linkages and thereby affect upstream and/or downstream industries. On the other hand, because they possess more advanced technology and have easier access to finance, foreign firms may impede existing local competition and the entry of potential competitors. In other words, DFI may crowd out or stimulate domestic investment to a certain degree.

Another area in which indirect effects can be important is trade. For example, foreign firms have gradually increased domestic sales over time, part of which has substituted for imports. Yet foreign firms may also stimulate import demand both directly and indirectly by increasing the demand for intermediate goods which have (at least initially) a high import content. To sort out these effects, it is necessary to model the activities and estimate the parameters in question. In order to illustrate the nature of these effects, an aggregate four-equation model of investment, consumption, exports, and imports is developed. The model is estimated by three-stage least squares for the 1958–1987 period (Table 6.12).[10]

The results of this model indicate that Taiwan's investment (total fixed capital formation) has been positively related to the change in total output, the change in

Table 6.11  Export Ratios and Employment Due to Exports for
Foreign Firms in Taiwan, 1975 and 1986[a] (percentage)

| Industry | Employment Due to Exports | | Average Export Ratio | |
|---|---|---|---|---|
| | 1975 | 1986 | 1975 | 1986 |
| Total | 75.57 | 65.18 | 56.09 | 49.07 |
| Food & beverages | 46.87 | 24.92 | 20.77 | 12.48 |
| Textiles | 75.51 | 46.36 | 77.61 | 46.43 |
| Apparel | 97.38 | 91.85 | 96.84 | 87.47 |
| Wood, bamboo & rattan | 94.75 | 98.86 | 93.89 | 97.37 |
| Paper & paper products | 22.90 | 20.33 | 16.69 | 15.86 |
| Leather & leather products | 99.99 | 76.14 | 99.96 | 59.36 |
| Rubber & plastics | 94.42 | 71.54 | 85.29 | 56.44 |
| Chemicals & petrol. products | 57.70 | 19.99 | 43.17 | 20.52 |
| Nonmetallic products | 32.60 | 35.58 | 8.58 | 19.39 |
| Basic metals & products | 62.92 | 49.88 | 50.13 | 44.08 |
| Nonelectric mach. and trans. eq. | 64.60 | 59.89 | 35.67 | 32.49 |
| Electric & electronic mach. | 77.08 | 76.72 | 63.56 | 75.02 |

[a]Exports include indirect exports (c.f. Table 6.7).

Source: Ministry of Economic Affairs, Investment Commission
(various years c).

the wage rate, and lagged investment, but negatively related to the user cost of capital. Of prime interest here is the significantly positive effect of DFI flows on total investment. The coefficient of 2.84 means that each NT$1 of DFI has induced a NT$1.84 of investment in addition to the direct contribution of DFI to total investment. This estimate is larger than that of the study by Areskoug (1976) which found an additional inducement of NT$1.39 for 1948–1968. This indicates that not only has the effect of DFI on investment been strongly positive, but the effect has increased in magnitude over time.

In contrast to investment, DFI flows apparently had no appreciable effect on consumption other than that imparted indirectly through income creation. Consumption was positively related to personal income and lagged consumption, and negatively influenced by the rate of interest.

Table 6.12 A Macroeconometric Model of DFI in Taiwan: Three-Stage Least Squares Estimates, 1958-1987[a]

Domestic investment

$$I = 23670.420 + 0.304(Y_t\text{-}Y_{t\text{-}1}) + 12.999(W_t\text{-}W_{t\text{-}1}) - 4498.467(U_t\text{-}U_{t\text{-}1}) + 2.840IF$$
$$\phantom{I = }(4.51) \qquad (4.06) \qquad\quad (1.66) \qquad\qquad (6.01) \qquad\qquad (2.76)$$

$$+ 0.963I_{t\text{-}1}$$
$$\phantom{+ }(37.73)$$

Adjusted $R^2$ = 0.993   Standard Error = 16040   Durbin-Watson stat. = 1.57

Domestic consumption

$$C = 47007.250 + 0.112YP - 1287.111R_{t\text{-}1} - 0.826IF + 0.876C_{t\text{-}1}$$
$$\phantom{C = }(4.83) \qquad (3.82) \qquad (3.47) \qquad (0.89) \qquad (20.6)$$

Adjusted $R^2$ = 0.999   Standard Error = 9707   Durbin-Watson stat. = 1.62

Exports

$$X = 28828.330 + 4.580YW - 968.06P + 4.07SF + 0.783X_{t\text{-}1}$$
$$\phantom{X = }(4.83) \qquad (1.16) \qquad (1.46) \qquad (3.05) \qquad (10.12)$$

Adjusted $R^2$ = 0.990   Standard Error = 43931   Durbin-Watson stat. = 2.62

Imports

$$M = 399473.3 + 0.285Y - 8056.067E - 2.424SF + 0.376M_{t\text{-}1}$$
$$\phantom{M = }(5.12) \qquad (3.23) \qquad (5.67) \qquad (1.62) \qquad (3.33)$$

Adjusted $R^2$ = 0.989   Standard Error = 33747   Durbin-Watson stat. = 1.64

Gross national product
$$Y = C + I + V + G + X - M$$

Personal income
$$YP = Y - D - IBT - RE + TP$$

Endogenous Variables

| | | |
|---|---|---|
| $C$ | = | private consumption (1981 NT$ millions) |
| $I$ | = | total fixed investment |
| $M$ | = | imports of goods and services |
| $X$ | = | exports of goods and services |
| $Y$ | = | gross national product |
| $YP$ | = | personal income |

## Table 6.12 (continued)

Exogeneous variables

| | | |
|---|---|---|
| $D$ | = | capital depreciation (1981 NT$ millions unless otherwise specified) |
| $E$ | = | real exchange rate (NT$/US$ adjusted by Taiwan and U.S. GDP deflators) |
| $G$ | = | government expenditures on goods and services |
| $IBT$ | = | indirect business taxes |
| $IF$ | = | net direct foreign investment inflow |
| $P$ | = | relative export price ratio (Taiwan's export price index divided by a weighted average of wholesale price indices of Australia, Canada, Japan, the United Kingdom, the United States, and West Germany. The weights used are the country's respective shares of Taiwan's exports.) |
| $R$ | = | interest rate (simple average of bank long-term deposit rate and black market rate, percent) |
| $RE$ | = | retained business earnings |
| $SF$ | = | direct foreign investment stock |
| $TP$ | = | government and foreign transfer payments |
| $U$ | = | user's cost of capital (percent) |
| $W$ | = | real wage rate (1981 NT$ thousands/month) |
| $YW$ | = | real world income, (the weighted average of real income in Australia, Canada, Japan, the United Kingdom, the United States, and West Germany. The weights used are the country's respective shares of Taiwan's exports.) |

[a]T-statistics are in parentheses. Sources for the data are Council for Economic Planning and Development (1989); Central Bank of China (various years b); International Monetary Fund (various years). Data on average wage rates and the user's cost of capital were complied by the authors.

As expected, Taiwan's exports were positively related to world income and lagged exports and negatively correlated with relative export prices. In addition, the stock of DFI is a positive and significant determinant of Taiwanese exports during this period. The coefficient indicates that an addition of NT$1 to the DFI stock increased exports by NT$4.07. On the other hand, according to survey data (Tables 6.3, 6.7, and sources), in 1976–1986 total foreign firm exports increased an average of NT$157.002 million annually while DFI stocks increased an average of NT$51.881 million in 1976–1987. Calculated as the ratio of these two nominal figures, the marginal export-capital stock ratio in foreign firms was only 3.02. The large difference between this ratio and the regression coefficient suggests that DFI imparted positive indirect effects on Taiwan's exports that are not reflected in the survey data.[11]

Imports are positively related to total income and lagged imports, and negatively correlated with the real exchange rate. The DFI stock also reduced total imports, but the coefficient was only weakly significant. Thus DFI did not stimulate imports in Taiwan and there is some weak evidence that it may have promoted net import substitution. Of course, both imports and consumption are indirectly stimulated by income creation which results from investment and export stimulation.

In short, these estimates suggest that DFI promoted investment and exports, had no effect on consumption, and may have reduced imports. Thus there is no evidence of net crowding out in investment and there is evidence of positive externalities imparted on domestic exporters. It should be noted that these results hold even after accounting for feedback among the variables in the model.

### The Future Role of DFI in Taiwan

This study has shown that DFI in Taiwan has generally increased since the mid-1960s, with the time trend reflecting both political and economic factors in Taiwan. About one-sixth of total DFI has come from Overseas Chinese, while Japan and the United States each account for about one-fourth. U.S. firms tend to be large and display a relatively large propensity for 100-percent ownership. On the other hand, Japanese and Overseas Chinese investors tend to be smaller and tend to be involved with local partners to a greater degree. Non-Chinese investors have concentrated on the manufacturing sector, and on the electrical and electronics industry in particular. In contrast, Overseas Chinese have focused on mature manufacturing industries or the service sector. It should also be noted that differences in industrial structure between non-Chinese and Overseas Chinese DFI have become more pronounced in the last decade.

Since 1965, DFI has never accounted for over 5 percent of Taiwan's total investment, though its share of manufacturing investment exceeded 10 percent between 1969 and 1972. If foreign firm activities are weighted by ownership shares, contributions to total GDP and employment were of a similar magnitude. However, foreign firm contributions to employment were substantially larger in the key electric and electronic machinery sector and also in the apparel and leather industries. The largest foreign contribution was to exports where weighted foreign firm exports accounted for 11–19 percent of all exports and 14–21 percent of manufacturing exports. Export activity was also concentrated in the electric and electronic machinery industry where the foreign contribution was 36–72 percent using weighted figures. The contributions of foreign firms tended to shrink over time largely as a result of expanded domestic firm activity. Thus foreign firms were clearly involved in the shift of Taiwan's industrial structure toward the electric and electronic machinery industry during the last decade though this involvement declined over time.

It was also shown that foreign firms used more labor-intensive technology than did domestic firms in 1976, mainly because they were more heavily concentrated in the labor-intensive industries than the latter. By 1986, however, foreign firms were generally more capital intensive despite their continued concentration in labor-intensive industries primarily because they adopted capital-intensive techniques relatively rapidly. Moreover, foreign firms tended to use much more labor-intensive technology in export production than in production for the domestic market. Thus market orientation was a crucial factor in determining the appropriate technology used by foreign firms, and the export orientation of foreign firms helped improve resource allocation efficiency in Taiwan in the 1970s and thereafter. Export-marketing assistance provided by foreign parent firms to their Taiwan subsidiaries is also likely to have played an important role in this regard.

A macroeconometric model of DFI in Taiwan illuminated the nature of DFI's indirect effects in the aggregate. It was seen that DFI had positive impacts upon local investment and exports, and may have stimulated import substitution as well. Moreover, close examination of the model's results indicate there were positive indirect effects on both investment and exports.

Thus this study suggests that Taiwan has used DFI successfully for promoting its investment, exports, and employment, and that foreign firms have played important roles in the structural changes of the Taiwanese economy, most notably the growth of the electric and electronic machinery sector. This experience resulted from several factors including: (1) favorable policies toward foreign (and domestic) firms which allowed them to operate more or less uninhibited and which fostered the emergence of positive externalities in the long run, and (2) an outward-oriented development strategy which apparently influenced foreign firms' choice of technology.

However Taiwan has undergone a number of important changes in recent years including: (1) the appreciation of the NT\$, (2) import liberalization, and (3) rapid growth of domestic demand. In this context, it is highly likely that the future contribution of foreign firms will be more diffused among industries and activities, and foreign firms will help to accelerate changes that have already begun. Moreover the 1987 liberalization of controls on outward capital movements has had an especially large effect on outward DFI which increased over tenfold in 1987 and almost fivefold in 1988. What is more, outward flows were over three times larger than the level of inward flows in the latter year (cf. Table 6.1) and data for 1989 indicate that the trend is continuing.[12] Thus it appears that Taiwan is making the transition to become a net exporter of DFI. This means that future DFI-structural change relationships in Taiwan may center more on outflows than inflows.[13] In any case, the recent increases in both outward and inward DFI suggest that multinationals from Japan, the United States, and Taiwan will have large effects on Taiwan's industrial structure in the years to come.

## Notes

Thanks are due to the other contributors to this volume, Eric D. Ramstetter in particular, for their useful comments and suggestions.

1. Through 1987, arrivals (as recorded in the balance-of-payments data) amounted to approximately 45 percent of approved DFI. The difference between the two series arises because: (1) there is a lag between DFI approvals and actual investment (paid-up capital is allowed to arrive up to 3–5 years after investment approvals), and (2) many approved investment plans never materialize. The latter factor is probably more important and nonrealized approvals include some multimillion dollar projects such as the proposed Swedish investment in the China Shipbuilding Company, the Austrian investment in China Steel, and the deferred and reduced investment by Toyota. Toyota's initial investment plans in 1983 anticipated a plant assembling 200,000 cars per year and total capital investment of US\$500 million. The project was dropped because of disputes over export requirements and a much smaller proposal was submitted two years later, this time with a total capital commitment of US\$6.3 million. Although it is preferable to use the balance-of-payments data, approval data provide detail on investing countries and sectors of investment that is not available in the balance-of-payments data.

2. Import duties on intermediate products were waived in EPZs and bonded factories, provided that all products were exported.

3. Paid-up capital data indicate that total arrivals were only 33 percent of total approvals. The foreign firm surveys used to gather the paid-up capital data covered all firms with a foreign capital share greater than 0 (Ministry of Economic Affairs, Investment Commission, various years a). However the extent of actual DFI (cf. balance-of-payments data in Table 6.2) is underestimated due to incomplete coverage. The number of firms covered in these surveys (coverage rates are in parentheses where available) were as follows: 1974–723 firms (73 percent), 1975–749 firms, 1976–766 firms, 1977–747 firms, 1978–839 firms, 1979–858 firms (78 percent), 1980–830 firms (77 percent), 1981–795 firms (76 percent), 1982–819 firms (76 percent), 1983–747 firms (72 percent), 1984–956 firms (78 percent), 1985–837 firms (74 percent), 1986–833 firms (73 percent), 1987–910 firms (79 percent).

4. The U.S. share tends to be underestimated because several U.S. investments were made through U.S. subsidiaries in other countries. For example, Ford's Taiwan venture was in association with Ford Canada, Gulf's investment in Taiwan was linked with that of Bermuda Gulf, and part of Singer's investment in Taiwan was financed by Swedish Singer. If such investments were included, the U.S. share of total investment would rise by approximately 4 percent (which is not enough to alter the basic patterns described).

5. Joint ventures are defined as firms with 99 percent or less foreign capital.

6. Indirect effects that work through macroeconomic relationships and through input-output relations among sectors are largely ignored here. The major exception to this is in the area of exports where indirect exports, i.e., sales to other local firms which end up embodied in exports, are accounted for.

7. Available data indicate that export-sales ratios were higher for U.S. firms than for their Japanese counterparts, both overall and in many individual industries. This is an apparent contradiction of the assertion that Japanese firms are more trade oriented than their U.S. counterparts in Taiwan. See Kojima (1985) for counterarguments on this.

8. Looking at these three exceptions more closely, we see that foreign firms in the wood industry were very export oriented (export ratios were over 93 percent) while firms in the paper industry were heavily oriented toward the domestic market (export ratios were under 17 percent). Although the former industry was highly export oriented while the latter was focused mainly on the local market, the marketing strategies used by foreign firms in these two industries caused few technological differences. The capital intensity of textiles firms in the 1970s was the result of a few large, export-oriented firms producing artificial fibers with very capital-intensive technology. The apparel and foods and beverages industries have marketing patterns similar to that of the wood and paper industries, but there are sharp technological differences depending on market orientation.

9. Textiles in 1975 and chemicals in 1986 are the major exceptions to this pattern. In addition, employment percentages and export ratios are very high in the apparel and wood industries.

10. See Tu and Schive (1989) for further details on specification and variable derivation.

11. Of course, there are other causes of differences between the discrete ratio calculated from the survey data and the regression coefficient including differences in sample, differences caused by using constant prices in the regression analysis and current prices in the calculation of discrete ratios, and a general tendency for discrete calculations and regression estimates to differ. Nonetheless the observed difference is substantial enough to suggest positive indirect export effects.

12. The total net outflow of DFI was US$7 billion in 1989, over three times the level of net inflows of DFI from abroad.

13. For more on DFI outflows from Taiwan, see Schive (forthcoming).

# References

Areskoug, Kaj. 1976. Private Foreign Investment and Capital Formation in Developing Countries. *Economic Development and Cultural Change* 24(3): 539–47.

Central Bank of China. Various years a. *Balance of Payments, Taiwan District, Republic of China,* various quarterly issues. Taipei: Central Bank of China.

_____ . Various years b. *Financial Statistics, Taiwan District, Republic of China,* various monthly issues. Taipei: Central Bank of China.

_____ . Various years c. Primary balance-of-payments data.

Committee on Industrial and Commercial Censuses of the Taiwan-Fukien District. 1978. *The Report of the Committee on Industrial and Commercial Censuses of the Taiwan-Fukien District of the Republic of China,* 1976 issue. Taipei: Committee on Industrial and Commercial Censuses.

_____ . 1989. *The Report of the Committee on Industrial and Commercial Censuses of the Taiwan-Fukien District of the Republic of China,* 1986 issue. Taipei: Committee on Industrial and Commercial Censuses.

Council for Economic Planning and Development. 1989. *Taiwan Statistical Data Book 1989.* Taipei: Council for Economic Planning and Development.

Directorate-General of Budget, Accounting and Statistics. 1988a. *National Income in 1988.* Taipei: Directorate-General of Budget, Accounting and Statistics.

_____ . 1988b. *Statistical Yearbook of the Republic of China 1988.* Taipei: Directorate-General of Budget, Accounting and Statistics.

Hymer, S. H. 1960. The International Operations of National Firms: A Study of Direct Foreign Investment. Ph.D. diss., Massachusetts Institute of Technology.

International Monetary Fund (IMF). 1979. *International Financial Statistics Yearbook 1979.* Washington, D.C.: International Monetary Fund.

Kojima, Kiyoshi. 1985. Japanese and American Direct Investment in Asia: A Comparative Analysis. *Hitotsubashi Journal of Economics* 26(1): 1–35.

Liu, T. Y., and C. C. Chien with P. W. Chang, J. H. Chiu, and C. J. Chuang. 1983. *The Effects of Japanese Investment on the National Economy.* (In Chinese). Taipei: Taiwan Institute of Economic Research.

Ministry of Economic Affairs, Investment Commission. Various years a. *An Analysis of Operations and Economic Effects of Foreign Enterprises in Taiwan.* (In Chinese). Taipei: Investment Commission.

_____ . Various years b. *Statistics On: Approved Overseas Chinese and Foreign Investment, Technical Cooperation, Outward Investment, and Outward Technical Cooperation.* Taipei: Investment Commission.

_____ . Various years c. Primary survey data.

Riedel, James. 1975. The Nature and Determinants of Export-Oriented Direct Foreign Investment in a Developing Country: A Case Study of Taiwan. *Weltwirtschlaftliches Archiv* 111(3): 505–28.

_____ . Forthcoming. Taiwan's Emerging Position in the International Division of Labor. In *Taiwan: Beyond Economic Miracle,* edited by Denis Simon. New York: Sharpe.

Tu, J. H., and Chi Schive. 1989. Direct Foreign Investment and its Effects on Taiwan's Investment. *Academia Economic Papers* 17(1): 63–92.

Wu, Rong I. 1987. U.S. Direct Investment in Taiwan: An Economic Appraisal. In *Asia Pacific Economies: Promises and Challenges,* Research in International Business and Management, Vol. 6, Part B: 185–98.

Wu, Rong I., L. C. H. Wong, T. C. Chou, and C. K. Li. 1980. *The Effects of United States' Investment on the National Economy.* (In Chinese). Taipei: Institute of American Culture, Academia Sinica.

# PART FOUR

# Outward Investment and Structural Change in Industrialized Economies

# 7

## The Rapid Increase of Direct Investment Abroad and Structural Change in Japan

*Shujiro Urata*

### Introduction

The rapid appreciation of the Japanese yen and the continuing trade friction between Japan and its trading partners have made further expansion of Japanese exports difficult. In order to cope with the situation, a large number of Japanese firms have adopted a globalization strategy which emphasizes the minimization of production costs and the maximization of market access. The globalization strategy takes various forms including direct foreign investment (DFI), production tie-ups, and outsourcing. Among the international arrangements involved, DFI has been the most conspicuous with approved DFI outflows from Japan more than tripling from 1985 to 1988 (US$12.2 to US$47.0 billion).[1] Developed countries have attracted the majority of Japanese DFI, approximately 60 percent through the end of fiscal 1988 (March 1989). Among developing countries, developing Asia has received the largest share. Forty-five percent of total DFI approvals in developing countries through fiscal year 1988 went to the Asian developing economies. Moreover, the Asian share of Japanese manufacturing DFI in developing countries is high at 64 percent.

The substantial amount of DFI undertaken by Japanese multinationals is expected to impart various impacts on the Japanese economy. Some argue that DFI causes unemployment in Japan as it shifts production activities from Japan to foreign countries. One frequently finds articles in Japanese newspapers and magazines about the "hollowing out" of the Japanese manufacturing industry. In spite of the tremendous amount of interest and concern, the effects of DFI on the Japanese economy have not been examined closely because Japan's outward DFI has been relatively small until only very recently and because detailed data on DFI are difficult to obtain. Although data necessary for detailed statistical analyses are still not available, it is nonetheless important to analyze DFI patterns and the effects of DFI on the Japanese economy to the greatest extent possible.

The objective of this paper is thus twofold. First, changes in the sectoral and geographical patterns of Japanese DFI are examined. Particular attention is given to Japanese DFI in the manufacturing sector of developing Asian economies. This

DFI has not only expanded rapidly in the last few years, but has also become an important element of structural adjustments in manufacturing, both in Japan and in developing Asia. Second, the effects of DFI on structural change in the Japanese economy are analyzed. The focus is on the effects of DFI on international trade flows, because trade flows are heavily influenced by DFI and because structural changes in the Japanese economy are often induced by changes in international trade patterns. In this respect, the paper focuses on the often-made assertion that Japanese multinationals divide a production process into a number of subprocesses and then allocate these subprocesses worldwide so as to minimize production costs. In particular, the relationship between this process and the expansion of intraindustry, intrafirm, interprocess trade between Japan and the developing Asian countries is explored.

To do this, the paper first provides an overview of the changing patterns of production and foreign trade in Japan. Second, it discusses the recent trends of Japan's DFI in Asia and then it statistically analyzes the determinants of Japanese DFI in Asia. Following this, the effects of Japanese DFI on Japanese exports and imports are examined, and some concluding comments are offered.

## Patterns of Structural Change in Japan's Economy

The post–World War Two period saw rapid structural change in a number of economies with Japan experiencing one of the fastest rates of structural change worldwide. Except for a period in the early 1970s when Japan's DFI in Asian textiles increased significantly as production facilities were shifted from Japan to developing Asia, DFI did not play an important role in the process of structural change until the 1980s. Although DFI has only recently become an important cause of structural change in Japan, a review of changes in the structure of production and foreign trade during the post–World War Two period highlights the interaction of long-run demand and supply factors which are the basic causes of structural change.

In 1950, food, textiles, and chemicals were the three sectors which had shares of total manufacturing shipments that exceeded 10 percent.[2] However, the shares of these three sectors have declined over time. Of particular note is the dramatic decline of the textiles' share, from 21.4 percent in 1950 to 3.0 percent in 1987; this experience is typical of labor-intensive, light industries. On the other hand, the share of iron and steel, a capital-intensive, heavy industry, increased to 10.6 percent in 1960, before beginning a substantial decline to 5.4 percent in 1987. In contrast to labor-and capital-intensive industries that have been losing shares, technology-or human capital-intensive sectors such as machinery have steadily increased their shares over time. Among the machinery subsectors, electrical machinery increased its share very rapidly, rising from 2.9 percent in 1950 to 16.5 percent in 1987. Electrical machinery had the largest share in total manufacturing shipments for 1987, followed by transport machinery at 12.9 percent. Furthermore, the increase in shipments of electrical machinery between 1980 and 1987 amounted to more than one-third of the increase in total manufacturing shipments.

Changes in the production structure are in turn reflected in changes in the structure of foreign trade. First, exports became less labor intensive and more capital intensive over time. For example, the share of textiles in total manufactured exports declined steadily from 37.3 percent in 1955 to 3.0 percent in 1987, while the share of iron and steel increased from 9.6 percent in 1960 to 18.2 percent in 1975 and then declined to 5.5 percent in 1987.[3] On the other hand, the share of machinery increased rapidly from 25.5 percent in 1960 to 71.2 percent in 1987. On the import side, raw materials have accounted for more than one-half of total imports throughout the postwar period. However, in recent years, the share of manufactures in total imports has started to increase rapidly, rising from 31.0 percent in 1985, to 41.8 percent in 1986, and to 49.0 percent in 1988. These statistics indicate that the drastic appreciation of the yen in recent years has brought about a major structural shift in the pattern of imports. Among manufactures, machinery imports have increased at quite a rapid rate. The fact that both exports and imports have been growing rapidly indicates that intraindustry trade in machinery has been expanding. I will argue below that, in addition to changes in relative prices due to the rapid appreciation of the yen, DFI has also been one of the most important factors leading to the expansion in intraindustry trade. One should note, however, that the share of manufactures in total imports and the share of intraindustry trade in overall trade are both still low in Japan when compared to those of other industrial countries.[4]

The changes in the structure of production and foreign trade in Japan can be largely explained by the interaction of changes in supply and demand factors.[5] Supply-side factors include the accumulation and efficient use of factors of production such as labor and capital, whereas demand-side factors include changes in the patterns of intermediate and final demand. The effects of supply-side and demand-side factors on structural changes in Japan are examined in three periods: the end of World War Two to the mid-1950s, the mid-1950s to the first oil crisis, and the first oil crisis to the present. This periodization is useful because the structure of exports was more or less dominated by labor-intensive products in the first period, by capital-intensive products in the second period, and by human capital-or technology-intensive products in the third period.

The rapid growth of the Japanese economy during the 1950s was quite significant, even if one discounts the fact that much of the growth in the first half of the decade simply recouped the economic losses sustained in World War Two. The rate of economic growth accelerated in the 1960s, and averaged over 10 percent annually in the last five years of the decade. This rapid growth was largely the result of increased fixed investment that was based on favorable expectations among private firms regarding the future economic performance of Japan. One should note that aggressive government policies, such as the National Income Doubling Plan, and the rapid growth of world trade were instrumental in the formation of private firm expectations.

Rapidly growing fixed investment contributed to economic growth not only through expansion of productive capacity, but also through creation of additional effective demand. These two effects led to a more capital-intensive production structure. Coupled with an increasingly severe labor shortage, expansion of fixed investment raised the capital-labor ratio and increased Japan's relative cost advantage in capital-intensive products. Moreover, booming fixed investment also resulted in increased demand for capital-intensive, heavy industrial products. It should also be mentioned that rapid economic growth increased household income and stimulated the demand for capital-intensive consumer durables such as electric refrigerators. Thus, as a result of increases in both supply and demand, the share of capital-intensive products in manufacturing production grew significantly.

Toward the end of the 1960s, the Japanese economy, which continued to perform well, began to encounter a number of problems. Among them, environmental problems and trade disputes with the United States had the largest influence on Japan's production and export structures. Increasing concern over environmental issues such as air and water pollution led to introduction of regulatory policies. As capital-intensive heavy and chemical industries were a major source of pollution, the regulatory policies resulted in increased production costs in these industries. At about the same time, Japan faced two distinct problems in its economic relations with the United States: (1) a growing bilateral trade surplus overall, and (2) increasingly frequent conflicts over trade in specific products such as textiles, iron, and steel. The large bilateral trade imbalance resulted in a substantial appreciation of the Japanese yen in the early 1970s while the trade problems in specific products resulted in export restrictions in various forms; for example, voluntary export restraints were imposed on exports of iron and steel, and textiles.

Increases in production costs due to regulatory policies and declines in export demand resulting from the yen's appreciation and export restraints led to reduced production and export of capital-intensive, heavy industrial products. In addition, the oil crisis in 1973, during which oil prices quadrupled, accelerated the production structure's shift away from capital-intensive, energy-intensive, heavy and chemical industries. The oil crisis and its aftermath reduced economic growth, which in turn led to a slowdown in fixed investment overall. Moreover, as a result of changes in factor endowments, Japan's comparative advantage in capital-intensive heavy industrial products began to shift to middle-income economies such as the Asian NICs (Hong Kong, Korea, Singapore, and Taiwan). The roots of the NICs' growing comparative advantage in heavy industrial products in the 1970s were (1) the same supply and demand factors that fostered Japan's growing comparative advantage in these products in the 1960s and (2) the slowed growth of Japan's capital endowment.

During the 1970s and 1980s, Japan gained comparative advantage in human capital-and technology-intensive products such as transport machinery and electric and electronic machinery. As early as the late 1960s, as further expansion of capital-intensive heavy industries became increasingly difficult, the Japanese government, as well as private firms, sought to expand human capital-intensive sectors through increased research and development (R&D) investment. R&D efforts were intensified following the two oil crises as the cost of producing capital-intensive heavy industrial products increased further. Increased R&D investment in both public and private sectors improved the technological level in Japan and contributed to increased energy efficiency. Coupled with expanding production capacity in human capital-intensive industries, increased demand for the products of these industries both in Japan and abroad led to increased shares of human capital-intensive products in Japan's production and export of manufactures.

The rapid appreciation of the yen in recent years has accelerated the globalization of Japanese firms which had already been taking place in the context of the changes described above. Specifically, many Japanese firms sought to divide the overall production process into a number of subprocesses and locate each subprocess in an economy so as to minimize the production costs of that subprocess. In this way, Japanese multinational parents and their affiliates have been able to specialize in the subprocesses they perform most efficiently. Affiliate operations in Asia have been an integral part of this division of labor. Although clear identification of this phenomenon is difficult because sufficiently detailed data do not exist, the sections below summarize existing information which can provide some insight into this trend.

### Changing Patterns of Japanese
### Multinational Activity in Asia

Japanese DFI in Asia has been growing steadily with few fluctuations. In particular, the rate of increase of Japanese DFI in Asia has been remarkably high since 1985, which is when the Japanese yen started to appreciate sharply (Ministry of Finance 1989). Annual reported Japanese DFI in Asia increased rapidly from US$2.3 billion in 1986, to US$4.9 billion in 1987, and US$6.4 billion in 1988. The total for these three years, US$13.6 billion, is more than the total for the entire 1951–1981 period (US$13.1 billion) and almost two-and-a-half times the total for the 1982–1984 period (US$5.5 billion).

Cumulative reported Japanese DFI in Asia from 1951 to 1988 amounted to US$32.2 billion, accounting for 17.3 percent of Japan's DFI worldwide and 44.9 percent of Japanese DFI in developing countries (Table 7.1). Cumulative manufacturing DFI in Asia was US$12.4 billion at the end of 1988 or 38.4 percent of all Japanese DFI in Asia. Correspondingly, Asia's share of Japanese manufacturing DFI worldwide was 24.8 percent and Asia accounted for 64.1 percent of Japanese manufacturing DFI in developing countries. These findings indicate that Japanese DFI in Asia has been concentrated in manufacturing to a greater extent than Japanese DFI in other regions, both developing and developed. On the other hand, although Japanese DFI in Asia has been increasing rapidly, Asia's shares of overall Japanese DFI, both in manufacturing and nonmanufacturing, declined over time as Japanese DFI in developed economies increased at an even greater rate.

Because Japan was faced with a balance-of-payments constraint, Japan's DFI outflows remained quite low until the late 1960s. Of the limited Japanese DFI in Asia, a large portion was devoted to securing supplies of natural resources. Examples of such DFI include petroleum drilling in Indonesia, iron ore mining in Malaysia, and copper mining in the Philippines. As for Japanese DFI in manufacturing, textiles was the first major sector to experience substantial DFI in Asia: Japanese DFI in textiles was directed to Thailand in the early 1960s and Taiwan, Malaysia, and Singapore in the late 1960s.

In the late 1960s, Japanese DFI in Asia, as well as in other parts of the world, increased rapidly. The rapid increase in Japanese DFI in Asia was realized through the interaction of supply factors in Japan and demand factors in the economies of Asia. In Japan, policies toward overseas investment were liberalized as balance-of-payments surpluses emerged. Moreover, as discussed earlier, Japanese production costs in manufacturing increased as a result of environmental problems and labor

Table 7.1 Cumulative Approvals of Japanese Direct Investment Abroad, 1978-1988
(fiscal yearend[a], US$ millions)

| Region /Country | Year | Total | Total Manuf. | Food | Textiles | Paper and Pulp | Chemi-cals | Ferrous and Nonfer. Metals | Gen-eral Mach. | Elec-trical Mach. | Trans-port Mach. | Other Manuf. |
|---|---|---|---|---|---|---|---|---|---|---|---|---|
| World | 1978 | 26,809 | 9,174 | 430 | 1,457 | 647 | 2,074 | 1,548 | 632 | 1,090 | 653 | 644 |
| | 1983 | 53,131 | 16,952 | 806 | 1,795 | 899 | 3,176 | 3,608 | 1,265 | 2,322 | 1,822 | 1,258 |
| | 1988 | 186,356 | 49,843 | 1,965 | 2,669 | 2,099 | 6,540 | 7,671 | 4,716 | 10,196 | 6,956 | 7,031 |
| Developing regions[b] | 1978 | 15,150 | 6,619 | 244 | 1,198 | 293 | 1,724 | 1,167 | 404 | 616 | 486 | 485 |
| | 1983 | 28,390 | 10,536 | 338 | 1,417 | 351 | 2,536 | 2,665 | 673 | 933 | 850 | 771 |
| | 1988 | 71,786 | 19,307 | 747 | 1,862 | 589 | 3,523 | 4,394 | 1,426 | 2,926 | 2,254 | 1,584 |
| Developing Asia | 1978 | 7,668 | 3,410 | 121 | 836 | 123 | 465 | 690 | 177 | 418 | 202 | 376 |
| | 1983 | 14,552 | 5,800 | 176 | 1,002 | 162 | 990 | 1,487 | 367 | 643 | 350 | 623 |
| | 1988 | 32,227 | 12,371 | 516 | 1,380 | 389 | 1,785 | 2,268 | 1,036 | 2,414 | 1,183 | 1,399 |
| Hong Kong | 1978 | 715 | 145 | 1 | 94 | 7 | 1 | 3 | 10 | 10 | 0 | 17 |
| | 1983 | 1,825 | 215 | 6 | 114 | 7 | 4 | 5 | 17 | 20 | 0 | 42 |
| | 1988 | 6,167 | 492 | 54 | 127 | 9 | 14 | 25 | 55 | 114 | 1 | 92 |
| Korea | 1978 | 1,007 | 697 | 11 | 163 | 1 | 225 | 65 | 32 | 125 | 16 | 56 |
| | 1983 | 1,312 | 839 | 18 | 166 | 2 | 269 | 82 | 47 | 162 | 29 | -64 |
| | 1988 | 3,248 | 1,589 | 75 | 201 | 7 | 334 | 113 | 127 | 435 | 160 | 138 |

| | | | | | | | | | | | | |
|---|---|---|---|---|---|---|---|---|---|---|---|---|
| Singapore | 1978 | 541 | 395 | 8 | 10 | 11 | 15 | 17 | 61 | 102 | 107 | 63 |
| | 1983 | 1,383 | 1,009 | 21 | 17 | 11 | 275 | 43 | 183 | 172 | 114 | 173 |
| | 1988 | 3,812 | 1,990 | 41 | 18 | 16 | 681 | 90 | 356 | 400 | 127 | 261 |
| Taiwan | 1978 | 284 | 266 | 4 | 37 | 4 | 23 | 9 | 40 | 105 | 4 | 40 |
| | 1983 | 479 | 439 | 6 | 47 | 5 | 56 | 34 | 62 | 157 | 15 | 57 |
| | 1988 | 1,791 | 1,473 | 29 | 55 | 10 | 140 | 126 | 140 | 428 | 256 | 288 |
| Indonesia | 1978 | 3,745 | 1,166 | 24 | 295 | 44 | 61 | 512 | 13 | 21 | 46 | 150 |
| | 1983 | 7,268 | 2,001 | 31 | 366 | 74 | 102 | 1,136 | 21 | 41 | 72 | 158 |
| | 1988 | 9,804 | 2,955 | 67 | 554 | 242 | 185 | 1,409 | 32 | 73 | 162 | 232 |
| Malaysia | 1978 | 471 | 302 | 15 | 91 | 42 | 57 | 26 | 9 | 37 | 5 | 18 |
| | 1983 | 764 | 533 | 20 | 120 | 46 | 177 | 59 | 9 | 66 | 10 | 26 |
| | 1988 | 1,833 | 1,350 | 38 | 143 | 60 | 214 | 188 | 52 | 382 | 184 | 89 |
| Philippines | 1978 | 434 | 152 | 14 | 20 | 7 | 59 | 25 | 3 | 6 | 8 | 9 |
| | 1983 | 721 | 290 | 15 | 21 | 8 | 66 | 75 | 5 | 8 | 72 | 21 |
| | 1988 | 1,120 | 510 | 57 | 27 | 9 | 89 | 86 | 10 | 55 | 136 | 41 |
| Thailand | 1978 | 309 | 233 | 39 | 121 | 4 | 19 | 12 | 8 | 4 | 15 | 13 |
| | 1983 | 521 | 390 | 49 | 146 | 5 | 30 | 30 | 19 | 8 | 36 | 67 |
| | 1988 | 1,992 | 1,456 | 107 | 218 | 24 | 83 | 182 | 237 | 350 | 80 | 173 |

[a]Fiscal year ends March 31 of the following calendar year.
[b]Regions excluding North America, Europe, and Oceania.

<u>Source:</u>  Ministry of Finance (1989).

shortages, and starting in 1971, costs increased further as a result of the appreciation of the yen. At the same time, a number of Asian economies were shifting the emphasis of their development strategies from import substitution towards export promotion. Correspondingly, DFI-promotion policies were adopted in some economies. Responding to these changes Japanese DFI in manufacturing, especially in textiles and electric machinery, expanded while flows of natural resource-related DFI remained rather constant.

The first oil shock brought the rapidly growing Japanese economy to a halt by increasing the rate of inflation and by worsening the balance-of-payments situation. Poor economic performance in Japan, coupled with a shift to restrictive DFI policies in a number of Asian economies, resulted in a decline of Japanese DFI flows to Asia. Restrictive DFI policies were adopted by some host economies to promote local firms and to deal with antiforeign, especially anti-Japanese, sentiment in these countries. Furthermore, in the early 1980s, a number of developing economies in Asia adopted tight fiscal and monetary policies to deal with balance-of-payments problems which were, in turn, primarily caused by aggressive development policies adopted since the late 1970s.[6] These contractionary economic policies resulted in slowdowns, and even recessions in some cases, and further discouraged inflows of DFI.

Although there were some ups and downs in the latter half of the 1970s and early 1980s, Japanese DFI in Asia did not increase substantially until the mid-1980s when the yen began to appreciate rapidly. A large share of Japan's DFI in the latter half of the 1970s and early 1980s was in ferrous and nonferrous metals such as aluminum refining in Indonesia and steel mills in Malaysia. Textiles, chemicals, electrical machinery, and transport machinery also accounted for substantial shares, especially in Asia's NICs.

The rapid increase in Japanese DFI in Asia since 1986 was undoubtedly prompted by the rapid and substantial appreciation of the yen. As was emphasized earlier, a large number of Japanese firms have undertaken DFI as part of a globalization strategy which seeks to cope with increases in Japanese production costs brought about by the appreciation. Globalization strategies have been further facilitated by the decreasing costs of communications and transportation services, which derive from technological advances and increased competition in these sectors. The rapid increase of Japanese DFI in Asia during this period is also attributable to the adoption of pro-DFI policies in several Asian economies, which reflects the shift towards export-promotion policies in these economies.

Electrical machinery led the rapid increase in Japanese DFI in Asia during the 1986–1988 period, followed by ferrous and nonferrous metals, and transport machinery. This recent surge in DFI has some notable characteristics that were not previously observed. One characteristic is its emphasis on export orientation. Although outward-looking trade policies were adopted off and on in most Asian economies since the 1960s, inward-looking policies emphasizing import substitution were the core of development strategies for most Asian economies (excluding the NICs). It was not until the mid-1980s that outward-looking policies become firmly planted in a number of Asian economies. To take advantage of the export-promoting measures adopted in these countries, a sizeable portion of Japanese affiliate production has been shipped overseas in recent years. It should be noted that exports of affiliates that are destined for Japan have also increased since the mid-1980s as the Japanese market has become more attractive with the appreciation of the yen. As will be detailed in the following discussion, another notable feature is the extensive division of production processes which was facilitated by Japanese DFI, especially in the machinery sectors. A third characteristic of Japan's recent DFI in Asia is that DFI by final producers is often accompanied with DFI by parts suppliers. In other words, DFI by final producers has led to DFI by their supporting industries. For example, electric wire producers followed electric appliance producers into a number of Asian economies. Finally, it should be noted that the countries in the Association of Southeast Asian Nations (ASEAN: Brunei, Indonesia, Malaysia, the Philippines, Singapore, and Thailand) appear to be attracting Japanese DFI more than the East Asian NICs in recent years as the NICs have lost some of their cost advantages due to rapid wage increases and currency appreciation. Moreover, the East Asian NICs and Singapore no longer receive special treatment of their exports to the United States under the Generalized System of Preferences. Thus export-oriented DFI has found the larger ASEAN countries a more attractive production locale.

Although the data give us a rough idea of the financial dimensions of Japan's DFI in Asia, the relationship between financial investment flows (as recorded in the Ministry of Finance figures on approved or reported DFI or as given in the balance of payments) and the production-related activities of multinational firms is often rather weak. Moreover these data are not compatible with data on capital formation or capital expenditures; thus it is very difficult to evaluate the scale of Japanese DFI relative to capital formation in either the host countries or Japan. Because the primary concern of this paper is to evaluate the role of Japan's multinationals in structural changes of the Japanese economy, it is helpful to ascertain the relative size of Japanese multinationals in various Japanese industries. A number of indicators may be used to do this, for example data on sales or production, employment and employee compensation, input procurement, and international trade activities.

Employment of multinational parents and their affiliates are perhaps the most relevant measure of the scale of multinational activity in Japan because the effect of outward DFI on Japan's employment is very often a subject of heated controversy. The debate centers around the belief that the transfer of production to foreign countries reduces domestic employment opportunities. Of course this argument ignores the positive indirect effect of reallocating productive resources in a more efficient manner. An important element of this debate is the effect of DFI on Japan's exports and how that feeds back to employment. Although a number of detailed investigations on employment impacts of outward DFI have been done for the United States (e.g., Ramstetter, this volume), similar industry- or firm-level detail is not available in the Japanese data to make comparable analyses possible.

It is possible, however, to examine the patterns of Japanese parent and affiliate employment in 12 manufacturing subsectors using surveys by the Ministry of International Trade and Industry (MITI) (Table 7.2), although these data tend to understate the true scope of Japanese multinational firm activities.[7] Approximately 2.0 million workers, or about 18 percent of all manufacturing employees, are employed by Japanese multinational parents in Japan but there are wide variations

Table 7.2 Employment of Japanese Parents, 1980-1986[a]

| | 1980 | | 1983 | | 1986 | |
|---|---|---|---|---|---|---|
| | Number of Employees | Share of Total Jap. Employ. (%) | Number of Employees | Share of Total Jap. Employ. (%) | Number of Employees | Share of Total Jap. Employ. (%) |
| Total manufacturing | 1,967,513 | 18.0 | 2,017,506 | 18.9 | 1,981,069 | 18.2 |
| Food | 63,364 | 5.5 | 70,313 | 6.2 | 16,967 | 1.4 |
| Textiles | 112,061 | 8.3 | 93,070 | 7.9 | 56,576 | 4.9 |
| Wood and pulp | 41,753 | 4.2 | 37,858 | 4.6 | 29,666 | 3.9 |
| Chemicals | 191,864 | 46.7 | 221,318 | 55.1 | 169,418 | 42.7 |
| Iron and steel | 227,823 | 52.7 | 190,774 | 46.9 | 165,400 | 44.9 |
| Nonferrous metals | 56,232 | 29.4 | 41,182 | 22.7 | 60,013 | 37.1 |
| General machinery | 217,085 | 20.1 | 202,377 | 18.6 | 199,112 | 17.8 |
| Electrical machinery | 475,046 | 35.0 | 497,718 | 30.6 | 526,024 | 28.2 |
| Transport machinery | 319,697 | 35.4 | 399,794 | 44.4 | 452,985 | 49.4 |
| Precision machinery | 48,915 | 17.7 | 42,733 | 16.1 | 91,005 | 35.2 |
| Coal and petro products | na | na | 19,124 | 45.8 | 8,978 | 24.3 |
| Others | 213,673 | 7.8 | 201,245 | 7.7 | 204,925 | 7.7 |

na = Not available.
[a]Parent data for fiscal years ending March 31 of the following calendar year.

Sources: MITI (various years a, various years b).

in the parents' shares of total Japanese employment in manufacturing subsectors. Generally, parent shares are high for heavy and chemical manufacturing and low for light manufacturing (food, textiles, wood and pulp, and miscellaneous manufacturing). For example, in 1986, parent shares in food, textiles, and wood and pulp were all below 5 percent, whereas the shares in the heavy and chemical subsectors (chemicals, metals, machinery, and coal and petroleum) were all greater than 17 percent. Shares were particularly high (greater than 40 percent) in chemicals, iron and steel, and transport machinery. These data indicate that multinationals constitute a disproportionately large share of Japanese economic activity in heavy and chemical sectors as theory would suggest (e.g., Markusen, this volume).

Employment of manufacturing affiliates abroad increased from 611,433 persons in 1980 to 725,810 persons in 1986. This amounted to 5.6 percent and 6.7 percent of total Japanese manufacturing employment, and 31.1 percent and 36.6 percent of manufacturing parent employment in each year, respectively. Employment of manufacturing affiliates in Asia declined from 374,457 persons in 1980 to 322,269 persons in 1983, but then increased rapidly to 391,156 persons in 1986 to represent approximately 20 percent of parent employment (Table 7.3). The rapid increase of employment in Asian manufacturing affiliates was mainly the result of increases in employment of affiliates in the non-ASEAN region, with activities of affiliates in the East Asian NICs (Hong Kong, Korea, and Taiwan) being particularly significant.[8]

Electrical machinery affiliates are by far the largest employers in both the ASEAN and non-ASEAN regions, followed by textiles and transport machinery. Another interesting characteristic is the high and increasing ratio of Asian affiliate employment to parent employment in textiles; indeed, in 1986 this ratio exceeded 100 percent. The increases in this ratio are particularly significant because the absolute level of affiliate employment was declining during this period. Thus the ratio's decline reflects an even more rapid decline in Japanese textile parent's employment during the period. Asian affiliate employment also declined in absolute terms in other light industries, specifically food and wood and pulp. In contrast, Asian affiliate employment increased in most heavy and chemical manufacturing sectors. Most notably, Asian affiliate employment in the four machinery sectors increased especially rapidly, particularly in non-ASEAN affiliates. This observation is consistent with changes in the pattern of reported DFI flows described earlier.

## Determinants of Japanese DFI in Asia

The steady increase of Japanese DFI in Asia over time and the changing focus of this DFI from resource-based and light manufacturing to heavy manufacturing have already been discussed. In order to further understand the nature of this DFI, it is also of interest to identify the factors that determine the timing and the sectoral pattern of Japanese DFI in Asia. There are a number of studies on this subject,[9] but there are very few econometric studies (in fact none to my knowledge) of the determinants of Japanese DFI's sectoral patterns.

A most comprehensive explanation of the determinants of DFI is the eclectic theory by Dunning (1979). According to this theory, DFI is hypothesized to be a function of three groups of "advantages" which are necessary conditions for DFI to

Table 7.3 Employment of Japanese Affiliates in Asian Regions, 1980-1986[a]

| | Asia | | | | | | ASEAN | | | | Non-ASEAN | | | |
|---|---|---|---|---|---|---|---|---|---|---|---|---|---|---|
| | 1980 | | 1983 | | 1986 | | 1983 | | 1986 | | 1983 | | 1986 | |
| Industry | Number of Employees | Share of Total Parent Employ. (%) | Number of Employees | Share of Total Parent Employ. (%) | Number of Employees | Share of Total Parent Employ. (%) | Number of Employees | Share of Total Parent Employ. (%) | Number of Employees | Share of Total Parent Employ. (%) | Number of Employees | Share of Total Parent Employ. (%) | Number of Employees | Share of Total Parent Employ. (%) |
| Total manufacturing | 374,457 | 19.0 | 322,269 | 18.0 | 391,156 | 19.7 | 166,916 | 8.3 | 177,977 | 9.0 | 155,353 | 7.7 | 213,179 | 10.8 |
| Food | 6,721 | 10.6 | 5,985 | 8.5 | 2,691 | 15.9 | 3,732 | 5.3 | 1,790 | 10.5 | 2,253 | 3.2 | 901 | 5.3 |
| Textiles | 92,385 | 82.4 | 80,798 | 86.8 | 70,227 | 124.1 | 54,692 | 58.8 | 37,623 | 66.5 | 26,106 | 28.0 | 32,604 | 57.6 |
| Wood and pulp | 4,742 | 11.4 | 3,487 | 9.2 | 3,130 | 10.6 | 3,372 | 8.9 | 2,757 | 9.3 | 115 | 0.3 | 373 | 1.3 |
| Chemicals | 15,942 | 8.3 | 17,119 | 7.7 | 20,831 | 12.3 | 10,953 | 4.9 | 9,525 | 5.6 | 6,166 | 2.8 | 11,306 | 6.7 |
| Iron and steel | 10,828 | 4.8 | 10,000 | 5.2 | 11,863 | 7.2 | 9,509 | 5.0 | 9,497 | 5.7 | 491 | 0.3 | 2,366 | 1.4 |
| Nonferrous metals | 8,013 | 10.7 | 8,232 | 20.0 | 9,202 | 15.3 | 3,352 | 8.1 | 2,661 | 4.4 | 4,880 | 11.8 | 6,541 | 10.9 |
| General machinery | 19,533 | 9.0 | 10,171 | 5.0 | 14,082 | 7.1 | 3,505 | 1.7 | 6,021 | 3.0 | 6,666 | 3.3 | 8,061 | 4.0 |
| Electrical machinery | 133,637 | 28.1 | 98,011 | 19.7 | 155,162 | 29.5 | 32,663 | 6.6 | 63,897 | 12.1 | 65,348 | 13.1 | 91,265 | 17.3 |
| Transport machinery | 24,718 | 7.7 | 42,553 | 10.8 | 54,075 | 11.9 | 24,556 | 6.1 | 25,039 | 5.5 | 17,997 | 4.5 | 29,036 | 6.4 |
| Precision machinery | 9,229 | 18.9 | 5,913 | 13.8 | 16,025 | 17.6 | 1,604 | 3.8 | 3,959 | 4.4 | 4,309 | 10.1 | 12,066 | 13.3 |
| Coal and petro products | na | na | 117 | 0.6 | 130 | 1.5 | 6 | 0.0 | 130 | 1.4 | 111 | 0.6 | 0 | 0.0 |
| Others | 50,709 | 23.7 | 39,883 | 19.8 | 33,738 | 16.5 | 18,972 | 9.4 | 15,078 | 7.4 | 20,911 | 10.4 | 18,660 | 9.1 |

na = Not available.

[a]Data refer to fiscal years ending March 31 of the following calendar year.

Sources: MITI (various years b).

occur: (1) ownership advantages, (2) internalization advantages, and (3) locational advantages. Ownership advantages arise from various market imperfections since firms are identical in perfectly competitive markets. Examples of ownership advantages are technological superiority, large size, and access to productive resources. Technological superiority may be obtained by extensive R&D activities. One notable characteristic of technological superiority is its public good nature and its subsequent relationship to the concept of multiplant economies of scale; in other words, the same technology can be used in several plants for essentially the same cost as in one plant (Markusen, this volume). Large firms are likely to have technological superiority because they are more likely to be able to exploit firm-level, multiplant economies of scale and then use the resulting profits to finance R&D activities. Thus, as Markusen (this volume) stresses, the mere existence of firm-level, multiplant scale economies encourages DFI. Moreover access to productive resources such as raw materials and financing, which are often influenced by government policies, may also enable a firm to gain further advantages over its competitors.

Internalization advantages arise when ownership advantages are best exploited through intrafirm as opposed to interfirm transactions. A firm has several alternative ways to gain from ownership advantages: DFI, exporting, licensing, patent sales, and others. In short, if transactions costs are higher for interfirm transactions than for intrafirm transactions, then DFI is likely to take place. Note that the presence of market imperfections such as imperfect information and government regulations tends to increase the cost of interfirm transactions. Imperfect or asymmetric information gives rise to DFI because the value of an ownership advantage such as management skill is not evaluated equivalently by the potential buyer and its owner. Since the owner of this management skill cannot sell it for the price sought, DFI becomes the best alternative if the desire is to exploit this skill in overseas markets. In addition, government regulations such as tariffs and taxes give a firm an incentive to manipulate prices by conducting intrafirm transactions: this practice is known as transfer pricing

Locational advantages refer to the advantages of locating production in a host country where wages are low, energy and/or raw materials are abundant and cheap, and policies that encourage DFI flows are found. These advantages essentially reflect the pattern of comparative advantage or distortions of it. In this regard, Kojima (1985) has characterized Japanese DFI as "trade-creating" and U.S. DFI as "trade-reducing." His characterization of Japanese and U.S. DFI is based on the observation that Japanese DFI is concentrated in industries in which Japan is losing a comparative advantage, whereas U.S. DFI is concentrated in those industries in which the United States has a comparative advantage. These observations, if true, imply that Japanese DFI promotes structural upgrading in Japan and that the same is not true in the United States. Kojima's insightful observation explains differences in patterns of Japanese and U.S. DFI in the 1960s and early 1970s, but the pattern of Japanese DFI appears to have become somewhat similar to that of the United States in recent years.

A model of Japanese DFI in Asia is constructed to test these hypotheses. The dependent variable, *DFIA*, is the annual approved or reported flow of Japanese DFI to Asia in constant 1985 prices (the Japanese investment goods price index was used as the deflator). Explanatory variables included in the model are: (1) *MES*, the mean size of the largest establishments accounting for one-half of an industry's employment (a proxy for minimum efficient scale); (2) *PD*, the ratio of advertisement expenditures to sales (a proxy for the degree of product differentiation); (3) *RD*, the ratio of R&D expenditures to sales (a proxy for technological superiority); (4) *EX*, the export-output ratio (a measure of export dependence); and (5) *IM*, the import-domestic absorption ratio (a measure of import penetration).[10] The first three variables are proxies for the different types of ownership advantages that were discussed; their coefficients are expected to be positive. According to Kojima, the coefficients on *EX* and *IM* should be negative and positive, respectively. However, if we interpret foreign trade variables as proxies for the level of technological superiority a la eclectic theory, we should expect these signs to be reversed.

A double-log specification of the model is estimated by generalized least squares to correct for heteroscedasticity and autocorrelation. The model is tested using pooled cross-section data of eight manufacturing sectors over a period of ten years, 1977–1986. The results of the model are reported in equation (7.1) below (t-values are in parentheses; * = significant at 0.05 level; ** = significant at 0.01 level).[11]

$$DFIA = 4.453 + 0.821 \ MES + 0.098 \ PD - 0.229 \ RD$$
$$\quad\quad\ \ (4.63)** \ \ (4.97)** \quad\quad (0.80) \quad\quad\ (0.79)$$

$$+ \ 0.312 \ EX + 0.335 \ IM \quad\quad\quad\quad\quad\quad (7.1)$$
$$(2.49)* \quad\ \ (3.81)**$$

$$R^2 = 0.554 \quad\quad F = 18.2**$$

The signs of the coefficients for *MES* and *PD* are positive as expected and consistent with the eclectic theory. However, the coefficient on *PD* is statistically insignificant and the coefficient on *RD* is both negative and statistically insignificant; thus the evidence suggests that neither product differentiation nor technological superiority were important determinants of Japanese DFI in Asia during this period although minimum efficient scale did impart a significant impact. Interestingly, the coefficients on both *EX* and *IM* are positive and statistically significant, indicating that high degrees of both export dependence and import penetration are associated with higher levels of DFI. This result is particularly interesting because it suggests that DFI in Asia is highest in industries where Japan has a large comparative disadvantage, industries in which Japan has a large comparative advantage, or industries in which a comparative advantage and disadvantage exist simultaneously (i.e., industries in which intraindustry trade is high).

As such, these results appear to indicate that neither ownership advantages in the eclectic theory nor the Kojima hypothesis conclusively explains the pattern of Japanese DFI in Asia. The roles of intraindustry trade and economies of scale appear to be particularly important. These observations are consistent with the view that the globalization of Japanese multinationals leads to the division of a production process into a number of subprocesses, and each subprocess is located where it can be performed at the least cost. As a result of this specialization within the multinational firm, intraindustry, intrafirm, interprocess trade is required to produce a finished product. Of course, these regression results are not robust enough to convince skeptics of this story; moreover, since there are several problems in the regressions, especially in the DFI data employed, more detailed analysis is required before firm conclusions can be made from such regressions. Nonetheless the story told here about the quest of Japanese multinationals to increase efficiency through globalization is an important one which figures prominently in analysis of trade activities as well.

## Japanese Multinationals and Foreign Trade

In light of the close association between changes in foreign trade and production structures in Japan, and the significant role of trade dependence in determining the timing and pattern of Japanese DFI in Asia, it is important to examine foreign trade activities of Japanese multinationals in the greatest detail possible. Manufactured exports of Japanese multinational parents grew steadily from 17 billion yen in 1980 to 23 billion yen in 1983 and to almost 25 billion yen in 1986 (Table 7.4). The slowdown in growth from 1983 to 1986 is mainly attributable to the rapid appreciation of the yen starting in 1985. However, despite this slowdown, the share of multinational parents' exports in total Japanese exports increased from 64 percent in 1980 to 73 percent in 1983 and to 82 percent in 1986.

In individual manufacturing sectors, two contrasting patterns are observed.[12] First, parent exports in nonferrous metals, electrical machinery, transport machinery, and precision machinery recorded substantial increases between 1980 and 1986 and, with the exception of precision machinery in 1980 and 1983, parent shares of total Japanese exports all exceeded 60 percent. Among these sectors, electrical machinery and transport machinery were by far the largest; their combined share of total parent exports increased steadily from 55 percent in 1980 to 72 percent in 1986. In other words, these sectors were the primary source of Japan's export boom in 1980–1986 and within these sectors, export growth was highly concentrated in multinational parents. On the other hand, parent exports declined in light manufacturing, as well as chemicals and iron and steel, and stagnated in general machinery. In light manufacturing (all years) and general machinery (1980 and 1983), parent shares of exports were generally low, while these ratios were substantially higher in iron and steel (all years) and chemicals (1980 and 1983).

An increasingly large portion of parent exports were shipped to their overseas affiliates (Table 7.5). From 2,803 billion yen in 1980, parent exports to overseas affiliates more than tripled to 9,657 billion yen in 1986. As the growth of these parent-to-affiliate exports exceeded the growth of parent exports, the intrafirm share of parent exports steadily increased from 16.4 percent in 1980 to 39.2 percent in 1986. Patterns of parent-to-affiliate exports among individual manufacturing sectors are rather similar to those found for parent exports overall. Parent-to-affiliate exports and intrafirm shares of parent exports grew rapidly in all machinery sectors, textiles, and iron and steel, but declined or stagnated in other light manufacturing, chemicals, and nonferrous metals. Moreover, intrafirm shares of parent exports were generally high in the four machinery sectors but low in light manufacturing, chemicals, and metals. By 1986, intrafirm shares of parent exports had reached 30–60 percent for the machinery sectors, but shares were under 10 percent in light manufacturing and

Table 7.4  Exports of Japanese Parents, 1980-1986[a]

| Industry | 1980 Parent Exports (billions of yen) | 1980 As a Share of Total Japanese Exports | 1983 Parent Exports (billions of yen) | 1983 As a Share of Total Japanese Exports | 1986 Parent Exports (billions of yen) | 1986 As a Share of Total Japanese Exports |
|---|---|---|---|---|---|---|
| Total manufacturing | 17,110.2 | 64.3 | 23,476.5 | 73.2 | 24,641.3 | 82.0 |
| Food | 26.1 | 10.0 | 32.9 | 12.9 | 0.7 | 0.4 |
| Textiles | 432.8 | 36.6 | 562.4 | 42.0 | 341.5 | 37.5 |
| Wood and pulp | 79.3 | 27.2 | 102.7 | 32.2 | 62.3 | 22.4 |
| Chemicals | 853.0 | 53.0 | 1,012.0 | 58.5 | 470.7 | 31.2 |
| Iron and steel | 2,937.7 | 71.5 | 2,457.4 | 65.4 | 1,578.3 | 64.7 |
| Nonferrous metals | 246.0 | 60.6 | 323.8 | 91.1 | 423.4 | 184.5 |
| General machinery | 1,446.8 | 37.5 | 1,880.2 | 36.1 | 1,581.9 | 27.9 |
| Electrical machinery | 4,253.1 | 97.3 | 5,744.3 | 91.0 | 6,434.1 | 102.2 |
| Transport machinery | 5,094.9 | 70.5 | 9,582.4 | 110.1 | 11,417.9 | 131.5 |
| Precision machinery | 574.2 | 39.8 | 431.3 | 23.7 | 1,245.1 | 69.0 |
| Coal and petro products | na | na | 275.9 | 495.4 | 30.5 | 54.7 |
| Others | 1,166.2 | 57.5 | 1,071.2 | 43.0 | 1,054.8 | 48.1 |

na = Not available.
[a]Parent data for fiscal years ending March 31 of the following calendar year.

Sources:  Institute of Developing Economies (1989); MITI (various years b).

Table 7.5  Exports of Japanese Parents to Their Affiliates Worldwide, 1980-1986[a]

| Industry | 1980 Parent Exports (billions of yen) | 1980 As a Share of Total Japanese Exports | 1983 Parent Exports (billions of yen) | 1983 As a Share of Total Japanese Exports | 1986 Parent Exports (billions of yen) | 1986 As a Share of Total Japanese Exports |
|---|---|---|---|---|---|---|
| Total manufacturing | 2,802,697 | 16.4 | 6,999,661 | 29.8 | 9,657,448 | 39.2 |
| Food | 4,413 | 16.9 | 6,035 | 18.3 | 51 | 7.8 |
| Textiles | 13,912 | 3.2 | 15,139 | 2.7 | 24,512 | 7.2 |
| Wood and pulp | 168 | 0.2 | 415 | 0.4 | 7 | 0.0 |
| Chemicals | 149,472 | 17.5 | 197,363 | 19.5 | 44,233 | 9.4 |
| Iron and steel | 78,397 | 2.7 | 53,931 | 2.2 | 130,729 | 8.3 |
| Nonferrous metals | 35,645 | 14.5 | 9,290 | 2.9 | 35,026 | 8.3 |
| General machinery | 281,962 | 19.5 | 236,305 | 12.6 | 508,737 | 32.2 |
| Electrical machinery | 1,012,960 | 23.8 | 1,425.282 | 24.8 | 2,788.914 | 43.4 |
| Transport machinery | 549,518 | 10.8 | 4,342,951 | 45.3 | 4,991.315 | 43.7 |
| Precision machinery | 226,255 | 39.4 | 166,700 | 38.7 | 742,590 | 59.6 |
| Coal and petro products | na | na | 116,887 | 42.4 | 22,423 | 73.6 |
| Others | 449,995 | 39.6 | 429,363 | 40.1 | 368,911 | 35.0 |

na = Not available.
[a]Data refer to fiscal years ending March 31 of the following calendar year.

Sources:  MITI (various years b).

material-producing manufacturing (chemicals, iron and steel, and nonferrous metals).

The contrasting patterns of parent-to-affiliate exports in machinery industries on the one hand and in nonmachinery industries on the other reflects the different production processes of the two sectors. The production of machinery requires a large number of manufactured parts, whereas the production of nonmachinery is more heavily based on the processing of mainly raw materials. For example, over 10,000 manufactured parts are required to produce an automobile, but the primary requirement for production of iron and steel is iron ore. The large manufactured-parts requirements of machinery industries create the possibility that different parts can be manufactured with vastly different technologies and factor requirements. As a result, the potential for division of production processes among different regions is greater in the machinery industries.

In recent years, two developments—the rise of protectionism centered in developed countries and the emphasis on cost reduction in the globalization strategy in Japanese multinationals—have added further incentives for machinery multinationals to locate different production processes in different economies, mainly in the form of overseas affiliates. As was noted earlier, exports of a number of commodities, including automobiles, to developed countries have come under voluntary export restraints or other types of export-limiting arrangements. To circumvent these restrictions on market access, Japanese multinationals have undertaken DFI to set up assembly and production plants in these countries. As local supplies of components are often not sufficient in the early stages of affiliate operations, Japanese parent exports of components to these newly established affiliates have been a major factor in the recent increase in parent-to-affiliate exports.

The automobile case is probably the best example of this point. Parent-to-affiliate exports in transport machinery increased rapidly from 0.5 billion yen in 1980 to 4.3 billion yen in 1983. This growth is highly correlated with the increased production by Japanese automobile affiliates abroad, especially in the United States. With the introduction of voluntary export restraints on automobile exports to the United States in 1981, Japanese auto producers sought to maintain their U.S. market shares by exporting automobile knockdown kits and assembling the automobiles in United States. However, as full production replaces assembly, these intrafirm exports are likely to decline in the future.

As stressed throughout this paper, the globalization strategy of Japanese multinationals has also led to different processes being located in different host economies with the aim of minimizing production costs. For example, electronic components such as semiconductors are shipped from Japanese parents to their overseas affiliates, where these components are used to produce household electric appliances such as microwave ovens and air conditioners. As these types of arrangements have increased, so has intrafirm trade. The rapid appreciation of the yen since 1985 and advances in transportation and communications services have further accelerated the trends toward the intrafirm division of production processes within Japanese multinationals. Although hard statistical evidence is lacking, intrafirm transactions of this type are thought to be increasing rapidly in Asia where good-quality, low-cost labor is abundant.

Thus far, only the export patterns of Japanese parents have been examined. In order to complete the analysis of Japanese multinational foreign trade activities, it is also necessary to examine the trade activities of multinational affiliates abroad, especially the imports of multinational parents from their Asian affiliates. Unfortunately, data on the trade activities of Japanese affiliates are only available at the regional level, though it is possible to distinguish affiliates in the ASEAN and non-ASEAN regions.

Exports from Japanese manufacturing affiliates in Asia to Japan increased slightly from 245 billion yen in 1980 to 252 billion yen in 1983, and skyrocketed to 506 billion yen in 1986 (Table 7.6). The increase reflects both increased affiliate activity in Asia and the increasing attractiveness of the Japanese market. Due to the yen appreciation in 1985–1986, the large 1983–1986 increase was actually much larger if measured in U.S. dollars. In addition, the 1983–1986 increase was highly concentrated in the non-ASEAN region, which accounted for 80 percent of this increase. By 1986, exports from non-ASEAN affiliates were 375 billion yen, or approximately 75 percent of the exports by all Asian affiliates to Japan.

Exports of affiliates abroad to Japan are highly concentrated in machinery industries, particularly electrical machinery which accounted for the largest share of affiliate exports to Japan for both the non-ASEAN and ASEAN region. However, Asian affiliate exports of electrical machinery increased relatively slowly during 1980–1986 and this sector's share of the total decreased steadily from 49 percent in 1980, to 45 percent in 1983, and to 27 percent in 1986. By 1986, the share of Asian affiliates' exports to Japan was also high in general machinery, transport machinery, textiles, and precision machinery in the non-ASEAN region, while the shares were high in nonferrous metals, transport machinery, and textiles in the ASEAN region.

The increased attractiveness of the Japanese market is also reflected by the increasing ratio of affiliate exports to Japan to total affiliate sales (Table 7.6). This ratio declined slightly from 1980 to 1983 but increased rapidly from 9.1 percent to 15.8 percent in 1986. Among individual manufacturing sectors, dependence on the Japanese market is highest in three machinery sectors (general, electrical, and precision machinery), food, wood and pulp, and nonferrous metals. However the degree of this dependence differs tremendously between industries in ASEAN and non-ASEAN. For ASEAN affiliates, a large portion of sales in wood and pulp and nonferrous metals were exports to Japan while affiliates in the food, nonferrous metals, general machinery, electrical machinery, and precision machinery industries in non-ASEAN countries exported a substantial portion of their sales to Japan. The differences in affiliate export patterns between ASEAN affiliates and non-ASEAN affiliates reflect differences in the pattern of comparative advantage in the two regions. In the non-ASEAN countries, there is a comparative advantage in the production of capital-intensive and human capital-intensive products such as machinery; in ASEAN, the comparative advantage lies in the production of natural resource-based and labor-intensive products.

More than 70 percent of Asian manufacturing affiliate exports to Japan were shipped to their parents in Japan (Table 7.7). These affiliate-to-parent exports were concentrated in the machinery sectors in the non-ASEAN region, especially electrical machinery (84 billion yen) and general machinery (61 billion yen) in 1986.

Table 7.6 Exports of Japanese Affiliates in Asian Regions to Japan, 1980-1986[a]

| Industry | Asia | | | | | | ASEAN | | | | Non-ASEAN | | | |
|---|---|---|---|---|---|---|---|---|---|---|---|---|---|---|
| | 1980 | | 1983 | | 1986 | | 1983 | | 1986 | | 1983 | | 1986 | |
| | Exports (millions of yen) | % of Total Asian Affiliate Sales | Exports (millions of yen) | % of Total Asian Affiliate Sales | Exports (millions of yen) | % of Total Asian Affiliate Sales | Exports (millions of yen) | % of Total Asian Affiliate Sales | Exports (millions of yen) | % of Total Asian Affiliate Sales | Exports (millions of yen) | % of Total Asian Affiliate Sales | Exports (millions of yen) | % of Total Asian Affiliate Sales |
| Total manufacturing | 244,917 | 9.8 | 251,907 | 9.1 | 506,039 | 15.8 | 82,166 | 5.7 | 130,932 | 10.0 | 169,741 | 12.8 | 375,107 | 19.8 |
| Food | 24,122 | 30.2 | 9,547 | 10.2 | 13,429 | 31.6 | 7,993 | 11.7 | 2,899 | 9.3 | 1,554 | 6.0 | 10,530 | 92.9 |
| Textiles | 17,349 | 4.0 | 20,892 | 4.7 | 37,693 | 10.3 | 6,330 | 2.8 | 11,171 | 8.1 | 14,662 | 6.4 | 26,522 | 11.6 |
| Wood and pulp | 7,539 | 30.8 | 6,791 | 38.1 | 5,085 | 25.5 | 6,627 | 39.5 | 5,621 | 32.6 | 164 | 16.0 | -536 | -19.9 |
| Chemicals | 19,303 | 8.9 | 24,385 | 8.3 | 13,933 | 3.8 | 6,239 | 4.0 | 9,890 | 5.6 | 18,146 | 13.0 | 4,043 | 2.1 |
| Iron and steel | 13,678 | 10.1 | 12,517 | 7.2 | 6,418 | 5.2 | 10,484 | 6.8 | 6,263 | 6.1 | 2,033 | 10.8 | 153 | 0.7 |
| Nonferrous metals | 1,729 | 2.8 | 446 | 0.3 | 34,445 | 31.8 | 0 | 0.0 | 26,800 | 33.2 | 446 | 0.6 | 7,645 | 27.7 |
| General machinery | 7,204 | 5.5 | 11,258 | 11.8 | 68,063 | 31.4 | 282 | 0.8 | 3,851 | 8.1 | 10,976 | 17.9 | 64,212 | 37.9 |
| Electrical machinery | 118,871 | 28.1 | 112,341 | 18.1 | 138,772 | 22.2 | 27,159 | 10.9 | 29,601 | 7.4 | 85,182 | 22.8 | 109,171 | 48.5 |
| Transport machinery | 4,645 | 1.9 | 19,300 | 3.8 | 50,624 | 5.3 | 8,097 | 2.5 | 15,045 | 7.9 | 11,203 | 5.9 | 35,579 | 4.7 |
| Precision machinery | 10,295 | 9.1 | 11,476 | 19.0 | 30,095 | 21.9 | 2,479 | 29.8 | 3,976 | 16.2 | 8,997 | 17.3 | 26,119 | 23.1 |
| Coal and petro products | na | na | 574 | 89.0 | 0 | 0.0 | 0 | 0.0 | 0 | 0.0 | 574 | 89.9 | 0 | 0.0 |
| Others | 20,182 | 6.0 | 22,280 | 6.7 | 18,520 | 7.7 | 6,476 | 3.6 | 4,770 | 4.8 | 15,804 | 10.2 | 13,750 | 9.7 |

[a]Data refer to fiscal years ending March 31 of following calendar year. Some of the figures were computed from rounded ratios from the sources and may not be consistent. Specifically, negative values for exports of non-ASEAN in wood and pulp is nonsensical, and the exports for 1986 do not add up to manufacturing total.

Sources: MITI (various years b).

Table 7.7 Exports of Japanese Affiliates in Asian Regions to Japanese Parents[a], 1980-1986

| Industry | Asia 1980 Total (millions of yen) | Asia 1980 % of Asian Aff. Exports to Sales | Asia 1983 Total (millions of yen) | Asia 1983 % of Asian Aff. Exports to Sales | Asia 1986 Total (millions of yen) | Asia 1986 % of Asian Aff. Exports to Sales | ASEAN 1983 Total (millions of yen) | ASEAN 1983 % of Asian Aff. Exports to Sales | ASEAN 1986 Total (millions of yen) | ASEAN 1986 % of Asian Aff. Exports to Sales | Non-ASEAN 1983 Total (millions of yen) | Non-ASEAN 1983 % of Asian Aff. Exports to Sales | Non-ASEAN 1986 Total (millions of yen) | Non-ASEAN 1986 % of Asian Aff. Exports to Sales |
|---|---|---|---|---|---|---|---|---|---|---|---|---|---|---|
| Total manufacturing | 218,378 | 89.2 | 187,410 | 74.4 | 387,120 | 76.5 | 52,362 | 63.7 | 102,782 | 78.5 | 135,048 | 79.6 | 284,338 | 75.8 |
| Food | 19,383 | 80.4 | 8,117 | 84.1 | 11,683 | 87.0 | 4,764 | 59.8 | 1,470 | 50.7 | 1,353 | 87.1 | 10,213 | 97.0 |
| Textiles | 14,961 | 86.2 | 15,729 | 74.9 | 21,749 | 57.7 | 2,971 | 46.9 | 11,171 | 100.0 | 12,758 | 87.0 | 10,578 | 39.9 |
| Wood and pulp | 7,539 | 100.0 | 8,075 | 89.5 | 1,409 | 27.7 | 5,911 | 89.2 | 1,478 | 28.3 | 164 | 100.0 | -89 | — |
| Chemicals | 15,338 | 79.4 | 12,144 | 49.8 | 12,386 | 83.9 | 6,239 | 100.0 | 7,467 | 75.5 | 5,905 | 32.5 | 4,919 | 121.7 |
| Iron and steel | 11,683 | 85.4 | 12,248 | 97.9 | 6,416 | 100.0 | 10,215 | 97.4 | 6,263 | 100.0 | 2,033 | 100.0 | 153 | 100.0 |
| Nonferrous metals | 1,613 | 93.3 | 344 | 77.1 | 34,189 | 99.2 | 0 | 0.0 | 28,800 | 100.0 | 344 | 77.1 | 7,389 | 98.4 |
| General machinery | 7,204 | 100.0 | 10,000 | 88.8 | 64,456 | 94.7 | 156 | 55.3 | 3,851 | 100.0 | 9,844 | 89.7 | 60,605 | 94.4 |
| Electrical machinery | 114,148 | 96.0 | 85,663 | 76.3 | 101,304 | 73.0 | 12,642 | 46.5 | 17,080 | 57.7 | 73,021 | 85.7 | 84,224 | 77.1 |
| Transport machinery | 2,380 | 51.2 | 12,962 | 67.3 | 23,287 | 46.0 | 2,036 | 25.1 | 6,770 | 45.0 | 10,946 | 97.7 | 18,517 | 48.4 |
| Precision machinery | 8,638 | 83.9 | 10,505 | 91.5 | 25,912 | 88.1 | 2,328 | 93.9 | 3,722 | 93.6 | 8,177 | 90.9 | 20,190 | 77.3 |
| Coal and petro products | na | na | 574 | 100.0 | 0 | 0.0 | 0 | 0.0 | 0 | 0.0 | 574 | 100.0 | 0 | 0.0 |
| Others | 15,493 | 76.8 | 15,029 | 67.5 | 16,390 | 88.5 | 5,100 | 78.8 | 3,849 | 80.7 | 9,929 | 62.8 | 12,541 | 91.2 |

na = Not available.
[a] Data refer to fiscal years ending March 31 of the following calendar year. Some of the figures were computed from rounded ratios from the sources and may not be consistent. Specifically, negative value in the exports of non-ASEAN in wood and pulp is non-sensical, and the exports for 1986 do not add up to manufacturing total.

Sources: MITI (various years b).

ASEAN affiliate-to-parent exports were large in textiles and nonferrous metals, as well as electrical machinery. Note, however, the declining trend in affiliate-to-parent exports as shares of all Asian manufacturing affiliate exports to Japan in 1980–1983. Moreover, in 1983–1986, these shares tended to decrease in the non-ASEAN region but increase in the ASEAN region, especially in textiles, electrical machinery, and transport machinery. As a result, although affiliate-to-parent exports accounted for a smaller share of ASEAN affiliate exports to Japan in 1983, this share became slightly larger for ASEAN in 1986.

Taken together, the above findings indicate that an increasingly large portion of Japanese trade with developing Asia has become intrafirm, intraindustry trade. It has been argued that such trade results from the pursuit of aggressive globalization strategies by Japanese multinationals which emphasize minimization of production costs through the division of production processes into a number of subprocesses and the subsequent location of each subprocess in a country where that process may be performed at least cost. As completion of a product requires a number of components from affiliates in different countries, intrafirm, intraindustry, interprocess trade expands. Intraindustry trade of this type differs substantially from the intraindustry trade that was analyzed extensively in the 1970s and 1980s[13] because these previous studies focused on intraindustry trade in differentiated, finished manufactures, which is essentially demand driven. In contrast, the intrafirm trade analyzed here is supply or production driven.

## Concluding Comments

A number of studies have argued that DFI reduces output in the home country. These studies first hypothesize that DFI reduces home output by lowering capital formation (i.e., the domestic investment displacement effect) and increasing imports from overseas affiliates in the home country (i.e., the boomerang effect). These output-reduction effects are then compared to the output-creation effect which is hypothesized to result from increased home country exports of capital goods and intermediate goods to host countries. According to most of these studies, the output-reduction effect outweighs the output-creation effect. The net negative effects of DFI are further magnified if interindustry effects are taken into account by using an input-output table. For example, one report by a Japanese labor union estimated that one yen of Japanese DFI would lead to a reduction of Japanese output by 4.4 yen if interindustry effects are ignored and 5.6 yen if such effects are included (Denki Rōren 1987). It is not surprising, therefore, to find these studies arguing for restricting DFI to save jobs in Japan. While the results of this report which was conducted by a labor union may not be wholly unbiased, a number of other studies that use more objective assumptions about the domestic investment displacement and the boomerang effects of DFI have come to similar conclusions, although the magnitude of the negative effects are smaller (Akiyama 1989).

But even these more objective studies suffer from a number of biases. One problem is that these studies do not take into account the interindustry effects and/or the multiplier effects of DFI in the host country. As was discussed in this paper, increases in the host country output that are due to DFI creates demand for intermediate goods through interindustry linkages and leads to an increase in the demand for intermediate goods from the home country. Moreover, as production and incomes rise, demand for the exports of the home country are likely to increase through a multiplier effect. Both of these effects add greater output to the output-creating effect of DFI.

Another problem with these studies is that they ignore the static and dynamic aspects of economies of scale which multinationals seek to exploit. In fact, one of the most important findings of this study is that DFI makes it possible for a multinational to exploit economies of scale. Specifically, we found that Japanese multinationals divide a production process into a number of subprocesses, and through DFI, locate each subprocess in countries where that subprocess may be performed at least cost. This type of production arrangement enables multinational parents and their affiliates to specialize in certain production processes, thereby enabling them to exploit scale economies. Such development is facilitated by a reduction in transportation and communication costs, thanks to rapid technological progress. Exploitation of scale economies results in increased efficiency and reduced production costs. With sufficient competition and/or appropriate regulatory policies, reduced costs result in reduced prices which then benefit both consumers and producers. If economies of scale and related efficiency gains are ignored, the positive effects of DFI on home and host country output are grossly underestimated. Moreover, the importance of multiplant economies of scale suggests the investment displacement effect would be greatly overestimated; in other words, domestic investment is often not a realistic alternative to DFI.

In view of these important points, this paper concludes that DFI helps both the home and the host countries expand their economic activities, and thereby makes structural change less painful. To assess the quantitative effect of DFI in the home and host countries more accurately, a model that explicitly incorporates economies of scale and process specialization should be used. One candidate would be an extension of computable general equilibrium models that have been used extensively in the analysis of trade liberalization.

## Notes

The author is grateful to the participants of the project, particularly E. Ramstetter, for comments and discussions. Able research assistance provided by K. Yokota of the Institute of Developing Economies is gratefully acknowledged.

1. The statistics on DFI used in this paper are based on "approved" or "reported" data from the Ministry of Finance (various years, 1989). Starting in 1980, approval is not required for outward DFI; thus the term "reported" may be more appropriate in recent years. Note also that the data differ significantly from those reported in the balance-of-payments accounts (Bank of Japan, various years a). Balance-of-payments totals for calendar 1965–1988 were only 61 percent of the approved total for fiscal 1965–1988; fiscal years end March 31 of the following calendar year. This ratio also varies depending on the country involved. For example, the ratio was approximately 72 percent in OECD countries and 44 percent in non-OECD countries (the former figure is slightly overestimated and the latter is slightly underestimated as South Africa is included in the OECD total in the balance of payments for 1965–1981).

2. The data employed in this paragraph refer to the value of shipments in nominal prices, which is a proxy for the value of total production, for 20 manufacturing sectors (Management and Coordination Agency 1987; MITI, various years a).

3. The foreign trade statistics in this section are taken from Management and Coordination Agency (various years a).

4. There are a number of studies analyzing manufactured imports and intraindustry trade in Japan. See Takeuchi (1989) for a comprehensive survey of these studies.

5. The following analysis draws on Kohama and Urata (1988).

6. For an analysis of economic performance of the developing economies in Asia in the 1980s, see Urata, Osada, Akiyama, and Torii (1989).

7. Comprehensive MITI surveys (MITI, various years b) are the most complete sources of data on the activities of Japanese multinationals. To date, three surveys (1980, 1983, and 1986) have been conducted; annual surveys have also been conducted for other years since 1970 but data included in annual surveys are much more limited in scope. One of the problems in the MITI surveys is that coverage differs markedly between surveys. For example, of the 3,247 parents that received questionnaires in the 1980 survey, 43.1 percent responded; of the 3,321 parents surveyed in 1983, 38.3 percent responded; and of the 3,425 parents in 1986, only 33.4 percent responded. Moreover, the figures reported in the surveys are apparently not adjusted for coverage. No attempt to make such an adjustment has been made here due to lack of sectoral information. Note that Lipsey (this volume) does attempt to make such an adjustment for 1974 and 1983. Thus the multinational figures cited in the text likely understate the true extent of multinational activities to a considerable extent. One indication of the extent the MITI survey tends to underestimate Japanese multinational activity comes from comparison of affiliate employment data for fiscal 1986 from MITI and for 1 July 1987 from Toyo Keizai (1988). MITI's estimates of total affiliate employment (921,138 persons) are only 60 percent of the Toyo Keizai estimate. MITI's estimate of manufacturing affiliate employment (725,810 persons) is only 63 percent of the Toyo Keizai estimate. For affiliates in Asia, these ratios were slightly higher, 68 percent overall and 64 percent in manufacturing. Since the Toyo Keizai estimates cover a slightly more recent period, these ratios likely overstate the degree to which MITI underestimates the scope of affiliate activity, but they do provide evidence that the degree of underestimation is substantial.

8. Note that the East Asian NICs account for the vast majority of non-ASEAN affiliate activity. For example, in all industries, East Asian NIC shares of total reported DFI in all of Asia were 26 percent in 1978, 25 percent in 1983, and 35 percent in 1988. Meanwhile, Brunei and other non-ASEAN countries accounted for only 2 percent of reported DFI in Asia in 1978 and 1983, and 8 percent in 1988. In manufacturing, corresponding East Asian NIC shares were 66 percent, 73 percent, and 67 percent, respectively while corresponding shares were 2 percent, 1 percent, and 4 percent for Brunei and other non-ASEAN countries.

9. See Agarwal (1980) for a survey of empirical studies on DFI.

10. Data come from the following sources: *DFIA* from Ministry of Finance (various years, 1989), *MES* from MITI (various years a), *PD* from the Bank of Japan (various years b), *RD* from the Management and Coordination Agency (various years b), and *EX* and *IM* from MITI (various years a) and Institute of Developing Economies (1989).

11. See Kmenta (1971) for details on estimation methodology. Note that since this is a double-log regression, the coefficients are elasticities.

12. Parent shares of total Japanese exports exceed 100 percent for some sectors. This is due to the fact that parent (and affiliate) exports as reported in the MITI survey are compiled on an enterprise basis while total trade data are compiled on a commodity basis. Since an enterprise can produce many different commodities, it is impossible to construct a perfect concordance between the two sets of data. Thus it is important to view these ratios as rough approximations of more qualitative than quantitative importance.

13. For more on intraindustry trade see, for example, Krugman and Obstfeld (1988).

## References

Agarwal, J. P. 1980. Determinants of Foreign Direct Investment: A Survey. *Welwirtschaftliches Archiv* 116(4): 739–73.

Akiyama, Y. 1989. Kaigai Chokusetsu Tōshi no Eikyō no Keisoku [Estimation of the effect of foreign direct investment]. In *Kikai Sangyō ni Okeru Kokusai Bungyōka ni Tomonau Kokunai Sangyōheno Eikyō Bunseki ni Kansuru Tokei Kenkyū Hōkokushō* [Report on the effect of international division of labor on the domestic industry: the machinery case]. Tokyo: Kikai Shinkō Kyōkai Kenkyūshō.

Bank of Japan. Various years a. *Balance of Payments Statistics Monthly*, 1967–1989 issues. Tokyo: Bank of Japan.

_____. Various years b. *Shuyō Kigyō Keiei Bunseki* [Analysis of managerial performance by major companies], 1977–1986 issues. Tokyo: Bank of Japan.

Denki Rōren. 1987. *Endaka to Kaigai Chokusetsu Tōshi: Kaden Sangyō ni Taisuru Eikyō no Bunseki* [Yen appreciation and overseas direct investment: an analysis of electric industry]. Tokyo: Denki Rōren.

Dunning, John H. 1979. Explaining Changing Patterns of International Production: In Defense of the Eclectic Theory. *Oxford Bulletin of Economics and Statistics* 41(4): 269–95.

Institute of Developing Economies. 1989. AIDXT trade data base.

Kmenta, J. 1971. *Elements of Econometrics*. New York: Macmillan.

Kohama, Hirohisa, and Shujiro Urata. 1988. The Impact of the Recent Yen Appreciation on the Japanese Economy. *Developing Economies* 26(4): 323–40.

Kojima, Kiyoshi. 1985. *Nihon no Kaigai Chokusetsu Tōshi: Keizaigakuteki Sekkin* [Japanese direct foreign investment]. Tokyo: Bunshindo.

Krugman, P. R., and M. Obstfeld. 1988. *International Economics*. Glenview, Ill.: Scott, Foresman and Company.

Management and Coordination Agency. Various years a. *Japan Statistical Yearbook*, 1971, 1975, 1977, 1982–1983, and 1986–1988 issues. Tokyo: Sorifu Tokeikyoku.

_____. Various years b. *Report on the Survey of Research and Development in Japan*, 1978 and 1987 issues. Tokyo: Sorifu Tokeikyoku.

_____. 1987. *Historical Statistics of Japan*, Vol. 2. Tokyo: Sorifu Tokeikyoku.

Ministry of Finance. Various years. *Zaisei Kinyū Tokei Geppō* [Fiscal and monetary statistics monthly], December issues 1981, 1983, 1985, and 1987. Tokyo: Ministry of Finance.

_____. 1989. Mimeos.

Ministry of International Trade and Industry (MITI). Various years a. *Census of Manufactures*, 1977, 1980, 1983, and 1986 issues. Tokyo: Ministry of International Trade and Industry.

_____. Various years b. *Kaigai Tōshi Tōkei Sōran* [A comprehensive survey of foreign investment statistics], 1980, 1983, and 1986 issues. Tokyo: Ministry of International Trade and Industry.

Takeuchi, K. 1989. Does Japan Import Less than it Should? A Review of the Econometric Literature. Mimeo, World Bank.

Toyo Keizai. 1988. *Gyōshubetsu Kaigai Shinshutsu Kigyō* [Firms with foreign affiliates by industry]. Tokyo: Tōyō Keizai Shinposha.

Urata, Shujiro, H. Osada, Y. Akiyama, and Y. Torii. 1989. Economic Growth and Structural Change in the Asian NIEs and ASEAN Economies. Paper presented at the Asia-Pacific Conference, 6–7 June, Tokyo, Japan.

# 8

## U.S. Direct Investment in Developing Asia and Structural Adjustment in the U.S. Manufacturing Industry

*Eric D. Ramstetter*

### Introduction

Since the 1960s U.S. firms, especially those within the manufacturing sector, have experienced strong challenges from firms based in Asia. The first and strongest challengers were firms from Japan, but in recent years challenges from firms based in the Asian newly industrializing countries (NICs: Hong Kong, Korea, Singapore, and Taiwan) have been formidable in many manufacturing industries. Moreover, the four larger economies of the Association of Southeast Asian Nations (ASEAN-4: Indonesia, Malaysia, the Philippines, and Thailand) have also begun to industrialize rapidly and there are indications that they may become another source of competition for U.S. industry.

The emergence of this competition is not undesirable for the United States. Not only is it a sign that these market economies are succeeding in their quest to raise their standards of living, but the process cannot help but lead to greater stability in a region where the United States has fought its last two wars. Aside from the political benefits, rising incomes in the region also create new demand for U.S. products and the increased competition provides incentives for U.S. industry to develop new products and improve efficiency.

Yet the process of Asian industrialization has also contributed to the need for restructuring in U.S. manufacturing industries which are losing comparative advantage to their Asian counterparts. For example, although total U.S. employment grew from 92 million in 1977 to 110 million in 1986, the share of employment in manufacturing fell more than 10 percent in all industries, except electric and electronic equipment and printing and publishing (Table 8.1). In fact, declines in the share of employment exceeded 35 percent in primary metals, tobacco, textiles and apparel, leather, and miscellaneous manufacturing. The share of value added also declined by more than 10 percent in most manufacturing industries. On the other hand, the share of total exports declined more than 10 percent in only a few industries including food, fabricated metals, textiles and apparel, lumber, stone, and

Table 8.1   Indicators of U.S. Structural Change, 1977-1986

| Industry | Nominal Value Added | | | Nominal Exports | | | Employment | | |
|---|---|---|---|---|---|---|---|---|---|
| | 1977 | 1982 | 1986 | 1977 | 1982 | 1986 | 1977 | 1982 | 1986 |
| Total economy (US$ billions; employment in millions) | 1,991 | 3,166 | 4,240 | 118 | 207 | 206 | 92 | 100 | 110 |
| Individual industry shares (%) | | | | | | | | | |
| Manufacturing, except petroleum | 28.6 | 25.3 | 24.0 | 79.3 | 78.2 | 84.9 | 21.1 | 19.0 | 16.6 |
| Food & kindred products | 2.8 | 2.8 | 2.6 | 6.2 | 5.3 | 5.5 | 1.7 | 1.5 | 1.3 |
| Chemicals & allied products | 2.8 | 2.4 | 2.4 | 9.0 | 9.7 | 10.9 | 1.0 | 0.9 | 0.7 |
| Metals | 4.2 | 2.9 | 2.5 | 6.3 | 6.4 | 5.0 | 2.9 | 2.3 | 1.9 |
| Primary metal products | 1.9 | 1.1 | 0.9 | 2.5 | 2.6 | 2.3 | 1.2 | 0.9 | 0.6 |
| Fabricated metal products | 2.3 | 1.9 | 1.6 | 3.8 | 3.7 | 2.7 | 1.7 | 1.5 | 1.3 |
| Nonelectric machinery | 3.4 | 3.2 | 2.6 | 18.2 | 18.8 | 17.6 | 2.3 | 2.2 | 1.7 |
| Electric & electronic equipment | 2.5 | 2.7 | 2.7 | 7.5 | 8.8 | 9.9 | 1.9 | 1.9 | 1.8 |
| Transportation equipment | 3.2 | 2.7 | 3.0 | 16.0 | 14.3 | 18.4 | 1.9 | 1.6 | 1.6 |
| Other manufacturing | 9.6 | 8.6 | 8.3 | 14.9 | 14.0 | 14.6 | 8.4 | 7.3 | 6.4 |
| Tobacco manufactures | 0.2 | 0.3 | 0.3 | 0.5 | 0.6 | 0.7 | 0.1 | 0.1 | 0.0 |
| Textile products & apparel | 1.8 | 1.4 | 1.2 | 2.0 | 1.5 | 1.4 | 2.4 | 1.9 | 1.5 |
| Lumber, wood, furniture, etc. | 1.3 | 0.9 | 1.0 | 2.0 | 1.7 | 1.7 | 1.3 | 1.0 | 1.0 |
| Paper & allied products | 1.1 | 1.1 | 1.0 | 2.1 | 2.0 | 2.2 | 0.7 | 0.6 | 0.6 |
| Printing & publishing | 1.6 | 1.7 | 1.8 | 0.6 | 0.7 | 0.6 | 1.2 | 1.3 | 1.3 |
| Rubber & plastics | 1.0 | 0.9 | 0.9 | 1.3 | 1.3 | 1.4 | 0.8 | 0.7 | 0.7 |
| Stone, clay, & glass products | 1.0 | 0.7 | 0.7 | 1.0 | 0.9 | 0.8 | 0.7 | 0.5 | 0.5 |
| Instruments & related products | 0.9 | 1.1 | 0.9 | 3.8 | 4.0 | 4.5 | 0.6 | 0.6 | 0.5 |
| Leather & leather products | 0.2 | 0.2 | 0.1 | 0.2 | 0.2 | 0.3 | 0.3 | 0.2 | 0.1 |
| Miscellaneous manufacturing | 0.5 | 0.4 | 0.3 | 1.3 | 1.1 | 1.0 | 0.5 | 0.4 | 0.3 |

Sources:   United States, Department of Commerce, Bureau of the Census (various years b).

miscellaneous manufacturing. Meanwhile export shares increased over 10 percent in chemicals, electric and electronic equipment, transportation equipment, tobacco, instruments, and leather. Note, however, that the growth of total merchandise exports was actually negative in 1982–1986 following a strong expansion in 1977–1982. Thus value added and employment structures moved toward nonmanufacturing more rapidly than did the structure of exports.

There is evidence suggesting that U.S. multinationals have remained extremely competitive in world markets and that the decline of U.S. competitiveness has been concentrated in nonmultinationals (Lipsey and Kravis 1985). Moreover there are several studies which indicate that foreign affiliate activity has generally been positively correlated with U.S. parent exports (Lipsey and Weiss 1981, 1984; Blomström,

Lipsey, and Kulchycky 1988). In short, direct foreign investment (DFI) appears to be an important means for U.S. firms to expand foreign market shares and develop new markets while maintaining their competitiveness by restructuring the geographical location of their activities.

Following a brief description of the financial aspects of U.S. DFI in Asia, this chapter analyzes the export and employment activities of U.S. multinationals with affiliates in the ASIA-8 (the NICs plus the ASEAN-4) in an attempt to ascertain the relationship between U.S. DFI in Asia and the structural changes experienced by the United States in the last decade. The first step is a simple comparison of exports and employment in U.S. industries overall, U.S. multinational parents, and Asian affiliates of U.S. multinationals. Second, using a cross-section of thirty-two industries, the relationships between growth in parent exports and employment from 1977 to 1982 on the one hand, and changes in the ratio of foreign affiliate value added to parent value added on the other, are analyzed. Finally, the study summarizes the implications of the quantitative results for evaluation of the relationship between DFI and structural adjustment problems in the United States.

## U.S. Direct Investment in Developing Asia:
## The Financial Dimensions

In a nutshell, financial data for 1977–1987 reveal that, with the exception of electric and electronic equipment and to a lesser extent petroleum, wholesale trade, and banking, U.S. DFI in Asia is quite small from the perspective of the United States. However U.S. DFI in Asia is relatively profitable compared to U.S. DFI in other regions. Moreover within Asia, U.S. DFI has been highly concentrated in the ASIA-8; for example, during this period 91 percent of U.S. DFI stocks in Asia and 98 percent of U.S. DFI income from the Asian region were in or came from these eight countries. The United States has been the largest investor in the ASIA-8 through 1987 though Japan, which is rapidly catching up, has been a more important source of DFI in the manufacturing sector in many of these ASIA-8 countries for a number of years.[1]

Petroleum accounted for 33 percent of the U.S. DFI stock in developing Asia in 1987, down from about 40 percent in 1977 and 1982 (Table 8.2). The vast majority of this DFI was in Indonesia with Thailand, Malaysia, Singapore, and Hong Kong also attracting substantial amounts. Despite the decrease of petroleum's share of U.S. DFI stocks in Asia, U.S. DFI stocks in petroleum in this region still accounted for 9 percent of U.S. petroleum DFI stocks worldwide in 1987. The decline in petroleum's share of U.S. DFI stocks in developing Asia has been accompanied by a surge in tertiary investment, primarily in trade, banking, and other finance. These three sectors accounted for 35 percent of total U.S. DFI stocks in developing Asia in 1987, up from 24 percent in 1977 and 28 percent in 1982. Hong Kong accounted for 51 percent of U.S. DFI stocks in the tertiary sectors in developing Asian countries in 1977 and 1982, and this share increased to 65 percent in 1987. By 1987, developing Asia's share of U.S. DFI stocks worldwide in wholesale trade (9 percent) and banking (10 percent) were comparable with developing Asia's shares of U.S. DFI stocks in petroleum worldwide.

In contrast, in manufacturing, U.S. DFI in developing Asia accounted for only 4 percent of U.S. manufacturing DFI stocks worldwide in 1987, which is up from 2 percent in 1977 and 3 percent in 1982. Of total U.S. DFI in Asia, however, manufacturing's share was 28 percent in 1987 which is a substantial increase over the 1982 share of 22 percent but only slightly larger than the 1977 share of 27 percent. Despite Asia's small share of total U.S. manufacturing DFI worldwide, Asia's electric and electronic equipment industry was an important industry for U.S. DFI and accounted for 21 percent of U.S. DFI stocks in this industry worldwide in 1987; moreover this sector accounted for 39 percent of total U.S. manufacturing DFI in Asia. All of these shares represent remarkable increases from 1977, with U.S. DFI stocks in Asian electric and electronic equipment growing more rapidly than U.S. DFI in electric and electronic equipment worldwide and U.S. DFI in Asian manufacturing. Most of this DFI was centered in Singapore with moderate amounts in Taiwan, Malaysia, and Thailand, and smaller sums in Korea and the Philippines.

U.S. DFI in Asian chemicals, nonelectric machinery, and food was much smaller from the United States' point of view but also grew rapidly. By 1987, chemicals accounted for 28 percent of U.S. DFI in Asian manufacturing, nonelectric machinery accounted for 12 percent, and food accounted for 7 percent. U.S. DFI stocks also increased rapidly in these industries; the Philippines was by far the largest recipient of food DFI; Singapore, Hong Kong, and Taiwan took the lion's share of nonelectric machinery DFI; and chemicals DFI was concentrated in Taiwan, Hong Kong, the Philippines, and Indonesia.

Developing Asia's share of worldwide U.S. DFI income is large relative to its shares of U.S. DFI stocks, reflecting relatively high rates of return on DFI in this region (Table 8.3). However this income is highly concentrated in a few countries and a few industries. For example, in 1977–1984; over one-half of the income from U.S. DFI in Asia came from the petroleum sector; with the fall in petroleum prices in the latter half of the 1980s, this share fell to 39 percent in 1985–1987. In all periods, the vast majority of petroleum income came from Indonesia. Moreover U.S. DFI in the Asian petroleum sector accounted for as much as 21 percent of total income from U.S. DFI in petroleum worldwide in 1981–1984. Trade, banking, and other finance accounted for roughly 21–23 percent of income on U.S. DFI in developing Asia in 1977–1984 and 27 percent in 1985–1987.[2] Over one-half of U.S. DFI income in these three sectors, mainly trade and other finance, came from Hong Kong; Singapore, the Philippines, and Korea were also important sources of banking income. In trade and banking, the Asian shares of U.S. DFI income from the world peaked at 15 percent and 13 percent, respectively, in 1981–1984.

Manufacturing income has grown very rapidly in recent years with its share of total income from U.S. DFI in developing Asia reaching 29 percent in 1985–1987 which is up from 15–16 percent in 1977–1984. Due to a decline in income from U.S. DFI worldwide in 1981–1984, the Asian share of total manufacturing income rose dramatically from 4 percent in 1977–1980 to 10 percent in 1981–1984; but this share fell back to 5 percent in 1985–1987. U.S. DFI income from Asian manufacturing was even more concentrated in electric and electronic equipment than U.S. DFI stocks in the region. U.S. DFI income from Asia in electric and electronic equipment, which came to be increasingly concentrated in Singapore, grew from 15

Table 8.2 Stock of U.S. Direct Investment Abroad in Selected Industries, 1977-1987 (yearend; US$ millions)

| Region/Country | Year | Total | Petroleum | Manufacturing, Excluding Petroleum | | | | | | | Trade[a] | Banking | Finance, Insurance & Real Estate |
|---|---|---|---|---|---|---|---|---|---|---|---|---|---|
| | | | | Subtotal | Food & Kindred Products | Chemicals | Primary & Fabricated Metals | Non-electric Machinery | Electric & Electronic Equipment | Trans-portation Equipment | | | |
| World | 1977 | 145,990 | 28,030 | 62,019 | 5,571 | 11,864 | 4,626 | 11,223 | 5,494 | 9,321 | 16,836 | 4,370 | 21,248 |
| | 1982 | 207,752 | 57,817 | 83,452 | 7,630 | 18,274 | 5,463 | 13,840 | 7,292 | 10,968 | 20,788 | 10,317 | 18,018 |
| | 1987 | 308,783 | 66,381 | 128,640 | 12,843 | 26,914 | 5,662 | 27,344 | 9,784 | 17,708 | 31,330 | 15,354 | 49,097 |
| Developing countries | 1977 | 31,800 | 1,518 | 11,545 | 1,286 | 2,874 | 1,115 | 1,034 | 1,273 | 1,127 | 3,305 | 1,924 | 9,534 |
| | 1982 | 48,058 | 17,777 | 19,315 | 2,097 | 4,489 | 1,602 | 2,069 | 2,279 | 2,160 | 4,566 | 5,252 | -3,469 |
| | 1987 | 71,174 | 19,009 | 21,881 | 2,474 | 5,150 | 1,066 | 2,681 | 2,943 | 2,850 | 6,430 | 6,001 | 13,150 |
| Developing Asia[b] | 1977 | 5,503 | 2,177 | 1,496 | 149 | 494 | 98 | 76 | 345 | na | 677 | 387 | 251 |
| | 1982 | 12,142 | 4,945 | 2,705 | 108 | 842 | 103 | 292 | 951 | 147 | 1,302 | 1,285 | 841 |
| | 1987 | 18,991 | 6,198 | 5,284 | 350 | 1,480 | 132 | 842 | 2,058 | 160 | 2,771 | 1,559 | 2,364 |
| Hong Kong | 1977 | 1,328 | 271 | 201 | 5 | 50 | na | 16 | 59 | 0 | 374 | 133 | 164 |
| | 1982 | 2,854 | 330 | 333 | 3 | 68 | 18 | 80 | 12 | 0 | 778 | 512 | 459 |
| | 1987 | 5,453 | 462 | 563 | na | 240 | 13 | 128 | 40 | 0 | 2,019 | 489 | 1,849 |
| Korea | 1977 | 395 | na | 164 | 8 | 90 | 1 | na | 17 | na | na | 17 | 11 |
| | 1982 | 690 | na | 187 | na | 58 | 7 | 0 | 48 | -8 | na | 132 | na |
| | 1987 | 1,018 | 7 | 339 | 41 | 78 | na | na | 115 | na | na | 370 | 180 |
| Singapore | 1977 | 516 | 232 | 106 | 5 | 3 | 28 | 15 | 45 | 1 | 75 | 49 | 18 |
| | 1982 | 1,720 | 553 | 615 | 4 | 32 | 8 | 119 | 313 | 130 | 191 | 288 | 36 |
| | 1987 | 2,521 | 579 | 1,493 | 22 | na | -3 | 208 | 966 | 61 | 150 | 163 | 72 |
| Taiwan | 1977 | 259 | 16 | 178 | 9 | 51 | 1 | 3 | 88 | 7 | 22 | 36 | 5 |
| | 1982 | 544 | na | 340 | 25 | 87 | na | na | 107 | na | 62 | 115 | 7 |
| | 1987 | 1,312 | -14 | 983 | 29 | 273 | 20 | 181 | 379 | 43 | 161 | 135 | 20 |
| Indonesia | 1977 | 984 | 738 | 97 | 2 | 30 | na | 0 | 13 | 0 | 9 | 8 | 5 |
| | 1982 | 2,295 | 1,958 | 134 | na | 38 | na | 3 | na | 0 | 30 | 7 | 17 |
| | 1987 | 3,929 | 3,251 | 234 | 7 | 196 | 7 | 9 | -2 | 0 | na | 3 | 195 |

| | | | | | | | | | | | | | | |
|---|---|---|---|---|---|---|---|---|---|---|---|---|---|---|
| Malaysia | 1977 | 464 | na | 86 | 3 | 15 | 2 | 4 | 46 | 0 | na | 8 | 2 |
| | 1982 | 1,221 | na | 245 | 6 | 20 | 5 | na | 161 | 0 | 45 | 13 | na |
| | 1987 | 1,111 | 704 | 329 | 4 | 21 | 5 | na | 246 | 0 | 52 | -8 | 11 |
| Philippines | 1977 | 837 | 273 | 317 | 100 | 88 | 14 | 1 | 34 | na | 76 | 93 | 26 |
| | 1982 | 1,315 | 410 | 366 | 23 | 153 | 8 | 0 | 123 | na | 81 | 149 | na |
| | 1987 | 1,211 | 101 | 602 | 222 | 213 | 14 | -4 | 91 | -2 | 84 | 237 | 1 |
| Thailand | 1977 | 237 | na | 51 | 9 | 9 | 4 | 0 | 11 | 0 | na | 27 | 6 |
| | 1982 | 780 | 484 | 181 | 8 | 23 | 5 | 0 | 105 | 0 | na | 36 | 5 |
| | 1987 | 1,282 | 857 | 256 | 6 | na | na | 4 | 172 | 0 | 49 | 87 | 9 |

na = Not available or not disclosed.
a Refers to wholesale trade only for 1982-1987; wholesale and retail trade for 1977-1981.
b Includes developing Pacific Island countries.

Sources: United States, Department of Commerce, Bureau of Economic Analysis (1985b, various years b).

Table 8.3 Income on U.S. Direct Investment Abroad in Selected Industries, 1977-1987 (annual averages; US$ millions)

| Region/Country | Year | Total | Petroleum | Manufacturing, Excluding Petroleum | | | | | | | Trade[a] | Banking | Finance, Insurance & Real Estate |
| --- | --- | --- | --- | --- | --- | --- | --- | --- | --- | --- | --- | --- | --- |
| | | | | Subtotal | Food & Kindred Products | Chemicals | Primary & Fabricated Metals | Non-electric Machinery | Electric & Electronic Equipment | Trans-portation Equipment | | | |
| World | 1977-80 | 30,115 | 9,454 | 10,186 | 1,054 | 2,234 | 573 | 2,268 | 790 | 1,171 | 3,222 | 1,984 | 3,066 |
| | 1981-84 | 23,911 | 10,267 | 5,887 | 866 | 1,434 | 284 | 1,171 | 672 | 204 | 2,130 | 2,905 | 1,274 |
| | 1985-87 | 41,309 | 8,500 | 19,876 | 2,165 | 3,862 | 782 | 5,459 | 1,329 | 2,444 | 4,762 | 2,511 | 3,587 |
| Developing countries | 1977-80 | 10,415 | 4,226 | 1,955 | 271 | 492 | 194 | 113 | 260 | 175 | 718 | 1,379 | 1,464 |
| | 1981-84 | 8,587 | 4,007 | 1,272 | 203 | 217 | 88 | 133 | 332 | -57 | 700 | 2,420 | -397 |
| | 1985-87 | 7,520 | 2,646 | 2,693 | 294 | 524 | 124 | 338 | 400 | 499 | 807 | 938 | -69 |
| Developing Asia[b] | 1977-80 | 2,295 | 1,276 | 376 | 43 | 108 | 16 | 28 | 117 | 8 | 209 | 236 | 75 |
| | 1981-84 | 3,641 | 2,178 | 545 | -15 | 105 | na | 79 | 264 | 56 | 316 | 373 | na |
| | 1985-87 | 3,203 | 1,247 | 931 | 40 | 198 | 21 | na | 320 | na | 427 | 289 | 153 |
| Hong Kong | 1977-80 | 487 | 47 | 58 | 1 | 20 | na | na | 13 | 0 | 136 | 115 | 67 |
| | 1981-84 | 573 | 57 | 70 | 2 | 15 | na | na | 22 | 0 | 214 | 118 | 80 |
| | 1985-87 | 719 | 49 | 133 | 3 | na | na | na | 12 | 0 | 307 | 74 | 108 |
| Korea | 1977-80 | 30 | na | 16 | na | 3 | 1 | 0 | 6 | na | na | na | na |
| | 1981-84 | 83 | 1 | 11 | 6 | -2 | 0 | 0 | 16 | na | na | 31 | na |
| | 1985-87 | 152 | 0 | 53 | 9 | 8 | na | -1 | 18 | na | na | na | 21 |
| Singapore | 1977-80 | 207 | 55 | 86 | na | 2 | 9 | 14 | 37 | na | 19 | 38 | 3 |
| | 1981-84 | 502 | 71 | 261 | -1 | na | na | 42 | 120 | na | 38 | 119 | 8 |
| | 1985-87 | 537 | 12 | 435 | 2 | na | -2 | 56 | 196 | na | 25 | 57 | -1 |
| Taiwan | 1977-80 | 79 | 3 | 53 | na | 15 | 0 | na | 26 | 4 | 7 | 13 | 0 |
| | 1981-84 | 137 | 3 | 96 | 5 | 17 | 1 | na | 48 | na | na | 21 | 1 |
| | 1985-87 | 200 | -3 | 140 | 7 | 44 | na | na | 54 | 5 | 31 | 25 | 4 |
| Indonesia | 1977-80 | 1,168 | 1,108 | 17 | 2 | 3 | -0 | 0 | 4 | na | 3 | na | 1 |
| | 1981-84 | 1,883 | 1,823 | na | 3 | 9 | na | 0 | 2 | 0 | na | 17 | na |
| | 1985-87 | 975 | 929 | 7 | 2 | 5 | 1 | 0 | 3 | 0 | na | -2 | na |

| | | | | | | | | | | | | |
|---|---|---|---|---|---|---|---|---|---|---|---|---|
| Malaysia | 1977-80 | 183 | na | 30 | 1 | 4 | 0 | 1 | 19 | 1 | na | na | na |
| | 1981-84 | 331 | na | na | 1 | 3 | na | na | 41 | 0 | na | 9 | na |
| | 1985-87 | 238 | na | na | 0 | 3 | -0 | 0 | 8 | 0 | na | 3 | 2 |
| Philippines | 1977-80 | 127 | -0 | 69 | 27 | 27 | 2 | 1 | 10 | na | 10 | 32 | 2 |
| | 1981-84 | 84 | na | -6 | -30 | 27 | 0 | 0 | 10 | na | -7 | 43 | na |
| | 1985-87 | 171 | na | na | 17 | 30 | 1 | 0 | 7 | na | na | 48 | na |
| Thailand | 1977-80 | 1 | -28 | 13 | 2 | 5 | 0 | 0 | 1 | 0 | 14 | 2 | -0 |
| | 1981-84 | 16 | -9 | 13 | 0 | 7 | -0 | na | na | 0 | 8 | 3 | 0 |
| | 1985-87 | 153 | na | 32 | 1 | 4 | 0 | na | 19 | 0 | 14 | na | 1 |

na = Not available or not disclosed.
a Refers to wholesale trade only for 1982-1987; wholesale and retail trade for 1977-1981.
b Includes developing Pacific island countries.

Sources: United States, Department of Commerce, Bureau of Economic Analysis (1985b, various years b).

percent of total U.S. DFI income from affiliates in this sector worldwide in 1977–1980, to 39 percent in 1981–1984, and fell back to 24 percent in 1985–1987 as a result of the recession in the Asian electric and electronic equipment sector. U.S. DFI income from the Asian chemicals industry, though rather small relative to U.S. DFI income in this sector worldwide, was also significant in terms of U.S. DFI income from Asia and grew rapidly in 1985–1987 after stagnating in 1977–1984; this income was more evenly distributed than in other industries with Taiwan, the Philippines, and Hong Kong generating the largest amounts.

Thus U.S. DFI in Asia is relatively minor in most respects, especially in manufacturing. Consequently, U.S. DFI in Asia may have little effect on structural adjustment in U.S. manufacturing industry overall. Yet in electric and electronic equipment, which is one of the United States' fastest growing industries, DFI in Asia has been an important force both from the Asian and U.S. perspectives. U.S. DFI in Asia in chemicals and nonelectric machinery are also important, though more modest.

## U.S. Multinational Activity and Changes in the Structure of Total U.S. Manufacturing Exports

One fact that is not brought out from the preceding analysis is the importance of U.S. multinational parents to the U.S. economy. Comparisons between exports of nonbank U.S. parents of nonbank affiliates (hereafter referred to simply as parents) and total U.S. exports by industry indicate that in many industries, multinationals literally dominate U.S. international trade (Table 8.4). In all industries, U.S. parents accounted for 79 percent of U.S. merchandise exports in 1977 with the share declining to 75 percent in 1982. For manufacturing as a whole, the shares were slightly smaller but remained large at 72 percent in 1977 and 68 percent in 1982.[3] The growth of parent exports slowed considerably in 1982–1986, but because total exports grew even more slowly, the share of parent exports in total industry and in manufacturing increased between 1982 and 1986.[4]

Among the major industry categories, parent shares varied from 37–38 percent in food to over 90 percent for electric and electronic equipment and transportation equipment in 1977 and 1982. More detailed examination reveals ratios over 90 percent in a large number of individual industries including drugs, soaps and cleansers, ferrous and nonferrous primary metals, construction and mining machinery, office and computing machinery, household appliances, radio and television, other electrical machinery, other transportation equipment, tobacco, rubber, and stone. Industries with exceedingly low ratios (under 35 percent) were other food and kindred products, other nonelectric machinery, textiles and apparel, printing and publishing, plastics, and leather and miscellaneous manufactures.

Activity in U.S. affiliates abroad has a direct bearing on U.S. parent exports precisely because those affiliates are an important destination of such exports (Table 8.5). In the aggregate, the share of parent exports going to their affiliates was 34 percent in 1977 and 31 percent in 1982; in manufacturing, the corresponding shares were 41 percent and 39 percent, respectively. More recent data show a large increase in these ratios in 1986 to 38 percent in all industries and 47 percent in manufactur-

## Table 8.4 Exports of Nonbank U.S. Parents, 1977-1986

| | 1977 | | 1982 | | 1986 |
|---|---|---|---|---|---|
| Industry | US$ Millions | As a Share of U.S. Exports | US$ Millions | As a Share of U.S. Exports | US$ Millions |
| All industries | 92,378 | 79.0 | 153,792 | 75.4 | 161,296 |
| Manufacturing | 65,877 | 72.7 | 105,967 | 68.3 | 122,182 |
| Food & kindred products | 2,683 | 38.3 | 3,884 | 36.7 | 7,675 |
| Grain mill & bakery products | 1,127 | 84.8 | 1,064 | 47.0 | 2,001 |
| Beverages | 162 | 132.7 | 142 | 69.0 | 1,732 |
| Other food & kindred products | 1,393 | 25.1 | 2,679 | 33.0 | 3,942 |
| Chemicals & allied products | 9,130 | 80.5 | 16,065 | 76.8 | 17,247 |
| Industrial chemicals & synthetics | 6,014 | 80.2 | 10,157 | 78.3 | 10,689 |
| Drugs | 1,406 | 130.4 | 2,554 | 107.3 | 3,705 |
| Soaps, cleansers, & toilet goods | 581 | 173.0 | 1,170 | 178.7 | 1,020 |
| Agricultural chemicals | 550 | 55.5 | 1,051 | 47.3 | 763 |
| Other chemicals & products | 580 | 40.4 | 1,132 | 42.1 | 1,070 |
| Primary & fabricated metals | 4,271 | 78.8 | 7,119 | 72.8 | 3,998 |
| Primary metal industries | 2,780 | 92.3 | 4,354 | 86.9 | 2,626 |
| Ferrous primary metals | 1,306 | 94.0 | 1,617 | 90.0 | 1,074 |
| Nonferrous primary metals | 1,474 | 90.9 | 2,737 | 85.2 | 1,552 |
| Fabricated metal products | 1,493 | 61.9 | 2,765 | 57.9 | 1,371 |
| Machinery, except electrical | 12,446 | 64.1 | 19,378 | 52.2 | 19,372 |
| Farm & garden machinery | na | na | 1,019 | 42.6 | na |
| Construction, mining, etc. | 4,347 | 96.6 | 6,084 | 69.3 | 4,160 |
| Office & computing machinery | 3,302 | 90.2 | 7,502 | 76.2 | na |
| Other machinery | na | na | 4,775 | 29.6 | 3,929 |
| Electric and electronic equipment | 7,701 | 81.7 | 16,234 | 93.8 | 18,289 |
| Household appliances | 644 | 93.6 | 512 | 56.4 | 593 |
| Radio, television, communication | 1,779 | 74.6 | 5,003 | 128.4 | 10,058 |
| Electric components, accessories | 1,438 | 71.0 | 3,605 | 72.8 | 3,899 |
| Other electrical machinery | 3,839 | 88.8 | 7,115 | 94.1 | 3,740 |
| Transportation equipment | 19,640 | 94.2 | 28,438 | 95.2 | 42,765 |
| Motor vehicles & equipment | 11,947 | 81.5 | 14,866 | 82.5 | 24,379 |
| Other transportation equipment | 7,694 | 124.3 | 13,572 | 114.4 | 18,387 |
| Other manufacturing | 10,005 | 58.5 | 14,849 | 50.3 | 12,836 |
| Tobacco manufactures | na | na | 2,129 | 164.2 | 698 |
| Textile products & apparel | 645 | 25.1 | 601 | 16.2 | 550 |
| Lumber, wood, furniture, etc. | 1,064 | 44.9 | 1,416 | 43.0 | 1,302 |
| Paper & allied products | 1,429 | 56.4 | 2,125 | 48.6 | 1,905 |
| Printing & publishing | 281 | 40.0 | 380 | 25.0 | 376 |
| Rubber products | 953 | 153.7 | 1,076 | 102.2 | 855 |
| Miscellaneous plastic products | 140 | 31.8 | 113 | 17.3 | 440 |
| Glass products | 330 | 64.4 | 471 | 56.2 | 406 |

**Table 8.4** (continued)

|  | 1977 | | 1982 | | 1986 |
| --- | --- | --- | --- | --- | --- |
| | | As a Share | | As a Share | |
| | US$ | of U.S. | US$ | of U.S. | US$ |
| Industry | Millions | Exports | Millions | Exports | Millions |
| Stone, clay, etc. | 417 | 93.6 | 543 | 68.5 | 383 |
| Instruments & related products | 3,061 | 68.2 | 5,492 | 59.8 | 5,173 |
| ·Leather & miscellaneous manuf. | na | na | 505 | 17.8 | 749 |

na = Not available or not disclosed.

Sources: United Nations (n.d.); United States, Department of Commerce, Bureau of Economic Analysis (1981, 1985a, various years a).

ing. Among the individual industries, the motor vehicle industry is the largest source of intrafirm exports; intrafirm exports in this industry accounted for 32 percent of total intrafirm manufacturing exports in 1977, 27 percent in 1982, and 37 percent in 1986. Office and computing machinery was the second largest source of intrafirm exports with corresponding shares of 10 percent, 15 percent, and 16 percent, respectively. Parent exports to their affiliates as a share of the parent's exports have always been over 70 percent and have been rising in both industries. By 1986, parent-to-affiliate exports in these two industries represented over one-half of all intrafirm exports in manufacturing, over one-fourth of U.S. manufacturing parent exports, and 17 percent of all U.S. manufacturing exports.[5] Relative to either total intrafirm exports or parent exports, intrafirm exports are also large in industries such as drugs, industrial chemicals, soaps and cleansers, construction and mining machinery, radio and television, electric components, and instruments. On the other hand, intrafirm exports are not large in food, agricultural chemicals, other chemicals, metals, other machinery, household appliances, other electric machinery, and most of the individual industries listed under other manufacturing.

With the exception of electric and electronic equipment, the absence of large DFI in Asian industries where intrafirm trade predominates is striking. Moreover, although the share of U.S. manufacturing exports destined for the ASIA-8 grew significantly from 8 percent in 1977 to 12 percent in 1982 (United Nations, n.d.), the NICs and the ASEAN-4 economies are still relatively small markets for U.S. exports. These two factors combined indicate that the direct trade between affiliates in Asia and U.S. parents is of small consequence for U.S. parent exports as a whole. Nonetheless it is possible that expansion of Asian affiliates led to indirect benefits by facilitating improvements in U.S. parent productivity and thereby indirectly stimulating the parent's exports.

Table 8.5  Exports of Nonbank U.S. Parents to Their Nonbank
Affiliates Worldwide, 1977-1986

| Industry | 1977 US$ Millions | 1977 As a Share of Exports of Nonbank Parents (%) | 1982 US$ Millions | 1982 As a Share of Exports of Nonbank Parents (%) | 1986 US$ Millions | 1986 As a Share of Exports of Nonbank Parents (%) |
|---|---|---|---|---|---|---|
| All industries | 31,319 | 33.9 | 47,126 | 30.6 | 61,607 | 38.2 |
| Manufacturing | 26,683 | 40.5 | 40,857 | 38.6 | 57,190 | 46.8 |
| Food & kindred products | 528 | 19.7 | 756 | 19.5 | 1,022 | 13.3 |
| Grain mill & bakery products | 138 | 12.2 | 131 | 12.3 | 557 | 27.8 |
| Beverages | 42 | 25.9 | 51 | 35.9 | 215 | 12.4 |
| Other food & kindred products | 347 | 24.9 | 575 | 21.5 | 250 | 6.3 |
| Chemicals & allied products | 4,067 | 44.5 | 6,079 | 37.8 | 7,832 | 45.4 |
| Industrial chemicals & synthetics | 2,373 | 39.5 | 3,147 | 31.0 | 4,331 | 40.5 |
| Drugs | 1,048 | 74.5 | 1,777 | 69.6 | 2,501 | 67.5 |
| Soaps, cleansers, & toilet goods | 328 | 56.5 | 671 | 57.4 | 580 | 56.9 |
| Agricultural chemicals | 123 | 22.4 | 118 | 11.2 | 95 | 12.5 |
| Other chemicals & products | 196 | 33.8 | 366 | 32.3 | 326 | 30.5 |
| Primary & fabricated metals | 1,070 | 25.1 | 1,279 | 18.0 | 1,034 | 25.9 |
| Primary metal industries | 636 | 22.9 | 612 | 14.1 | 571 | 21.7 |
| Ferrous primary metals | 219 | 16.8 | 133 | 8.2 | 47 | 4.4 |
| Nonferrous primary metals | 417 | 28.3 | 479 | 17.5 | 524 | 33.8 |
| Fabricated metal products | 435 | 29.1 | 667 | 24.1 | 463 | 33.8 |
| Machinery, except electrical | 5,268 | 42.3 | 9,863 | 50.9 | 13,404 | 69.2 |
| Farm & garden machinery | na | na | 606 | 59.5 | 662 | na |
| Construction, mining, etc. | 1,032 | 23.7 | 1,620 | 26.6 | 1,974 | 47.5 |
| Office & computing machinery | 2,674 | 81.0 | 6,297 | 83.9 | 9,341 | na |
| Other machinery | na | na | 1,341 | 28.1 | 1,427 | 36.3 |
| Electric and electronic equipment | 2,625 | 34.1 | 5,208 | 32.1 | 6,616 | 36.2 |
| Household appliances | 208 | 32.3 | 127 | 24.8 | 132 | 22.3 |
| Radio, television, communication | 719 | 40.4 | 2,259 | 45.2 | 3,420 | 34.0 |
| Electric components, accessories | 915 | 63.6 | 1,702 | 47.2 | 2,293 | 58.8 |
| Other electrical machinery | 783 | 20.4 | 1,121 | 15.8 | 771 | 20.6 |
| Transportation equipment | 9,166 | 46.7 | 12,105 | 42.6 | 22,169 | 51.8 |
| Motor vehicles & equipment | 8,634 | 72.3 | 11,225 | 75.5 | 21,280 | 87.3 |
| Other transportation equipment | 533 | 6.9 | 880 | 6.5 | 889 | 4.8 |
| Other manufacturing | 3,959 | 39.6 | 5,567 | 37.5 | 5,113 | 39.8 |
| Tobacco manufactures | na | na | 207 | 9.7 | 4 | 0.6 |
| Textile products & apparel | 186 | 28.8 | 144 | 24.0 | 126 | 22.9 |
| Lumber, wood, furniture, etc. | 85 | 8.0 | 98 | 6.9 | 127 | 9.8 |
| Paper & allied products | 559 | 39.1 | 294 | 13.8 | 294 | 15.4 |
| Printing & publishing | 123 | 43.8 | 127 | 33.4 | 142 | 37.8 |

## Table 8.5 (continued)

| Industry | 1977 | | 1982 | | 1986 | |
|---|---|---|---|---|---|---|
| | US$ Millions | As a Share of Exports of Nonbank Parents (%) | US$ Millions | As a Share of Exports of Nonbank Parents (%) | US$ Millions | As a Share of Exports of Nonbank Parents (%) |
| Rubber products | 384 | 40.3 | 486 | 45.2 | 440 | 51.5 |
| Miscellaneous plastic products | 43 | 30.7 | 33 | 29.2 | 173 | 39.3 |
| Glass products | 80 | 24.2 | 152 | 32.3 | 107 | 26.4 |
| Stone, clay, etc. | 121 | 29.0 | 204 | 37.6 | 179 | 46.7 |
| Instruments & related products | 1,977 | 64.6 | 3,623 | 66.0 | 3,345 | 64.7 |
| Leather & miscellaneous manuf. | na | na | 200 | 39.6 | 175 | 23.4 |

na = Not available or not disclosed.

Sources: United States, Department of Commerce, Bureau of Economic Analysis (1981, 1985a, various years a).

In order to estimate the total effect of U.S. affiliate activity on parent exports, the growth in parent exports in industry $j$ from 1977 to 1982 is estimated as a function of the growth of total U.S. exports in industry $j$ and the change in the ratio of affiliate value added to parent value added in industry $j$ using cross-section data for thirty-two industries (i.e., $j = 1$–32). To isolate the impact of affiliate activity in the Asian region, the ratio of affiliate value added to parent value added has been disaggregated by region to see if changes in affiliate-to-parent value added ratios of Asian affiliates impart different effects than changes in affiliate-to-parent value added ratios of affiliates in other regions. The intuition behind this approach is that deviations from the linear relationship between the growth of parent exports and the growth of total industry exports is due to changes in the portion of multinational production undertaken by affiliates.[6] The primary difficulty with the approach is that, as discussed earlier, parents account for a large portion of exports in a number of industries. Consequently, coefficients on foreign affiliate value added variables will tend to be insignificant if there is great similarity between the variation of parent export changes and the variation of total export changes across industries. However, as seen above, the variation in parent shares of total exports is substantial across industries, so it is believed that this problem is not severe.

Equations (1c)–(1d) in Table 8.6 indicate that changes in the shares of Asian affiliate value added to parent value added are not statistically significant determinants of parent export growth, even at the 0.10 level of significance. Indeed, in equations (1b)–(1d), none of the developing economy variables are significant, though increases

Table 8.6  The Effect of Increased Affiliate Production on Growth of Exports of Nonbank Parents to the World, 1977-1982:  Ordinary Least Squares Estimates

(1a)  $XP_{82}/XP_{77} = 0.242621 + 0.704352(XT_{82}/XT_{77}) - 1.133169(YAW_{82}-YAWP_{77})$
$(0.67)$ $(3.49)^{***}$ $(2.76)^{***}$

Adjusted $R^2 = 0.45677$  Sum of squared residuals $= 4.00032$  $F = 14.0^{***}$

(1b)  $XP_{82}/XP_{77} = 0.198965 + 0.723782(XT_{82}/XT_{77}) - 1.370150(YAMP_{82}-YAMP_{77})$
$(0.53)$ $(3.47)^{***}$ $(2.15)^{**}$

$- 0.396503(YALP_{82}-YALP_{77})$
$(0.26)$

Adjusted $R^2 = 0.44220$  Sum of squared residuals $= 3.96602$  $F = 9.19^{***}$

(1c)  $XP_{82}/XP_{77} = 0.224040 + 0.705966(XT_{82}/XT_{77}) - 1.359677(YAMP_{82}-YAMP_{77})$
$(0.58)$ $(3.29)^{***}$ $(2.11)^{**}$

$- 4.382432(YAAP_{82}) - 0.192882(YAOP_{82}-YAOP_{77})$
$(0.52)$ $(0.12)$

Adjusted $R^2 = 0.42640$  Sum of squared residuals $= 3.93269$  $F = 6.76^{***}$

(1d)  $XP_{82}/XP_{77} = 0.350020 + 0.639156(XT_{82}/XT_{77}) - 1.227680(YAMP_{82}-YAMP_{77})$
$(0.90)$ $(2.99)^{***}$ $(1.93)^{*}$

$- 5.644354(YAMP_{82}-YAMP_{77}) + 25.72761(YASP_{82}-YASP_{77})$
$(0.68)$ $(1.21)$

$- 0.259148(YAO_{82}-YAOP_{77})$
$(0.16)$

Adjusted $R^2 = 0.45349$  Sum of squared residuals $= 3.60815$  $F = 6.14^{***}$

Variable definitions:

| | |
|---|---|
| $XP_t$ | = Exports of U.S. parents in year $t$ |
| $XT_t$ | = Exports of all U.S. firms in year $t$ |
| $YAAP_t$ | = Ratio of value added of U.S. affiliates in the ASIA-8 to value added of U.S. parents in year $t$ |
| $YALP_t$ | = Ratio of value added of U.S. affiliates in developing countries to value added of U.S. parents in year $t$ |
| $YAMP_t$ | = Ratio of value added of U.S. affiliates in developed countries to value added of U.S. parents in year $t$ |
| $YANP_t$ | = Ratio of value added of U.S. affiliates in the NICs to value added of U.S. parents in year $t$ |
| $YAOP_t$ | = Ratio of value added of U.S. affiliates in developing countries other than the ASIA-8 to value added of U.S. parents in year $t$ |
| $YASP_t$ | = Ratio of value added of U.S. affiliates in the ASEAN-4 to value added in U.S. parents in year $t$ |
| $YAWP_t$ | = Ratio of value added of all U.S. affiliates in worldwide to value added of U.S. parents in year $t$ |
| $^{*}, ^{**}, ^{***}$ | = Significant at 0.10, 0.05, and 0.01 levels, respectively (t-tests are two-tailed; absolute t-values are in parentheses) |

Source:  United States, Department of Commerce, Bureau of Economic Analysis (1989).

in the developed country affiliate-to-parent value added ratio has a negative and statistically significant effect on the growth of parent exports. Rigorous F-tests of null hypotheses that the affiliate activity in all regions has the same effect cannot be rejected at the 0.10 level or better. Thus, equation (1a) is the most appropriate equation to base the analysis upon.

According to equation (1a), a 1 point increase in the change of the affiliate-to-parent value added ratio in any region decreases the growth of parent exports by 1.1 points. Although the elasticity of parent export growth to the change in the affiliate-to-parent value added ratio is quite low in absolute value, -0.127 at the means, the finding of a negative and statistically significant relationship between foreign affiliate activity and parent exports is in marked contrast to the findings of previous static analyses where non-negative relationships were the rule (Lipsey and Weiss 1981, 1984; Blomström et al. 1988). These differences are not necessarily contradictory as it is entirely possible that greater affiliate production may lead to greater parent exports at a given point in time while, over time, an increased level of affiliate production relative to parent production may lead to a lower rate of growth in parent exports. Nonetheless, to check the robustness of these results, it would be very helpful to have similar equations re-estimated using firm-level, cross-section data that are grouped by industry.[7]

## U.S. Multinational Activity and Changes in the Structure of U.S. Exports to Developing Asia

Because it is reasonable to expect that affiliate activity would have a larger impact on bilateral trade than on multilateral trade, this section looks at the bilateral trade relationship between the United States and Asia. Examination of U.S. parent exports to the ASIA-8 reveals that the ratio of U.S. parent exports to total U.S. exports destined for the NICs and ASEAN-4 is smaller than the ratio of U.S. parent exports to U.S. exports to the world (Table 8.7). Nonetheless, parents do account for the majority of exports to these two country groups both in all industries and in manufacturing. Parents have accounted for over 85 percent of U.S. exports to the NICs in a wide range of industries including drugs, primary metals, farm and garden machinery, household appliances, radio and television, and transportation equipment in 1977 and/or 1982. For parent exports to the ASEAN-4, similarly high ratios have been observed in beverages, soaps and cleansers, primary ferrous metals, office and computing machinery, household appliances, radio and television, electric components, other transportation equipment, and lumber. Industries with low parent shares of exports (under 25 percent) in either of the two years were other food, other nonelectric machinery, textiles and apparel, lumber, paper, plastics, and stone for the NICs, and grain mill and bakery products, fabricated metals, farm and garden machinery, other machinery, household appliances, motor vehicles, textiles and apparel, paper, plastics, and stone for the ASEAN-4.

Moreover there are wide fluctuations in a number of ratios. For example, the ratio varied widely in household appliances and electric components, especially in the ASEAN-4. One explanation for these fluctuations is undoubtably the mismatch between the data on trade and the data obtained from the DFI surveys. The problem is especially severe in the ASEAN-4 data where several ratios exceed 100 percent by a large margin. Another reason for the wide fluctuations is that the effects of new exports are magnified because of the small scale of parent exports to Asia.

In industries such as electric components, new exports through intrafirm trade are directly related to the rapid growth of DFI in these regions (Table 8.8). In the case of parent-to-affiliate trade, the differences between activity in the NICs and in the ASEAN-4 are quite conspicuous. First, in manufacturing overall, the affiliate share of parent exports was 32 percent in both 1977 and 1982 for the NICs, but increased from 30 percent to 45 percent in the ASEAN-4. Second, the increase in the affiliate share in ASEAN-4 was primarily due to a more than fivefold increase in intrafirm exports in radio and television and electric components, two industries in which the affiliate share of parent exports exceeded 85 percent in both years. Third, the significance of these two industries differed over time in the NICs and ASEAN-4 although both industries accounted for large shares of intrafirm exports of manufactures in the two country groups. The ratio of intrafirm electric component exports to intrafirm manufacturing exports decreased from 36 percent to 9 percent in the NICs but increased from 39 percent to 50 percent in the ASEAN-4; corresponding ratios for radio and television grew much more rapidly in the NICs, rising from 8 percent to 22 percent, than in the ASEAN-4 for which the ratio increased from 20 percent to 26 percent. In addition, affiliate shares of total parent exports to the NICs declined substantially in electric components and increased markedly in radio and television; in the ASEAN-4, these shares remained relatively high in both industries for both years. Fourth, no individual industry other than radio and television and electric components, accounted for more than 10 percent of intrafirm exports of manufactures to the ASEAN-4; in the NICs, this threshold was also exceeded by industrial chemicals for 1977 and office and computing equipment for 1982. Although intrafirm exports of office and computing machinery to the ASEAN-4 increased over tenfold between 1977 and 1982, this industry's share of all intrafirm manufactured exports remained relatively small, rising from 2 percent in 1977 to 4 percent in 1982.

There are a large number of industries in which affiliate shares of parent exports are very low. In the NICs, single-digit affiliate shares are observed in all food industries, ferrous primary metals, farm and garden machinery, household appliances, other electrical machinery, other transportation equipment, textiles and apparel, lumber, paper, plastics, and stone. In the ASEAN-4, the corresponding list includes grain mill and bakery products, primary metals, farm and garden machinery, construction machinery, other nonelectric machinery, household appliances, other electrical machinery, other transportation equipment, textiles and apparel, lumber, plastics, glass, and stone. In contrast, in a few individual industries, exports to affiliates accounted for more than one-half of parent exports. For the NICs, these industries were drugs, soaps and cleansers, rubber, glass, and instruments, and for the ASEAN-4 these industries include beverages, drugs, soaps and cleansers, nonferrous primary metals, office and computing machinery, printing and publishing, and rubber products.

In short, the clearest direct link between U.S. exports and U.S. affiliates in the NICs and ASEAN-4 is in office and computing equipment, radio and television,

Table 8.7 Exports of Nonbank U.S. Parents to the NICs and ASEAN-4, 1977 and 1982

| Industry | NICs 1977 Parent Exports (US$ millions) | NICs 1977 As a Share of Total U.S. Exports to the NICs | NICs 1982 Parent Exports (US$ millions) | NICs 1982 As a Share of Total U.S. Exports to the NICs | ASEAN-4 1977 Parent Exports (US$ millions) | ASEAN-4 1977 As a Share of Total U.S. Exports to ASEAN-4 | ASEAN-4 1982 Parent Exports (US$ millions) | ASEAN-4 1982 As a Share of Total U.S. Exports to ASEAN-4 |
|---|---|---|---|---|---|---|---|---|
| All industries | 4,223 | 60.0 | 9,493 | 56.9 | 1,832 | 65.7 | 4,576 | 60.2 |
| Manufacturing | 2,755 | 58.6 | 6,250 | 50.7 | 1,269 | 59.7 | 3,290 | 55.8 |
| Food & kindred products | 138 | 37.0 | 228 | 29.1 | 24 | 15.3 | 49 | 32.4 |
| Grain mill & bakery products | na | na | 66 | 55.9 | na | na | 4 | 19.6 |
| Beverages | na | na | 11 | 72.5 | na | na | 4 | 89.7 |
| Other food & kindred products | na | na | 150 | 23.1 | na | na | 40 | 31.7 |
| Chemicals & allied products | 402 | 70.2 | 1,067 | 58.8 | 220 | 53.9 | 433 | 42.1 |
| Industrial chemicals & synthetics | 283 | 76.0 | 770 | 57.5 | 151 | 77.8 | 300 | 45.9 |
| Drugs | 39 | 78.2 | 91 | 122.0 | 28 | 74.5 | 41 | 58.0 |
| Soaps, cleansers, & toilet goods | 17 | 58.0 | 41 | 59.0 | 12 | 102.5 | 38 | 171.2 |
| Agricultural chemicals | na | na | na | na | na | na | na | na |
| Other chemicals & products | na | na | na | na | na | na | na | na |
| Primary & fabricated metals | 126 | 69.6 | 498 | 50.7 | 90 | 42.3 | 148 | 28.3 |
| Primary metal industries | 98 | 93.1 | 274 | 91.1 | 62 | 78.2 | 88 | 44.1 |
| Ferrous primary metals | 56 | 132.5 | 99 | 74.6 | 49 | 97.8 | 36 | 28.1 |
| Nonferrous primary metals | 42 | 66.7 | 175 | 104.1 | 13 | 44.5 | 51 | 71.4 |
| Fabricated metal products | 27 | 35.7 | 224 | 32.8 | 28 | 21.0 | 59 | 18.2 |

| | | | | | | | | |
|---|---|---|---|---|---|---|---|---|
| Machinery, except electrical | 360 | 43.9 | 1,054 | 39.4 | 134 | 25.3 | 350 | 24.1 |
| Farm & garden machinery | 6 | 172.1 | 9 | 62.8 | 6 | 24.3 | 5 | 32.2 |
| Construction, mining, etc. | 146 | 73.4 | 425 | 70.6 | 49 | 27.5 | 183 | 38.7 |
| Office & computing machinery | 74 | 74.0 | 390 | 60.9 | 10 | 34.9 | 75 | 96.2 |
| Other machinery | 134 | 25.9 | 231 | 16.3 | 70 | 23.5 | 88 | 9.9 |
| Electric and electronic equipment | 885 | 67.1 | 1,603 | 61.5 | 375 | 113.1 | 1,501 | 100.5 |
| Household appliances | 34 | 166.5 | 20 | 36.7 | 1 | 12.9 | 9 | 110.3 |
| Radio, television, communication | 119 | 97.6 | 556 | 105.1 | 89 | 164.9 | 452 | 470.7 |
| Electric components, accessories | 378 | 64.8 | 423 | 34.1 | 151 | 487.5 | 788 | 83.2 |
| Other electrical machinery | 354 | 59.6 | 604 | 77.1 | 134 | 56.1 | 253 | 57.3 |
| Transportation equipment | 605 | 108.7 | 1,138 | 91.1 | 319 | 138.7 | 517 | 77.6 |
| Motor vehicles & equipment | na | na | 283 | 102.3 | na | na | 51 | 23.4 |
| Other transportation equipment | na | na | 855 | 87.9 | na | na | 466 | 104.0 |
| Other manufacturing | 240 | 27.2 | 662 | 29.9 | 107 | 41.9 | 292 | 50.0 |
| Tobacco manufactures | na | na | na | na | na | na | na | na |
| Textile products & apparel | 13 | 17.7 | 22 | 12.9 | 3 | 15.6 | 3 | 7.2 |
| Lumber, wood, furniture, etc. | 8 | 9.1 | 31 | 16.6 | 9 | 235.5 | 21 | 327.9 |
| Paper & allied products | 21 | 15.8 | 74 | 21.0 | 11 | 18.9 | 31 | 20.3 |
| Printing & publishing | 5 | 27.4 | 17 | 35.9 | 7 | 54.2 | 9 | 30.4 |
| Rubber products | 13 | 87.7 | 31 | 53.0 | 13 | 76.8 | 24 | 69.5 |
| Miscellaneous plastic products | 7 | 46.6 | 3 | 6.2 | 3 | 35.9 | 1 | 4.9 |
| Glass products | 11 | 76.5 | 47 | 71.7 | 3 | 42.6 | 9 | 48.1 |
| Stone, clay, etc. | 7 | 49.6 | 11 | 23.8 | 2 | 12.5 | 7 | 37.0 |
| Instruments & related products | 95 | 38.6 | 216 | 33.6 | 31 | 33.9 | 95 | 49.3 |
| Leather & miscellaneous manufactures | na | na | na | na | na | na | na | na |

na = Not available or not disclosed.

Sources: United Nations (n.d.); United States, Department of Commerce, Bureau of Economic Analysis (1989).

Table 8.8 Exports of Nonbank U.S. Parents to Their Nonbank Affiliates in the NICs and ASEAN-4, 1977 and 1982

| Industry | NICs | | | | ASEAN-4 | | | |
|---|---|---|---|---|---|---|---|---|
| | 1977 | | 1982 | | 1977 | | 1982 | |
| | Parent Exports to Affiliates in NICs (US$ millions) | As a Share of Parent Exports to the NICs | Parent Exports to Affiliates in NICs (US$ millions) | As a Share of Parent Exports to the NICs | Parent Exports to Affiliates in ASEAN-4 (US$ millions) | As a Share of Parent Exports to ASEAN-4 | Parent Exports to Affiliates in ASEAN-4 (US$ millions) | As a Share of Parent Exports to ASEAN-4 |
| All industries | 986 | 23.3 | 2,368 | 24.9 | 356 | 19.4 | 1,764 | 38.5 |
| Manufacturing | 890 | 32.3 | 1,978 | 31.6 | 375 | 29.6 | 1,481 | 45.0 |
| Food & kindred products | 4 | 2.9 | 15 | 6.6 | 7 | 29.2 | 17 | 34.7 |
| Grain mill & bakery products | na | na | 0 | 0.0 | na | na | 0 | 0.0 |
| Beverages | na | na | 1 | 9.1 | na | na | 2 | 50.0 |
| Other food & kindred products | | | 13 | 8.7 | | | 14 | 35.0 |
| Chemicals & allied products | 153 | 38.1 | 262 | 24.6 | 64 | 29.1 | 112 | 25.9 |
| Industrial chemicals & synthetics | 103 | 36.4 | 178 | 23.1 | 34 | 22.5 | 66 | 22.0 |
| Drugs | 21 | 53.8 | 48 | 52.7 | 21 | 75.0 | 24 | 58.5 |
| Soaps, cleansers, & toilet goods | 9 | 52.9 | 16 | 39.0 | 9 | 75.0 | 20 | 52.6 |
| Agricultural chemicals | na | na | na | na | na | na | na | na |
| Other chemicals & products | na | na | na | na | na | na | na | na |
| Primary & fabricated metals | 23 | 18.3 | 123 | 24.7 | 12 | 13.3 | 2 | 1.4 |
| Primary metal industries | 18 | 18.4 | 93 | 33.9 | 10 | 16.1 | 1 | 1.1 |
| Ferrous primary metals | 1 | 1.8 | 9 | 9.1 | 2 | 4.1 | 0 | 0.0 |
| Nonferrous primary metals | 17 | 40.5 | 85 | 48.6 | 8 | 61.5 | 1 | 2.0 |
| Fabricated metal products | 5 | 18.5 | 30 | 13.4 | 2 | 7.1 | 0 | 0.0 |

| | | | | | | | |
|---|---|---|---|---|---|---|---|
| Machinery, except electrical | 134 | 37.2 | 536 | 50.9 | 17 | 12.7 | 67 | 19.1 |
| Farm & garden machinery | 0 | 0.0 | 1 | 11.1 | 0 | 0.0 | 0 | 0.0 |
| Construction, mining, etc. | 49 | 33.6 | 170 | 40.0 | 0 | 0.0 | 5 | 2.7 |
| Office & computing machinery | 52 | 70.3 | 320 | 82.1 | 6 | 60.0 | 61 | 81.3 |
| Other machinery | 33 | 24.6 | 46 | 19.9 | 12 | 17.1 | 2 | 2.3 |
| Electric and electronic equipment | 464 | 52.4 | 681 | 42.5 | 230 | 61.3 | 1,173 | 78.1 |
| Household appliances | 2 | 5.9 | 0 | 0.0 | 0 | 0.0 | 0 | 0.0 |
| Radio, television, communication | 71 | 59.7 | 445 | 80.0 | 76 | 85.4 | 399 | 88.3 |
| Electric components, accessories | 322 | 85.2 | 182 | 43.0 | 148 | 98.0 | 755 | 95.8 |
| Other electrical machinery | 69 | 19.5 | 54 | 8.9 | 6 | 4.5 | 20 | 7.9 |
| Transportation equipment | 28 | 4.6 | 162 | 14.2 | 10 | 3.1 | 41 | 7.9 |
| Motor vehicles & equipment | na | na | 109 | 38.5 | na | na | 11 | 21.6 |
| Other transportation equipment | na | na | 52 | 6.1 | na | na | 30 | 6.4 |
| Other manufacturing | 84 | 35.0 | 199 | 30.1 | 35 | 32.7 | 69 | 23.6 |
| Tobacco manufactures | na | na | na | na | na | na | na | na |
| Textile products & apparel | 1 | 7.7 | 7 | 31.8 | 0 | 0.0 | 0 | 0.0 |
| Lumber, wood, furniture, etc. | 0 | 0.0 | 0 | 0.0 | 2 | 22.2 | 2 | 9.5 |
| Paper & allied products | 5 | 23.8 | 0 | 0.0 | 4 | 36.4 | 6 | 19.4 |
| Printing & publishing | 2 | 40.0 | 3 | 17.6 | 4 | 57.1 | 4 | 44.4 |
| Rubber products | 3 | 23.1 | 16 | 51.6 | 8 | 61.5 | 17 | 70.8 |
| Miscellaneous plastic products | 0 | 0.0 | 0 | 0.0 | 1 | 33.3 | 0 | 0.0 |
| Glass products | 3 | 27.3 | 27 | 57.4 | 0 | 0.0 | 1 | 11.1 |
| Stone, clay, etc. | 1 | 14.3 | 1 | 9.1 | 0 | 0.0 | 0 | 0.0 |
| Instruments & related products | 47 | 49.5 | 97 | 44.9 | 15 | 48.4 | 20 | 21.1 |
| Leather & miscellaneous manufactures | na | na | na | na | na | na | na | na |

na = Not available or not disclosed.

Sources: United States, Department of Commerce, Bureau of Economic Analysis (1989).

and electric components. These industries are those in which U.S. firms export components manufactured in the United States to their NIC and ASEAN-4 affiliates for assembly; the finished product is then re-exported back to the United States under sections 806 and 807 of the U.S. tariff code. These sections of the tariff code stipulate that re-imports of products that have been processed or assembled abroad using U.S. components are to be taxed only on the foreign value added embodied in the product and not on the total market value.

The large scale of U.S. DFI activity is also reflected in data on sales by majority-owned nonbank affiliates of nonbank parents (hereafter referred to as majority-owned affiliates). For example, in the NICs in 1977, 1982, and 1986, and in the ASEAN-4 in 1986, export sales to the United States by majority-owned electric and electronic machinery affiliates alone accounted for 69–76 percent of total sales by majority-owned electric and electronic machinery affiliates and 37–44 percent of total sales by all majority-owned manufacturing affiliates. For majority-owned non-electric machinery affiliates in the NICs in 1986, corresponding shares were 55 percent and 10 percent, respectively (United States, Department of Commerce, Bureau of Economic Analysis 1981, 282–83 and 321; 1985a, 217–18 and 228; various years a, Tables 29–30 and 37).

Although detailed industry breakdowns of majority-owned affiliate sales are not published separately for the ASEAN-4 and NICs, published data indicate that sales of U.S. majority-owned affiliates in developing Asia accounted for a substantial share of sales of U.S. majority-owned affiliates worldwide in electric components (36 percent in 1977, 46 percent in 1982, and 35 percent in 1986), and in radio and television (9 percent and 23 percent in 1982 and 1986, respectively). For office equipment and machinery, the sales share of U.S. majority-owned affiliates in Asia was lower at 2 percent in 1986. Nonetheless, because sales of these industries are concentrated in the ASIA-8 affiliates,[8] and because the combined shares of these three individual industries in parent exports to these regions were large (40–45 percent in the NICs and 65–69 percent in the ASEAN-4 in 1977 and 1982; cf. Table 8.7 and sources), it is clear that U.S. DFI activity in Asian affiliates has large implications for U.S. trade with these Asian countries.

In order to investigate the overall impact of changes in affiliate production on U.S. exports to the NICs and the ASEAN-4, bilateral export models that are similar to the multilateral model employed earlier have been estimated (Table 8.9, equations (2a)–(2d) and (3a)–(3d)). Interestingly, the results indicate that the rapid growth of parent exports to the NICs and the ASEAN-4 has not been significantly affected by affiliate activity in the region. Another striking result is the total lack of any significant correlation between changes in affiliate-to-parent value added ratios in any region worldwide and the growth of parent exports to the NICs. In other words, once the factors accounting for growth of all U.S. exports are included, changes in affiliate production relative to parent production had no effect on parent exports to the NICs. This result indicates that the strong relationships between parents and NICs affiliates in office and computing machinery, radio and television, and electric components were exceptions to the rule in the thirty-two industry cross-section data set.

On the other hand, the calculations indicate that increases in NIC affiliate-to-parent value added ratios stimulate the growth of exports to the ASEAN-4 a great

Table 8.9   The Effect of Increased Affiliate Production on Growth of Exports from Nonbank U.S. Parents to the NICs and ASEAN-4, 1977 and 1982:   Ordinary Least Squares Estimates

Exports to the NICs

(2a)   $XPN_{82}/XPN_{77}$ = 0.593247 + 0.692196$(XTN_{82}/XTN_{77})$
           (1.24)        (4.95)***

              - 0.511113$(YAWP_{82}\text{-}YAWP_{77})$
              (0.42)

       Adjusted $R^2$ = 0.43455   Sum of squared residuals = 38.61643   $F$ = 12.9***

(2b)   $XPN_{82}/XPN_{77}$ = 0.584774 + 0.686906$(XTN_{82}/XTN_{77})$
           (1.20)        (4.82)***

              - 1.186705$(YAMP_{82}\text{-}YAMP_{77})$
              (0.59)

              + 1.429938$(YALP_{82}\text{-}YALP_{77})$
              (0.31)

       Adjusted $R^2$ = 0.41823   Sum of squared residuals = 38.36140   $F$ = 9.19***

(2c)   $XPN_{82}/XPN_{77}$ = 0.628551 + 0.677736$(XTN_{82}/XTN_{77})$
           (1.24)        (4.61)***

              - 1.237698$(YAMP_{82}\text{-}YAMP_{77})$
              (0.61)

              + 10.58699$(YAAP_{82}\text{-}YAAP_{77})$ + 0.891349$(YAOP_{82}\text{-}YAOP_{77})$
              (0.40)                        (0.18)

       Adjusted $R^2$ = 0.39949   Sum of squared residuals = 38.18304   $F$ = 6.16***

(2d)   $XPN_{82}/XPN_{77}$ = 0.548281 + 0.697041$(XTN_{82}/XTN_{77})$
           (1.01)        (4.80)***

              - 1.583692$(YAMP_{82}\text{-}YAMP_{77})$
              (0.78)

              + 11.87641$(YANP_{82}\text{-}YANP_{77})$ - 75.56593$(YASP_{82}\text{-}YASP_{77})$
              (0.46)                       (1.12)

              - 0.796956$(YAOP_{82}\text{-}YAOP_{77})$
              (0.16)

       Adjusted $R^2$ = 0.41896   Sum of squared residuals = 35.57633   $F$ = 5.47***

## Table 8.9 (continued)

Exports to the ASEAN-4

(3a) $XPS_{82}/XPS_{77} - XTS_{82}/XTS_{77} = -0.491024 - 2.323211(YAMP_{82}-YAMP_{77})$
$\qquad\qquad\qquad\qquad\qquad\quad (0.55) \qquad (0.44)$

Adjusted $R^2 = -0.02670$   Sum of squared residuals $= 751.02447$   $F = 0.19$

(3b) $XPS_{82}/XPS_{77} - XTS_{82}/XTS_{77} = -0.770325 - 5.201396(YAMP_{82}-YAMP_{77})$
$\qquad\qquad\qquad\qquad\qquad\quad (0.17) \qquad (0.62)$

$\qquad\qquad\qquad\qquad\quad + 24.24542(YALP_{82}-YALP_{77})$
$\qquad\qquad\qquad\qquad\qquad (1.22)$

Adjusted $R^2 = -0.01608$   Sum of squared residuals $= 718.48501$   $F = 0.75$

(3c) $XPS_{82}/XPS_{77} - XTS_{82}/XTS_{77} = 0.080435 - 6.839622(YAMP_{82}-YAMP_{77})$
$\qquad\qquad\qquad\qquad\qquad\quad (0.17) \qquad (1.59)$

$\qquad\qquad\qquad\qquad\quad + 517.7254(YAAP_{82}-YAAP_{77})$
$\qquad\qquad\qquad\qquad\qquad (9.35)^{***}$

$\qquad\qquad\qquad\qquad\quad - 5.519306(YAOP_{82}-YAOP_{77})$
$\qquad\qquad\qquad\qquad\qquad (0.52)$

Adjusted $R^2 = 0.73269$ Sum of squared residuals $= 182.50116$   $F = 29.3^{***}$

(3d) $XPS_{82}/XPS_{77} - XTS_{82}/XTS_{77} = -0.025604 - 8.886937(YAMP_{82}-YAMP_{77})$
$\qquad\qquad\qquad\qquad\qquad\quad (0.07) \qquad (2.57)^{**}$

$\qquad\qquad\qquad\qquad\quad + 527.7167(YANP_{82}-YANP_{77})$
$\qquad\qquad\qquad\qquad\qquad (12.0)^{***}$

$\qquad\qquad\qquad\qquad\quad + 70.34125(YASP_{82}-YASP_{77})$
$\qquad\qquad\qquad\qquad\qquad (0.61)$

$\qquad\qquad\qquad\qquad\quad - 6.057714(YAOP_{82}-YAOP_{77})$
$\qquad\qquad\qquad\qquad\qquad (0.72)$

Adjusted $R^2 = 0.83213$   Sum of squared residuals $= 110.5173$   $F = 39.4^{***}$

Variable definitions:

| | | |
|---|---|---|
| $XPN_t$ | = | Exports of U.S. parents to the NICs in year $t$ |
| $XPS_t$ | = | Exports of U.S. parents to the ASEAN-4 in year $t$ |
| $XTN_t$ | = | Exports of all U.S. firms to the NICs in year $t$ |
| $XTS_t$ | = | Exports of all U.S. firms to the ASEAN-4 in year $t$ |

all other variables are defined in table 8.6

Source: United States, Department of Commerce, Bureau of Economic Analysis (1989).

deal. Note that interpretation of the coefficients in equations (3a)–(3d) is somewhat different from the coefficients in equations (1a)–(2d) because the total U.S. export variable was moved to the left-hand side of the equation (i.e., its coefficient is forced to equal 1). This transformation was used because it improved the fit of equations (3c)–(3d) markedly. From equation (3d),[9] a 1 point increase in the change of the NICs affiliate-to-parent value added ratio is seen to result in a differential between parent and total export growth rates that is 528 points higher than it otherwise would have been. In contrast, a 1 point increase in the change of the developed country affiliate-to-parent value added ratio leads to an export growth rate differential that is 9 points lower than it otherwise would have been. At the means, these coefficients imply elasticities of 1.197 with respect to NIC affiliate-to-parent value added ratios and -0.362 for developed country ratios. Affiliate production in the ASEAN-4 and in other developing countries has no statistically significant effect on the differential between parent and total U.S. export growth to the ASEAN-4.

These results indicate that expanded production in NIC affiliates assists with developing markets for U.S. parents in the ASEAN-4. This is a perfectly plausible result especially in view of the high level of U.S. DFI in Singapore, a country with especially close links to the Indonesian and Malaysian markets. Increased production in NIC affiliates may also increase the demand for intermediate inputs produced by ASEAN-4 affiliates such as electric components and thereby increase demand for parent shipments of raw materials to ASEAN-4 affiliates. Nonetheless, these results differ significantly from previous studies of bilateral trade flows in that affiliate production in partner regions themselves impart no significant impacts on the growth of parent exports (e.g., Lipsey and Weiss 1981, 1984). Moreover it is difficult to explain why increased developed country production leads to reduced growth of parent exports to the ASEAN-4 though it is possible to conceive of a situation where increased developed country activity leads parents to neglect ASEAN-4 markets. At any rate, as in the multilateral case, it would clearly be desirable to follow this industry-level analysis with firm-level analyses to further explore the relationships involved.

## U.S. Multinational Activity and Changes in
## the Structure of U.S. Employment

The crux of any discussion of structural adjustment typically revolves around the issue of employment. Indeed some of the strongest opposition to outward DFI from the United States comes from U.S. labor unions and other related groups which assert that DFI results in the export of jobs from the United States. These criticisms are based on observation of direct effects, including the loss of jobs when U.S. factories shut down and transfer production abroad.

However the indirect effects, in particular those which work through exports, have been argued to be more important than the direct effects (e.g., Bergsten, Horst, and Moran 1978, 102–103). If foreign affiliate production stimulates U.S. exports, then the negative effect on U.S. employment can be mitigated to a significant degree. Yet despite the fact that previous analyses have generally revealed a non-negative relationship between foreign affiliate production and parent exports (see discussion above), a recent firm-level study by Kravis and Lipsey (1988) indicated that affiliate production and parent employment were, in general, negatively correlated in 1982. This section further examines the role of multinationals in U.S. employment creation and in particular the effects of Asian affiliate activity on U.S. parent employment.

As in the case of exports, U.S. parents account for the majority of employment in many manufacturing industries (Table 8.10).[10] However, for all industries, employment shares (38 percent in 1977 and 30 percent in 1982) are much smaller than export shares (79 percent in 1977 and 75 percent in 1982). In total manufacturing, parent shares of U.S. employment are larger, 55 percent and 48 percent in 1977 and 1982, respectively, but the shares are still significantly below parent shares of U.S. exports. This is a pattern similar to that observed in Asia's developing economies where foreign (including U.S.) affiliate shares of host-country exports are generally much larger than their shares of host-country employment (e.g., Plummer and Ramstetter, this volume). In other words, multinationals are generally more involved in trade than in other economic activities. This pattern implies that multinationals possess relatively large firm-specific advantages in international marketing and that a primary motive for DFI is market expansion.

Another reason for the relatively large parent shares of U.S. exports in all industries as a whole is that multinationals are often concentrated in industries with large amounts of exports. For example, motor vehicles was the largest individual exporting industry in our thirty-two industry classification in both 1977 and 1982 (United Nations, n.d.) and this industry was also characterized by high parent export-to-total export ratios (Table 8.4) and high parent employment-to-total employment ratios (Table 8.10). The combination of relatively high export levels, high parent export-to-total export ratios, and high parent employment-to-total employment ratios also characterizes industrial chemicals, drugs, office and computing machinery, and other transportation equipment (mainly aircraft). Among the smaller exporting industries, the combination of high parent export-to-total export ratios and high parent employment-to-total employment ratios is observed in household appliances and soaps and cleansers. Industries in which smaller parent employment-to-total employment ratios coexist with larger parent export-to-total export ratios are grain mill and bakery products, beverages, fabricated metals, radio and television, electric components, rubber, and stone. On the other hand, only two industries, other food and other chemicals, were characterized by large parent employment-to-total employment ratios but small parent export-to-total export ratios. The remaining industries have both low parent employment-to-total employment and parent export-to-total export ratios.

Although the relationship between affiliate employment and parent employment is a complicated one, ratios of affiliate employment to parent employment are a helpful guide to isolating industries in which affiliate employment is quantitatively important relative to U.S. employment. Data indicate that employment in Asian affiliates appears to be of little consequence in terms of parent employment in most U.S. industries (Table 8.11). Indeed affiliates in the NICs accounted for 5 percent or more of U.S. parent employment in only one industry, electric components. Moreover in this industry, employment in NIC affiliates declined dramatically from 37,400 in 1977 to only 14,500 in 1982 and the ratio of NIC affiliate employment to parent employment fell from 24 percent to only 5 percent. In 1977, electric

Table 8.10  Employment of Nonbank U.S. Parents, 1977-1986

| Industry | 1977 | | 1982 | | 1986 |
|---|---|---|---|---|---|
| | Employ- ment of Nonbank Parents | As a Share of Total U.S. Employ- ment | Employ- ment of Nonbank Parents | As a Share of Total U.S. Employ- ment | Employ- ment of Nonbank Parents |
| All industries | 18,884,636 | 37.9 | 18,704,600 | 30.3 | 17,861,000 |
| Manufacturing | 11,775,031 | 54.9 | 10,532,800 | 47.9 | 10,384,700 |
| Food & kindred products | 1,016,702 | 49.3 | 1,011,200 | 43.9 | 1,215,500 |
| Grain mill & bakery products | 199,016 | 34.0 | 176,400 | 30.1 | 348,700 |
| Beverages | 122,782 | 41.6 | 86,300 | 29.1 | 180,400 |
| Other food & kindred products | 694,904 | 58.9 | 748,500 | 52.6 | 686,400 |
| Chemicals & allied products | 1,207,675 | 96.9 | 1,364,600 | 107.9 | 1,264,100 |
| Industrial chemicals & synthetics | 652,827 | 110.4 | 660,100 | 115.7 | 537,700 |
| Drugs | 253,902 | 79.5 | 299,400 | 87.3 | 342,100 |
| Soaps, cleansers, & toilet goods | 167,363 | 95.1 | 207,400 | 96.5 | 215,600 |
| Agricultural chemicals | 21,277 | 73.4 | 90,400 | 250.7 | 39,900 |
| Other chemicals & products | 112,306 | 86.2 | 107,400 | 107.3 | 128,800 |
| Primary & fabricated metals | 1,484,236 | 53.7 | 976,200 | 39.9 | 657,300 |
| Primary metal industries | 990,625 | 70.7 | 523,400 | 48.7 | 349,300 |
| Ferrous primary metals | 732,657 | 74.0 | 351,400 | 45.8 | 195,900 |
| Nonferrous primary metals | 257,968 | 62.7 | 171,900 | 55.9 | 153,400 |
| Fabricated metal products | 493,611 | 36.3 | 452,800 | 33.1 | 307,900 |
| Machinery, except electrical | 1,546,343 | 67.0 | 1,457,900 | 56.2 | 1,237,900 |
| Farm & garden machinery | 90,583 | 39.3 | 68,300 | 44.9 | 52,200 |
| Construction, mining, etc. | 312,997 | 74.6 | 244,300 | 57.9 | 136,300 |
| Office & computing machinery | 502,823 | 102.7 | 680,700 | 87.5 | 695,300 |
| Other machinery | 639,940 | 54.8 | 464,600 | 37.4 | 354,200 |
| Electric and electronic equip. | 1,274,090 | 60.6 | 1,619,500 | 65.0 | 1,559,800 |
| Household appliances | 169,644 | 118.0 | 91,900 | 68.6 | 109,200 |
| Radio, television, communication | 320,321 | 44.3 | 609,900 | 58.6 | 850,400 |
| Electric components, accessories | 157,109 | 46.8 | 290,100 | 63.7 | 271,900 |
| Other electrical machinery | 627,016 | 69.7 | 627,600 | 72.9 | 328,200 |
| Transportation equipment | 2,289,002 | 85.7 | 1,687,300 | 73.0 | 2,310,800 |
| Motor vehicles & equipment | 1,356,856 | 96.4 | 828,000 | 85.4 | 1,180,700 |
| Other transportation equipment | 932,146 | 73.8 | 859,400 | 64.0 | 1,130,100 |
| Other manufacturing | 2,956,983 | 35.6 | 2,416,000 | 31.0 | 2,139,300 |
| Tobacco manufactures | 97,993 | 86.5 | 161,000 | 96.2 | 59,100 |
| Textile products & apparel | 667,753 | 30.8 | 437,700 | 22.6 | 397,000 |
| Lumber, wood, furniture, etc. | 268,438 | 25.1 | 174,100 | 18.6 | 142,700 |
| Paper & allied products | 341,630 | 42.4 | 293,500 | 41.2 | 289,100 |
| Printing & publishing | 253,418 | 20.5 | 276,800 | 18.5 | 309,000 |
| Rubber products | 293,693 | 72.3 | 200,400 | 64.5 | 172,000 |
| Miscellaneous plastic products | 67,268 | 18.9 | 35,700 | 9.8 | 97,100 |

## Table 8.10 (continued)

| Industry | 1977 | | 1982 | | 1986 |
|---|---|---|---|---|---|
| | Employ-ment of Nonbank Parents | As a Share of Total U.S. Employ-ment | Employ-ment of Nonbank Parents | As a Share of Total U.S. Employ-ment | Employ-ment of Nonbank Parents |
| Glass products | 131,090 | 55.2 | 108,800 | 45.9 | 91,600 |
| Stone, clay, etc. | 170,639 | 37.2 | 140,100 | 31.8 | 106,000 |
| Instruments & related products | 414,688 | 63.5 | 427,600 | 70.4 | 363,700 |
| Leather & miscellaneous manuf. | 250,373 | 31.1 | 160,400 | 27.1 | 112,000 |

Sources: United States, Department of Commerce, Bureau of the Census (various years a); Bureau of Economic Analysis (1981, 1985a, various years a).

components affiliates were by far the largest employers among U.S. affiliates in the NICs with other electric machinery and radio and television being the only other individual industries where affiliate employment exceeded 10,000. In 1982, these three electric and electronic machinery industries still led this list but radio and television moved to the top position followed by electric components and other electric machinery; employment in office and computing machinery affiliates also grew to over 10,000 in this year.

In the ASEAN-4, affiliate employment levels have been higher relative to parent employment in a number of industries with the ratio of affiliate employment to parent employment exceeding 5 percent in beverages, electric components, tobacco, and rubber, both in 1977 and 1982. In contrast to the trend in NICs affiliates, employment in ASEAN-4 affiliates in electric components grew rapidly from 20,700 in 1977 to 37,800 in 1982, a rate of increase roughly equal to that observed in parents. Employment in ASEAN-4 radio and television affiliates, though small relative to parent employment, also grew rapidly to reach 23,900 in 1982. Following affiliates in these two industries, affiliates in other food, rubber, tobacco, beverages, and drugs all had employment levels over 10,000 in 1982. In contrast, this list was much shorter in 1977 consisting of only other food, rubber, and electric components. Thus affiliate employment in both the NICs and the ASEAN-4 has become highly concentrated in electric components and radio and television, industries in which U.S. parent employment also grew rather rapidly between 1977 and 1982.

Important as this observation may be it does not establish a general relationship between increased affiliate activity and parent employment. For the purpose of investigating this relationship, a simple model similar to those employed in the study of the impact of affiliate activity on parent exports is also estimated for parent employment (Table 8.12). Equation (4a) reveals a negative relationship between the increase of affiliate production relative to parent production and the growth of parent employment growth; this negative relationship is somewhat similar to the negative relationship observed in the static analysis of Kravis and Lipsey (1988). However an F-test of the null hypothesis that changes in affiliate-to-parent value added ratios for developed and developing country affiliates affect the growth of employment in the same way is rejected at the 0.01 level. On the other hand, affiliate production in Asian regions apparently has the same effects as production in other developing country affiliates making it most appropriate to focus on equation (4b).[11] From this equation, it can be seen that a 1 point increase in the change of the developed country affiliate-to-parent value added ratio increases employment growth in parents by 1.3 points while a 1 point increase in the change of the developing economy affiliate-to-parent value added ratio results in a 11 point decrease of employment growth in parents. The respective elasticities are both very low in absolute value, however, 0.03 and 0.05 at the means.[12]

In short, increased affiliate activity can affect parent employment in two ways: (1) through its impacts on the factor intensity of parent operations, and (2) through its impact on the level of parent operations. The observation of a negative correlation between the ratio of developing country affiliate production relative to parent production and employment growth in parents is consistent with the assertion that parents reduce their demand for labor in the United States by transferring labor-intensive activities to developing country affiliates to take advantage of the cheaper cost of labor in developing countries. This factor intensity element has been stressed in previous studies and is likely to be very important with respect to developing country affiliate production (e.g., Kravis and Lipsey 1988, 7–8). On the other hand, the positive correlation between increased developed country affiliate production relative to parent production and employment growth in parents indicates that increased production in developed country affiliates facilitates the expansion of parent activities because differences in factor prices are not so pronounced. The interesting element here is that the expansion of parent operations must have been oriented toward the U.S. market, since a negative relationship between changes in affiliate-to-parent value added ratios in all regions and the growth of parent exports was indicated above (Table 8.6, and equation (1a)). That is, parents in industries in which developed country affiliate production grew more rapidly than parent production experienced relatively slow export growth at the same time their employment expanded relatively rapidly, indicating relatively fast growth in the U.S. market. This pattern suggests there may be an efficiency gain associated with expanding foreign affiliate operations in developed economies that makes a parent become more competitive in the U.S. market.[13]

## Multinationals, Structural Adjustment, and Policy

There are several important findings in the analysis above. First, multinational parents are a very important source of total U.S. exports, with intrafirm exports accounting for a large share of parent exports. On the other hand, increased production in affiliates worldwide relative to parent production reduced the growth of U.S. parent exports in 1977–1982.

Table 8.11 Employment of Nonbank Affiliates of Nonbank U.S. Parents in the NICs and ASEAN-4, 1977 and 1982

| Industry | NICs 1977 Employment of Affiliates | NICs 1977 As a Share of Total Parent Employment | NICs 1982 Employment of Affiliates | NICs 1982 As a Share of Total Parent Employment | ASEAN-4 1977 Employment of Affiliates | ASEAN-4 1977 As a Share of Total Parent Employment | ASEAN-4 1982 Employment of Affiliates | ASEAN-4 1982 As a Share of Total Parent Employment |
|---|---|---|---|---|---|---|---|---|
| All industries | 188,129 | 1.0 | 181,900 | 1.0 | 227,539 | 1.2 | 252,100 | 1.3 |
| Manufacturing | 143,800 | 1.2 | 131,100 | 1.2 | 155,900 | 1.3 | 204,800 | 1.9 |
| Food & kindred products | 4,800 | 0.5 | 3,600 | 0.4 | 35,600 | 3.5 | 38,200 | 3.8 |
| Grain mill & bakery products | 1,300 | 0.7 | 500 | 0.3 | 100 | 0.1 | 1,900 | 1.1 |
| Beverages | 100 | 0.1 | 700 | 0.8 | 7,500 | 6.1 | 14,100 | 16.3 |
| Other food & kindred products | 3,500 | 0.5 | 2,300 | 0.3 | 28,000 | 4.0 | 22,200 | 3.0 |
| Chemicals & allied products | 15,100 | 1.3 | 16,200 | 1.2 | 17,700 | 1.5 | 19,700 | 1.4 |
| Industrial chemicals & synthetics | 8,200 | 1.3 | 8,600 | 1.3 | 6,300 | 1.0 | 4,600 | 0.7 |
| Drugs | 3,000 | 1.2 | 4,000 | 1.3 | 7,800 | 3.1 | 10,100 | 3.4 |
| Soaps, cleansers, & toilet goods | 700 | 0.4 | 900 | 0.4 | 3,300 | 2.0 | 4,600 | 2.2 |
| Agricultural chemicals | 700 | 3.3 | 100 | 0.1 | 0 | 0.0 | 0 | 0.0 |
| Other chemicals & products | 2,400 | 2.1 | 2,600 | 2.4 | 200 | 0.2 | 300 | 0.3 |
| Primary & fabricated metals | 4,600 | 0.3 | 3,000 | 0.3 | 3,500 | 0.2 | 6,900 | 0.7 |
| Primary metal industries | 3,200 | 0.3 | 1,400 | 0.3 | 3,000 | 0.3 | 2,500 | 0.5 |
| Ferrous primary metals | 600 | 0.1 | 800 | 0.2 | 700 | 0.1 | na | na |
| Nonferrous primary metals | 2,600 | 1.0 | 700 | 0.4 | 2,300 | 0.9 | na | na |
| Fabricated metal products | 1,400 | 0.3 | 1,600 | 0.4 | 500 | 0.1 | 4,400 | 1.0 |
| Machinery, except electrical | 9,700 | 0.6 | 15,100 | 1.0 | 3,700 | 0.2 | 4,000 | 0.3 |
| Farm & garden machinery | 0 | 0.0 | 100 | 0.1 | 0 | 0.0 | 0 | 0.0 |

| | | | | | | | |
|---|---|---|---|---|---|---|---|
| Construction, mining, etc. | 600 | 0.2 | 1,700 | 0.7 | 1,200 | 0.4 | 400 | 0.2 |
| Office & computing machinery | 7,400 | 1.5 | 11,600 | 1.7 | 1,500 | 0.3 | 3,400 | 0.5 |
| Other machinery | 1,700 | 0.3 | 1,700 | 0.4 | 1,000 | 0.2 | 200 | 0.0 |
| Electric and electronic equipment | 77,100 | 6.1 | 54,700 | 3.4 | 39,400 | 3.1 | 69,200 | 4.3 |
| Household appliances | 1,800 | 1.1 | 0 | 0.0 | 5,500 | 3.2 | 0 | 0.0 |
| Radio, television, communication | 15,000 | 4.7 | 25,900 | 4.2 | 7,800 | 2.4 | 23,900 | 3.9 |
| Electric components, accessories | 37,400 | 23.8 | 14,500 | 5.0 | 20,700 | 13.2 | 37,800 | 13.0 |
| Other electrical machinery | 22,900 | 3.7 | 14,300 | 2.3 | 5,400 | 0.9 | 7,500 | 1.2 |
| Transportation equipment | 15,400 | 0.7 | 16,400 | 1.0 | 4,600 | 0.2 | 8,300 | 0.5 |
| Motor vehicles & equipment | 9,700 | 0.7 | na | na | 4,300 | 0.3 | na | na |
| Other transportation equipment | 5,700 | 0.6 | na | na | 300 | 0.0 | na | na |
| Other manufacturing | 17,000 | 0.6 | 22,200 | 0.9 | 51,400 | 1.7 | 58,500 | 2.4 |
| Tobacco manufactures | 500 | 0.5 | 2,600 | 1.6 | 5,200 | 5.3 | 17,600 | 10.9 |
| Textile products & apparel | 1,500 | 0.2 | 5,700 | 1.3 | 7,800 | 1.2 | 3,100 | 0.7 |
| Lumber, wood, furniture, etc. | 900 | 0.3 | 0 | 0.0 | 6,600 | 2.5 | na | na |
| Paper & allied products | 1,400 | 0.4 | na | na | 2,600 | 0.8 | na | na |
| Printing & publishing | 1,100 | 0.4 | 600 | 0.2 | 800 | 0.3 | 700 | 0.3 |
| Rubber products | 500 | 0.2 | 500 | 0.2 | 23,100 | 7.9 | 21,800 | 10.9 |
| Miscellaneous plastic products | 0 | 0.0 | 0 | 0.0 | 300 | 0.4 | 0 | 0.0 |
| Glass products | 1,600 | 1.2 | na | na | 500 | 0.4 | na | na |
| Stone, clay, etc. | 300 | 0.2 | 800 | 0.6 | 1,800 | 1.1 | 900 | 0.6 |
| Instruments & related products | 3,600 | 0.9 | 3,600 | 0.8 | 2,600 | 0.6 | 2,000 | 0.5 |
| Leather & miscellaneous manufactures | 5,600 | 2.2 | na | na | 100 | 0.0 | na | na |

na = Not available or not disclosed.

Sources: United States, Department of Commerce, Bureau of Economic Analysis (1981, 1985a, 1989).

Table 8.12  The Effect of Increased Affiliate Production on Growth of Employment of Nonbank U.S. Parents, 1977-1982:  Ordinary Least Squares Estimates

(4a)  $EP_{82}/EP_{77} = -0.236184 + 1.227623(ET_{82}/ET_{77}) - 1.688054(YAW_{82}\text{-}YAWP_{77})$
   (0.54)  (2.87)[***]  (2.92)[***]

Adjusted $R^2$ = 0.43769  Sum of squared residuals = 7.62172  $F$ = 13.1[***]

(4b)  $EP_{82}/EP_{77} = -0.060260 + 1.165979(ET_{82}/ET_{77}) - 1.347366(YAMP_{82}\text{-}YAMP_{77})$
   (0.24)  (4.96)[***]  (2.77)[**]

   $- 10.64877(YALP_{82}\text{-}YALP_{77})$
   (9.39)[***]

Adjusted $R^2$ = 0.82984  Sum of squared residuals = 2.22691  $F$ = 51.4[***]

(4c)  $EP_{82}/EP_{77} = -0.079716 + 1.193017(ET_{82}/ET_{77}) + 1.344035(YAMP_{82}\text{-}YAMP_{77})$
   (0.32)  (4.98)[***]  (2.74)[**]

   $- 6.077947(YAAP_{82}\text{-}YAAP_{77}) - 10.90631(YAOP_{82}\text{-}YAOP_{77})$
   (0.97)  (9.13)[***]

Adjusted $R^2$ = 0.82707  Sum of squared residuals = 2.18233  $F$ = 38.1[***]

(4d)  $EP_{82}/EP_{77} = -0.054977 + 1.170732(ET_{82}/ET_{77}) - 1.380597(YAMP_{82}\text{-}YAMP_{77})$
   (0.22)  (4.79)[***]  (2.76)[**]

   $- 6.403026(YAMP_{82}\text{-}YAMP_{77}) + 3.871008(YASP_{82}\text{-}YASP_{77})$
   (1.01)  (0.24)

   $- 10.90311(YAO_{82}\text{-}YAOP_{77})$
   (9.03)[***]

Adjusted $R^2$ = 0.82335  Sum of squared residuals = 2.14670  $F$ = 29.9[***]

Variable definitions:
$EP_t$  =  Employment by U.S. parents in year $t$
$ET_t$  =  Employment by all U.S. firms in year $t$
all other variables are as defined in table 8.6

Source:  United States, Department of Commerce, Bureau of Economic Analysis (1989).

Second, in the case of exports to the NICs and the ASEAN-4, the share of parents in total exports and the share of intrafirm exports in parent exports are not generally as large as in the case of multilateral trade. Moreover, multinational activity in the NICs and the ASEAN-4 has been very heavily concentrated in a few industries, notably electric components and radio and television. Partly due to this heavy concentration, variation in the growth of parent exports to the NICs seems unrelated to variation in the ratio of affiliate-to-parent production in any region across industries. On the other hand, the increase of NIC affiliate production relative to parent production has apparently stimulated the growth of U.S. parent exports to the ASEAN-4.

Third, ratios of parent employment to total U.S. employment are generally lower than ratios of parent exports to total U.S. exports. Moreover, employment in NIC and ASEAN-4 affiliates is generally quite small relative to parent employment. Nonetheless, increased production in developing country affiliates (including Asian affiliates) relative to production in parents depresses employment growth in parents while increased production in developed country affiliates relative to production in parents has the opposite effect.

These findings suggest that multinational parents are very heavily involved in U.S. structural changes and that affiliate activity has important effects on U.S. parents. Unfortunately, these findings alone (1) cannot establish whether multinational activity is a cause or a result of structural changes and (2) cannot facilitate an unambiguous evaluation of the relative efficiency of structural changes facilitated by multinational activity.

Yet it should be clear from the analysis above that it would be very difficult, if not impossible, to establish a clear relationship between the degree of multinational involvement and the nature of structural change at the industry level. This is reflected in the wide variety of adjustment experiences in U.S. industries which are characterized by large multinational parent involvement. As examples, consider the adjustment experiences in primary metals (mainly steel), motor vehicles (mainly automobiles), office and computing machinery, radio and television, and electric components, industries where U.S. parents accounted for more than 60 percent of U.S. employment in 1977 and/or in 1982.

Primary metals industries have clearly been declining in the United States with multinational parents contracting especially fast in 1977–1986 (parent employment in 1986 was only 35 percent of 1977 levels). Some argue that steel (the largest component of primary metals) is an example of an industry undergoing structural adjustment that is too little, too late (Cline 1986). In contrast, parents and nonmultinationals have both expanded employment rapidly in office and computing machinery, radio and television, and electric components. Of course, there have also been adjustment problems in these rapidly changing industries, but they have been mitigated by the emergence of new opportunities. The motor vehicle industry represents an intermediate case where parent employment, which dominates the industry, contracted in 1977–1982 but recovered somewhat in 1982–1986. Clearly, as in primary metals, there have been large adjustment difficulties in this industry, but there have also been large investments in recent years which may help the industry to regain some of its lost competitiveness in the future (Cline 1986).

Interestingly, U.S. investment in developing Asia has been limited in primary metals and motor vehicles but has been relatively large in the other three industries considered here. In contrast, multinationals from Japan have been very active in primary metals and motor vehicles in developing Asia. Like primary metals and motor vehicles, textiles and apparel is another industry characterized by significant adjustment problems in the United States (Cline 1986) and relatively large Japanese DFI but relatively small U.S. DFI in developing Asia (e.g., Plummer and Ramstetter, this volume).

Five factors seem important in describing the relative lack of U.S. DFI in developing Asia in these three industries: (1) the relatively long distances between the United States and Asia, (2) developing host-country policies which promote joint ventures in some industries, (3) competition from Japanese firms, (4) a historical tendency for U.S. firms to pay little attention to Asian markets, and (5) protection from foreign competition in the U.S. market. First, locational factors are clearly important in some cases, especially in industries like primary metals where transportation costs are large. Second, the relatively large Japanese involvement in primary metals and motor vehicles may also be related to a relatively high propensity for Japanese affiliates to get involved in large government-related joint ventures like the Asahan Aluminum Project in Indonesia and the Proton Saga Project in Malaysia. Third, competition from Japanese firms has complicated the entry of U.S. multinationals into some Asian markets. Yet Japanese competition has also been very strong in industries such as office and computing machinery, radio and television, and electric components where U.S. firms have been extremely active in Asia. Fourth, it is clear that U.S. firms have sometimes been slow to exploit opportunities in developing Asia and other foreign markets. Nonetheless, these four factors alone seem incapable of explaining the relative lack of U.S. DFI in developing Asia's primary metals, motor vehicles, and textiles and apparel industries.

These three industries all share an important trait; that is, they have all been major beneficiaries of import protection in the United States, especially in the case of imports from developing Asia and Japan. By reducing competitive pressures, protection has clearly reduced the motive for U.S. firms to compete head-to-head with Asian producers in Asia (and other foreign) markets and probably had adverse effects on the ability to compete in the U.S. market as well. Moreover, the effectiveness of lobbying for protection in these U.S. industries has accentuated inefficiencies in U.S. firms by encouraging them to devote resources to lobbying efforts rather than to upgrading their operations. This contrasts markedly with experiences in office and computing machinery, radio and television, and electric components, industries which have been relatively free of protection. Indeed in these industries, corporate lobbies often worked in the opposite direction and promoted the establishment and maintenance of sections 806 and 807 in the U.S. tariff code, measures that increase the motive for internationalizing production by reducing tariffs on intrafirm trade.

These patterns suggest that, in industries where lobbying for protection remains a viable alternative, U.S. firms may not have fully availed themselves of opportunities to improve efficiency and expand markets through the establishment or expansion of affiliates in developing Asia. Thus, policies which de-emphasize protection would not only impart well-known benefits on U.S. consumers but would also be likely to encourage increased U.S. DFI in Asia as many firms would be forced to internationalize their operations in order to become more efficient. On the other hand, both theory (e.g., Markusen, this volume) and empirics suggest that the prospects for efficiency gains through DFI vary greatly across industries. Namely, the scope for increased DFI in Asia (and elsewhere) would seem most promising in industries like high-end textiles and apparel and perhaps motor vehicles, where knowledge-based assets and multiplant economies of scale are relatively important. In contrast, the room for increased DFI is probably limited in industries like primary metals where these factors are generally less important.

## Notes

Special thanks go to Robert E. Lipsey for research guidance, comments, and suggestions; to the Bureau of Economic Analysis of the U.S. Department of Commerce for provision of unpublished data; and to Arnold Gilbert of the Bureau of Economic Analysis for programming and other assistance with the data.

1. Japan has always been the largest investor in Korea and became the largest investor in Thailand in 1987. However, through the mid-1980s, the United States was a larger investor in all other NICs and ASEAN-4 countries (see Lee and Ramstetter, this volume; Naya and Ramstetter 1987; Tambunlertchai and Ramstetter, this volume).

2. Due to nondisclosure, it is impossible to determine the share for 1981–1984. However, excluding finance income in Korea, Indonesia, Malaysia, and the Philippines, the share was 21 percent. Inclusion of the unavailable data would almost certainly not raise the share over 22 percent.

3. Some of the decline in these ratios is due to a reduction of coverage in the benchmark surveys between 1977 and 1982. Specifically, a large number of smaller firms were dropped from the sample; the number of nonbank parents (of nonbank affiliates) dropped from 3,425 to 2,110 and the number of nonbank affiliates (of nonbank parents) declined from 23,641 to 17,213 (United States, Department of Commerce, Bureau of Economic Analysis 1981, 20; 1985a, 27). Note also that exports to U.S. nonbank affiliates of nonbank parents (hereafter referred to as affiliates) by unaffiliated U.S. persons accounted for another 5–7 percent of total U.S. exports and 4–6 percent of U.S. manufacturing exports in 1977 and 1982. Thus the share of all multinational-related exports in U.S. exports is somewhat larger than shown in Table 8.3. Some of the individual industry ratios are over 100 percent due to incompatibilities between commodity trade and industrial classifications. The trade data used were adjusted in accordance with a methodology developed by Robert Lipsey (e.g., Blomström et al. 1988, 16–20) to fit the industrial classification used in the U.S. DFI surveys. However, there are mismatches between commodity and industrial classifications due the existence of multiproduct firms.

4. Using U.S. government calculations of SIC-based exports at the 2-digit SIC level, parent shares of total exports were 78.3 percent in 1977, 75.4 percent in 1982, and 78.2 percent in 1986. In manufacturing, these shares were 69.4 percent, 62.9 percent, and 68.1 percent, respectively (Table 8.4; United States, Department of Commerce, Bureau of the Census, various years b).

5. For total manufacturing exports, see United States, Department of Commerce, Bureau of the Census (various years b). The total export classification used by the U.S. Department of Commerce is somewhat different from that used here; thus these data are not strictly comparable with those for 1977 and 1982 in Tables 8.4 and 8.5.

6. The approach is essentially an industry-level adaptation of a model proposed by Lipsey (1987, 14) to study the effects of the growth in affiliate-to-parent value added ratios on parent compensation per employee at the firm level.

7. However, this would be a very costly exercise since it would require that the Department of Commerce be contracted to match firm-level data from different benchmark surveys.

8. For example, the sales of ASIA-8 affiliates were 96–97 percent of sales of all majority-owned Asian affiliate sales in electric and electronic equipment in 1982 and 1986, and at least 87 percent in nonelectric machinery in 1986 (the latter figure excludes Indonesia, the Philippines, and Thailand for which data were not disclosed).

9. In equation (3c), all ASIA-8 affiliates are also shown to have the same effect. However, F-tests of hypothesis that all affiliates in the NICs and the ASEAN-4 impart the same impact is rejected at the 0.01 level. Hence equation (3d) is used as the basis of this discussion.

10. The Bureau of Economic Analysis classification used in the multinational parent and affiliate employment data differs somewhat from the Bureau of Census classification used in the total enterprise employment data. Hence the ratios sometimes exceed 100 percent in Table 8.10.

11. Equations (4c) and (4d) indicate that Asian affiliate activity has no statistically significant effect on the growth of U.S. employment, but F-tests of the null hypothesis that Asian affiliates impart different effects than affiliates in other developing regions cannot be rejected at the 0.10 level. Thus the differences between the effects of Asian affiliates and affiliates in other developing regions observed in equations (4c) and (4d) are not statistically significant.

12. Absolute values are used here because the mean of $(YAMP_{82} - YAMP_{77})$ is negative making the elasticity of opposite sign than the coefficient at the means.

13. Although negative, the elasticity of employment growth with respect to the ratio of developing country affiliate production to parent production (-0.05) is also greater than the the corresponding elasticity for export growth (-0.13). Thus, the reduction of parent export growth caused by expanded affiliate production is relatively greater than the corresponding reduction of parent employment growth, regardless of whether the affiliate is located in developed or developing regions.

# References

Bergsten, C. Fred, Thomas Horst, and Theodore H. Moran. 1978. *American Multinationals and American Interests*. Washington, D.C.: Brookings Institution.

Blomström, Magnus, Robert E. Lipsey, and Ksenia Kulchycky. 1988. U.S. and Swedish Direct Investment and Exports. In *Trade Policy Issues and Empirical Analysis*, edited by Robert E. Baldwin. Chicago: University of Chicago Press.

Cline, William R. 1986. U.S. Trade and Industrial Policy: The Experience of Textiles, Steel, and Automobiles. In *Strategic Trade Policy and the New International Economics*, edited by Paul Krugman. Cambridge: MIT University Press.

Kravis, Irving B., and Robert E. Lipsey. 1988. The Effect of Multinational Firms' Foreign Operations on Their Domestic Employment. Working Paper No. 2760. Cambridge, Mass.: National Bureau of Economic Research.

Lipsey, Robert E. 1987. Direct Foreign Investment and Structural Change in Asian Economies and the U.S.: Possibilities for Research. Mimeo.

Lipsey, Robert E., and Irving B. Kravis. 1985. The Competitive Position of U.S. Manufacturing Firms. *Banca Nazionale del Lavoro Quarterly Review* 38(153): 127–54.

Lipsey, Robert E., and Merle Y. Weiss. 1981. Foreign Production and Exports in Manufacturing Industries. *Review of Economics and Statistics* 63(4): 488–94.

_____. 1984. Foreign Production and Exports of Individual Firms. *Review of Economics and Statistics* 66(2): 304–308.

Naya, Seiji, and Eric D. Ramstetter. 1987. United States Direct Foreign Investment in Asia's Developing Economies. Paper presented at the Seminar on Cooperation through Foreign Investment among Asian and Pacific Countries (Phase II), 19–22 May, Bangkok, Thailand.

United Nations (UN). N.d. Commodity Trade Statistics, computer tapes.

United States, Department of Commerce, Bureau of the Census. Various years a. *Enterprise Statistics*, 1977 and 1982 issues. Washington, D.C.: Bureau of the Census.

_____. Various years b. *Statistical Abstract of the United States*, 1985–1989 issues. Washington, D.C.: Bureau of the Census.

United States, Department of Commerce, Bureau of Economic Analysis. 1981. *United States Direct Investment Abroad 1977.* Washington, D. C.: Bureau of Economic Analysis.

_____. 1985a. *U.S. Direct Investment Abroad: 1982 Benchmark Survey Data.* Washington, D.C.: Bureau of Economic Analysis.

_____. Various years a. *U.S. Direct Investment Abroad: Operations of U.S. Parent Companies and Their Foreign Affiliates*, Revised Estimates 1983, 1984, and 1985 issues, and Preliminary Estimates 1986 issue. Washington, D.C.: Bureau of Economic Analysis.

_____. Various years b. *Survey of Current Business*, August issues, 1986–1988. Washington, D.C.: Department of Commerce.

_____. 1985b, 1989. Mimeos.

# PART FIVE

# Regional and Global Perspectives

# 9

## Multinational Affiliates and the Changing Division of Labor in the Asia-Pacific Region

*Michael G. Plummer and Eric D. Ramstetter*

### Foreign Investment, Multinationals, and the International Division of Labor

This chapter takes a regional view of some of the issues brought out in previous country studies. The relationship between direct foreign investment (DFI) and the process of structural adjustment is examined by focusing on recent changes in the division of labor among Asia-Pacific economies in a number of important sectors. Industrial growth in Asia's newly industrializing countries (NICs: Hong Kong, Korea, Singapore, and Taiwan) is shown to have been an important factor in the restructuring of several Japanese and U.S. industries in the last decade, and this process is likely to continue in the future. Moreover, although industrial development is less advanced in the four larger members of the Association of Southeast Asian Nations (ASEAN-4: Indonesia, Malaysia, the Philippines, and Thailand), certain industries have grown very rapidly and there are indications that they will begin to put substantial pressure on certain sectors in the NICs, Japan, and the United States in the near future.

Furthermore, the role of multinational corporations has been substantial in a number of industries, although some industries involved in the regional restructuring of the Asia-Pacific economies—for example, metals—are not heavily dominated by multinationals. Of course, the observation of a correlation (or lack of it) between heavy multinational involvement and a rapid (or slow) pace of restructuring does not establish (negate) the multinational as the cause of the restructuring. Rather, it seems more appropriate to view multinationals as one of several avenues through which restructuring of the regional division of labor is possible with changes in prices, incomes, productivity, technology, and government policies being additional sources of restructuring.

This chapter focuses on the experiences of five manufacturing industries to describe how the regional division of labor has changed in the last decade and the extent that multinational firms are associated with this process. The focus on manufacturing reflects the fact that (1) multinationals have played a major role in several manufacturing sectors, and (2) changes in these sectors are a major cause of concern for policy makers and researchers. Of course manufacturing cannot be looked at in a vacuum; multinational-structural adjustment relationships are also important to the services and primary production sectors, and are related to the patterns observed in manufactures. In order to put the experiences of the individual manufacturing industries in perspective, the following section looks at the role of multinationals in the region's economywide and manufacturing aggregates.

Finally, a caveat about the data used in this study must be issued. Because the study brings together data from a wide variety of sources, there are inconsistencies and classification problems.[1] As a result, several figures in this paper, especially the ratios of multinational affiliate employment to host or investing country employment and the ratios of multinational affiliate exports to host country exports, should be viewed as first approximations. Thus the interested reader is strongly encouraged to refer to the original sources for more details as warranted. On the other hand, the data are very helpful in revealing a number of pervasive characteristics that have important implications and it is unlikely that the major conclusions of this study would be greatly altered even if all the data problems were solved.

## An Overview

The period following the first oil shock has been subject to vicissitudes, with the global macroeconomy including the Asia-Pacific region experiencing large imbalances. First, there was the overheating of the world economy which resulted in a substantial increase in inflation and a significant rise in real interest rates in the late 1970s. This was followed by a period of severe contraction that was exacerbated by the second oil shock and its aftermath in the early 1980s. Also at this time, persistently high interest rates contributed to the emergence of a severe debt crisis in the developing world and pushed the value of the U.S. dollar so high that many U.S. exports lost their competitiveness, resulting in large U.S. trade deficits. Despite a robust recovery in the mid-1980s, the U.S. dollar continued to remain at high levels and the United States became the world's largest net importer of capital by 1985. Since late 1985, however, there have been moves toward a more balanced position. First, the dollar has depreciated while the yen, the deutsche mark, and the New Taiwanese dollar among other currencies have appreciated. Second, throughout the late 1980s there was a gradual reduction in the U.S. government budget and external deficits. Third, there has been substantial growth of domestic demand in conjunction with the liberalization of several restrictive economic policies in Japan and Taiwan.

Given this background, it is perhaps surprising to note that the 1980s have witnessed persistently rapid growth in the NICs, followed by the ASEAN-4, as they catch up with the developed countries of the region. Nonetheless, many of the region's economies have not performed as well in the 1980s as they did in the 1970s, and there have been some wide fluctuations in economic activity in a number of countries. Difficulties were greatest in Southeast Asia in the mid-1980s. Malaysia and Indonesia were severely affected by the downturn in primary product prices, and the recession in the region's electric and electronic machinery industry hit

Malaysia and Singapore hard. Yet, except for the Philippines which due to political difficulties grew at an annual rate of only 2 percent, the production growth record for the Asia-Pacific economies during the 1976–1987 period is quite respectable (Table 9.1 and sources). For example, during this period the United States and Japan grew at 3–4 percent annually; the NICs at 7–9 percent; and Indonesia, Malaysia, and Thailand at 6 percent. With the exception of Hong Kong, Singapore, and the Philippines, growth was more rapid in manufacturing, especially in Korea, Taiwan, and Indonesia where manufacturing output grew by more than 10 percent year.

This growth in production supported the substantial expansion of employment in the region. Employment rose 4 percent annually in Thailand, the Philippines, Indonesia, and Hong Kong; 3 percent in Malaysia, Singapore, and Taiwan; 2 percent in Korea and the United States; and 1 percent in Japan. In developing economies, manufacturing employment generally grew much faster than total employment and the developing country share of the region's manufacturing employment increased rapidly, rising from 28 percent to 37 percent as compared to an increase from 45 percent to 49 percent in the aggregate.

Furthermore, despite the rise of protectionist pressures in the early and mid-1980s, nominal exports continued to expand very rapidly. Nominal exports increased 9.9 percent annually overall and 10.3 percent in manufacturing. Note that the real increase in total exports was greater than the growth in total GDP for all countries except Indonesia, whose exports were greatly reduced by the fall in oil prices (Table 9.1 and sources). Despite the rising value of exports, the United States, Indonesia, and the Philippines experienced a decline in their shares of the region's exports. The U.S. decrease was especially large, both in total exports (from 50 percent to 36 percent) and in manufactures (from 47 percent to 34 percent). In contrast, Japan's export shares grew from 29 percent to 35 percent overall, and from 35 percent to 41 percent in manufacturing. The NICs' shares also increased from 13 percent to 22 percent in total exports and from 14 percent to 20 percent in manufacturing exports; the ASEAN-4 shares remained largely unchanged at 7–8 percent in total exports and 4 percent in exports of manufactures.

With the exception of the United States, fixed investment accounted for over 19 percent of total value added in all countries for the period 1976–1986/87. New productive capacity was being added at particularly high rates in Japan, Korea, Singapore, and Malaysia where these ratios were over 29 percent. The investment-to-value added ratios were generally much lower in manufacturing than in the aggregate; these ratios were under 11 percent in the United States, Japan, and Hong Kong. Only in Korea, Singapore, and Indonesia were these ratios higher than 20 percent. Thus new capacity was generally being added most rapidly in nonmanufacturing and in developing countries.

Data on employment of foreign multinational affiliates reveal that their role is generally limited in the aggregate (Table 9.2 and sources). In Korea and Taiwan, two economies that are popularly thought to be major beneficiaries of DFI, the ratio of multinational employment to total domestic employment was under 6 percent, with the ratio increasing in Korea but decreasing in Taiwan.[2] Looking at individual investors, Japanese and U.S. affiliates combined account for 2 percent of Korea's employment and 2–3 percent of Taiwan's employment. Unfortunately, in the other

Table 9.1  Economic Indicators of All Industries and Manufacturing, 1976-1987

| Country | Employment (Thousands) | | Nominal Exports (US$ millions) | | Compound Annual Growth of Real GDP, 1976-1987[c] (%) | Average Fixed Investment/ Value Added, 1976-1985[d] (%) |
|---|---|---|---|---|---|---|
| | 1976 | Latest Year[a] | 1976 | 1986[b] | | |
| **All industries** | | | | | | |
| Group total | 235,627 | 307,019 | 232,939 | 601,162 | na | na |
| Share of group total (%) | | | | | | |
| United States | 33.0 | 32.0 | 49.5 | 36.2 | 2.9 | 16.1 |
| Japan | 22.4 | 19.3 | 28.9 | 34.8 | 4.2 | 29.4 |
| Hong Kong | 0.8 | 0.9 | 3.7 | 5.9 | 8.8 | 25.7 |
| Korea | 5.3 | 5.3 | 3.3 | 5.8 | 7.8 | 30.0 |
| Singapore | 0.4 | 0.4 | 2.8 | 3.7 | 7.0 | 41.4 |
| Taiwan | 2.4 | 2.6 | 3.5 | 6.6 | 8.2 | 23.4 |
| Indonesia | 20.1 | 22.3 | 3.7 | 2.5 | 5.8 | 21.9 |
| Malaysia | 1.9 | 1.9 | 2.3 | 2.3 | 5.7 | 29.6 |
| Philippines | 6.0 | 6.7 | 1.1 | 0.8 | 2.4 | 19.4 |
| Thailand | 7.8 | 8.7 | 1.3 | 1.5 | 5.8 | 23.1 |
| **Manufacturing** | | | | | | |
| Group total | 44,639 | 51,818 | 188,155 | 501,240 | na | na |
| Share of group total (%) | | | | | | |
| United States | 41.5 | 35.9 | 47.2 | 34.3 | 3.1 | 8.3 |
| Japan | 30.1 | 27.5 | 35.0 | 41.1 | 6.6 | 9.7 |
| Hong Kong | 1.8 | 1.8 | 3.5 | 3.9 | 7.7 | 10.6 |
| Korea | 6.0 | 8.5 | 3.8 | 6.6 | 10.9 | 24.1 |
| Singapore | 0.5 | 0.6 | 2.9 | 3.9 | 6.9 | 20.1 |
| Taiwan | 3.6 | 5.4 | 4.1 | 5.9 | 10.0 | 17.2 |
| Indonesia | 8.9 | 10.8 | 0.5 | 0.9 | 11.0 | 31.6 |
| Malaysia | 1.4 | 1.8 | 1.4 | 1.6 | 7.8 | 17.4 |
| Philippines | 3.6 | 3.7 | 0.8 | 0.5 | 2.2 | 15.4 |
| Thailand | 2.6 | 4.0 | 0.9 | 1.2 | 6.9 | na |

na = Not available.

[a]For all industries: 1986 in Indonesia, the Philippines, and Thailand; and 1987 in all others. For manufacturing: 1985 in the Philippines; 1986 in Indonesia and Thailand; and 1987 in all others.

[b]1985 for Taiwan manufacturing.

[c]GNP in Japan; 1976-1986 in Indonesia and 1976-1986 in Hong Kong, manufacturing only (proxied with nominal manufacturing GDP deflated by total GDP deflator).

[d]For all industries 1976-1986 in Indonesia. For manufacturing: 1976-1984 in Japan, Hong Kong, Korea, and Indonesia; 1976, 1978-1984 in the Philippines; 1976, 1978, and 1983 in Malaysia.

Sources: Asian Development Bank (1988); Australian National University (1989); Japan, Management and Coordination Agency (various years); Japan, Economic Planning Agency (1989); Republic of China, Directorate-General of Budget, Accounting and Statistics (1988); United Nations (various years a, various years b); United States, Department of Commerce, Bureau of Economic Analysis (1986, various years a).

economies, data paucity precludes calculation of the total multinational employment-to-domestic employment ratio. However, U.S. data show that U.S. affiliates alone accounted for 2 percent of total employment in Hong Kong and 4–5 percent in Singapore though comparable ratios were much smaller in other countries.

Multinational employment-to-total employment ratios were generally much larger in manufacturing than in the aggregate reflecting the importance of manufacturing DFI in the region. These ratios were 46–48 percent in Singapore, 30–33 percent in Malaysia, 9–17 percent in Taiwan, and 8–11 percent in Hong Kong and Korea. U.S. affiliate shares of total host-economy manufacturing employment were as high as 15 percent in Singapore, and in the 2–6 percent range for Hong Kong, Malaysia, the Philippines, and Taiwan. On the other hand, Japanese affiliates accounted for up to 4 percent of Thai manufacturing employment. It is notable, however, that these ratios have generally declined over time with the total foreign share in Korea and the U.S. share in Malaysia being exceptions to this pattern.

The role of multinationals in trade has been relatively large. The ratio of multinational exports to total exports exceeds 20 percent for a number of years in Korea and Taiwan, with the bulk of multinational exports accounted for by Japanese and U.S. investors (Table 9.2 and sources). Moreover, in 1986, U.S. affiliates alone accounted for as much as 32 percent of Singapore's exports, 29 percent of Indonesia's exports, and 16 percent of Malaysia's exports.

Because manufactures account for the bulk of total exports, the multinational export-to-total export ratios for manufacturing are not much higher than for the aggregate in the NICs. In Korea and Taiwan, ratios of manufacturing multinational affiliate exports to total manufactured exports were 19–31 percent, and in Singapore, ratios were 74–85 percent. Singapore and Thailand, like Taiwan but in contrast to Korea, experienced a drop in the multinational share. Investing country data also indicate that either Japanese or U.S. multinationals alone accounted for over 10 percent of manufacturing exports from Malaysia, the Philippines, and Thailand; note that the U.S. ratios increased in Malaysia and the Philippines.

From a regional point of view, Japan and U.S. affiliates combined account for 23–25 percent of Asia's merchandise exports with Japanese affiliate exports growing rapidly in 1977–1986 to overtake U.S. affiliate exports. Nonetheless official sources indicate that aggregate employment remained slightly smaller in Japanese affiliates. However, the official figures used in Table 9.2 likely understate the true extent of Japanese affiliate activity as suggested by the references to private figures in the notes to the table.[3] From the investing country's point of view, affiliate activity abroad is much larger for the United States than it is for Japan, but affiliate activity in Asia has been much more significant for Japan. For example, Japan's affiliates in Asia accounted for 0.8 percent of Japanese employment and 50–54 percent of Japanese affiliate employment worldwide, while corresponding ratios were only 0.5–0.7 percent and 7–8 percent, respectively, for the United States (Table 9.2).

## Textiles and Apparel

In employment terms, textiles and apparel are stagnant industries in the Asia-Pacific economies with employment decreasing in both industries over the 1976–

Table 9.2 Employment and Exports of Foreign Affiliates in All Industries and Manufacturing, Selected Years

| Host Economy | Investing Economy | Foreign Affiliate Employment | | | | Foreign Affiliate Exports | | |
|---|---|---|---|---|---|---|---|---|
| | | Year | Number of Employees | As a Share of Host-Country Employment (%) | As a Share of Home-Country Employment (%) | Year | Exports (US$ millions) | As a Share of Host-Country Exports[a] (%) |
| All industries: Host-economy data[b] | | | | | | | | |
| Korea | World | 1976 | 225,679 | 1.8 | na | 1976 | 1,962 | 25.4 |
| Korea | World | 1986 | 418,166 | 2.7 | na | 1986 | 10,061 | 29.0 |
| Korea | Japan | 1986 | 263,000 | 1.7 | 0.4 | 1986 | 6,226 | 17.9 |
| Korea | U.S. | 1986 | 87,000 | 0.6 | 0.1 | 1986 | 1,694 | 4.9 |
| Taiwan | World | 1976 | 290,084 | 5.1 | na | 1976 | 2,334 | 28.6 |
| Taiwan | World | 1986 | 263,708 | 3.4 | na | 1986 | 6,493 | 16.3 |
| Taiwan | Japan | 1976 | 125,637 | 2.2 | 0.2 | 1976 | 998 | 12.2 |
| Taiwan | Japan | 1986 | 133,790 | 1.7 | 0.2 | 1986 | 2,990 | 7.5 |
| Taiwan | U.S. | 1976 | 69,834 | 1.2 | 0.1 | 1976 | 620 | 7.6 |
| Taiwan | U.S. | 1986 | 53,125 | 0.7 | 0.1 | 1986 | 1,174 | 3.0 |
| All industries: Investing-economy data[c] | | | | | | | | |
| World | Japan | 1977 | 769,893 | na | 1.4 | 1977 | 50,359 | 4.5 |
| World | Japan | 1986[d] | 921,138 | na | 1.6 | 1986 | 91,427 | 4.3 |
| World | U.S. | 1977 | 7,196,691 | na | 9.0 | 1977 | 193,712 | 17.2 |
| World | U.S. | 1986 | 6,262,700 | na | 6.6 | 1986 | 248,560 | 11.7 |
| Asia | Japan | 1977 | 416,183 | na | 0.8 | 1977 | 5,457 | 7.6 |
| Asia | Japan | 1986[e] | 456,898 | na | 0.8 | 1986 | 26,610 | 13.5 |

| Country | Partner | Year | | | | Year | | |
|---|---|---|---|---|---|---|---|---|
| Asia | U.S. | 1977 | 528,614 | na | 0.7 | 1977 | 11,408 | 15.8 |
| Asia | U.S. | 1986 | 509,600 | na | 0.5 | 1986 | 21,917 | 11.1 |
| ASEAN-6 | Japan | 1986 | 225,267 | na | 0.4 | 1986 | 6,972 | 10.5 |
| Hong Kong | U.S. | 1977 | 44,847 | 2.4 | 0.1 | 1977 | 3,822 | 39.7 |
| Hong Kong | U.S. | 1986 | 46,800 | 1.8 | 0.0 | 1986 | 4,899 | 13.8 |
| Korea | U.S. | 1977 | 31,058 | 0.2 | 0.0 | 1977 | 128 | 1.3 |
| Korea | U.S. | 1986 | 46,700 | 0.3 | 0.0 | 1986 | 406 | 1.2 |
| Singapore | U.S. | 1977 | 44,184 | 4.9 | 0.1 | 1977 | 1,423 | 17.3 |
| Singapore | U.S. | 1986 | 47,200 | 4.1 | 0.0 | 1986 | 7,276 | 32.3 |
| Taiwan | U.S. | 1977 | 68,040 | 1.1 | 0.1 | 1977 | 591 | 6.3 |
| Taiwan | U.S. | 1986 | 62,100 | 0.8 | 0.1 | 1986 | 1,576 | 4.0 |
| Indonesia | U.S. | 1977 | 52,465 | 0.1 | 0.1 | 1977 | 4,426 | 40.8 |
| Indonesia | U.S. | 1986 | 38,300 | 0.1 | 0.0 | 1986 | 4,294 | 29.0 |
| Malaysia | U.S. | 1977 | 35,969 | 0.8 | 0.0 | 1977 | 508 | 8.4 |
| Malaysia | U.S. | 1986 | 62,800 | 1.1 | 0.1 | 1986 | 2,249 | 16.2 |
| Philippines | U.S. | 1977 | 111,768 | 0.8 | 0.1 | 1977 | 355 | 11.3 |
| Philippines | U.S. | 1986 | 92,100 | 0.4 | 0.1 | 1986 | 625 | 12.9 |
| Thailand | Japan | 1983 | 42,650 | 0.2 | 0.1 | 1983 | 754 | 11.8 |
| Thailand | U.S. | 1977 | 27,337 | 0.1 | 0.0 | 1977 | 104 | 3.0 |
| Thailand | U.S. | 1986 | 29,700 | 0.1 | 0.0 | 1986 | 524 | 6.0 |

Manufacturing: Host-economy data[b]

| Country | Partner | Year | | | | Year | | |
|---|---|---|---|---|---|---|---|---|
| Hong Kong | World | 1976 | 63,000 | 8.0 | na | 1976 | na | na |
| Hong Kong | World | 1983 | 96,046 | 10.9 | na | 1983 | na | na |
| Hong Kong | Japan | 1983 | 25,569 | 2.9 | 0.2 | 1983 | na | na |
| Hong Kong | U.S. | 1983 | 40,379 | 4.6 | 0.2 | 1983 | na | na |
| Korea | World | 1976 | 218,000 | 8.2 | na | 1976 | 1,927 | 27.0 |
| Korea | World | 1986 | 372,000 | 9.7 | na | 1986 | 8,621 | 26.1 |
| Singapore | World | 1977 | 117,941 | 47.9 | na | 1977 | 3,807 | 84.7 |
| Singapore | World | 1985 | 134,452 | 45.7 | na | 1985 | 8,177 | 74.1 |
| Singapore | Japan | 1977 | 20,377 | 8.3 | 0.2 | 1977 | 253 | 5.6 |
| Singapore | Japan | 1985 | 41,003 | 13.9 | 0.3 | 1985 | 1,405 | 12.7 |

Table 9.2 (continued)

| Host Economy | Investing Economy | Foreign Affiliate Employment | | | | Foreign Affiliate Exports | | |
|---|---|---|---|---|---|---|---|---|
| | | Year | Number of Employees | As a Share of Host-Country Employment (%) | As a Share of Home-Country Employment (%) | Year | Exports (US$ millions) | As a Share of Host-Country Exports[a] (%) |
| Singapore | U.S. | 1977 | 31,891 | 13.0 | 0.2 | 1977 | 1,543 | 34.3 |
| Singapore | U.S. | 1985 | 42,502 | 14.5 | 0.2 | 1985 | 2,845 | 25.8 |
| Taiwan | World | 1976 | 269,256 | 16.8 | na | 1976 | 2,214 | 31.3 |
| Taiwan | World | 1986 | 246,313 | 9.4 | na | 1986 | 6,241 | 19.1 |
| Taiwan | Japan | 1976 | 118,023 | 7.3 | 0.9 | 1976 | 962 | 13.6 |
| Taiwan | Japan | 1986 | 129,154 | 5.2 | 0.9 | 1986 | 2,903 | 8.9 |
| Taiwan | U.S. | 1976 | 62,831 | 3.9 | 0.3 | 1976 | 573 | 8.1 |
| Taiwan | U.S. | 1986 | 48,492 | 1.9 | 0.3 | 1986 | 1,106 | 3.4 |
| Malaysia | World | 1973 | 96,827 | 32.5 | na | 1973 | na | na |
| Malaysia | World | 1979 | 138,727 | 33.3 | na | 1979 | na | na |
| Malaysia | World | 1985 | 140,972 | 29.6 | na | 1985 | na | na |
| Malaysia | Japan | 1973 | 2,351 | 0.8 | 0.0 | 1973 | na | na |
| Malaysia | U.S. | 1973 | 16,885 | 5.7 | 0.1 | 1973 | na | na |
| Thailand | World | 1975 | na | na | na | 1975 | 192 | 16.7 |
| Thailand | World | 1984 | na | na | na | 1984 | 329 | 6.8 |
| Thailand | Japan | 1975 | na | na | na | 1975 | 49 | 4.3 |
| Thailand | Japan | 1984 | na | na | na | 1984 | 82 | 1.3 |
| Thailand | U.S. | 1975 | na | na | na | 1975 | 8 | 0.7 |
| Thailand | U.S. | 1984 | na | na | na | 1984 | 61 | 1.0 |

| Manufacturing: | Investing-economy data[c] | | | | | | | |
| --- | --- | --- | --- | --- | --- | --- | --- | --- |
| World | Japan | 1977 | 656,586 | na | 4.9 | 1977 | 4,758 | na |
| World | Japan | 1986[f] | 725,810 | na | 5.0 | 1986 | 16,355 | na |
| World | U.S. | 1977 | 4,848,957 | na | 25.2 | 1977 | 59,773 | na |
| World | U.S. | 1986 | 4,175,100 | na | 22.6 | 1986 | 128,901 | na |
| Asia | Japan | 1977 | 378,149 | na | 2.8 | 1977 | 2,689 | na |
| Asia | Japan | 1986[g] | 391,156 | na | 2.7 | 1986 | 9,880 | na |
| Asia | U.S. | 1977 | 398,408 | na | 2.1 | 1977 | 2,921 | na |
| Asia | U.S. | 1986 | 390,000 | na | 2.1 | 1986 | 7,956 | na |
| ASEAN-6 | Japan | 1986 | 177,977 | na | 1.2 | 1986 | 6,972 | na |
| Hong Kong | U.S. | 1977 | 32,775 | 4.3 | 0.2 | 1977 | 600 | 8.1 |
| Hong Kong | U.S. | 1986 | 27,000 | 2.9 | 0.1 | 1986 | 863 | 4.5 |
| Korea | U.S. | 1977 | 23,537 | 0.9 | 0.1 | 1977 | 128 | 1.4 |
| Korea | U.S. | 1986 | 41,500 | 1.1 | 0.2 | 1986 | 341 | 1.0 |
| Singapore | U.S. | 1977 | 35,330 | 14.4 | 0.2 | 1977 | 822 | 12.3 |
| Singapore | U.S. | 1986 | 35,200 | 12.1 | 0.2 | 1986 | 2,771 | 14.1 |
| Taiwan | U.S. | 1977 | 65,364 | 3.8 | 0.3 | 1977 | 558 | 7.1 |
| Taiwan | U.S. | 1986 | 55,000 | 1.9 | 0.3 | 1986 | 1,321 | 4.0 |
| Indonesia | U.S. | 1977 | 14,454 | 0.3 | 0.1 | 1977 | 107 | 8.3 |
| Indonesia | U.S. | 1986 | 7,600 | 0.1 | 0.0 | 1986 | 46 | 1.0 |
| Malaysia | U.S. | 1977 | 28,608 | 4.3 | 0.1 | 1977 | 339 | 11.2 |
| Malaysia | U.S. | 1986 | 54,600 | 6.3 | 0.3 | 1986 | 1,700 | 21.1 |
| Philippines | U.S. | 1977 | 80,221 | 5.3 | 0.4 | 1977 | 260 | 14.6 |
| Philippines | U.S. | 1985 | 71,600 | 3.7 | 0.4 | 1986 | 498 | 19.7 |
| Thailand | Japan | 1976 | 50,822 | 4.4 | 0.4 | 1976 | 130 | 11.3 |
| Thailand | Japan | 1983 | 37,507 | 2.0 | 0.3 | 1983 | 141 | 3.5 |
| Thailand | U.S. | 1977 | 15,130 | 1.1 | 0.1 | 1977 | na | na |
| Thailand | U.S. | 1986 | 22,200 | 1.1 | 0.1 | 1986 | 370 | 6.0 |

Table 9.2 (continued)

na = Not available or not disclosed.

[a]Host exports refer to merchandise exports; ratios tend to be overstated because foreign affiliate exports often include some service exports.

[b]Singapore's export data refer to direct exports only; Thai data refer to promoted firms only; total exports for Taiwan and Singapore were taken from foreign firm surveys and for all others from independent trade data.

[c]U.S. data refer to employment of nonbank affiliates of nonbank parents and exports of majority-owned nonbank affiliates of nonbank parents; manufacturing excludes petroleum and coal products; data for Asia include developing Pacific economies.

[d]Only 60 percent of the estimate for 7/1/87 by Toyo Keizai (1988).

[e]Only 63 percent of the estimate for 7/1/87 by Toyo Keizai (1988).

[f]Only 68 percent of the estimate for 7/1/87 by Toyo Keizai (1988).

[g]Only 64 percent of the estimate for 7/1/87 by Toyo Keizai (1988).

Sources: Hong Kong, Industry Department (1983); International Monetary Fund (1988); Japan, Bangkok Chamber of Commerce (1978, 1981, 1984); Koo and Bark (1988, 39-43); Lee and Ramstetter (this volume); Lin and Mok (1985, 248-49); Malaysia, Department of Statistics (1973, various years); MITI (1979, 1989); Republic of China, Ministry of Economic Affairs (various years); Singapore, Department of Statistics (various years); Sibunruang and Brimble (1987, 335-36 and 344); Toyo Keizai (1988); United States, Department of Commerce, Bureau of Economic Analysis (1981, various years b); sources of Table 9.1.

Table 9.3 Economic Indicators of the Textiles and Apparel Industry, 1976-1986

| Country | Employment (Thousands) 1976 | Employment (Thousands) 1985[a] | Nominal Exports (US$ millions) 1976 | Nominal Exports (US$ millions) 1986[b] | Compound Annual Growth of Industrial Production, 1976-1985[c] (%) | Average Fixed Investment/ Value Added, 1976-1984[d] |
|---|---|---|---|---|---|---|
| **Textiles (ISIC) 321)** | | | | | | |
| Group total | 3,220 | 2,805 | 9,058 | 17,692 | na | na |
| Share of group total (%) | | | | | | |
| United States | 32.4 | 29.9 | 24.6 | 15.8 | 0.3 | 7.3 |
| Japan | 27.2 | 24.0 | 36.7 | 30.0 | -0.2 | 4.9 |
| Hong Kong | 3.6 | 3.9 | 9.0 | 8.0 | na | 11.3 |
| Korea | 11.1 | 13.1 | 13.3 | 22.2 | 7.3 | 22.2 |
| Singapore | 0.4 | 0.1 | 2.3 | 2.4 | -13.3 | 16.5 |
| Taiwan | 9.5 | 11.0 | 11.1 | 14.8 | 6.5 | na |
| Indonesia | 6.6 | 8.5 | 0.0 | 2.0 | 1.1 | 63.8 |
| Malaysia | 1.1 | 1.0 | 0.8 | 1.2 | na | 15.3 |
| Philippines | 2.7 | 2.3 | 0.5 | 0.6 | 17.5 | 22.6 |
| Thailand | 5.5 | 6.2 | 1.8 | 3.0 | 8.2 | na |
| **Apparel (ISIC 322)** | | | | | | |
| Group total | 2,350 | 2,301 | 7,016 | 19,125 | na | na |
| Share of group total (%) | | | | | | |
| United States | 47.5 | 38.6 | 8.5 | 5.2 | -0.2 | 2.2 |
| Japan | 18.7 | 19.0 | 5.0 | 3.6 | -0.1 | 2.6 |
| Hong Kong | 11.3 | 11.5 | 39.5 | 34.8 | na | 6.4 |
| Korea | 8.5 | 10.5 | 23.2 | 24.8 | 8.6 | 8.3 |
| Singapore | 0.9 | 1.1 | 2.4 | 3.6 | 1.4 | 10.7 |
| Taiwan | 4.0 | 6.9 | 18.7 | 17.8 | 9.4 | na |
| Indonesia | 0.2 | 1.6 | 0.1 | 2.5 | na | 21.9 |
| Malaysia | 0.5 | 1.4 | 0.7 | 2.1 | 5.4 | 13.8 |
| Philippines | 3.6 | 3.7 | 0.9 | 1.2 | 19.5 | 8.3 |
| Thailand | 4.8 | 5.9 | 1.1 | 4.3 | 11.7 | na |

na = Not available.

[a]1984 for Japan, Indonesia, and Thailand.

[b]1985 for Taiwan.

[c]Growth of real value added for Thailand.

[d]In nominal terms: 1976-1985 for United States and Singapore; 1976, 1978 and 1983 for Malaysia; and 1976 and 1978-1984 for Philippines.

Sources: Australian National University (1989); Republic of China, Directorate-General of Budget, Accounting and Statistics (1988); Republic of China, Council for Economic Planning and Development (1988); Thailand, National Economic and Social Development Board (various years); United Nations (various years a); United Nations Industrial Development Organization (1989).

1984/85 period (Table 9.3). In textiles, employment declined in all countries except Korea, Taiwan, and Indonesia, with the declines being most rapid in Singapore, the Philippines, Japan, the United States, and Malaysia. In apparel, employment declined most rapidly in the United States and remained virtually unchanged in Japan, Hong Kong, and the Philippines. Employment in the apparel industry grew slowly in Korea, Singapore, and Thailand, and rapidly in Malaysia and especially Indonesia although it remained at very low levels in the latter two countries. Thus while employment growth in the textiles subsector was anemic, it was larger, though still modest, in apparel.

Textile production plummeted in Singapore, stagnated in the United States, Japan, and Indonesia, and grew at a robust pace in Taiwan, Korea, Thailand, and especially the Philippines. In apparel, production stagnated in the United States, Japan, and Singapore but boomed in the Philippines,[4] Thailand, Taiwan, and Korea. The expansion in production, and to some extent employment, in textiles and apparel in the ASEAN-4 is consistent with the perception that much of the textiles and apparel industry which is labor-intensive has shifted production to labor-abundant locations. This perception is supported by the observation that ratios of fixed investment to value added in these two industries were relatively high in the ASEAN-4, especially in Indonesia, and relatively low in the United States and Japan.

With respect to trade, textile exports doubled in nominal terms in 1976–1985/86. Japan continued to be the largest exporter at the end of the period, and Korea replaced the United States as the number two exporter, with Taiwan close behind. The ASEAN-4 countries, except the Philippines, increased exports rapidly, albeit from a small base. Exports of apparel almost tripled over the period to become slightly larger than the value of textile exports. Hong Kong had the largest share of apparel exports throughout the period, followed by Korea and Taiwan. Taken together, these three NICs accounted for over three-fourths of total apparel exports in 1985/86. The ASEAN-4 countries all increased their share of the total region's exports of apparel, with growth being particularly strong in Indonesia.

In 1977, Japanese textiles and apparel affiliates in Asia had 122,778 employees or 70 percent of the employment of all Japanese textiles affiliates worldwide, 19 percent of the employment of all Japanese manufacturing affiliates abroad, and 10 percent of total Japanese employment in these sectors (Table 9.4). By 1986, employment by textiles and apparel affiliates in Asia had fallen substantially but continued to account for about 6 percent of total Japanese employment in the two sectors. In contrast, textiles and apparel have never been major areas of U.S. investment in Asia.

Although host-country data are scarce, foreign affiliate shares of host-country employment in textiles and apparel have been rather limited, under 6 percent in Hong Kong and Korea and 6–12 percent in Taiwan. Both foreign affiliate employment levels and shares of host-country employment decreased in Korea and Taiwan as did corresponding figures for Japanese firms in Thailand. Foreign affiliate export shares have also fallen in Taiwan and Thailand as a result of reduced Japanese activity, although affiliates still accounted for 8 percent and 29 percent of total exports in each country, respectively, in the mid-1980s. This pattern of reduced multinational presence over time is to be expected in a relatively competitive industry where entry barriers are relatively small and the response of domestic firms to foreign competition can be rapid and effective. Moreover, since technology in these industries tends to be standardized, domestic firms can upgrade rather rapidly.

Japan's investment in the textiles and apparel industries is interesting because it has occurred in conjunction with Japan's efforts to rationalize its own domestic productive capacity. Since Japanese textiles and apparel firms were generally small and inexperienced in the operation of foreign affiliates, they sought to minimize risks by investing in groups that were typically centered around banks and trading companies (providers of finance and international trade expertise) and very rarely assumed 100 percent ownership of affiliates. The role of the trading company partners is particularly conspicuous since trading companies have historically handled most foreign transactions (trade and investment) for textiles and apparel firms (Yoshihara 1978, Ch. 4). A government policy which stressed rationalization of production capacity (Yamazawa 1988) and a limited amount of financial aid to foreign investors (Billerbeck and Yasugi 1979) were other factors that led to the large amount of Japanese DFI in this sector in the late 1960s and early 1970s. This institutional setting helped minimize risks that often preclude DFI by small firms operating in relatively competitive industries like textiles and apparel. Furthermore, the ability of textiles and apparel firms to profit from DFI has undoubtedly weakened pressure for import protection in this industry. In contrast, the U.S. textiles and apparel industry has been more effective in obtaining protection from import competition. In this respect, it is interesting that indigineous textiles and apparel firms in the NICs, especially in Taiwan, have also begun to rapidly move productive capacity abroad through DFI in recent years.

## Chemicals

Chemicals[5] was also a generally stagnant industry with the region's employment in this industry remaining virtually unchanged between 1976 and the mid-1980s (Table 9.5). In 1976–1984/85, the decline in employment was largest in Japan while employment in total chemicals grew fastest in Indonesia. In short, there was moderate change in the regional division of labor with decreases in the shares of Japan and the United States and increases in the shares of the NICs and ASEAN-4. The contraction in employment was concentrated in industrial chemicals, while employment in other chemicals grew throughout the region. In the industrial chemicals subsector, production grew in all countries, despite decreases in employment in some countries. Double-digit annual growth rates are observed in Singapore, Taiwan, Indonesia, and the Philippines, with significant growth in Korea and Malaysia as well. Average fixed investment-to-value added ratios were at double-digit levels throughout the region, and were especially high in Korea and Singapore (over 40 percent). Nominal exports of chemicals more than doubled, with the United States continuing to account for a majority of the total although its share decreased from 66 percent to 58 percent. The decline in the U.S. export share was particularly steep in the other chemicals category, falling from over three-fourths to under two-thirds of total exports. The Japanese share stagnated at about 30 percent, with the NICs and ASEAN-4 (except the Philippines) increasing their shares somewhat

As shown in Table 9.6, Japanese affiliate activity in this industry is limited. U.S. affiliates in Asia employed well over two times the number of workers employed by

Table 9.4 Employment and Exports of Foreign Affiliates in the Textiles and Apparel Industry, Selected Years

| Host Economy | Investing Economy | Year | Foreign Affiliate Employment | | | Foreign Affiliate Exports | | |
|---|---|---|---|---|---|---|---|---|
| | | | Number of Employees | As a Share of Host-Country Employment (%) | As a Share of Home-Country Employment (%) | Year | Exports (US$ millions) | As a Share of Host-Country Exports[a] (%) |
| Textiles and apparel: Host-economy data[b] | | | | | | | | |
| Hong Kong | World | 1976 | 13,500 | 3.5 | na | 1976 | na | na |
| Hong Kong | World | 1983 | 21,946 | 6.0 | na | 1983 | na | na |
| Hong Kong | Japan | 1983 | 8,766 | 2.4 | 0.7 | 1983 | na | na |
| Hong Kong | U.S. | 1983 | 6,174 | 1.7 | 0.3 | 1983 | na | na |
| Korea | World | 1976 | 32,725 | 5.8 | na | 1976 | 211 | 7.5 |
| Korea | World | 1986 | 23,907 | 3.3 | na | 1986 | 1,099 | 12.7 |
| Taiwan | World | 1976 | 47,474 | 11.9 | na | 1976 | 500 | 22.3 |
| Taiwan | World | 1986 | 28,661 | 6.3 | na | 1986 | 529 | 7.6 |
| Taiwan | Japan | 1976 | 16,886 | 4.2 | 1.3 | 1976 | 202 | 9.0 |
| Taiwan | Japan | 1986 | 6,030 | 1.3 | 0.5 | 1986 | 61 | 0.9 |
| Taiwan | U.S. | 1976 | 3,869 | 1.0 | 0.2 | 1976 | 78 | 3.5 |
| Taiwan | U.S. | 1986 | 12,103 | 2.6 | 0.7 | 1986 | 246 | 3.6 |
| Thailand | World | 1975 | na | na | na | 1975 | 50 | 35.7 |
| Thailand | World | 1984 | na | na | na | 1984 | 121 | 28.7 |
| Textiles and apparel: Investing-economy data[c] | | | | | | | | |
| World | Japan | 1977 | 175,275 | na | 14.1 | 1977 | 1,045 | na |
| World | Japan | 1986[d] | 83,096 | na | 7.2 | 1986 | 1,435 | na |

| | | | | | | | | |
|---|---|---|---|---|---|---|---|---|
| World | U.S. | 1977 | 51,754 | na | 2.3 | 1977 | na | na |
| World | U.S. | 1986 | 87,300 | na | 5.3 | 1982-1986 | na | na |
| Asia | Japan | 1977 | 122,778 | na | 9.9 | 1977 | 803 | na |
| Asia | Japan | 1986[c] | 70,227 | na | 6.1 | 1986 | 1,353 | na |
| Asia | U.S. | 1977 | 24,861 | na | 1.1 | 1977 | na | na |
| Asia | U.S. | 1986 | 19,600 | na | 1.2 | 1982-1986 | na | na |
| ASEAN-6 | Japan | 1986 | 37,623 | na | 3.3 | 1983 | 381 | na |
| Thailand | Japan | 1976 | 32,096 | 11.1 | 2.4 | 1976 | 87 | 36.1 |
| Thailand | Japan | 1983 | 18,372 | 6.3 | 1.6 | 1983 | 94 | 12.7 |
| **Textiles: Host-economy data[b]** | | | | | | | | |
| Korea | World | 1976 | 19,156 | 5.3 | na | 1976 | 136 | 11.3 |
| Taiwan | World | 1976 | 26,877 | 8.8 | na | 1976 | 344 | 37.8 |
| Taiwan | World | 1986 | 15,644 | 5.2 | na | 1986 | 322 | 12.9 |
| Taiwan | Japan | 1976 | 11,307 | 3.7 | 1.3 | 1976 | 163 | 17.9 |
| Taiwan | Japan | 1986 | 3,618 | 1.2 | 0.6 | 1986 | 50 | 2.0 |
| Taiwan | U.S. | 1976 | 1,709 | 0.6 | 0.2 | 1976 | 56 | 6.1 |
| Taiwan | U.S. | 1986 | 10,051 | 3.4 | 1.6 | 1986 | 220 | 8.8 |
| Thailand | World | 1975 | na | na | na | 1975 | 36 | 42.0 |
| Thailand | World | 1984 | na | na | na | 1984 | 69 | 12.5 |
| **Apparel: Host-economy data[b]** | | | | | | | | |
| Korea | World | 1976 | 13,569 | 6.6 | na | 1976 | 75 | 4.6 |
| Taiwan | World | 1976 | 20,597 | 22.1 | na | 1976 | 156 | 11.7 |
| Taiwan | World | 1986 | 13,017 | 8.3 | na | 1986 | 207 | 4.7 |
| Taiwan | Japan | 1976 | 5,579 | 6.0 | 1.2 | 1976 | 39 | 2.9 |
| Taiwan | Japan | 1986 | 2,412 | 1.5 | 0.4 | 1986 | 10 | 0.2 |
| Taiwan | U.S. | 1976 | 2,160 | 2.3 | 0.2 | 1976 | 22 | 1.7 |
| Taiwan | U.S. | 1986 | 2,052 | 1.3 | 0.2 | 1986 | 26 | 0.6 |
| Thailand | World | 1975 | na | na | na | 1975 | 14 | 25.8 |
| Thailand | World | 1984 | na | na | na | 1984 | 52 | 9.5 |

Table 9.4 (continued)

na = Not available or not disclosed.

[a]Host exports refer to merchandise exports; ratios tend to be overstated because foreign affiliate data often include some service exports.

[b]Apparel includes footwear for Taiwan, leather products for Thailand; for Thailand all figures refer to promoted firms only; total exports from foreign firm surveys for Taiwan, from trade data for all others.

[c]U.S. data refer to employment of nonbank affiliates of nonbank parents and exports of majority-owned nonbank affiliates of nonbank parents; manufacturing excludes petroleum and coal products; U.S. data for Asia include developing Pacific island economies.

[d]Only 54 percent of the estimate for 7/1/87 by Toyo Keizai (1988).

[e]Only 61 percent of the estimate for 7/1/87 by Toyo Keizai (1988).

Sources: Asian Development Bank (1988); Hong Kong, Industry Department (1983); International Monetary Fund (1988); Japan, Bangkok Chamber of Commerce (1978, 1981, 1984); Japan, Prime Minister's Office (1988); Koo (1982, 97-102); Lee and Ramstetter (this volume); Lin and Mok (1985, 248-49); MITI (1979, 1989); Republic of China, Ministry of Economic Affairs (various years); Sibunruang and Brimble (1987, 335-36); Toyo Keizai (1988); United States, Department of Commerce, Bureau of the Census (various years); United States, Department of Commerce, Bureau of Economic Analysis (1981, 1985, various years b); sources of Tables 9.1, 9.2, and 9.3.

Table 9.5  Economic Indicators of the Chemicals Industry, 1976-1986

| Country | Employment (Thousands) | | Nominal Exports (US$ millions) | | Compound Annual Growth of Industrial Production, 1976-1985[c] | Average Fixed Investment/ Value Added, 1976-1984[d] |
|---|---|---|---|---|---|---|
| | 1976 | 1985[a] | 1976 | 1986[b] | (%) | (%) |
| Industrial chemicals (ISIC 351) | | | | | | |
| Group total | 833 | 743 | 11,942 | 29,502 | na | na |
| Share of group total (%) | | | | | | |
| United States | 54.8 | 54.0 | 63.5 | 56.8 | 3.3 | 15.9 |
| Japan | 29.4 | 25.6 | 33.1 | 30.6 | 2.1 | 16.4 |
| Hong Kong | 0.1 | 0.3 | 0.1 | 0.3 | na | 27.2 |
| Korea | 5.0 | 5.0 | 0.9 | 3.5 | 8.9 | 42.6 |
| Singapore | 0.2 | 0.4 | 1.0 | 3.4 | 17.3 | 44.9 |
| Taiwan | 4.9 | 7.5 | 1.0 | 2.9 | 15.0 | na |
| Indonesia | 1.2 | 3.1 | 0.0 | 0.7 | 19.1 | 18.4 |
| Malaysia | 0.5 | 0.8 | 0.1 | 0.7 | 5.3 | 22.1 |
| Philippines | 1.4 | 1.2 | 0.2 | 0.7 | 13.9 | 21.2 |
| Thailand | 2.4 | 2.2 | 0.1 | 0.4 | na | na |
| Other chemicals (ISIC 352) | | | | | | |
| Group total | 820 | 917 | 3,600 | 10,143 | na | na |
| Share of group total (%) | | | | | | |
| United States | 52.4 | 50.8 | 76.4 | 63.5 | 4.3 | 5.8 |
| Japan | 24.9 | 22.8 | 16.4 | 27.0 | 5.9 | 6.9 |
| Hong Kong | 0.6 | 0.6 | 1.0 | 1.1 | na | 6.3 |
| Korea | 5.7 | 6.3 | 0.5 | 1.4 | 13.3 | 12.1 |
| Singapore | 0.4 | 0.5 | 3.3 | 4.0 | 9.9 | 12.3 |
| Taiwan | 4.3 | 5.9 | 0.8 | 1.1 | 6.2 | na |
| Indonesia | 3.8 | 5.7 | 0.7 | 0.7 | 7.9 | 20.8 |
| Malaysia | 0.9 | 1.1 | 0.5 | 0.6 | na | 9.5 |
| Philippines | 2.7 | 2.5 | 0.1 | 0.2 | na | 8.1 |
| Thailand | 4.2 | 3.7 | 0.2 | 0.3 | na | na |

na = Not available.
[a]1984 for Japan, Indonesia, and Thailand.
[b]1985 for Taiwan.
[c]Growth of real value added for Thailand.
[d]1976-1985 for the United States and Singapore; 1976, 1978 and 1983 for Malaysia; and 1976 and 1978-1984 for the Philippines.

Sources: Sources of Table 9.3.

Table 9.6 Employment and Exports of Foreign Affiliates in the Chemicals Industry, Selected Years

| Host Economy | Investing Economy | Year | Foreign Affiliate Employment | | | Foreign Affiliate Exports | | |
|---|---|---|---|---|---|---|---|---|
| | | | Number of Employees | As a Share of Host-Country Employment (%) | As a Share of Home-Country Employment (%) | Year | Exports (US$ millions) | As a Share of Host-Country Exports[a] (%) |
| **Chemicals: Host-economy data[b]** | | | | | | | | |
| Hong Kong | World | 1976 | 700 | 12.5 | na | 1976 | na | na |
| Hong Kong | World | 1983 | 1,381 | 16.8 | na | 1983 | na | na |
| Hong Kong | U.S. | 1983 | 562 | 6.9 | 0.0 | 1983 | na | na |
| Korea | World | 1976 | 25,525 | 12.3 | na | 1976 | 371 | 43.5 |
| Korea | World | 1986 | 28,683 | 6.9 | na | 1986 | 591 | 12.2 |
| Taiwan | World | 1976 | 18,466 | 21.5 | na | 1976 | 261 | 93.9 |
| Taiwan | World | 1986 | 16,797 | 13.5 | na | 1986 | 344 | 30.8 |
| Taiwan | Japan | 1976 | 4,433 | 5.2 | 0.0 | 1976 | 45 | 16.3 |
| Taiwan | Japan | 1986 | 2,646 | 2.1 | 0.0 | 1986 | 37 | 3.3 |
| Taiwan | U.S. | 1976 | 2,589 | 3.0 | 0.0 | 1976 | 34 | 12.3 |
| Taiwan | U.S. | 1986 | 1,846 | 1.5 | 0.0 | 1986 | 51 | 4.6 |
| Thailand | World | 1975 | na | na | na | 1975 | 1 | 6.0 |
| Thailand | World | 1984 | na | na | na | 1984 | 12 | 6.3 |
| **Chemicals: Investing-economy data[c]** | | | | | | | | |
| World | Japan | 1977 | 23,980 | na | 5.5 | 1977 | 193 | na |
| World | Japan | 1986[d] | 34,862 | na | 8.8 | 1986 | 1,546 | na |
| World | U.S. | 1977 | 614,086 | na | 69.8 | 1977 | 8,447 | na |
| World | U.S. | 1986 | 571,800 | na | 71.3 | 1986 | 19,931 | na |
| Asia | Japan | 1977 | 14,505 | na | 3.3 | 1977 | 77 | na |
| Asia | Japan | 1986[e] | 20,831 | na | 5.3 | 1986 | 537 | na |
| ASEAN-6 | Japan | 1986 | 9,525 | na | 2.4 | 1986 | 291 | na |

| | | | | | | | | |
|---|---|---|---|---|---|---|---|---|
| Asia | U.S. | 1977 | 55,751 | na | 6.3 | 1977 | 139 | na |
| Asia | U.S. | 1986 | 49,200 | na | 6.1 | 1984 | 326 | na |
| Hong Kong | U.S. | 1977 | 982 | 16.9 | 0.1 | 1977 | 42 | 73.3 |
| Hong Kong | U.S. | 1985 | 1,100 | 13.6 | 0.1 | 1986 | 91 | 42.9 |
| Korea | U.S. | 1977 | 3,448 | 3.9 | 0.4 | 1977 | 1 | 0.4 |
| Korea | U.S. | 1985 | 2,500 | 2.6 | 0.3 | 1986 | 0 | 0.0 |
| Singapore | U.S. | 1977 | 359 | 6.8 | 0.0 | 1977 | 2 | 0.7 |
| Singapore | U.S. | 1985 | 1,200 | 15.5 | 0.1 | 1982 | 42 | 5.2 |
| Taiwan | U.S. | 1977 | 3,623 | 4.6 | 0.4 | 1977 | 53 | 26.4 |
| Taiwan | U.S. | 1985 | 3,300 | 3.0 | 0.4 | 1985 | 29 | 3.0 |
| Indonesia | U.S. | 1977 | 2,224 | 5.1 | 0.3 | 1977 | 0 | 0.0 |
| Indonesia | U.S. | 1984 | 2,900 | 3.8 | 0.3 | 1986 | 3 | 1.1 |
| Malaysia | U.S. | 1977 | 1,100 | 8.8 | 0.1 | 1977 | 7 | 20.8 |
| Malaysia | U.S. | 1985 | 1,300 | 8.0 | 0.2 | 1986 | 20 | 7.7 |
| Philippines | U.S. | 1977 | 7,696 | 18.2 | 0.9 | 1977 | 23 | 47.9 |
| Philippines | U.S. | 1985 | 7,700 | 23.7 | 0.9 | 1986 | 9 | 3.7 |
| Thailand | Japan | 1976 | 3,923 | 7.2 | 0.9 | 1976 | 3 | 25.7 |
| Thailand | Japan | 1983 | 2,077 | 3.9 | 0.5 | 1983 | 6 | 10.3 |
| Thailand | U.S. | 1977 | 1,211 | 1.8 | 0.1 | 1977 | 5 | 27.0 |
| Thailand | U.S. | 1984 | 1,900 | 3.8 | 0.2 | 1986 | 3 | 2.2 |

na = Not available or not disclosed.

[a]Host exports refer to merchandise exports; ratios tend to be overstated because foreign affiliates data often include some service exports.

[b]Includes rubber and plastics for Korea; includes petroleum and coal products for Taiwan and Thailand; Thai data refer only to promoted firms; total exports from foreign firm surveys for Taiwan, from trade data for all others.

[c]U.S. data refer to employment of nonbank affiliates of nonbank parents and exports of majority-owned nonbank affiliates of nonbank parents; manufacturing excludes petroleum and coal products; U.S. data for Asia include developing Pacific island economies.

[d]Only 62 percent of the estimate for 7/1/87 by Toyo Keizai (1988).

[e]Only 64 percent of the estimate for 7/1/87 by Toyo Keizai (1988).

<u>Sources</u>: Sources of Table 9.4.

Japanese affiliates in Asia , despite accounting for only 9 percent of total employment in U.S. chemicals affiliates worldwide. However, Japanese affiliates exported much more in 1977 and Japanese affiliate employment in Asia as a share of total chemicals affiliate employment worldwide was much larger. From the host country point of view, U.S. chemicals affiliates account for large shares of chemicals employment (7–24 percent) in Hong Kong, Singapore, Malaysia, and the Philippines. Japanese chemicals affiliates employ more people than their U.S. counterparts in Taiwan and Thailand but their shares of host-country chemicals employment are relatively low (2–7 percent). There are also a number of European affiliates that are active in Asia in this industry as indicated by the fact that non-U.S., non-Japanese multinationals account for over one-half of the employment by chemicals affiliates in Taiwan and a large portion in Hong Kong.[6] Foreign firms in the chemicals industry were generally much more significant in terms of exports, especially in the mid-1970s when foreign firm shares of exports exceeded 40 percent in Hong Kong, Korea, Taiwan, and the Philippines. However, in the 1980s, these shares have generally fallen dramatically.

## Metals

Overall, metals is yet another stagnant sector in which regional employment fell in 1976–1984/85 (Table 9.7 and sources). The decline was largely a result of the contraction in U.S. and Japanese basic metals industries. In this industry, the U.S. share of regional employment fell from 57 percent to 47 percent, while the developing country share jumped from 9 percent to 17 percent. U.S. and Japanese employment declined 5 percent and 2 percent annually, respectively, while annual increases were 5 percent or better in Korea, Taiwan, Malaysia, and Indonesia. Iron and steel accounted for most of the employment in basic metals (70–75 percent regionwide) and the changes of basic metals employment in these countries were thus concentrated in this subsector. In contrast, regional employment grew slightly and changes in the regional division of labor were less pronounced in metal products, though Korea and Taiwan both increased their employment shares significantly.

These changes are also reflected in the production data. In basic metals, iron and steel production grew rapidly in Indonesia and Korea, moderately in Singapore and Malaysia, and rather slowly in Japan, but plummeted in the United States. In metal products, growth was again relatively rapid in Indonesia, Korea, Taiwan, Malaysia, and the Philippines. Average fixed investment was relatively high in all of the countries in the basic metals subsector and in the developing countries for metal products. In particular, the extraordinarily high ratios for Korea, 57 percent in basic metals and 24 percent in metal products, indicate the high priority this sector has received in the allocation of investment funds in that country.

Regional exports of basic metals and metal products combined increased relatively slowly with Japan dominating in both subsectors. However, the Japanese share of basic metals dropped somewhat from 69 percent to 62 percent. On the other hand, exports have grown particularly rapidly in Korea and Taiwan; their combined share grew from 4 percent to 13 percent in basic metals and from 5 percent to 20 percent in metal products. Interestingly, Korea has specialized in basic metals while Taiwan has focused on metal products. Rapid export share increases are also observed for

## Table 9.7  Economic Indicators of the Metals Industry, 1976-1986

| Country | Employment (Thousands) 1976 | Employment (Thousands) 1985[a] | Nominal Exports (US$ millions) 1976 | Nominal Exports (US$ millions) 1986[b] | Compound Annual Growth of Industrial Production, 1976-1985[c] (%) | Average Fixed Investment/ Value Added, 1976-1984[d] (%) |
|---|---|---|---|---|---|---|
| **Basic metals (ISIC 371 + ISIC 372)** | | | | | | |
| Group total | 1,846 | 1,468 | 16,476 | 24,245 | na | na |
| Share of group total (%) | | | | | | |
| United States | 57.2 | 47.2 | 21.8 | 17.0 | na | 12.0 |
| Japan | 33.9 | 36.0 | 68.7 | 62.1 | na | 16.9 |
| Hong Kong | 0.2 | 0.3 | 0.1 | 0.2 | na | 15.3 |
| Korea | 2.9 | 6.7 | 2.8 | 9.8 | na | 56.7 |
| Singapore | 0.1 | 0.1 | 0.6 | 2.0 | na | 18.1 |
| Taiwan | 2.4 | 4.6 | 0.8 | 3.2 | 13.3 | na |
| Indonesia | 0.3 | 1.0 | 0.1 | 2.1 | na | 20.0 |
| Malaysia | 0.4 | 0.9 | 3.7 | 1.6 | na | 30.9 |
| Philippines | 0.8 | 1.2 | 0.4 | 1.0 | na | 25.7 |
| Thailand | 1.8 | 2.0 | 1.0 | 0.9 | 6.2 | na |
| **Metal products (ISIC 381)** | | | | | | |
| Group total | 2,457 | 2,608 | 7,281 | 15,112 | na | na |
| Share of group total (%) | | | | | | |
| United States | 54.6 | 52.1 | 53.3 | 32.6 | 1.7 | 5.7 |
| Japan | 32.5 | 29.5 | 35.6 | 40.1 | 1.6 | 5.0 |
| Hong Kong | 2.6 | 2.8 | 3.4 | 4.1 | na | 11.8 |
| Korea | 2.4 | 4.8 | 1.9 | 8.5 | 15.0 | 24.4 |
| Singapore | 0.5 | 0.7 | 1.2 | 2.6 | 3.2 | 25.3 |
| Taiwan | 3.4 | 5.9 | 3.4 | 11.0 | 7.2 | na |
| Indonesia | 1.3 | 1.6 | 0.6 | 0.2 | 7.8 | 26.4 |
| Malaysia | 0.6 | 0.8 | 0.3 | 0.4 | 10.2 | 15.3 |
| Philippines | 1.2 | 0.6 | 0.1 | 0.1 | 29.1 | 11.3 |
| Thailand | 0.9 | 1.2 | 0.2 | 0.5 | 4.2 | na |

na = Not available.
[a]1984 for Japan, Indonesia, and Thailand.
[b]1985 for Taiwan.
[c]Growth of real value added for Thailand.
[d]1976-1985 for the United States and Singapore; 1976, 1978 and 1983 for Malaysia; and 1976 and 1978-1984 for the Philippines.

Sources:  Sources of Table 9.3.

260

Table 9.8 Employment and Exports of Foreign Affiliates in the Metals Industry, Selected Years

| Host Economy | Investing Economy | Year | Foreign Affiliate Employment | | | Foreign Affiliate Exports | | |
|---|---|---|---|---|---|---|---|---|
| | | | Number of Employees | As a Share of Host-Country Employment (%) | As a Share of Home-Country Employment (%) | Year | Exports (US$ millions) | As a Share of Host-Country Exports[a] (%) |
| All metals: Host-economy data[b] | | | | | | | | |
| Korea | World | 1976 | 10,272 | 9.0 | na | 1976 | 48 | 8.1 |
| Korea | World | 1986 | 20,286 | 8.2 | na | 1986 | 347 | 9.5 |
| Taiwan | World | 1976 | 11,132 | 8.8 | na | 1976 | 58 | 15.4 |
| Taiwan | World | 1986 | 9,961 | 4.5 | na | 1986 | 211 | 6.9 |
| Taiwan | Japan | 1976 | 6,504 | 5.1 | 0.5 | 1976 | 39 | 10.3 |
| Taiwan | Japan | 1986 | 6,664 | 3.0 | 0.5 | 1986 | 160 | 5.2 |
| Taiwan | U.S. | 1976 | 1,926 | 1.5 | 0.1 | 1976 | 11 | 3.0 |
| Taiwan | U.S. | 1986 | 1,571 | 0.7 | 0.1 | 1986 | 8 | 0.3 |
| Thailand | World | 1975 | na | na | na | 1975 | 118 | 89.9 |
| Thailand | World | 1984 | na | na | na | 1984 | 3 | 0.9 |
| All metals: Investing-economy data[c] | | | | | | | | |
| World | U.S. | 1977 | 396,241 | na | 15.9 | 1977 | 3,094 | na |
| World | U.S. | 1986 | 271,600 | na | 12.9 | 1986 | 5,259 | na |
| Asia | U.S. | 1977 | 15,773 | na | 0.6 | 1977 | 69 | na |
| Asia | U.S. | 1986 | 10,100 | na | 0.5 | 1985 | 79 | na |
| Hong Kong | U.S. | 1977 | 532 | 0.7 | 0.0 | 1977 | na | na |
| Hong Kong | U.S. | 1985 | 600 | 0.9 | 0.0 | 1984 | 2 | 0.3 |

| | | | | | | | | |
|---|---|---|---|---|---|---|---|---|
| Korea | U.S. | 1977 | na | na | na | 1977 | 0 | 0.0 |
| Korea | U.S. | 1985 | 800 | 0.4 | 0.0 | 1986 | 0 | 0.0 |
| Singapore | U.S. | 1977 | 1,965 | 13.4 | 0.1 | 1977 | na | na |
| Singapore | U.S. | 1985 | 200 | 0.9 | 0.0 | 1986 | 11 | 1.2 |
| Taiwan | U.S. | 1977 | na | na | na | 1977 | 0 | 0.0 |
| Taiwan | U.S. | 1985 | 800 | 0.4 | 0.0 | 1985 | 11 | 0.5 |
| Indonesia | U.S. | 1977 | 293 | 0.8 | 0.0 | 1977 | 0 | 0.0 |
| Indonesia | U.S. | 1984 | 200 | 0.4 | 0.0 | 1986 | 0 | 0.0 |
| Malaysia | U.S. | 1977 | na | na | na | 1977 | 0 | 0.0 |
| Malaysia | U.S. | 1985 | 100 | 0.3 | 0.0 | 1986 | 0 | 0.0 |
| Philippines | U.S. | 1985 | 1,300 | 4.0 | 0.1 | 1986 | 4 | 2.3 |
| Thailand | Japan | 1976 | 2,947 | 5.3 | 0.2 | 1976 | 0 | 0.0 |
| Thailand | Japan | 1983 | 1,442 | 2.4 | 0.1 | 1983 | 0 | 0.0 |
| Thailand | U.S. | 1977 | 998 | 1.5 | 0.0 | 1977 | 0 | 0.0 |
| Thailand | U.S. | 1983 | 200 | 0.3 | 0.0 | 1986 | 0 | 0.0 |
| **Basic metals: Host-economy data[b]** | | | | | | | | |
| Korea | World | 1976 | 6,022 | 11.1 | na | 1976 | 36 | 7.9 |
| Thailand | World | 1975 | na | na | na | 1975 | 115 | 96.2 |
| Thailand | World | 1984 | na | na | na | 1984 | 3 | 1.1 |
| **Basic metals: Investing-economy data[c]** | | | | | | | | |
| World | Japan | 1977 | 131,503 | na | 21.5 | 1977 | 960 | na |
| World | Japan | 1986[d] | 79,311 | na | 14.9 | 1986 | 1,300 | na |
| World | U.S. | 1977 | 171,915 | na | 16.2 | 1977 | 1,302 | na |
| World | U.S. | 1986 | 93,900 | na | 13.6 | 1986 | 2,148 | na |
| Asia | Japan | 1977 | 28,234 | na | 4.6 | 1977 | 76 | na |
| Asia | Japan | 1986[e] | 21,065 | na | 4.0 | 1986 | 566 | na |
| ASEAN-6 | Japan | 1986 | 12,158 | na | 2.3 | 1986 | 449 | na |
| Asia | U.S. | 1977 | 8,331 | na | 0.8 | 1977 | na | na |
| Asia | U.S. | 1986 | 3,100 | na | 0.4 | 1982-1986 | na | na |

Table 9.8 (continued)

| Host Economy | Investing Economy | Foreign Affiliate Employment | | | | Foreign Affiliate Exports | | |
|---|---|---|---|---|---|---|---|---|
| | | Year | Number of Employees | As a Share of Host-Country Employment (%) | As a Share of Home-Country Employment (%) | Year | Exports (US$ millions) | As a Share of Host-Country Exports[a] (%) |
| Metal products: Host-economy data[b] | | | | | | | | |
| Hong Kong | World | 1976 | 1,800 | 2.6 | na | 1976 | na | na |
| Hong Kong | World | 1983 | 2,900 | 4.4 | na | 1983 | na | na |
| Hong Kong | U.S. | 1983 | 1,547 | 2.3 | 0.1 | 1983 | na | na |
| Korea | World | 1976 | 4,250 | 7.0 | na | 1976 | 12 | 8.8 |
| Thailand | World | 1975 | na | na | na | 1975 | 2 | 21.2 |
| Thailand | World | 1984 | na | na | na | 1984 | 0 | 0.0 |
| Metal products: Investing-economy data[c] | | | | | | | | |
| World | U.S. | 1977 | 224,326 | na | 15.7 | 1977 | 1,792 | na |
| World | U.S. | 1986 | 177,700 | na | 12.0 | 1986 | 3,111 | na |
| Asia | U.S. | 1977 | 7,442 | na | 0.5 | 1977 | na | na |
| Asia | U.S. | 1982 | 6,100 | na | 0.4 | 1982-1986 | na | na |

na = Not available or not disclosed.

[a] Host exports refer to merchandise exports; ratios tend to be overstated because foreign affiliate data often include some service exports.

[b] Thai data refer only to promoted firms; total exports from foreign firm surveys for Taiwan, from trade data for all others.

[c] U.S. data refer to employment of nonbank affiliates of nonbank parents and exports of majority-owned nonbank affiliates of nonbank parents; manufacturing excludes petroleum and coal products; U.S. data for Asia include developing Pacific island economies.

[d] Only 63 percent of the estimate for 7/1/87 by Toyo Keizai (1988).

[e] Only 85 percent of the estimate for 7/1/87 by Toyo Keizai (1988).

Sources: Sources of Table 9.4.

Indonesia in basic metals and for Singapore in both basic metals and metal products, but these shares remain relatively small.

Multinational affiliate shares of developing Asian metals industries have generally been modest (Table 9.8). Only in Singapore in the mid-1970s was the ratio of foreign affiliate employment to host employment over 10 percent in this sector. On the export side, foreign firms are somewhat more significant, but Thailand is the only country in which metals affiliates are estimated to have accounted for over 20 percent of total exports. Asian metals affiliates are also very small from the United States' point of view, representing less than 1 percent of U.S. employment in that industry. On the other hand, Asian basic metals affiliates are somewhat more significant for Japan.

In short, although the metals industry has experienced extensive adjustment in the last decade, multinationals have played a limited role in the adjustment. Among the numerous reasons for this, the most important are (1) the high policy-priority given to developing the domestic metals sector by many Asian governments, and (2) technology, in particular the importance of single-plant economies of scale, which made it inefficient to decentralize production.

### Electric and Electronic Machinery

The Asia-Pacific electric and electronic machinery industry provides perhaps the most interesting case of multinational involvement because it exhibits rapid growth in employment, production, and exports, and heavy involvement of multinationals. As Chen (1987) stresses, an important reason for the large multinational involvement is technological. The combination of a manufacturing process that is characterized by different production stages with distinctly diverse factor requirements, low transportation costs, rapid technological progress, and institutional arrangements which facilitate the division of production processes among many countries,[7] has led to the development of a highly internationalized industry. In Markusen's (this volume) terminology, this industry is subject to pervasive multiplant economies of scale.

Regionally, electric and electronic machinery employment grew at a robust pace for the period 1976–1984/85. In all of the countries except Thailand, employment growth exceeded 2.5 percent annually (Table 9.9). Employment in electric and electronic machinery grew 3–4 percent annually in Japan and the United States, 3–6 percent annually in the NICs, and 4–10 percent annually in Indonesia, Malaysia, and the Philippines. As a result, the U.S. share of regional employment dropped from 45 percent to 43 percent, the developing country share rose from 19 percent to 22 percent, and the Japanese share remained unchanged.

Production also grew rapidly. Annual growth rates were 5 percent in the United States, 9–15 percent in Thailand, Japan, Taiwan, Singapore, Indonesia, and Malaysia, and 18–22 percent in Korea and the Philippines. Average fixed investment-to-value added ratios were relatively low in the United States, Japan, and Hong Kong, but exceeded 20 percent in Korea, Singapore, Indonesia, Malaysia, and the Philippines.

Electric and electronic machinery exports boomed for the region as a whole, growing 14 percent annually in the period 1976–1985/86. Although U.S. exports

Table 9.9  Economic Indicators of the Electric and Electronic Machinery Industry, 1976-1986

| Country | Employment (Thousands) | | Nominal Exports (US$ millions) | | Compound Annual Growth of Industrial Production, 1976-1985[c] | Average Fixed Investment/ Value Added, 1976-1984[d] |
|---|---|---|---|---|---|---|
| | 1976 | 1985[a] | 1976 | 1986[b] | (%) | (%) |
| Electric and electronic machinery (ISIC 383) | | | | | | |
| Group total | 3,529 | 4,762 | 21,863 | 82,008 | na | na |
| Share of group total (%) | | | | | | |
| United States | 45.4 | 42.6 | 36.0 | 22.0 | 5.2 | 8.1 |
| Japan | 35.6 | 35.9 | 44.7 | 51.0 | 14.1 | 10.6 |
| Hong Kong | 2.5 | 2.3 | 4.1 | 3.7 | na | 12.1 |
| Korea | 5.1 | 6.1 | 4.2 | 7.1 | 18.3 | 23.8 |
| Singapore | 1.4 | 1.7 | 4.1 | 5.7 | 10.9 | 20.2 |
| Taiwan | 6.0 | 7.1 | 5.8 | 5.6 | 15.2 | na |
| Indonesia | 0.5 | 0.8 | 0.1 | 0.1 | 9.3 | 23.6 |
| Malaysia | 1.3 | 1.7 | 0.9 | 3.6 | 9.7 | 20.4 |
| Philippines | 0.7 | 0.8 | 0.0 | 0.4 | 22.4 | 24.0 |
| Thailand | 1.4 | 1.0 | 0.2 | 0.9 | 9.8 | na |

na = Not available.
[a]1984 for Japan, Indonesia, and Thailand.
[b]1985 for Taiwan.
[c]Growth of real value added for Thailand.
[d]1976-1985 for the United States and Singapore; 1976, 1978 and 1983 for Malaysia; and 1976 and 1978-1984 for the Philippines.

Sources: Australian National University (1989); Republic of China, Directorate-General of Budget, Accounting and Statistics (1988); Republic of China, Council for Economic Planning and Development (1988); Thailand, National Economic and Social Development Board (various years); United Nations (various years a); United Nations Industrial Development Organization (1989).

more than doubled, the U.S. share of the region's exports fell from 36 percent to 22 percent, while Japan's share increased from 45 percent to 51 percent. The NICs' share increased from 18 percent to 23 percent and the ASEAN-4 share grew from 1 percent to 5 percent as exports grew more than 30 percent annually in Malaysia, the Philippines, and Thailand.

Multinationals had a large, if not dominant, hand in the rapid growth of this industry (Table 9.10 and sources). In Hong Kong and Taiwan, foreign affiliate employment shares fell over time but remained high in the 1980s at 29 percent and 37 percent, respectively. In Korea, the share of foreign affiliate employment in the electric and electronic machinery industry increased from 37 percent in 1976 to 57 percent in 1986. Japanese affiliates were larger than their U.S. counterparts in Taiwan, while U.S. affiliates dominated in Hong Kong and were somewhat larger in

Table 9.10 Employment and Exports of Foreign Affiliates in the Electric and Electronic Machinery Industry, Selected Years

| Host Economy | Investing Economy | Foreign Affiliate Employment | | | | Foreign Affiliate Exports | | |
|---|---|---|---|---|---|---|---|---|
| | | Year | Number of Employees | As a Share of Host-Country Employment (%) | As a Share of Home-Country Employment (%) | Year | Exports (US$ millions) | As a Share of Host-Country Exports[a] (%) |
| **Electric and electronic machinery: Host-economy data[b]** | | | | | | | | |
| Hong Kong | World | 1976 | 28,800 | 32.7 | na | 1976 | na | na |
| Hong Kong | World | 1983 | 38,086 | 28.9 | na | 1983 | na | na |
| Hong Kong | Japan | 1983 | 6,039 | 4.6 | 0.4 | 1983 | na | na |
| Hong Kong | U.S. | 1983 | 24,043 | 18.3 | 1.3 | 1983 | na | na |
| Korea | World | 1976 | 66,546 | 36.5 | na | 1976 | 622 | 68.2 |
| Korea | World | 1986 | 205,007 | 56.5 | na | 1986 | 4,229 | 72.6 |
| Taiwan | World | 1976 | 127,118 | 59.8 | na | 1976 | 1,057 | 82.9 |
| Taiwan | World | 1986 | 134,099 | 36.8 | na | 1986 | 3,876 | 43.6 |
| Taiwan | Japan | 1976 | 68,545 | 32.2 | 5.5 | 1976 | 510 | 40.0 |
| Taiwan | Japan | 1986 | 86,646 | 23.8 | 4.6 | 1986 | 1,926 | 21.7 |
| Taiwan | U.S. | 1976 | 45,192 | 21.3 | 2.4 | 1976 | 406 | 0.8 |
| Taiwan | U.S. | 1986 | 24,637 | 6.8 | 1.3 | 1986 | 658 | 0.2 |
| Thailand | World | 1975 | na | na | na | 1975 | 1 | 4.2 |
| Thailand | World | 1984 | na | na | na | 1984 | 45 | 11.2 |
| **Electric and electronic machinery: Investing-economy data[c]** | | | | | | | | |
| World | Japan | 1977 | 152,574 | na | 12.6 | 1977 | 966 | na |
| World | Japan | 1986[d] | 239,438 | na | 12.8 | 1983 | 3,847 | na |
| World | U.S. | 1977 | 756,324 | na | 43.4 | 1977 | 6,293 | na |
| World | U.S. | 1986 | 745,700 | na | 38.4 | 1986 | 12,585 | na |
| Asia | Japan | 1977 | 114,413 | na | 9.5 | 1977 | 787 | na |

| | | | | | | | | |
|---|---|---|---|---|---|---|---|---|
| Asia | Japan | 1986[e] | 155,162 | na | 8.3 | 1986 | 2,448 | na |
| Asia | U.S. | 1977 | 158,421 | na | 9.1 | 1977 | na | na |
| Asia | U.S. | 1986 | 165,300 | na | 8.5 | 1986 | 5,416 | na |
| ASEAN-6 | Japan | 1986 | 63,897 | na | 3.4 | 1986 | 1,553 | na |
| Hong Kong | U.S. | 1977 | 18,791 | 21.0 | 1.1 | 1977 | 360 | 31.7 |
| Hong Kong | U.S. | 1985 | 9,800 | 8.8 | 0.5 | 1986 | 386 | 12.8 |
| Korea | U.S. | 1977 | 8,459 | 4.5 | 0.5 | 1977 | na | na |
| Korea | U.S. | 1985 | 15,500 | 5.4 | 0.8 | 1983 | 299 | 10.0 |
| Singapore | U.S. | 1977 | 25,162 | 46.2 | 1.4 | 1977 | 650 | 55.4 |
| Singapore | U.S. | 1985 | 20,500 | 24.8 | 1.0 | 1986 | 1,384 | 29.7 |
| Taiwan | U.S. | 1977 | 47,723 | 20.0 | 2.7 | 1977 | 442 | 30.3 |
| Taiwan | U.S. | 1985 | 36,600 | 10.8 | 1.8 | 1985 | 910 | 20.0 |
| Indonesia | U.S. | 1977 | 5,250 | 25.5 | 0.3 | 1982 | 109 | 84.5 |
| Indonesia | U.S. | 1984 | 3,100 | 8.5 | 0.2 | 1986 | 40 | 67.6 |
| Malaysia | U.S. | 1977 | 23,586 | 48.1 | 1.4 | 1982 | 1,283 | 84.2 |
| Malaysia | U.S. | 1985 | 47,100 | 57.6 | 2.3 | 1986 | 1,626 | 54.4 |
| Philippines | U.S. | 1977 | 8,922 | 22.9 | 0.5 | 1977 | 28 | 107.4 |
| Philippines | U.S. | 1985 | 14,700 | 39.1 | 0.7 | 1986 | 324 | 94.7 |
| Thailand | Japan | 1983 | 4,960 | 9.8 | 0.3 | 1983 | 8 | 2.8 |
| Thailand | U.S. | 1984 | 12,200 | 26.2 | 0.6 | 1985 | 256 | 59.6 |

na = Not available or not disclosed.

[a]Host exports refer to merchandise exports; ratios tend to be overstated because foreign affiliate data often include some service exports.

[b]Thai data refer only to promoted firms; total exports from foreign firm surveys for Taiwan, from trade data for all others.

[c]U.S. data refer to employment of nonbank affiliates of nonbank parents and exports of majority-owned nonbank affiliates of nonbank parents; U.S. data for Asia include developing Pacific economies.

[d]Only 80 percent of the estimate for 7/1/87 by Toyo Keizai (1988).

[e]Only 70 percent of the estimate for 7/1/87 by Toyo Keizai (1988).

Sources: Sources of Table 9.4.

Thailand as well. Moreover, U.S. affiliates accounted for at least one-fourth of domestic employment in Singapore, Indonesia, Malaysia, and the Philippines in 1977. By the mid-1980s, U.S. affiliate employment shares declined in Singapore and Indonesia but increased in Malaysia and the Philippines.

Significant as the employment shares are, export shares have been even larger. For example, all multinationals accounted for over two-thirds of Korean electric and electronic machinery exports. A similarly high share was observed in 1976 for Taiwan but this share fell to 44 percent by 1986. Also, U.S. affiliates alone accounted for 30 percent or more of Singapore's exports and over 50 percent of exports from each of the ASEAN-4 countries. Asian affiliates were also very significant from the investing country's viewpoint, accounting for 43 percent of all exports by U.S. affiliates in this industry worldwide and 64 percent of all exports by Japanese affiliates in the industry worldwide in 1986. Moreover, Asian affiliate employment represented 8–9 percent of both Japanese and U.S. employment in this industry. It is also interesting to note that Japanese multinationals have generally been concentrated in consumer electronics and nonsemiconductor components, while U.S. multinationals are more active in industrial electronics and semiconductors.[8]

## Transportation Equipment

From 1976 to the mid-1980s, the transportation equipment industry grew moderately in the region and continues to be a critical sector especially in terms of exports (Table 9.11). In the mid-1980s, the United States was still the largest employer in this sector, accounting for 58 percent of regional employment. The developing country share increased from 10 percent in 1976 to more than 14 percent in the mid-1980s. Employment levels remained largely unchanged in the United States, Japan, Hong Kong, and Singapore, but increased 11 percent annually in Korea, and 3–7 percent annually in Taiwan, Indonesia, Malaysia, and Thailand. The Philippines, on the other hand, experienced a large drop of 7 percent annually, and employment fell slightly in Singapore.

Average annual production growth rates were largest in Korea (20 percent), followed by the Philippines (16 percent), Taiwan (12 percent), and Malaysia (11 percent); production growth was slowest in Indonesia (under 2 percent). Average fixed investment-to-value added ratios were highest in Korea, lowest in the United States, and relatively high in the developing countries of the region. As in basic metals, the relatively high investment-to-value added ratios in the developing countries reflects the fact that this sector has received high priority in a number of Asia's developing countries.

Over the 1976–1985/86 period, the region's exports grew 11 percent annually for all transportation equipment and 13 percent annually in the important motor vehicles subsector. U.S. exports grew only 7 percent annually compared to 13 percent for Japan, with the differential being even greater in motor vehicles, 5 percent versus 8 percent. As a result, Japan's shares of regional exports grew rapidly in both categories. Korean export expansion was also impressive, more than 28 percent annually overall and 55 percent annually in motor vehicles, and Korea's share of regional exports also grew rapidly, as did Taiwan's.

Table 9.11 Economic Indicators of the Transportation Equipment Industry, 1976-1986

| Country | Employment (Thousands) | | Nominal Exports (US$ millions) | | Compound Annual Growth of Industrial Production, 1976-1985[c] | Average Fixed Investment/ Value Added, 1976-1984[d] |
|---|---|---|---|---|---|---|
| | 1976 | 1985[a] | 1976 | 1986[b] | (%) | (%) |
| Transportation equipment (ISIC 384) | | | | | | |
| Group total | 3,019 | 3,268 | 38,820 | 106,534 | na | na |
| Share of group total (%) | | | | | | |
| United States | 60.5 | 58.1 | 52.3 | 37.8 | 3.2 | 8.2 |
| Japan | 30.0 | 27.7 | 45.4 | 56.6 | 3.5 | 13.2 |
| Hong Kong | 0.4 | 0.4 | 0.0 | 0.0 | na | 13.7 |
| Korea | 2.3 | 5.3 | 0.6 | 3.4 | 19.6 | 32.2 |
| Singapore | 0.8 | 0.7 | 0.9 | 0.6 | 5.0 | 14.1 |
| Taiwan | 2.0 | 3.2 | 0.5 | 1.2 | 11.6 | na |
| Indonesia | 0.9 | 1.3 | 0.0 | 0.0 | 1.9 | 30.2 |
| Malaysia | 0.4 | 0.6 | 0.1 | 0.2 | 10.6 | 16.9 |
| Philippines | 0.8 | 0.4 | 0.0 | 0.0 | 16.4 | 19.7 |
| Thailand | 1.9 | 2.3 | 0.0 | 0.0 | 7.5 | na |
| Motor vehicles (ISIC 3843) | | | | | | |
| Group total | 1,596 | 1,733 | 22,228 | 75,173 | na | na |
| Share of group total (%) | | | | | | |
| United States | 57.6 | 50.3 | 53.7 | 26.6 | 3.4 | 10.9 |
| Japan | 38.3 | 41.4 | 45.7 | 70.3 | na | 15.1 |
| Hong Kong | 0.0 | 0.0 | 0.0 | 0.0 | na | 7.2 |
| Korea | 1.5 | 3.7 | 0.1 | 2.4 | na | 25.3 |
| Singapore | 0.1 | 0.1 | 0.2 | 0.1 | na | 12.7 |
| Taiwan | 1.3 | 2.4 | 0.2 | 0.6 | 18.4 | na |
| Indonesia | 0.7 | 1.2 | 0.0 | 0.0 | 6.0 | 21.6 |
| Malaysia | 0.5 | 0.7 | 0.0 | 0.0 | na | 15.6 |
| Philippines | na | 0.2 | 0.0 | 0.0 | na | na |
| Thailand | na | na | 0.0 | 0.0 | na | na |

na = Not available.
[a]For ISIC 384 data refer to 1984 for Japan, Indonesia, and Thailand. For ISIC 3843 data refer to 1983 for Hong Kong and 1984 for Japan and Korea.
[b]1985 for Taiwan.
[c]Growth of real value added for Thailand.
[d]1976-1985 for the United States and Singapore; 1976, 1978 and 1983 for Malaysia and 1976 and 1978-1984 for the Philippines.

Sources: Sources of Table 9.3.

Table 9.12 Employment and Exports of Foreign Affiliates in the Transportation Equipment Industry, Selected Years

| Host Economy | Investing Economy | Year | Number of Employees | Foreign Affiliate Employment | | Year | Foreign Affiliate Exports | |
|---|---|---|---|---|---|---|---|---|
| | | | | As a Share of Host-Country Employment (%) | As a Share of Home-Country Employment (%) | | Exports (US$ millions) | As a Share of Host-Country Exports[a] (%) |
| Transportation equipment: Host-economy data[b] | | | | | | | | |
| Hong Kong | World | 1983 | 1,834 | 12.6 | na | 1983 | na | na |
| Hong Kong | U.S. | 1983 | 430 | 3.0 | 0.0 | 1983 | na | na |
| Korea | World | 1976 | 6,806 | 9.7 | na | 1976 | 12 | 5.3 |
| Korea | World | 1986 | 48,195 | 26.7 | na | 1986 | 1,575 | 44.1 |
| Thailand | World | 1975 | na | na | na | 1975 | 0 | 33.3 |
| Thailand | World | 1984 | na | na | na | 1984 | 3 | 17.5 |
| Transportation equipment: Investing-economy data[c] | | | | | | | | |
| World | Japan | 1977 | 32,964 | na | 3.7 | 1977 | 188 | na |
| World | Japan | 1986[d] | 110,882 | na | 12.1 | 1986 | 2,236 | na |
| World | U.S. | 1977 | 909,628 | na | 47.0 | 1977 | 18,871 | na |
| World | U.S. | 1986 | 751,300 | na | 42.4 | 1986 | 39,458 | na |
| Asia | Japan | 1977 | 19,579 | na | 2.2 | 1977 | 137 | na |
| Asia | Japan | 1986[e] | 54,075 | na | 5.9 | 1986 | 1,665 | na |
| Asia | U.S. | 1977 | 21,018 | na | 1.1 | 1977 | na | na |
| Asia | U.S. | 1986 | 25,200 | na | 1.4 | 1984 | 202 | na |
| ASEAN-6 | Japan | 1986 | 25,039 | na | 2.7 | 1986 | 311 | na |

| | | | | | | | |
|---|---|---|---|---|---|---|---|
| Hong Kong | U.S. | 1977 | na | na | na | 1977 | 0 | 0.0 |
| Hong Kong | U.S. | 1985 | 0 | 0.0 | 0.0 | 1986 | 0 | 0.0 |
| Korea | U.S. | 1977 | na | na | na | 1977 | 0 | 0.0 |
| Korea | U.S. | 1982 | 6,300 | 4.8 | 0.4 | 1986 | 0 | 0.0 |
| Singapore | U.S. | 1985 | 1,800 | 8.3 | 0.1 | 1984 | 196 | 22.6 |
| Taiwan | U.S. | 1977 | 4,601 | 6.9 | 0.2 | 1977 | na | na |
| Taiwan | U.S. | 1985 | 3,300 | 3.1 | 0.2 | 1986 | 0 | 0.0 |
| Indonesia | U.S. | 1977 | na | na | na | 1977 | 0 | 0.0 |
| Indonesia | U.S. | 1984 | 0 | 0.0 | 0.0 | 1986 | 0 | 0.0 |
| Malaysia | U.S. | 1977 | na | na | na | 1977 | 1 | 3.0 |
| Malaysia | U.S. | 1985 | 0 | 0.0 | 0.0 | 1986 | 0 | 0.0 |
| Philippines | U.S. | 1977 | na | na | na | 1977 | 2 | 12.3 |
| Philippines | U.S. | 1986 | 300 | na | 0.0 | 1986 | 0 | 0.0 |
| Thailand | Japan | 1976 | 4,693 | 8.1 | 0.5 | 1976 | 1 | 18.2 |
| Thailand | Japan | 1983 | 5,783 | 7.0 | 0.6 | 1983 | 3 | 22.6 |
| Thailand | U.S. | 1977 | na | na | na | 1977 | 0 | 0.0 |
| Thailand | U.S. | 1984 | 0 | 0.0 | 0.0 | 1986 | 0 | 0.0 |

na = Not available or not disclosed.

[a]Host exports refer to merchandise exports; ratios tend to be overstated because foreign affiliate data often include some service exports.

[b]Thai data refer only to promoted firms.

[c]U.S. data refer to employment of nonbank affiliates of nonbank parents and exports of majority-owned nonbank affiliates of nonbank parents; U.S. data for Asia include developing Pacific economies.

[d]69 percent of the estimate for 7/1/87 by Toyo Keizai (1988).

[e]61 percent of the estimate for 7/1/87 by Toyo Keizai (1988).

Sources: Sources of Table 9.4.

In this industry, Japanese affiliates came to dominate multinational activity in Asia employing over twice as many people and exporting eight times as much as U.S. affiliates by 1986 (Table 9.12 and sources). Employment in Japan's Asian affiliates also represented 6 percent of Japanese employment in this industry while the comparable figure was 1 percent for U.S. affiliates in Asia. Moreover, in 1986 Japanese affiliate exports from Asia amounted to US$1.7 billion, which is over one-fourth of the US$5.9 billion in total transportation equipment exports from the NICs and ASEAN-4. Host-country data are scarce but multinationals have been heavily involved in the export boom and employment creation in the transport equipment industry in Korea. It is difficult to further quantify the significant multinational involvement in the Asian transportation equipment industry due to the lack of country-level detail on Japanese affiliate activity. However it is clear that this activity is highly concentrated in the motor vehicle industry. Urata (1987) provides data which suggest that major Japanese motor vehicle producers have captured market shares of over 80 percent in Hong Kong, Singapore, Indonesia, Malaysia, and Thailand. Of course, these shares reflect the high level of exports from Japan as well as local assembly and manufacture. Nevertheless, there were 20 DFI cases in the region (two cases each in Korea and Taiwan, five cases each in Malaysia and the Philippines, and six cases in Thailand) in 1958–1985, or 57 percent of Japanese DFI cases in developing countries and 39 percent of the world total in this industry (Urata 1987). Furthermore, large market shares for Japanese firms in Indonesia, Malaysia, and Thailand, countries in which the automobile industry is heavily promoted and imports of finished automobiles are severely restricted, are primarily due to high levels of production and assembly in Japanese affiliates in these countries.

## Conclusion

The 1980s was a decade of large and swift economic changes in the world as a whole with the Asia-Pacific economies deeply involved in and affected by these changes. A major focus of this chapter has been on the extent to which manufacturing industries in Japan and the United States have been affected by competition from Asia's developing economies. This has been illustrated by comparing the growth of employment, production, and exports in the economies involved. In all sectors, developing countries of the region have increased their shares of regional employment, production, and exports. This trend is observed not only in those sectors characterized by standard technologies (e.g., textiles) but also in the more sophisticated sectors (e.g., electric and electronic machinery).

The degree to which Japanese and U.S. multinationals have been involved in the growth of industries in Asia's developing economies was also examined. Theory suggests that multinationals can play important catalytic roles primarily through the provision of production technology, management skills, and marketing know-how. The relatively large share of affiliates in exports from the NICs and ASEAN-4 suggests that the latter factor may have been particularly important in the cases studied here. The large contributions of multinational activity in technology-intensive industries such as electric and electronic machinery also indicate that multinationals possess key technological advantages.

## Notes

The authors would like to thank Prue Philipps of the International Economic Data Bank, Australian National University and Youngil Lim of the United Nations Industrial Development Organization for assistance with trade and industrial data and to thank project participants for their comments and suggestions. However, the authors remain solely responsible for all errors and opinions expressed.

1. Some of the problems are: (1) Industry indicators are taken primarily from censuses/surveys of manufacturing, the coverage of which often differs substantially across countries and time. Moreover, industry definitions are not always consistent across countries or time; (2) A similar warning applies to data on multinational affiliate activity. To obtain a comprehensive data set, we spliced together information from many different surveys, among which the coverage, methodology, and sectoral or regional definitions often differ substantially. Again, it is crucial to refer to original sources for details on these differences as all of them could not be detailed here; (3) In order to get an idea of the relative size of multinational activity, we have compared censuses/surveys of manufacturing, which are conducted on an establishment basis, and surveys of multinational affiliate activity which are usually conducted on an enterprise basis. This discrepancy can be another important source of inaccuracy since establishment-and enterprise-based industrial classifications can be quite different; and (4) Country trade data have generally been converted from the SITC classification to the ISIC classification. As is well known, the existence of multiproduct firms (and plants) makes any conversion method imprecise.

2. These low ratios may be due to the differential sequencing of investment policies that were pursued in the two countries. In Korea, recent liberalization of DFI restrictions has led to an increase in the ratio. In Taiwan, the more liberal policy in the past allowed multinational saturation and the response of domestic competition to occur earlier.

3. This underestimation is primarily due to the fact that survey coverage is incomplete and not adjusted for in the official figures. The coverage of the private surveys cited in the notes to Table 9.2 appears to be somewhat more complete.

4. Philippine production indexes often display a high level of growth that seems inconsistent with the sluggish overall performance in manufacturing and the slow or negative growth of sectoral employment levels. We suspect that the indexes are inflated to some extent, perhaps affected by the high rate of inflation experienced during the mid-1980s.

5. The chemicals industry consists of industrial chemicals (ISIC 351) and "other" chemicals (ISIC 352). Petroleum and coal products, rubber, and plastics are excluded.

6. In Hong Kong chemicals in 1983, U.S. firms accounted for 41 percent of all foreign affiliate employment.

7. For example, some of the arrangements are: (1) The existence of export processing zones or bonded factories in host countries which allow free imports of intermediate goods to be processed and re-exported; and (2) The existence of Sections 806 and 807 in the U.S. tariff code which only tax the portion of value added contributed by foreign processing.

8. See the reports by the United Nations Economic and Social Commission for Asia and the Pacific/Centre on Transnational Corporations Joint Unit (1987, 20-37), the United Nations Centre on Transnational Corporations (1986, 383-423), and Ishii (1988) for more details.

## References

Asian Development Bank. 1988. *Key Indicators of Developing Member Countries of ADB.* Manila: Asian Development Bank.

Australian National University. 1989. Mimeos from the International Economic Data Bank.

Billerbeck, K., and Y. Yasugi. 1979. Private Direct Foreign Investment in Developing Countries. World Bank Working Paper No. 348. Washington, D.C.: World Bank.

Chen, Edward K. Y. 1987. Industrial Development, Foreign Direct Investment and Economic Cooperation: A Study of the Electronics Industry in the Asian Pacific. Mimeo.

Hong Kong, Industry Department. 1983. Mimeos, 31 December.

International Monetary Fund (IMF). 1988. *International Financial Statisitics Yearbook 1988*. Washington, D.C.: International Monetary Fund.

Ishii, S. 1988. Wagakuni Denshi Denki Sangyō no Ajia ni Okeru Kokusai Bungyō no Tenkai [The development of the international division of labor in Asia and the national electric and electronic machinery industry]. *Kaigai Tōshi Kenkyūjo Hō* [Report of the institute of overseas investment] 14(2): 11-42

Japan, Bangkok Chamber of Commerce. 1978. *Dai 7 kai Nikkeikigyō (Seizōgyō) no Tai Keizai ni Taisuru Kōkendo Chōsa Kekka* [The results of the seventh survey of the contributions of Japanese (manufacturing) firm activities to the Thai economy]. Bangkok: Japan, Bangkok Chamber of Commerce.

———. 1981. *Dai 8 Kai Nikkeikigyō Jittai Chōsa (Kōkendo Chōsa) Kekka* [The results of the eighth survey of the state of Japanese firms (survey of contributions)]. Bangkok: Japan, Bangkok Chamber of Commerce.

———. 1984. *Dai 9 Kai Nikkeikigyō no Jittai Chōsa* [The ninth survey of the state of Japanese firms]. Bangkok: Japan, Bangkok Chamber of Commerce.

Japan, Economic Planning Agency. 1989. *Annual Report on National Accounts*. Tokyo: Economic Planning Agency.

Japan, Management and Coordination Agency. Various years. *Monthly Statistics of Japan*, November issues, 1981-1988. Tokyo: Management and Coordination Agency.

Japan, Prime Minister's Office. 1988. *Japan Statistical Yearbook 1988*. Tokyo: Statistics Bureau, Management and Coordination Agency.

Koo, Bohn-Ho, and Taeho Bark. 1988. The Role of Direct Foreign Investment in Korea's Recent Growth. Paper presented at the First Conference on Asia-Pacific Relations, sponsored by the Foundation for Advanced Information and Research, 20-22 April, Tokyo, Japan

Koo, Bohn Young. 1982. Status and Changing Forms of Foreign Investment in Korea. Paper presented at the Conference on the "New Forms" of Investment in Developing Countries, sponsored by the Organisation for Economic Co-operation and Development, 15-19 March, Paris, France.

———. 1985. The Role of Foreign Direct Investment in Korea's Economic Growth. In *Foreign Trade and Investment: Economic Development in the Newly Industrializing Asian Countries*, edited by Walter Galenson. Madison: University of Wisconsin Press

Lin, Tzong-Biau, and Victor Mok. 1985. Trade, Foreign Investment, and Development in Hong Kong. In *Foreign Trade and Investment: Economic Development in the Newly Industrializing Asian Countries*, edited by Walter Galenson. Madison: University of Wisconsin Press.

Malaysia, Department of Statistics. 1973. *Census of Manufacturing Industries 1973*, Vol. 1. Kuala Lumpur: Department of Statistics.

———. Various years. *Industrial Survey*, 1979 and 1985 issues. Kuala Lumpur: Department of Statistics.

Ministry of International Trade and Industry (MITI). 1979. *Wagakuni Kaigai Jigyō no Katsudō* [Foreign activities of national firms], Survey 8 (1977 issue). Tokyo: Ministry of International Trade and Industry.

———. 1989. *Kaigai Tōshi Tōkei Sōran* [A comprehensive survey of foreign investment statistics], No. 3. Tokyo: Ministry of International Trade and Industry.

Republic of China, Council for Economic Planning and Development. 1988. *Industry of Free China*, October issue. Taipei: Council for Economic Planning and Development.

Republic of China, Directorate-General of Budget, Accounting and Statistics. 1988. *Statistical Yearbook of the Republic of China 1988*. Taipei: Directorate-General of Budget, Accounting and Statistics.

Republic of China, Ministry of Economic Affairs, Investment Commission. Various years. *A Survey of Overseas Chinese and Foreign Firms and Their Effects on National Economic Development*, (In Chinese) 1982–1986 issues. Taipei: Investment Commission.

Sibunruang, Atchaka, and Peter Brimble. 1987. Foreign Investment and Export Orientation: A Thai Perspective. In *Direct Foreign Investment and Export Promotion: Policies and Experiences in Asia*, edited by Seiji Naya, Vinyu Vichit-Vadakan, and Udom Kerdpibule. Honolulu and Kuala Lumpur: East-West Center and Southeast Asian Central Banks Research and Training Centre.

Singapore, Department of Statistics. Various years. *Report on the Census of Industrial Production*, 1977–1985 issues. Singapore: Department of Statistics.

Thailand, National Economic and Social Development Board (NESDB). Various years. *National Income of Thailand*, 1985 and 1986 issues. Bangkok: NESDB.

Toyo Keizai. 1988. *Gyōshubetsu Kaigai Shinshutsu Kigyō* [Firms with foreign affiliates by industry]. Tokyo: Tōyō Keizai Shinposha.

United Nations. Various years a. *Industrial Statistics Yearbook*, 1980–1985 issues. New York: United Nations.

———. Various years b. *Yearbook of International Trade Statistics*, 1980–1986 issues. New York: United Nations.

United Nations Centre on Transnational Corporations. 1986. *Transnational Corporations in the International Semiconductor Industry*. New York: United Nations Centre on Transnational Corporations.

United Nations Economic and Social Commission for Asia and the Pacific/Centre on Transnational Corporations Joint Unit. 1987. *Transnational Corporations and the Electronics Industries of ASEAN Economies*. New York: United Nations Centre on Transnational Corporations.

United Nations Industrial Development Organization (UNIDO). 1989. Mimeos.

United States, Department of Commerce, Bureau of the Census. Various years. *Statistical Abstract of the United States*, 1985–1989 issues. Washington, D.C.: Bureau of the Census.

United States, Department of Commerce, Bureau of Economic Analysis. 1981. *United States Direct Investment Abroad 1977*. Washington, D.C.: Bureau of Economic Analysis.

———. 1985. *U.S. Direct Investment Abroad: 1982 Benchmark Survey Data*. Washington, D.C.: Bureau of Economic Analysis.

———. 1986. *National Income and Product Accounts 1929–82*. Washington, D.C.: Bureau of Economic Analysis.

———. Various years a. *Survey of Current Business*, July issues, 1986–1988. Washington, D.C.: Bureau of Economic Analysis.

———. Various years b. *U.S. Direct Investment Abroad: Operations of U.S. Parent Companies and Their Foreign Affiliates*, Revised Estimates 1983, 1984, and 1985 issues, and Preliminary Estimates 1986 issue. Washington, D.C.: Bureau of Economic Analysis.

Urata, Shujiro. 1987. The Development of the Motor Vehicle Industry in Post-Second World War Japan. Mimeo, Resource Systems Institute, East-West Center.

Yamazawa, Ippei. 1988. The Textile Industry. In *Industrial Policy of Japan*, edited by R. Komiya, M. Okuno, and K. Suzumura. Tokyo: Academic Press.

Yoshihara, Kunio. 1978. *Japanese Investment in Southeast Asia*. Honolulu, Hawaii: University of Hawaii.

# 10

## Direct Foreign Investment and Structural Change in Developing Asia, Japan, and the United States

*Robert E. Lipsey*

### Introduction

Since Japan and many of the developing countries in Asia are among the most successful in the world with respect to growth of per capita income and ability to export, one might be inclined to ask if and why any restructuring is called for. In addition to the universal problem of adapting to changes in world markets, some of these countries also need to adapt to the results of their own past success in raising per capita incomes and the price of labor, particularly unskilled and semiskilled labor. For example, real gross domestic product (GDP) per capita in Hong Kong which was a little over the world average in 1950 increased to twice the world average in 1984. The increase in real GDP per capita in Korea was even larger, rising from 38 percent to 91 percent of the world average. The high rates of economic growth are not only a record of spectacular successes, but they are also a measure of the need for adaptation of these countries' economies. The accompanying rise in the price of labor has already or will at some point make the production of the most labor-intensive products uneconomical and force these countries toward more capital-intensive or skill-intensive industries.

The precise nature of the future changes in comparative advantage is difficult to predict. The analysis would be simplest in a two-factor world in which, for example, the abundance of land and labor determined the composition of trade and the changes in factor abundance were the outcome of fairly predictable trends. As Leamer (1987) has shown, however, the introduction of even one additional resource can add considerable complexity to paths of development. Thus the numerous factors of production that are likely to be important for the developing Asian economies (such as several types of labor skill, various natural resources, and physical capital) would add still further complications, although they are dealt with to some extent in Leamer (1984). If we add the likely circumstance that availability of some resources such as educated labor are not predetermined but depend to a considerable degree on deliberate policies of the countries involved, the difficulties multiply.

One reason why multinationals might play an important role in structural change is that, according to most of the literature on the subject, they possess their own comparative advantages or sources of competitiveness which they bring to the countries in which they operate. These advantages may originate in the multinationals' home countries but are specific to the firm. They are transferable to the firms' foreign operations and, indeed, are the basis for the multinationals' ability to operate in many locations where local firms have the advantages of familiarity with local conditions and the favor of local governments. These are the types of assets that Markusen (this volume) refers to as "knowledge-based assets." At least among U.S. multinationals and to some extent Swedish multinationals, these firm-specific assets are related to the research and development (R&D) activities of the parents as well as to the parents' size, growth, and profitability. In the case of the United States, we can say that multinational firms are R&D-intensive, large, profitable, and fast-growing relative to other firms in their industries. Furthermore, their industries exhibit the same characteristics relative to industry as a whole (Lipsey, Blomström, and Kravis 1990). Both Swedish and U.S. multinationals are concentrated in industries in which exports grew relatively rapidly over the last twenty years or so (Lipsey and Kravis 1987a; Blomström and Lipsey 1989). There is evidence that multinationals adapt their methods of production or their selection of lines of production to the factor costs in the different host countries. In particular, multinationals tend to locate labor-intensive production in countries in which labor is cheap (Lipsey, Kravis, and Roldan 1982). One might guess from this fact that the multinationals do not change their host countries so much as they adapt their own operations to local conditions. However the multinationals' operations, combining the comparative advantages and competitiveness of the parent firms with those of the host countries, might move the host countries to become more like the multinationals themselves. This process may involve altering the comparative advantages of the host countries or reducing the costs of adjustment to the inevitable changes in comparative advantage.

If the multinationals' influence on host countries involves the transfer of technology and expertise to locations outside their home countries, there must be some impact on home-country economies as well as on host-country economies. The early home-country discussion revolved around the fear that the multinationals were moving jobs and income out of the home countries by substituting overseas production for exports from the home countries (for further references, see Bergsten, Horst, and Moran 1978). However the lack of substantial empirical evidence for such substitution has shifted the nature of that discussion.

There are still some fears that the multinationals are giving technology away too cheaply (from the point of view of the home country, if not that of the multinational itself). However, there is also the realization that by moving segments of their operations, such as those that are labor intensive, to foreign locations, the multinationals may be preserving markets for the more capital-intensive or technology-intensive elements of home-countries' production. In this way, they may be aiding the inevitable shift of their home-country production up the technology scale. Thus a major question with respect to home-country impacts is whether the multinationals are speeding these required changes in the composition of home-country employment, output, and trade.

In discussing the role of multinationals in the Asian countries, this paper focuses on their activities in the manufacturing sector and more specifically on their international trade. Multinationals play a larger part in manufacturing than they do in most service sectors and play a much larger part in international trade than in employment or output destined for domestic consumption. Thus if multinationals have been and are to continue to be important actors in structural change in Asian countries, their influence should appear most clearly in the trade sector.

## Multinationals in Developing Country Trade

One of the advantages hoped for by host countries from investment by multinationals is increased access to foreign markets. This might come from the enhanced technological level brought to the host countries by the multinationals or more directly from the links that multinationals have to their home markets or to other markets.

In the last twenty or thirty years, U.S. multinationals have not played a very large role overall in the exports of developing countries but their role was growing, at least up to the early 1980s (Table 10.1). Although the data for Japanese affiliates are much weaker,[1] they do indicate that Japanese affiliates account for a substantial and rising share of developing country exports, 3.5 percent in 1974 and over 5 percent in 1983. The combined share of U.S. and Japanese multinationals was about 12 percent in 1983 and is probably higher now. In terms of employment, in the mid-1980s, multinationals from the two countries accounted for more than 60 percent of employment in all manufacturing foreign firms in Hong Kong, Korea, Singapore, and Taiwan (Plummer and Ramstetter, this volume).

The role of U.S. firms in developing country exports has varied widely among industries. Exports of U.S. firms are more significant in chemicals, transport equipment, and machinery, especially the last two industries, than in other industries, reaching in some instances one-quarter or one-third of total developing countries' exports (Table 10.2). Thus it is in these industries that we might expect to find an impact of the multinational firms' operations. The importance of U.S. multinationals has varied by geographical location as well as by industry. Historically, more U.S. direct investment has been directed towards Latin America rather than Asia, and U.S. multinationals have always played a larger role in Latin America. Japanese investment, on the other hand, has typically been more concentrated in Asia.

The share of U.S. multinationals in Asian exports grew rapidly between 1966 and 1977, and then was quite stable until it declined in 1986. The multinationals' share of Asian exports was close to their worldwide share of developing-country exports in 1966 and 1977, and fell below the average thereafter (Table 10.3). The decline in the export share of multinationals was not due to slow export growth in multinationals. In fact, export growth rates for U.S. multinationals' affiliates in Latin America and Asia were similar, but the export performances of other firms (local and non-U.S. multinationals) were very different in the two regions. In Latin America, the growth of exports by other firms was much slower than that of the U.S. multinationals; in Asia, it was faster.

The share of Japanese multinationals in the exports of developing Asia as a whole was close to that of U.S. multinationals in the 1970s and may have moved above

Table 10.1 Share of U.S. Majority-Owned Foreign Affiliates In Developing-Country Exports of Manufactures[a], Selected Years

| Year | Percentage |
|------|------------|
| 1957 | 3.0[b] |
| 1966 | 3.9 |
| 1977 | 6.2 |
| 1982 | 7.5 |
| 1983 | 6.8 |
| 1984 | 7.4 |
| 1985 | 7.7 |
| 1986 | 7.1 |

[a]Manufactures defined to match definition in United States, Department of Commerce (1985). It thus includes manufactured food products, but excludes petroleum refining and coal products.
[b]Estimate.

Source: Lipsey, Blomström, and Kravis (1990, Tables 12.5 and 12.6); United States, Department of Commerce, Bureau of Economic Analysis (various years, Tables 37 and 38 of 1986 issue).

that of the U.S. companies in the 1980s, to judge by these very rough figures. However, the larger increase in exports that is estimated for Japanese affiliates is due almost entirely to an unreliable coverage correction; exports as reported in the original data source grew at about the same rate as exports by U.S. affiliates.

The host-country data for exports by all foreign-owned firms suggest a considerably larger role for multinationals. They also confirm the impression drawn from the U.S. and Japanese data that the role of multinationals is greater, the smaller the host economy is. The host-country data for Singapore and Taiwan also support the suggestion from the U.S. and Japanese data that the importance of multinationals in the exports of developing Asian countries decreased somewhat between the 1970s

Table 10.2   Shares of U.S. and Japanese Multinationals in
Developing-Country Exports of Manufactures, Selected Years

| Year | Total | Foods | Chemi-icals | Metals | Non-Elec. Mach. | Elec. Mach. | Transport Equip. | Other Manuf. |
|------|-------|-------|-------------|--------|-----------------|-------------|------------------|--------------|
| U.S. multinationals[a] | | | | | | | | |
| 1966 | 3.9 | 12.2 | 2.6 | 13.7 | na | na | 5.2 | 2.2 |
| 1977 | 2.4 | 10.2 | 4.6 | 31.8 | 18.6 | 36.4 | 13.5 | 2.0 |
| 1982 | 2.6 | 11.3 | 3.4 | 29.3 | 18.8 | 33.7 | 10.8 | 2.0 |
| 1985 | 3.0 | 8.5 | 1.7 | 23.8 | 18.8 | 26.3 | 17.5 | 1.8 |
| 1986 | 2.3 | 8.2 | 2.4 | 19.6 | 14.4 | 21.8 | 25.9[b] | 1.5 |
| Japanese multinationals[c] | | | | | | | | |
| 1974 | 1.3 | 2.3 | 0.9 | 12.3 | 3.3 | 16.0 | 5.7 | 4.0 |
| 1983 | 1.0 | 4.1 | 4.8 | 12.0 | 3.1 | 15.4 | 6.3 | 4.6 |

na = Not available.
[a]Majority-owned affiliates.
[b]The jump of almost 50 percent reflected mainly the fall in developing-country exports
of ships, particularly from Korea. U.S. affiliates have never been a factor in the
shipbuilding industry.
[c]The industry group data are rough estimates based on the assumption that the
coverage in the survey was identical across industries.

Source: Lipsey, Blomström, and Kravis (1990, Tables 12.5 and 12.6); United States,
Department of Commerce, Bureau of Economic Analysis (various years, Tables 37 and
38).

and the 1980s. However, the coverage of data for Taiwan varies substantially from
year to year and the 1985 figures probably exaggerate the decline because coverage
for that year was particularly poor.

For 1983, we can calculate shares in exports within industry groups for U.S. and
Japanese affiliates in Asia as a whole, U.S. affiliates in each country, and all countries'
affiliates in Taiwan. While the overall share of U.S. multinationals was between 6
and 7 percent of exports, they accounted for about 15 percent or more in a few
countries (Table 10.4). U.S. multinationals were particularly significant in machinery
exports; in electrical machinery and equipment, the U.S. multinationals' share was

over one-quarter overall and more than one-half in three countries. On the other hand, in food, metals, and miscellaneous manufacturing, which accounted for over 70 percent of developing Asia's exports, the U.S. multinationals' exports were only about 1 percent of the total. Japanese affiliates' exports were also most important, by far, in the electrical machinery industry. Chemicals and transportation equipment are the only other industries in which the export share was over 5 percent for Japanese affiliates.

The industry breakdown available for all countries' multinational in Taiwan suggests that for that country at least, U.S. and Japanese home-country data cover about two-thirds of exports by foreign-owned manufacturing firms overall and more than two-thirds in most industries. The major gaps appear to be in chemicals and in "other manufacturing." The omitted exports could be exports of minority-owned firms or by firms from countries other than the United States or Japan. Data on exports to the United States by U.S. affiliates that were not majority-owned show that they did little or no exporting to the United States (United States, Department of Commerce, Bureau of Economic Analysis, various years, Tables 17 and 53). Thus, the multinationals' exports that have been omitted from our calculations must be from non-U.S. firms, from non-Japanese firms, or from minority-owned U.S. affiliates exporting to countries other than the United States.

Host-country data on exports, such as those in Table 10.4 for Taiwan, where available, have a considerable advantage. The comparison between exports by U.S. affiliates, as reported in the U.S. direct investment data, and exports by the country as a whole always suffers from incomparabilities between the two sets of data. The incomparibilities are inevitable, partly because the exports by affiliates can be allocated to detailed industries only by the industry of the affiliate, but not by the nature of the product that is actually exported. The more detailed the classification used, the greater is the likelihood of errors. This problem is avoided if host-country data that report exports by foreign-owned and domestic firms on the same basis exist.

All in all, the impact of both U.S. and Japanese multinationals on the exports of developing Asian countries seems to have been concentrated in the machinery industry, and in particular in electrical machinery and equipment. In the case of the Asian countries, this means mainly the electronics industry.

Another way of looking at the influence or potential influence of multinationals on Asian economies is by asking what comparative advantages they seem to bring with them. Do they follow the existing comparative advantages of the host countries or do they bring with them some of the comparative advantages associated with their home countries?

One way of answering this question is by comparing patterns of exports of affiliates in Asian countries with those of their host and home countries (Table 10.5). Relative to the United States and Japan, local firms in developing Asian countries, to judge by their exports, have comparative advantages in foods and especially in other manufacturing (mainly textiles and apparel) and comparative disadvantages in chemicals, machinery, and transport equipment. How do the U.S. and Japanese affiliates affect the export pattern of these countries? The influence of the U.S. affiliates is to move the Asian countries toward machinery exports, an area of U.S. home-country comparative advantage. The influence of Japanese affiliates is to move

282

Table 10.3  Shares of Multinationals in Exports of Manufactures from Developing Asia, Selected Years (percentage)

| Host country | 1966 | 1974 | 1976 | 1977 | 1982 | 1983 | 1984 | 1985 | 1986 |
|---|---|---|---|---|---|---|---|---|---|
| **Home-country data[a]** | | | | | | | | | |
| <u>U.S. multinationals</u> | | | | | | | | | |
| Developing Asia | 3.8 | na | na | 6.2 | 6.4 | 6.2 | 6.7 | 6.5 | 5.7 |
| Hong Kong | na | na | na | 8.1 | 6.5 | 5.6 | 5.7 | 5.6-6.4 | 4.5 |
| Korea | na | na | na | 1.4 | 1.2 | 1.3 | 1.1-2.0 | 1.2-2.0 | 1.0 |
| Singapore | na | na | na | 18.7 | 14.5 | 17.5 | 18.4-20.2 | 20.1 | 18.1 |
| Taiwan | na | na | na | 6.2 | 4.2 | 4.0 | 3.7-6.3 | 4.1-5.7 | 3.4 |
| **Japanese multinationals** | | | | | | | | | |
| Developing Asia | na | 6.2 | na | 5.7 | na | 6.9 | na | na | 7.1 |
| **Host-country data** | | | | | | | | | |
| <u>All foreign firms</u> | | | | | | | | | |
| Korea | na | 24.3 | 27.0 | 25.3 | na | na | 19.9 | 21.5 | 26.1 |
| Singapore | na | na | na | 84.7 | 72.1 | 71.6 | 73.9 | 74.1 | na |
| Taiwan | na | 30.6 | 31.3 | 32.5 | 27.7 | 20.9 | 26.5 | 18.2 | 19.1 |

| U.S. multinationals | | | | | | | | |
|---|---|---|---|---|---|---|---|---|
| Singapore | na | na | na | 34.3 | 18.1 | 21.6 | 23.7 | 25.8 | na |
| Taiwan | na | 8.9 | 8.1 | 7.7 | 8.4 | 5.6 | 7.2 | 4.1 | 3.4 |
| Japanese multinationals | | | | | | | | |
| Singapore | na | na | na | 5.6 | 8.7 | 9.7 | 11.5 | 12.7 | na |
| Taiwan | na | 12.7 | 13.6 | 14.2 | 10.6 | 8.8 | 8.4 | 6.5 | 8.9 |

na = Not available.
aMajority-owned affiliates.

Source: Lipsey, Blomström, and Kravis (1990, Table 12.4); Lee and Ramstetter (this volume); Plummer and Ramstetter (this volume); Republic of China, Investment Commission (1981, 1983, 1985, 1986, 1987); Singapore, Department of Statistics (1978-1986); United Nations (n.d.); United States, Department of Commerce, Bureau of Economic Analysis (various years, Tables 29, 36, 37, and 38).

Table 10.4 Shares of Multinationals in Exports of Manufactures by Developing Asian Countries[a], 1983 and 1985 (percentage)

| | Total | Foods | Chemicals | Metals | Non-elec. Mach. | Elec. Mach. & Equip. | Transport Equip. | Other Manuf. |
|---|---|---|---|---|---|---|---|---|
| **All multinationals, 1985** | | | | | | | | |
| Taiwan[c] | 20.9[d] | 3.0 | 51.6[d] | 8.5 | 17.3[e] | 42.3 | na[f] | 12.6 |
| **U.S. multinationals, 1983[g]** | | | | | | | | |
| All countries | 6.2 | 0.9 | 4.6-6.6 | <0.4 | 14.7 | 27.2 | 3.7-4.1 | 0.7 |
| Hong Kong | 5.6 | 2.0 | 34.5 | 0.0 | 6.7-8.2 | 19.8 | 0.0 | 1.5 |
| India | <0.1 | 0.0 | 0.6 | 0.0 | 3.0-12.7 | <16.4 | 0.0 | <0.1 |
| Indonesia | 1.4 | 0.1 | 1.2 | <8.4 | 0.0 | <11.8 | 0.0 | <0.1 |
| Malaysia | 15.9 | 0.1 | 5.3 | 0.0 | 0.0 | 61.2 | 0.0 | <0.6 |
| Philippines | 17.4 | 8.1 | 31.2 | 3.0 | 0.0 | 94.5-100.0 | 8.3 | 3.3-6.0 |
| Singapore | 17.5 | 0.8 | 5.6-7.4 | 0.7 | 35.7-36.7 | 31.3 | 23.5 | 0.4 |
| Korea | 1.3 | 0.2 | 0.0 | 0.0 | 0.0 | 9.6 | 0.0 | <0.1 |
| Taiwan | 4.0 | 0.0 | 3.5 | <1.6 | 4.6 | 16.6 | <4.0 | 2.7 |
| Taiwan[c] | 4.1[d] | 0.0 | 5.8[d] | 0.7 | 3.4[e] | 13.7 | na[f] | 3.6 |
| Thailand | 4.2-6.6 | 0.6 | 5.6 | 0.0 | 0.0 | 82.5 | 0.0 | <2.0 |
| Other | <0.4 | <0.1 | 21.6 | 0.0 | 0.0 | 11.6 | 0.0 | 0.0 |
| **Japanese multinationals, 1983** | | | | | | | | |
| All countries | | | | | | | | |
| As reported | 3.9 | 1.3 | 4.8 | 1.7 | 2.1 | 10.3 | 5.6 | 2.9 |
| As estimated | 6.9 | 2.3 | 8.4 | 3.0 | 3.6 | 18.0 | 9.8 | 5.0 |
| Taiwan, 1985[c] | 6.5[d] | 1.5 | 3.0[d] | 4.4 | na | 15.6 | na | 2.4[e] |

na = Not available.
[a]Excluding the Middle East.
[b]Exports by affiliates are assigned to industries by the main industry of the affiliate. It is possible that they could belong in a different industry.
[c]Host country data.
[d]Including petroleum and coal products.
[e]Including transport equipment.
[f]Included with non-electrical machinery.
[g]Majority-owned manufacturing affiliates.

Sources: Blomström, Kravis, and Lipsey (1988); Republic of China, Investment Commission (1987); United Nations (n.d.); United States, Department of Commerce (various years, Tables 29, 36, 37, 38).

Table 10.5 Distribution of Exports of Manufactures by the United States, Japan, Developing Asia, and U.S. and Japanese Affiliates in Developing Asia, 1983 (percentage)

| | United States | Japan | Developing Asian countries (excl. affil.) | Affiliates in Developing Asia Based in: | | Difference Between Developing Asia (excl. affiliates) and Affiliates Based in: | |
|---|---|---|---|---|---|---|---|
| | | | | United States | Japan | United States | Japan |
| Foods | 6.9 | 1.0 | 13.7 | 1.7 | 4.1 | -12.0 | -9.6 |
| Chemicals | 13.8 | 5.4 | 3.5 | 2.6-3.7 | 4.4 | -0.4 | 0.9 |
| Metals | 7.2 | 13.8 | 11.2 | <0.6 | 4.4 | -10.9 | -6.8 |
| Machinery | | | | | | | |
| Nonelectrical | 20.9 | 14.5 | 5.2 | 13.2 | 2.9 | 8.0 | -2.3 |
| Electrical | 11.2 | 21.1 | 10.3 | 72.2 | 42.6 | 62.1 | 32.3 |
| Trans. equip. | 21.7 | 27.8 | 5.2 | 3.1-4.0 | 7.4 | -1.6 | 2.2 |
| Other manuf. | 18.5 | 16.4 | 50.9 | 5.1 | 34.1 | -45.8 | -16.8 |
| Total | 100.0 | 100.0 | 100.0 | 100.0 | 100.0 | | |
| Average absolute difference | | | | | | 20.1 | 10.1 |

Sources: Lipsey, Blomström, and Kravis (1990); United Nations (n.d.); United States, Department of Commerce, Bureau of Economic Analysis (various years).

these countries toward both electrical machinery and, to a smaller extent, toward transport equipment.

While both U.S. and Japanese affiliates move the export patterns of the Asian countries closer to their own, and to that of the developed countries in general, there is a striking difference between them: the export distribution of the Japanese affiliates is much closer to that of local firms than is the distribution of exports by U.S. affiliates. This is especially true of the concentration of Japanese affiliate exports in other manufacturing and their lesser concentration than U.S. affiliates in machinery. The average difference across industries between affiliate shares and those of local firms is twice as great for U.S. affiliates as for those from Japan. Thus U.S. affiliates seem to be altering the export patterns of Asian countries more than Japanese affiliates, and Japanese affiliates seem to be taking greater advantage of the existing comparative advantages of these countries.

The concentration in electrical machinery by both U.S. and Japanese affiliates in developing Asian countries is far beyond that of the home countries, the host countries, or any other group of countries or affiliates we have examined. Presumably, there is some unusually advantageous combination of the firm-specific advantages of U.S. and Japanese multinationals with the location-specific advantages of the Asian countries.

## Who Invests in Asia?

The potential for transfer of technology to host countries is partly a function of the sources of direct investment. If most of the direct investment is from companies with low technological levels that seek to take advantage of low labor costs, there might be little gain to the host country.

Although we know relatively little about the factors that determine which companies invest in which areas, some evidence can be drawn from special tabulations of U.S. Department of Commerce data. The data suggest that, relative to U.S. investors in general, American companies investing in the developing Asian countries in 1977 were heavily concentrated in electrical machinery, transport equipment, and chemicals (Table 10.6). On the other side, there was relatively little investment from companies in foods, metals, nonelectrical machinery, or other manufacturing. Other manufacturing includes industries, such as textiles and apparel, in which the Asian countries have had major comparative advantages. These comparative advantages are centered in locally owned firms but are threatened by rising income levels and wage costs in the developing Asian countries.

Aside from the industry distribution of U.S. parent firms investing in Asia, we can also learn something about their technological activities from three characteristics of the firms: (1) R&D expenditures as a percent of total sales, (2) the ratio of license fees received from firms not controlled by the parent to total parent sales, and (3) the ratio to total parent sales of sales under license from the parent by foreign firms not controlled by the parent.

Our measure of parent R&D intensity, the ratio of R&D expenditures to sales, reveals a surprising relationship (Table 10.7). Investors in developing Asian countries were the group with the highest R&D intensity for manufacturing as a whole.

Table 10.6 Industry Distribution[a] of Aggregate Assets of U.S. Parents Investing in Each Area[b], 1977

| | All Manuf. | Foods | Chem-icals | Metals | Non-Elec. Mach. | Elec. Mach. | Transport Equip. | Other Manuf. |
|---|---|---|---|---|---|---|---|---|
| Developed countries | 100.0 | 7.6 | 22.1 | 7.6 | 13.2 | 7.3 | 24.2 | 18.0 |
| Developing countries | | | | | | | | |
| Latin America | 100.0 | 7.5 | 25.3 | 8.7 | 8.7 | 5.9 | 26.9 | 17.0 |
| Asia | 100.0 | 5.0 | 28.8 | 5.5 | 6.0 | 11.7 | 30.8 | 12.3 |

[a]A given parent may appear in several countries but in only one industry.
[b]The distribution for an area is the unweighted average of country distributions.

Source: Lipsey, Blomström, and Kravis (1990, Table 12.13). Data are from United States, Department of Commerce, Bureau of Economic Analysis (n.d.).

Table 10.7 Measures of Technological Intensity of Parent Companies by Location of Investment, 1977

| | All Manuf. | Foods | Chem-icals | Metals | Non-Elec. Mach. | Elec. Mach. | Transport Equip. | Other Manuf. |
|---|---|---|---|---|---|---|---|---|
| R&D expenditures as percentage of sales | | | | | | | | |
| Developed countries | 2.36 | 0.71 | 3.51 | 1.09 | 2.69 | 2.90 | 2.20 | 2.02 |
| Developing countries | | | | | | | | |
| Latin America | 2.42 | 0.76 | 3.56 | 1.06 | 2.56 | 3.00 | 2.18 | 2.10 |
| Asia | 2.87 | 0.68 | 3.62 | 1.13 | 4.37 | 4.18 | 2.23 | 2.20 |
| Fees and royalties received from uncontrolled foreign persons as percentage of sales | | | | | | | | |
| Developed countries | 0.15 | 0.04 | 0.20 | 0.16 | 0.17 | 0.17 | 0.15 | 0.12 |
| Developing countries | | | | | | | | |
| Latin America | 0.17 | 0.05 | 0.27 | 0.15 | 0.19 | 0.11 | 0.10 | 0.14 |
| Asia | 0.15 | 0.01 | 0.11 | 0.12 | 0.15 | 0.22 | 0.04 | 0.25 |
| Uncontrolled product sales as percentage of sales | | | | | | | | |
| Developed countries | 2.11 | 0.69 | 1.78 | 1.84 | 2.83 | 3.66 | 0.63 | 2.58 |
| Developing countries | | | | | | | | |
| Latin America | 2.40 | 1.32 | 2.10 | 2.16 | 3.72 | 1.54 | 0.78 | 3.60 |
| Asia | 2.37 | 0.12 | 1.42 | 1.12 | 2.25 | 1.55 | 0.40 | 7.33 |

Source: Lipsey, Blomström, and Kravis (1990, Table 12.14). Data are from United States, Department of Commerce, Bureau of Economic Analysis (n.d.).

Investors in Asia also had the highest R&D intensity in every industry group except foods, with the R&D intensity particularly high in the two machinery sectors.

The high R&D intensity of machinery industry investors in developing Asian countries reflects the fact that they are heavily concentrated in two R&D-intensive subgroups within nonelectrical machinery and electrical machinery; namely, office and computing machines, and electronic components and accessories. The ability of semiconductor companies to split stages of production between labor-intensive operations, which are carried out in developing countries, and skill-and technology-intensive operations, which are carried out in developed countries, is partly responsible for this apparently paradoxical choice of host countries by R&D-intensive parents (Finan 1975).

The two measures of technology sales included in Table 10.7 represent a mixture of two elements. The first element is the technological level of the parent, which determines whether it possesses technology to sell to others. If the parent does have such technological assets, the second element is the preference for exploiting them outside the United States by selling the technology itself rather than producing the goods that embody the technology. A firm or industry with little technology to sell, such as the food industry, would presumably show low ratios to total sales of fees and royalties and of uncontrolled product sales under license. On the other hand, a firm or industry at a fairly high technological level might still show low ratios if it chose to exploit its technological capital by producing abroad rather than by sales of the technology itself. This might be the case for the motor vehicle industry; it is only slightly below average in R&D expenditure, but is far below average in terms of the importance of uncontrolled product sales under license.

In most industries, firms investing in developing Asia were less involved in sales of technology than were those investing in developed and other developing countries, although they were relatively R&D intensive. The major exception is in the other manufacturing group, where investors in developing Asia reported both relatively high sales by uncontrolled companies under license and high income from fees and royalties from such sales, even though investors in these countries were no more research intensive than were investors in Europe. The reason may be that the group includes firms in industries such as apparel that are licensing the use of fashion designs or other nontechnological assets, the creation of which is not called R&D, rather than patents or other products of R&D.

This analysis of the characteristics of U.S. companies investing in Asian production is a very crude one. It classifies companies only as investors or noninvestors and ignores differences in the size and type of their operations. It would be useful to know the characteristics of parent companies investing in each Asian country, weighted by some measure of the size of their affiliates' operations, such as employment, value added, or at least output minus imports. The idea behind the weighting would be that the impact of the parent on a host-country economy would depend on the extent of its operations there. Thus, for example, the R&D intensity of companies investing in country $i$ would be,

$$(R\&D/Sales)_{pi} = (\sum_{j=1}^{n} ANS_{ij} (R\&D/Sales)_{pij})/(\sum_{j=1}^{n} ANS_{ij}) \quad (10.1)$$

where

$(R\&D/Sales)_{pi}$ = the R&D intensity of U.S. parents investing in country $i$

$ANS_{ij}$ = the net sales of affiliates of parent $j$ in country $i$

$(R\&D/Sales)_{pij}$ = the R&D/sales ratio of parent $j$ investing in country $i$.

The data on individual parents and affiliates that are needed for such a calculation are not published, of course, although R&D-to-sales ratios are publicly available from consolidated company accounts. However, these measures for U.S. parents can be calculated from company reports to the U.S. Department of Commerce and could be done for each Asian host country and for each major industry group in each Asian host country.

## Direct Investment and the Technological Development of Host-Country Industries

There have been relatively few systematic analyses of the impact of direct investment on the development of industries within host countries. There are quite a few channels of such influence and some of them are difficult to trace.

One of the major questions at issue is the extent to which affiliates from developed countries raise the technological level of locally owned firms. There is a wide range of possible effects. There could be, at one extreme, a negative effect if the foreign-owned firms simply displace local firms from profitable local markets and take over the rents formerly accruing to local owners. If the foreign firms force their way into local markets by higher levels of efficiency, local consumers, at least, may gain from their presence. But if the foreign firms enter through political pressure or through the exercise of monopoly power, there may even be losses to consumers.

Since technology is to some extent a public good, a more likely outcome is that some spillovers to local firms will occur. Among the possible channels for such spillovers, aside from pure imitation, are:

1. Through the provision of management and technical training to local person-nel who then transfer this human capital to existing local firms or use it to establish new ones.
2. Through the training of local suppliers of intermediate products to meet the higher standards of quality control, reliability, and speed of delivery required by the technology and method of operation of the foreign-owned operation. The motivation may be to procure lower-cost components or raw materials or, in some cases, to meet local content requirements imposed by host countries.
3. Through intensifying the degree of competition faced by local firms, forcing them to become more efficient or to leave the industry. This effect is treated as an unfavorable one in some development literature, but it does produce efficiency gains that could be important.

Although there has been some discussion of technological spillovers in the literature, there has not been a great deal of empirical evidence beyond case studies, aside from a study for Australia by Caves (1974), for Canada by Globerman (1979) and for Mexico by Blomström (1986a, 1986b) and by Blomström and Persson (1983). A possible source of material for such an investigation would be detailed industrial census data for a host country, tagged by ownership, for a period that is long enough for technological change to be observed. For any country in which access to census data of this type could be arranged, foreign-owned establishments could be compared with locally owned ones with respect to productivity and other characteristics, such as physical capital intensity, scale of operations, and average skill levels of employees.

If data were available for a period of five or ten years, further analyses could be performed. It would be possible to ask whether rates of change in inputs, outputs, and productivity were different according to the nationality of the firms' owners. Do foreign-owned and locally owned firms tend to converge with respect to factor proportions, average skill of employees, productivity, etc.?

If establishment-level data were available, several additional types of studies would be possible. One would be to fit separate production functions or efficiency frontiers to the domestically owned and foreign-owned establishments to compare not only their average performance, but also the effect of foreign participation on the dispersion of productivity and other variables.[2] If the data were available over a sufficient period of time, it would also be possible to study of the effect of foreign takeovers on the characteristics of establishments. Given the initial characteristics at the time of the takeover, did a change to foreign ownership have any effect on productivity, profitability, growth, exporting or importing behavior, capital intensity, or the range of products?

Even if access to such detailed data were not feasible, it should still be possible to infer some effects of foreign participation from industry data, as long as the extent of foreign participation in each industry was known. One question that could be asked is whether industries with high degrees of foreign participation grew more rapidly than others, increased their productivity or their exports more, or shifted toward more capital-intensive or skill-intensive operations. These industry characteristics could also be related to changes in the degree of foreign participation.

It would be preferable for these studies to use host-country data on the extent of foreign participation in local industries, especially if the data distinguished among the countries of origin of the participation. Host-country data on foreign participation would be preferable because they are likely to match the industry classification of other host-country data better than foreign data would and they are likely to cover all home countries. However, where they are not available, it might be possible to work with data from the U.S. and a few other home countries.

The effects of foreign participation on industries outside those in which their affiliates are established may be important but would be harder to quantify because it is unlikely that suppliers to foreign firms can be identified separately. An alternative would be to use input-output tables, where they exist, to correlate the behavior of industries with the extent of foreign participation in the industries they sell to. Does productivity, for example, rise faster in the steel industry if its customers are mainly in industries with large foreign participation? Some implicit assumption must be made that foreign-owned firms buy from local supplying industries in the same proportions as locally owned firms do. That is probably a risky assumption. An alternative assumption, if U.S. investment data were used, would be that U.S. firms purchase inputs other than imports, rather than all inputs, in the same proportions as the industry as a whole.

## R&D by Multinational Firms and the Technology Level
## of Host-Country Exports

While R&D performed by parents may be the main potential source of technology for affiliates, there is no certainty that the fruits of such R&D are in fact transferred. To the extent that multinationals perform R&D within a host country, however, the effects on the affiliates' production are likely to be very direct, and the likelihood of spillovers to other firms within the country is greater.

In 1982, majority-owned affiliates of U.S. multinationals spent about US$3.6 billion for R&D (United States, Department of Commerce, Bureau of Economic Analysis 1985, Table III.H3), about 10 percent of the R&D expenditures by the parents of these affiliates (United States, Department of Commerce, Bureau of Economic Analysis 1985, Table III.Q1). Over 90 percent of the spending by affiliates was done by those in developed countries. Of the US$260 million that was performed in developing countries, the overwhelming majority was by manufacturing affiliates. Among the developing countries, US$205 million was concentrated in five countries: Brazil, Mexico, Hong Kong, Singapore, and Argentina. An additional US$25 million was spent by affiliates in Venezuela, Israel, Colombia, and Taiwan. (United States, Department of Commerce 1985, Table III.H3).

The R&D intensity of the manufacturing operations, measured by the ratio of R&D expenditures to sales in 1982 (United States, Department of Commerce, Bureau of Economic Analysis 1985, Tables III.D3 and III.H3), was 0.46 in developing country affiliates which is only one-third the level of affiliates in developed countries (1.31). The ratios in developing Asia (0.62) were above the developing country average and were higher in Hong Kong and Singapore (1.49) than the developed country average. However the ratio was relatively low in Taiwan (0.33). Both developing and developed country affiliates were, in turn, much less R&D intensive than their parent companies which allocated 3 percent of their sales receipts to R&D (United States, Department of Commerce, Bureau of Economic Analysis 1985, Tables III.N1 and III.Q1).

Aside from any effects of U.S. firms' R&D in a country, it would seem likely, a priori, that the technological level of a country's exports would be explained to a substantial degree by per capita real income or output, because per capita income reflects the country's endowment of both human and nonhuman capital.[3]

Although R&D expenditures of developing country affiliates are small relative to R&D expenditures of parents, they may be large relative to the host country's R&D efforts and may play some role in determining the composition of the host country's exports. If this were true, we might expect that locally performed R&D by multinationals would tilt the production and exports of a country toward higher-technology products.

To examine these possibilities we use a characterization of each country's exports in 1982 as originating in high-, medium-, and low-technology industries, following an OECD classification based on the R&D intensity of industries (OECD 1986). These designations are always somewhat misleading unless one can use a very detailed industry classification, and even then, there remains the problem that even the highest-tech industry includes some relatively low-technology products.[4]

Using the OECD technology classification, it was found that the higher the level of real per capita output in a country, the greater the share of both high-tech and medium-tech industries in the country's total exports, and the smaller the share of low-tech industries (Lipsey, Blomström, and Kravis 1990). The level of per capita income explains the share of medium-tech exports better than that of high-tech exports, and that of low-tech exports best of all.

The technology level of a country's exports could be a reflection of its endowment of human resources, particularly in the form of technically trained personnel. We have tested whether that factor has some impact beyond what is incorporated in the income per capita by adding to the equations a measure of the share of the labor force that consists of professional and technical workers.[5] For no class of exports is this technical labor endowment significant. Thus, as far as we can tell from this comparison across countries, the effects of endowment differences on the technological level of exports, to the extent that there is any, is captured by the per capita income level.

Another possible factor determining the composition of a country's exports might be the extent of U.S. multinationals' operations in the country. This is based on the theory that the exploitation of a parent firm's technology is the main basis for direct investment. Two measures, the ratio of U.S. affiliate sales to output and the share of U.S. affiliate exports in a country's total exports, were added to the equations. However neither variable added much to the equations' explanatory power.

Finally, the impact of R&D conducted locally by affiliates was tested using two measures of the R&D intensity of the local operations—R&D expenditures as a percent of sales and R&D employment as a percent of total employment. The result of adding these two variables to the estimates was our measure of the effect of the local R&D operations of the multinationals on the composition of exports.

For high-tech exports, the addition of the R&D variables, especially the employment variable, added considerably to the explanation of the share of high-tech industries in exports. The larger the local R&D expenditure relative to affiliate sales or the larger R&D employment relative to total employment in U.S. affiliates in a country, the higher was the proportion of the country's exports originating in high-tech industries. However per capita income is not significant once either R&D variable is included.

In the case of medium-tech exports, the addition of a variable for U.S. affiliates' R&D to the export equations added nothing to the explanation offered by per capita income; the same was true for low-tech exports, which were the ones best explained by per capita income levels alone. As expected, both R&D coefficients were negative in the medium-tech equation, but were not statistically significant at the 5 percent level (Lipsey, Blomström, and Kravis 1990).

The conclusion that more R&D-intensive production in a host country by U.S. affiliates is associated with a higher proportion of high-tech products in the country's total exports is not necessarily implied by the fact that U.S. multinationals tend to be concentrated in R&D-intensive industries. The essence of multinational operations is that firm-specific assets, such as technology, are expected to flow relatively freely from country to country within the firm even though they are not mobile among firms. It would, therefore, be conceivable for manufacturing operations to produce outside the home country using technology developed entirely in the home country. The association we find suggests several possibilities. One is that high-technology production is attracted to locations in which it is economical to perform R&D, or to locations where there are other, nonprice inducements to undertake R&D. Another is that high-technology industries tend to need some local R&D activity to support their production or their sales and service activities. However, the country endowment characteristics that were included in the equations did not explain the share of high-tech exports to the same degree as the size of U.S. affiliates' R&D effort. Since our measure of R&D investment does not include R&D by non-U.S. multinationals and by local firms, and is therefore seriously incomplete, the explanatory power of the variable suggests that host-country R&D activity by multinationals has an influence that is independent of the other factors.

A different approach to examining the impact of multinationals in different countries would be to use the latest rounds of the U.N. International Comparison Program (Kravis and Lipsey, forthcoming) to determine whether domestic prices in an industry tend to be lower than prices in general in countries where there is substantial production by multinationals. Presumably, lower relative prices would imply greater efficiency in production. The 1980 survey included only seven developing Asian countries—Hong Kong, India, Indonesia, Pakistan, Philippines, Korea, and Sri Lanka—and only covered final output. Nevertheless the survey includes a substantial number of industries that would be of interest.

The extent of direct foreign investment in a country should itself be treated as an endogenous variable to some extent. Some countries have clearly been more hospitable to foreign investors than others and some are more attractive to investors than others because their markets are larger, their governments are more stable, their wages are lower, or their unions are weaker. The level of hospitality to investment may itself be treated as endogenous. The more attractive the country is as a location for production, the less willing it may be to share its advantages with foreign companies. There is some evidence that the frequency of local content requirements and other regulations on foreign investors is, among developing countries, positively related to income levels and sizes of local markets.[6]

## Multinationals' Impact on Home Countries

Some of the possible impacts of multinationals on the host country economy have been discussed above. The other side of their contribution to the restructuring of the world economy is their impact on their home country.

If multinationals have had some influence on the structure of production in host countries by transferring technology or, more generally, speeding the adaptation of these countries to changing economic circumstances, they are likely to have affected their home countries as well. If they have shifted their labor-intensive operations to developing countries, they may have reduced the demand for unskilled labor at home or they may have been reacting to increased prices of such labor in their home countries. At the same time, their reallocation of production may have increased their demand at home for higher-skill management or technical labor.

Of the two major Pacific region home countries, the United States has a longer record of data and more information with which to trace the impact of its multina-

## Table 10.8  Average Technology Level of U.S. Trade[a], Selected Years

|              | 1970 | 1978 | 1982 | 1985 | 1986 |
|--------------|------|------|------|------|------|
| U.S. exports | 2.02 | 2.05 | 2.10 | 2.17 | 2.17 |
| U.S. imports | 1.68 | 1.76 | 1.84 | 1.87 | 1.89 |

[a]High-tech = 3; medium-tech = 2; and low-tech = 1. Note that the ordering of the three technology groups is reversed in this table from that of the source.

Source: Blomström, Lipsey, and Ohlsson (1989).

tionals on the home-country economy. The earliest concern in the United States was that production abroad by U.S. multinationals would reduce employment at home by substituting foreign production for exports from the United States. There has been very little empirical evidence that such substitution takes place in any home country, and there is now a fairly strong collection of evidence that suggests that production overseas has an impact on home-country exports that lies somewhere between no effect at all and some increase in exports (Bergsten, Horst, and Moran 1978; Lipsey and Weiss 1981, 1984; Blomström, Lipsey, and Kulchycky 1988; Swedenborg 1979, 1982).

There is evidence for the United States and Sweden that multinationals based in both countries have been supplying more and more of their export markets from operations outside their home countries (Lipsey and Kravis 1985, 1987a; Blomström and Lipsey 1989). In that sense, they have been shifting their production for the world market away from home, although their exports from home production have continued to grow in an absolute sense. What, then, is being shifted from the home countries? Is the United States moving away from relatively high-tech production and exports as the multinationals shift more of such production to their foreign operations? Or is production of more labor-intensive and lower-tech segments of the high-tech industries being shifted, with the highest portion of the technology range for production being retained in the United States? If this is the case, both the United States and the developing host countries would be moving up the technology scale in their production and exports.

A comparison of changes in the average technology level of U.S. exports and imports indicates that what is taking place is a shift of lower-tech segments of production (Table 10.8). U.S. exports are, throughout the period, at a higher technology level than U.S. imports, but both exports and imports have been moving

**Table 10.9  R&D Content of U.S. Trade, Selected Years (R&D per $100 of trade)**

|        | Exports | Imports |
|--------|---------|---------|
| 1970   | 3.10    | 2.23    |
| 1978   | 3.18    | 2.52    |
| 1982   | 3.48    | 2.92    |
| 1985   | 3.97    | 3.27    |
| 1986   | 4.02    | 3.32    |

Source: Blomström, Lipsey, and Ohlsson (1989).

toward higher-technology classes. The margin between exports and imports has narrowed over the 16 years, but only slightly.

Another way of describing the changes in U.S. export trade is through a calculation of the R&D content of exports and imports, applying the average U.S. ratio of R&D-to-sales in each industry to that industry's value of exports and imports (Table 10.9). Again U.S. exports embody an increasing amount of R&D and embody considerably more R&D than do U.S. imports, but the R&D content of imports (as measured by U.S. R&D intensities) has also been increasing. Thus there is no hint that the composition of U.S. exports has been shifted away from high-technology products by the expansion of the overseas operations of U.S. multinationals.

If U.S. multinationals are engaged in reallocating production around the world, what is the nature of that reallocation? U.S. multinationals operate in a more labor intensive way in their foreign affiliates than they do at home, and in a more labor intensive way in affiliates in developing countries than in those located in developed countries (Lipsey, Kravis, and Roldan 1982). To some extent, the difference may simply represent an adaptation to labor prices by producing the same products differently in countries with different costs of labor. However, it seems more likely that the multinationals produce different parts of their product lines or different stages of production in the various countries according to the labor intensity or unskilled labor intensity of the operation and the labor resources of the host country. Another way of observing the effects of U.S. multinational firms' operations on the United States is to compare the shares of world trade across industries for the United States, for U.S. multinationals, for U.S. multinational firms' parents, and for foreign affiliates of U.S. multinationals, and to try to explain differences among these shares. A previous study (Kravis and Lipsey 1989) has found that a higher R&D intensity of an industry is associated with a higher U.S. export share. When U.S. multinational firms are distinguished from U.S. firms that are not multinationals, R&D intensity favors the U.S. exports of multinational firms but not that of nonmultinationals.

Furthermore, within the multinational firms, high R&D intensity of an industry promotes parent exports from the United States to a much larger degree than exports from overseas affiliates. Thus, multinationals seem to be involved in the shift of both the affiliates' host countries and the United States as a home country toward R&D-intensive industries.

## Conclusions

The role of multinationals in the export trade of manufactured goods of developing Asian countries, and of developing countries in general, has increased over the last thirty years. The multinationals' activities are concentrated in chemicals, machinery, and transport equipment, particularly electrical and electronic machinery and equipment. In these industries, foreign-owned firms have been the source of one-third or more of total exports from these countries as a group, and 80 percent or more of total exports from individual countries.

The comparative advantages of U.S. and Japanese affiliates in developing Asia, relative to other firms in these countries, are mainly in electrical and electronic machinery and equipment, and, in the case of U.S. affiliates, in nonelectrical machinery to a much smaller extent. The multinationals, particularly the American multinationals, have thus pulled the host countries toward these industries and away from the food, metals, and textiles and apparel industries. Textiles and apparel, in particular, have represented the comparative advantage of the nonmultinational sectors of the developing Asian economies.

The mechanism for this pull toward the more technologically advanced sectors of the economy can be thought of, at least for the U.S. firms, as beginning with the selection of firms investing in developing Asia. They are not only concentrated in the technology-oriented sectors but, within these sectors, they were the more R&D-intensive firms. That selection was the case in all industries except foods, and it was particularly clear in the machinery industries. Although the firms investing in developing Asian countries were R&D intensive relative to other firms in their industries, they were not heavily involved in the sale of their technology through licensing but tended to exploit their technology by producing the high-tech products themselves. The only exception among the industries was "other manufacturing," in which the U.S. affiliates did extensive licensing despite their relatively low R&D investment. This may have been because these firms were licensing designs or other nontechnological knowledge rather than the results of R&D, although there is no evidence to substantiate this hypothesis.

While R&D performed in home countries by parents is undoubtedly the source of most of the technology advantages of the multinationals investing in the Asian countries, some R&D was performed by U.S. affiliates in the developing countries. In fact, U.S. affiliates in developing Asian countries were relatively R&D intensive as compared with those in other developing countries.

As small as the R&D effort in U.S. affiliates may have been, it did seem to have an impact on the composition of host-country exports. The proportion of exports that came from high-tech and low-tech industries could be partly explained by a country's real per capita income, but that was much more true for low-tech than for high-tech exports. In particular, the higher the real income per capita in a country, the smaller the proportion of exports from low-tech industries. The R&D intensity within the affiliates of U.S. multinationals went a considerable way toward explaining the share of a country's exports that came from high-tech industries. Considering that the measure covers only R&D in U.S.-owned affiliates and omits that performed by affiliates of non-U.S. firms, by local firms, and by governments, the strong relationship to high-tech exports suggests that affiliate R&D may be an important force in changing the character of industry in the host country.

While U.S. multinationals have been increasing the share of their export markets that they supply from their foreign operations, the export trade of the United States itself has moved steadily toward products of more R&D-intensive industries. The United States has moved towards greater concentration on high-tech exports than most of the developed world, despite the expansion of overseas operations in these industries. The only close rival in this direction is Japan. U.S. multinationals in particular appear to be promoting a shift of their affiliates' host countries toward R&D-intensive products and are also leading the way in moving the United States itself up the technological scale toward more R&D-intensive exports. Thus U.S. multinationals appear to be pushing their rapidly growing host countries to adapt to competition from new generations of low-tech producers. At the same time, in the United States, U.S. multinationals are also facilitating necessary adaptation to the shift of the more advanced Asian countries into higher-tech product markets, a shift that the multinationals themselves are contributing to.

## Notes

1. The Japanese data cover a shorter period, a smaller part of the universe of investors, and fewer aspects of affiliate operations than the U.S. data.
2. For an experiment along these lines for Canada, comparing foreign-owned with Canadian-owned firms, see Corbo and Havrylyshyn (1982). Comparisons of two sets of foreign firms in Taiwan are made in Chen and Tang (1986, 1987).
3. For example, across 34 countries for which Leamer and Bowen calculated endowments of various inputs, physical capital per capita explained more than 95 percent of the variation in real output per capita. Human capital per worker was, in turn, highly correlated with physical capital per capita (Lipsey and Kravis 1987b, 58).
4. The degree of industry detail is more limited across many countries than it is for countries such as the United States. Even the level of industry detail available for the United States mixes products of very different technological levels in a single industry. A warning about the interpretation of industry data on exports is provided in a recent U.S. Bureau of the Census analysis of U.S. trade. See Abbott, McGuckin, Herrick, and Norfolk (1989).
5. We are grateful to Harry Bowen for providing the factor abundance data originally prepared for use in Leamer (1984).
6. Some evidence for the motor vehicle industry is given in Kulchycky and Lipsey (1984).

## References

Abbott, Thomas, Robert McGuckin, Paul Herrick, and Leroy Norfolk. 1989. Measuring the Trade Balance in Advanced Technology Products. Discussion Paper CES 89-1 (January),

Center for Economic Studies, U.S. Bureau of the Census. Washington, D.C.: Bureau of the Census.

Bergsten, C. Fred, Thomas Horst, and Theodore H. Moran. 1978. *American Multinationals and American Interests*. Washington, D.C.: Brookings Institution.

Blomström, Magnus. 1986a. Multinationals and Market Structure in Mexico. *World Development* 14(4): 523–30.

_____. 1986b. Foreign Investment and Productive Efficiency: The Case of Mexico. *Journal of Industrial Economics* 35(1): 97–110.

_____. 1989. *Foreign Investment and Spillovers*. New York: Routledge.

Blomström, Magnus, Irving B. Kravis, and Robert E. Lipsey. 1988. Multinational Firms and Manufactured Exports from Developing Countries. National Bureau of Economic Research Working Paper 2493 (January). Cambridge, Mass.: National Bureau of Economic Research.

Blomström, Magnus, and Robert E. Lipsey. 1989. The Export Performance of Swedish and U.S. Multinationals. *Review of Income and Wealth* 35(3): 245–64.

Blomström, Magnus, and Håkan Persson. 1983. Foreign Investment and Spillover Efficiency in an Underdeveloped Economy: Evidence from the Mexican Manufacturing Industry. *World Development* 11(6): 493–501.

Blomström, Magnus, Robert E. Lipsey, and Ksenia Kulchycky. 1988. U.S. and Swedish Direct Investment and Exports. In *Trade Policy Issues and Empirical Analysis*, edited by Robert E. Baldwin. Chicago: University of Chicago Press.

Blomström, Magnus, Robert E. Lipsey, and Lennart Ohlsson. 1989. What Do Rich Countries Trade with Each Other? R&D and the Composition of U.S. and Swedish Trade. National Bureau of Economic Research Working Paper No. 3140. Cambridge, Mass.: National Bureau of Economic Research.

Caves, Richard E. 1974. Multinational Firms, Competition, and Productivity in Host-Country Markets. *Economica* 41(162): 176–93.

Chen, Tain-Jy, and De Piao Tang. 1986. The Production Characteristics of Multinational Firms and the Effects of Tax Incentives. *Journal of Development Economics* 24(1): 119–29.

_____. 1987. Comparing Technical Efficiency Between Import-Substitution-Oriented and Export-Oriented Foreign Firms in a Developing Economy. *Journal of Development Economics* 26(2): 277–89.

Corbo, Vittorio, and Oli Havrylyshyn. 1982. Production Technology Differences between Canadian-Owned and Foreign-Owned Firms using Translog Production Functions. National Bureau of Economic Research Working Paper No. 981. Cambridge, Mass.: National Bureau of Economic Research.

Finan, William F. 1975. The International Transfer of Semiconductor Technology Through U.S.-Based Firms. National Bureau of Economic Research Working Paper No. 118. Cambridge, Mass.: National Bureau of Economic Research.

Globerman, Steven. 1979. Foreign Direct Investment and 'Spillover' Efficiency Benefits in Canadian Manufacturing Industries. *Canadian Journal of Economics* 12(1): 42–56.

Kravis, Irving B., and Robert E. Lipsey. 1989. Technological Characteristics of Industries and the Competitiveness of the U.S. and Its Multinational Firms. National Bureau of Economic Research Working Paper 2933 (April). Cambridge, Mass.: National Bureau of Economic Research.

_____. Forthcoming. The International Comparison Program: Current Status and Problems. In *International Economic Transactions: Studies in Income and Wealth*, edited by Peter Hooper and J. David Richardson. Chicago: University of Chicago Press.

Kulchycky, Ksenia, and Robert E. Lipsey. 1984. Host-Country Regulation and Other Determinants of Overseas Operations of U.S. Motor Vehicle and Parts Companies. National

Bureau of Economic Research Working Paper 1463 (September). Cambridge, Mass.: National Bureau of Economic Research.

Leamer, Edward E. 1984. *Sources of International Comparative Advantage, Theory and Evidence.* Cambridge: MIT Press.

————. 1987. Paths of Development in the Three Factor, n-Good General Equilibrium Model. *Journal of Political Economy* 95(5): 961–99.

Lipsey, Robert E., Magnus Blomström, and Irving B. Kravis. 1990. R&D by Multinational Firms and Host Country Exports. In *Science and Technology: Lessons for Development Policy,* edited by Robert Evenson and Gustav Ranis. Boulder, Colo.: Westview Press.

Lipsey, Robert E., and Irving B. Kravis. 1985. The Competitive Position of U.S. Manufacturing Firms. *Banca Nazionale del Lavoro Quarterly Review* 38(153): 127–54.

————. 1987a. The Competitiveness and Comparative Advantage of U.S. Multinationals, 1957–1984. *Banca Nazionale del Lavoro Quarterly Review* 40(161): 147–65.

————. 1987b. *Saving and Economic Growth: Is the U.S. Really Falling Behind?* New York: The Conference Board.

Lipsey, Robert E., Irving B. Kravis, and Linda O'Connor. 1983. Characteristics of U.S. Manufacturing Companies Investing Abroad and Their Choice of Production Locations. National Bureau of Economic Research Working Paper 1104 (April). Cambridge, Mass.: National Bureau of Economic Research.

Lipsey, Robert E., Irving B. Kravis, and Romualdo Roldan. 1982. Do Multinational Firms Adapt Factor Proportions to Relative Factor Prices? In *Trade and Employment in Developing Countries: Factor Supply and Substitution,* Vol. II, edited by Anne Krueger. Chicago: University of Chicago Press for the National Bureau of Economic Research.

Lipsey, Robert E., and Merle Y. Weiss. 1981. Foreign Production and Exports in Manufacturing Industries. *Review of Economics and Statistics* 63(4): 488–94.

————. 1984. Foreign Production and Exports of Individual Firms. *Review of Economics and Statistics* 66(2): 304–308.

Naya, Seiji, and Eric D. Ramstetter. 1988. Direct Foreign Investment in Asia's Developing Economies and Trade in the Asia-Pacific Region. Paper presented at the Conference on Economic Cooperation through Foreign Investment in the ESCAP Region, 20–23 September, Beijing, China.

Organisation for Economic Co-operation and Development (OECD). 1986. *OECD Science and Technology Indicators, No. 2: R&D, Invention, and Competitiveness.* Paris: OECD.

Republic of China, Investment Commission. 1981, 1983, 1985, 1986, 1987. *A Survey of Overseas Chinese and Foreign Firms and Their Effects on National Economic Development,* 1980, 1982–1985 issues. Taipei: Investment Commission.

Singapore, Department of Statistics. Various years. *Report on the Census of Industrial Production,* 1977–1985 issues. Singapore: Department of Statistics.

Swedenborg, Birgitta. 1979. *The Multinational Operations of Swedish Firms: An Analysis of Determinants and Effects.* Stockholm: Industriens Utredningsinstitut.

————. 1982. *Svensk Industri i Utlandet: En Analys av Drivkrafter och Effeckter.* Stockholm: Industriens Utredningsinstitut.

United Nations. N.d. United Nations Trade Tapes.

United States, Department of Commerce, Bureau of Economic Analysis. 1985. *U.S. Direct Investment Abroad, 1982: Benchmark Survey Data.* Washington, D.C.: U.S. Department of Commerce, Bureau of Economic Analysis.

————. Various years. *U.S. Direct Investment Abroad: Operations of U.S. Parent Companies and Their Foreign Affiliates,* Revised Estimates 1983, 1984, 1985, and 1986 issues. Washington, D.C.: Bureau of Economic Analysis.

Appendix Table 10.A  Total Exports of Manufactured Goods by All Firms and by U.S. and Japanese Multinationals in Developing Asian Countries[a], 1983 (US$ millions)

| | | | | | Industry Group | | | |
|---|---|---|---|---|---|---|---|---|
| | Total | Foods | Chemicals | Metals | Non-Elec. Mach. | Elec. Mach. & Equip. | Transport Equip. | Other Manuf. |
| **Exports by all firms[b]** | | | | | | | | |
| Total | 102,950 | 12,611 | 3,595 | 9,774 | 5,680 | 16,829 | 5,383 | 49,079 |
| Hong Kong | 13,896 | 200 | 139 | 367 | 849 | 2,502 | 32 | 9,807 |
| India | 5,656 | 1,314 | 173 | 234 | 165 | 110 | 299 | 3,361 |
| Indonesia | 3,369 | 1,159 | 161 | 451 | 9 | 144 | 2 | 1,443 |
| Malaysia | 8,129 | 1,967 | 225 | 858 | 203 | 2,057 | 140 | 2,679 |
| Philippines | 2,559 | 990 | 96 | 134 | 12 | 218 | 24 | 1,085 |
| Singapore | 12,458 | 1,053 | 1,036 | 1,214 | 1,898 | 3,862 | 834 | 2,561 |
| South Korea | 23,376 | 962 | 777 | 4,375 | 661 | 3,115 | 3,346 | 10,140 |
| Taiwan | 24,239 | 1,642 | 829 | 1,716 | 1,819 | 4,476 | 678 | 3,079 |
| Thailand | 4,111 | 1,875 | 71 | 349 | 36 | 302 | 13 | 1,465 |
| Other | 5,157 | 1,449 | 88 | 76 | 28 | 43 | 15 | 3,459 |
| **Exports by U.S. multinationals[b,c]** | | | | | | | | |
| Total | 6,337 | 109 | 165-237 | <92 | 837 | 4,576 | 199-222 | 322 |
| Hong Kong | 783 | 4 | 48 | 0 | 57-70 | 496 | 0 | 144 |
| India | <24 | 0 | 1 | 0 | 5-21 | <18 | 0 | 1 |
| Indonesia | 48 | 1 | 2 | <38 | 0 | <17 | 0 | 1 |
| Malaysia | 1,296 | 2 | 12 | 0 | 0 | 1,258 | 0 | <17 |
| Philippines | 445 | 80 | 30 | 4 | 0 | 206-292 | 2 | 36-65 |
| Singapore | 2,185 | 8 | 58-77 | 8 | 678-697 | 1,210 | 196 | 9 |
| South Korea | 303 | 2 | 0 | 0 | 0 | 299 | 0 | <15 |
| Taiwan | 964 | 0 | 29 | <27 | 83 | 743 | <27 | 83 |
| Thailand | 171-270 | 12 | 4 | 0 | 0 | 249 | 0 | <29 |
| Other | 23 | * | 19 | 0 | 0 | 5 | 0 | 0 |
| **Exports by Japanese multinationals** | | | | | | | | |
| Total | | | | | | | | |
| As reported | 4,086 | 168 | 181 | 180 | 119 | 1,740 | 303 | 1,395 |
| Adjusted for coverage | 7,131 | 293 | 316 | 314 | 208 | 3,037 | 529 | 2,435 |

* = Less than US$500,000.
[a]Excluding the Middle East.
[b]Data by SITC commodity allocated to industries by concordance described in Blomström, Kravis, and Lipsey (1988).
[c]Majority-owned manufacturing affiliates.

Sources: Blomström, Kravis, and Lipsey (1988); United Nations (n.d.); United States, Department of Commerce (various years, Tables 29, 36, 37, 38).

# 11

# Multinationals and Structural Change: Implications of the Asia-Pacific Experience

*Seiji Naya and Eric D. Ramstetter*

### Industrial Structure, Multinationals, and Multiplant Economies of Scale

This chapter summarizes some of the more important issues raised by the studies in this volume and highlights those areas in which future research may be particularly helpful. As in many studies of this nature, more questions have been raised throughout the course of this volume than have been answered. Moreover, given the breadth of experiences studied here, this short chapter cannot hope to do justice to all of the issues involved. Rather our more modest goal is to highlight some the issues which we believe are at the core of the relationship between direct foreign investment (DFI) and structural change in the Asia-Pacific region.

Although the terms structural change or structural adjustment have numerous meanings depending on the context in which they are used, in this volume these terms are generally used to refer to changes in the industrial distribution of economic activities such as financial flows of DFI, fixed capital formation, employment, production, and trade. The degree and indeed the very nature of structural changes often depends heavily on the activity which is being analyzed. For example, trade structures generally changed relatively rapidly while employment structures changed rather slowly. Nevertheless without exception, the six economies that were studied in parts 2, 3, and 4 of this volume (Indonesia, Thailand, Korea, Taiwan, Japan, and the United States) experienced significant changes in economic structure between the mid-1970s and the mid-1980s. There have also been significant structural changes in Malaysia and Singapore during this period while the pace of structural change has been arguably slower in Hong Kong and the Philippines. Moreover, the ten countries that are the focus of this volume—namely, the ASEAN-4 (the four larger members of the Association of Southeast Asian Nations: Indonesia, Malaysia, the Philippines, and Thailand), the NICs (Newly Industrializing Countries: Hong Kong, Korea, Singapore, and Taiwan), Japan, and the United States—are becoming increasingly interdependent with changes experienced in one economy invariably affecting some, if not all, of the other countries in the group in important respects. Of course there is an asymmetry with changes in the larger economies (the United States and Japan) having much larger effects on the smaller economies (the NICs and ASEAN-4). Yet it is ironic that adjustment problems have been perhaps the most severe in the largest economy, the United States.

The focus of this volume has been to quantify the role of multinationals in the structural changes experienced, especially those changes that have taken place in the manufacturing sector. Throughout the volume, we have seen that in general multinationals were limited sources of economywide investment, employment, and production in host economies. However multinationals were significant factors in manufacturing, reflecting the concentration of DFI in this sector in these countries. For example, foreign firm shares of host-country manufacturing employment were at one time or another almost one-half in Singapore, close to one-third in Malaysia, and nearly one-fourth in Indonesia.[1] In the other countries for which data have been gathered (Hong Kong, Korea, Taiwan, and Thailand), these shares were markedly lower, about one-sixth or less, but they still tended to be relatively large in manufacturing compared to other sectors.

A similar pattern is also observed from the investing country viewpoint with ratios of foreign affiliate employment to investing-country employment being much larger in manufacturing than in the aggregate. Ratios of employment in manufacturing affiliates worldwide to investing-country employment were much larger for the United States than for Japan though ratios of employment in Asian affiliates to investing-country employment were somewhat larger for Japan. However, Asian affiliates accounted for under 3 percent of Japanese and U.S. employment.

Ratios like these were often even higher in a number of individual manufacturing industries, most notably electric and electronic machinery, transport machinery, chemicals, and textiles and apparel. As has been stressed throughout this volume, the predominance of multinationals in the first three of these industries is the result of the advantages multinationals have in industries where high research and development (R&D) outlays result in multiplant economies of scale. On the other hand, there is a relative lack of foreign firm activity in industries such as food, paper, and metals, in which R&D outlays are relatively low and/or single-plant economies of scale are probably more important. Thus the theoretical concepts outlined by Markusen (this volume) appear to be particularly relevant to the Asia-Pacific experience in many respects.

However, the importance of textiles and apparel investments from Japan and more recently from Taiwan raises some important theoretical issues since textiles and apparel firms often operate in very competitive markets. Much of the theoretical literature generally assumes that multinationals operate in imperfectly competitive, often oligopolistic, markets (e.g., Caves 1982). Noting the large involvement of Japanese firms in textiles and apparel, Kojima (1978) and Ozawa (1979) have argued that theories of DFI which assume that multinationals operate in imperfectly competitive markets are not general enough to explain the large amount of Japanese DFI in this relatively competitive industry. On the other hand, as Plummer and Ramstetter (this volume) point out, there are a number of special institutional characteristics related to Japanese DFI in this industry—most importantly, the tendency for firms to invest in groups which are often related to a trading firm that provides marketing expertise and a bank which provides finance. Thus it is possible to argue that Japanese textiles and apparel firms investing abroad behave in an imperfectly competitive manner in several respects. Nevertheless the rapid growth of Taiwanese DFI in these industries in recent years, which has occured in a different different institutional setting, suggests that further exploration into the nature and the implications of DFI in Asia's textiles and apparel industries is still needed.

Of course, textiles and apparel are industries in which multiplant economies are probably important. More specifically, the development of fabric technology and apparel designs are important stages that can often be performed in isolation from actual production. Moreover it is relatively easy for affiliates of textiles and apparel multinationals to rely on the abundant supplies of unskilled labor affiliates in Asia because production processes in these industries are generally rather standardized. Thus control of assets such as technology and the knowledge of the markets in the investing country and previous export destinations (notably the United States and Europe) become the basis for parent-firm operations while production is concentrated in overseas affiliates. In industries like electric machinery and transportation equipment, the story is somewhat more complicated because, as emphasized by Urata (this volume) and Lipsey (this volume), the production processes themselves are often characterized by different stages with different factor requirements. In these cases, the more capital-and/or technology-intensive production stages may be performed in the investing country or developed country affiliates. Moreover where there are large numbers of interrelated production processes in multiproduct firms, production is often spread across several countries. For example, as of mid-1989, Matsushita Electric had nine affiliates in Malaysia, seven affiliates in Singapore, four affiliates each in Taiwan and Thailand, three affiliates in the Philippines, and two affiliates each in Hong Kong and Indonesia; Sanyo Electric had eight affiliates in Hong Kong, seven affiliates in Singapore, four affiliates in Korea, and two affiliates each in Taiwan, Indonesia, Malaysia, and the Philippines; and Toshiba had eight affiliates in Thailand, four affiliates each in Hong Kong and Malaysia, and two affiliates each in Korea and Singapore (Toyo Keizai 1990). Thus, although the hypothesis that multiplant scale economies are an important determinant of multinational firm production has not been formally tested in this volume, a large body of evidence that is generally consistent with this hypothesis has been assembled. Moreover, emphasizing the roles of R&D and multiplant scale economies clearly helps to explain why multinationals are highly involved in the growth of industries such as electric machinery and transport machinery, in both the host and the investing countries.

## Multinationals, International Trade, and the Nature of Firm-Specific Assets

The relationship between multinationals and international trade has long been a concern of economic theory (e.g., Mundell 1957, Purvis 1972, Kojima 1978, Markusen 1983) as well as a concern for empirical analyses (e.g., Blomström, Lipsey, and Kulchycky 1988, Helleiner 1973, Nayyar 1978, Lipsey and Weiss 1981 and

1984, Naya and Ramstetter 1988b). Much of this literature has focused on whether foreign production is a substitute for or a complement to international trade activities. The theoretical literature has shown that the Heckscher-Ohlin trade model generally leads to the substitution case (e.g., Mundell 1957) while relaxation of key assumptions regarding technology, perfect competition, and tastes can result in DFI and trade becoming complements. Previous empirical literature has in turn generally shown that expanded U.S. affiliate activity is either positively correlated with U.S. parent exports or is unrelated to them. In contrast, the findings of Ramstetter (this volume) suggest that the growth of parent exports was negatively correlated with increased ratios of affiliate value added to parent value added in some cases. Although these two findings are not necessarily contradictory, further investigation of these relationships in a dynamic context appears warranted. Moreover, since most of the empirical evidence that has been gathered thus far deals with U.S. multinationals, similar studies of other multinationals in the region, particularly Japanese multinationals, would add further insights. Yet, as should be clear from Urata (this volume), the data problems encountered in such an attempt would be enormous. Indeed the large problems with existing data make compiling an accurate and comprehensive data base on the activities of Japanese parents and affiliates perhaps the most important and difficult challenge facing researchers attempting to analyze the behavior of Japanese multinationals in more detail.

Despite the data problems involved in Japan and a number of the host countries studied here, it is clear that multinational parents and their affiliates account for a large portion of trade in the Asia-Pacific region. Indeed the evidence assembled throughout this volume suggests a much stronger relationship between multinational activity and international trade than between multinational activity and investment, employment, or production. For example, the data in Plummer and Ramstetter (this volume) indicate that Japanese and U.S. affiliates alone accounted for 23 percent of all Asian exports in 1977 and 25 percent in 1986. Since this activity is highly concentrated in the NICs and the ASEAN-4 and investment from other regions (mainly Europe and Asia's NICs) is also significant, these figures would suggest that all foreign affiliates in the NICs and the ASEAN-4 probably account for more than one-third of the exports from these countries. If similar ratios were calculated for manufacturing they would probably be somewhat higher, though the differences between the aggregate and the manufacturing ratios would likely be relatively small in the export case since manufacturing accounts for the vast majority of NICs' exports and a large share of ASEAN-4 exports.

From the investing country point of view, Urata (this volume) and Ramstetter (this volume) show that multinational parents account for two-thirds or more of investing country exports. Moreover, in 1986, if one adds the US$50 billion of exports from affiliates of foreign multinationals in the United States (United States, Department of Commerce, Bureau of Economic Analysis 1989) to the US$161 billion in exports from U.S. parents in that year, a figure exceeding the US$206 billion in total U.S. merchandise exports for that year is obtained (Ramstetter, this volume). Clearly there is an accounting problem since the sum of exports from foreign affiliates and domestic parents should not exceed the U.S. total; nevertheless it should suffice to say that multinationals, domestic and foreign, probably account for almost all of U.S. exports. Given the low level of foreign multinational activity, this extreme level of domination is not found in Japan but nonmultinationals are nonetheless relatively small sources of exports. It is more difficult to ascertain the degree to which local multinationals export from the NICs. Yet given the rapid expansion of DFI from the NICs in recent years (especially from Hong Kong, Singapore, and Taiwan), it is likely that multinational parents are substantial sources of exports from these economies.

In short, it is not at all far-fetched to assert that multinationals account for two-thirds or more of all exports from the ten economies studied in this volume. In addition, it is very likely that the portion of trade conducted through multinationals will rise in the early-and mid-1990s as multinationals, especially those from Japan and the NICs, have been rapidly expanding investment in Asia in recent years.

Why are multinationals so involved in trade in comparison to other activities? We would suggest that it is due in large part to the possession of very significant firm-specific advantages (FSAs) in marketing, especially international marketing. In our discussion of industrial structure, we discussed another interrelated FSA, production technology, and its relation to multiplant economies of scale. While this connection has been frequently emphasized in the literature (e.g., Markusen, this volume), we would suggest that marketing know-how is another very important FSA leading to multiplant scale economies. Moreover the role of marketing know-how seems particularly crucial to understanding the success of multinationals in industries such as textiles and apparel where production technology is relatively standardized. Of course, there is at least one more important FSA in this regard, management know-how; but here again we would expect the differences between management in multinationals and management in nonmultinationals to be relatively small in standardized industries such as textiles and apparel. On the other hand, it is clear that multinationals have much more experience in international marketing and this experience often seems to be the crucial advantage multinationals have over nonmultinationals in standardized industries.

Of course, we must acknowledge that the assertions made above are based more on casual empiricism and intuition than on irrefutable logic and/or empirical analysis. Moreover the possession of superior marketing know-how is clearly useless unless a firm can produce a competitive product; this in turn requires a reasonably efficient production technology and management system. However, we also believe that FSAs have constituted one of several "black boxes" in the literature which should be pried open to the greatest extent possible. To this end, work similar to that undertaken by Lipsey (this volume) is exceedingly important if there is to be greater understanding of the role played by technology-related activities, both in parents and affiliates. In addition to this, we would also like to see a similar effort at measuring and analyzing the marketing and management abilities of multinationals so as to further illuminate the nature and effects of different FSAs possessed by multinationals.

### Policies, Multinationals, and the Costs of Structural Change

The evidence summarized above suggests that multinationals have indeed played large roles in some of the large structural changes experienced by the ten Asia-

Pacific economies over the last decade and a half. Variation in the scope of multinational involvement across industries and economic activities (e.g., employment versus exports) was partially attributed to variation in the distribution of FSAs across firms. However there is another element which is also very important in this respect, namely, economic policy. In general, this volume has been more concerned with positive rather than normative issues, but policies have figured prominently in several parts of the discussion. What follows is a synthesis of these discussions.

First, the strong desire to industrialize among the NICs and the ASEAN-4 has led many of these countries to adopt relatively liberal policies toward DFI in manufacturing. As a result, manufacturing multinationals have been relatively free to locate in Asia when they found it advantageous to do so. In contrast, restrictions have generally much stricter in other industries, especially services. Indeed, restrictions on DFI in service industries have been so strict in Asia and other regions that the United States has made liberalization of DFI in services a priority in the Uruguay Round negotiations of the GATT (General Agreement on Tariffs and Trade). However, even within manufacturing, some of the variation in multinational activity is due to policy. For example, the ASEAN-4, Korea, and Taiwan have all made development of their indigenous steel industries a high priority. Although the prevalence of single-plant scale economies in many parts of the steel industry is an important reason explaining why DFI has been limited, policies which promote indigenous firms have also constrained DFI in steel in these countries.

Second, the relatively large multinational shares of exports are also partly attributable to policy biases. Indeed many of the incentives offered to foreign investors in Asia are tied to export performance. For example, if a multinational agrees to export over 80 percent of its output from a Thai affiliate, the Thailand Board of Investment will drop all limits on the share of foreign ownership. Another indication of the concern with exports is the plethora of export processing zones and bonded factories in Korea, Taiwan, the Philippines, Malaysia, and more recently, Indonesia. In addition to the special incentives provided for export-oriented multinationals, it is important to realize that anti-export policy biases have been minimal in the NICs since the late 1960s. Moreover the ASEAN-4 have all moved toward more liberal trade regimes in recent years making them among the more open developing economies in the world (e.g., Naya and Ramstetter 1988a; World Bank 1987, 83).

Third, an emphasis on self-reliance in some of Asia's developing economies has resulted in policies that are so restrictive that multinationals have not been able or willing to invest (e.g., Burma, China, India, North Korea, and Vietnam). Even in Korea (South), a country with a relatively open trade regime since the 1960s, the liberalization of restrictive industrial and DFI policies in the early-and mid-1980s was apparently an important factor in the sharp increase of inward DFI since that time. At the same time, liberalization of restrictions on outward DFI were major factors in the increase of outward DFI from Japan in the early 1970s and from Taiwan since 1987. Thus variation in policies helps to explain the variation in the level of multinational activities across countries and time as well as across industries and economic activities.

In the context of this volume, we would like to know how the costs of structural adjustment are related to policies affecting DFI. As was detailed in the introductory chapter, structural adjustment is a costly process and one of the important roles of government policy should be to reduce the costs involved wherever this is possible. However, after compiling this volume, we are very skeptical about the potential of policies that are focused on multinationals alone to have much of an effect in this area. One fundamental problem is that it has been impossible to establish whether multinational activity is a cause or a result of structural change. Indeed, we would argue that the causation is likely to be mutual with the changing factor intensities (FSAs are included as factors of production here) in multinational firms leading to structural change on the one hand and multinationals adjusting their factor intensities in reaction to changing prices and incomes on the other.

If this view is accepted, there is little logic to making multinationals the focus of a policy designed to reduce the costs of structural change. In short, even if the large presence of multinationals has contributed to relatively low structural adjustment costs in industries such as electric machinery and Japanese textiles and apparel as suggested by Plummer and Ramstetter (this volume), it does not follow that adjustment difficulties in industries such as steel and U.S. textiles and apparel can be reduced by encouraging multinationals to enter the industries. Indeed the U.S. automobile industry has been characterized by both a high level of multinational activity and large adjustment problems. Moreover we believe that government incentives to elicit DFI are often ineffective. For example, even if substantial incentives for DFI were offered (by either the investing country or the host country), it is unlikely that U.S. steel firms would have found it profitable to undertake DFI in Asia on a scale similar to that of electric machinery firms. In other words, the promotion of DFI as a means to reduce adjustment costs in investing or host countries is at best a haphazard practice.

On the other hand, given the large role of multinationals in many countries and industries, it is crucial to be cognizant of how multinationals are likely to react to more general policies that are designed to smooth adjustment. In this respect, the importance of FSAs in multinationals (such as production technology, management know-how, and marketing know-how) can produce reactions that are different than those in nonmultinationals. For example, given the importance of international trade to multinationals, protectionism is likely to have greater adverse effects on multinationals than on nonmultinationals, at least in a direct sense. Other measures which affect trade prices, such as the appreciation of the yen and the New Taiwanese dollar after the Plaza Accord, have also had especially large effects on multinational activities. Indeed this volume has not been able to analyze the ostensibly large effects of this currency realignment in the detail which may be desired. In this respect, analyses similar to those performed here that compare data (when they become available) from the mid-1980s and the early-1990s will be extremely valuable.

Other measures which are likely to have disproportionately large effects on multinationals are public support of education, R&D, and other measures spurring the development of technology. These measures are likely to affect multinationals more than nonmultinationals since the former depend relatively heavily on skilled labor and the ability to generate technology in a given economy. Likewise the public provision of transportation and communication infrastructure may also benefit multinationals more than nonmultinationals since multinationals often rely more heavily on the transport of goods, services, and information. Thus, it should be clear that a large number of policies have had important implications for the DFI-structural change relationship and that a systematic analysis of the implications of various policies would be helpful.

Finally, we must emphasize the need to study countries other than the ten countries studied here. As was noted throughout this volume, economic performance in these countries over the last two to three decades has been remarkable in many respects. Much of the rapid economic growth and the rapid pace of structural change experienced in these economies can be attributed to rather special interactions of economic policies and economic institutions in the countries involved. More specifically, we believe that the relatively outward-looking and market-oriented economic policies employed by all of the economies studied have been an important element in the region's success (e.g., James, Naya, and Meier 1989). It is also clear that these policies and comparatively favorable policies toward DFI combine to make the Asia-Pacific experience unique in some respects. As a result, closer study of the relationships between DFI and structural change in other countries and regions would be highly beneficial to help isolate the more general elements of the Asian experience. However, we agree with Markusen (this volume) in cautioning against trying to construct country-or region-specific theories of behavior in multinationals or other economic agents. Rather the efforts of volumes like this should be focused on illustrating how relatively general concepts apply in a particular setting.

## Notes

1. See the chapters by Pangestu (Ch. 3) and Plummer and Ramstetter (Ch. 9) in this volume. Of course, as emphasized at several points throughout the volume, ratios of multinational activity to total activity, whether that activity is in investment, employment, or exports, do not indicate the net impact of DFI on the activity in question. This is because multinationals may suppress or stimulate activities by domestic firms in both the host country and the investing country depending on the nature of the activity involved. However the ratios do provide a rough guide to the scale of multinational activity in the region.

## References

Blomström, Magnus, Robert E. Lipsey, and Knesia Kulchycky. 1988. U.S. and Swedish Direct Investment and Exports. In *Trade Policy Issues and Empirical Analysis*, edited by Robert E. Baldwin. Chicago: University of Chicago Press.

Caves, Richard E. 1982. *Multinational Enterprise and Economic Analysis*. Cambridge: Cambridge University Press.

Helleiner, G. K. 1973. Manufactured Exports from Less Developed Countries and Multinational Firms. *Economic Journal*, 83(329): 21–47.

James, William E., Seiji Naya, and Gerald M. Meier. 1989. *Asian Development*. Madison: University of Wisconsin Press.

Kojima, Kiyoshi. 1978. *Japanese Direct Foreign Investment: A Model of Multinational Business Operations*. Tokyo: Tuttle.

Lipsey, Robert E., and Merle Y. Weiss. 1981. Foreign Production and Exports in Manufacturing Industries. *Review of Economics and Statistics* 63(4): 488–494.

————. 1984. Foreign Production and Exports of Individual Firms. *Review of Economics and Statistics*, 66(2): 304–308.

Markusen, James R. 1983. Factor Movements and Commodity Trade as Complements. *Journal of International Economics*, 14(3/4): 341–355.

Mundell, Robert. 1957. International Trade and Factor Mobility. *American Economic Review*, 47(3): 321–335.

Naya, Seiji, and Eric D. Ramstetter. 1988a. Policy Interactions and Direct Foreign Investment in East and Southeast Asia. *Journal of World Trade*, 22(2): 57–71.

————. 1988b. Direct Foreign Investment in Asia's Developing Economies and Trade in the Asia-Pacific Region. Paper presented at the Conference on Economic Cooperation through Foreign Investment in the ESCAP Region, 20–23 September, Beijing, China.

Nayyar, Deepak. 1978. Transnational Corporations and Manufactured Exports from Poor Countries. *The Economic Journal*, 88(349): 59–84.

Ozawa, Terutomo. 1979. *Multinationalism, Japanese Style: The Political Economy of Outward Dependency*. Princeton: Princeton University Press.

Purvis, Douglas D. 1972. Technology, Trade, and Factor Mobility. *The Economic Journal*, 82(327): 991–999.

Toyo Keizai. 1990. *Gyōshubetsu Kaigai Shinshutsu Kigyō Sōran* [A comprehensive survey of firms overseas by industry], 1990 issue. Tokyo: Toyo Keizai.

United States, Department of Commerce, Bureau of Economic Analysis. 1989. *Foreign Direct Investment in the United States: Operations of U.S. Affiliates of Foreign Companies*, Revised 1986 Estimates. Washington, D.C.: Bureau of Economic Analysis.

World Bank. 1987. *World Development Report 1987*. New York: Oxford University Press.

# Contributors

**Chung H. Lee:** Research Associate, Institute for Economic Development and Policy, East-West Center, 1777 East-West Road, Honolulu, Hawaii, 96848, U.S.A.; Professor, Department of Economics, University of Hawaii, Honolulu, Hawaii, 96822, U.S.A.

**Robert E. Lipsey:** Research Associate, National Bureau of Economic Research, 269 Mercer Street, 8th Floor, New York, New York, 10003, U.S.A.; Professor, Queens College and The Graduate Center, Flushing, New York, 11367, U.S.A.

**James R. Markusen:** Professor, Department of Economics, University of Colorado, Boulder, Colorado, 80309, U.S.A.

**Seiji Naya:** Professor, Department of Economics, University of Hawaii, Honolulu, Hawaii, 96822, U.S.A.

**Mari Pangestu:** Centre for Strategic and International Studies, Jl. Tanah Abang III/23-27, Jakarta, 10160, Indonesia; Research Director, CFPST, Harvard Institute for International Development, P.O. Box 2707/Jkt., Jakarta, Indonesia

**Michael G. Plummer:** Research Associate, Institute for Economic Development and Policy, East-West Center, 1777 East-West Road, Honolulu, Hawaii, 96848, U.S.A.

**Eric D. Ramstetter:** Associate Professor, Faculty of Economics, Kansai University, 3-3-35 Yamatecho, Suita, Osaka, 564, Japan; Adjunct Research Associate, Institute for Economic Development and Policy, East-West Center, 1777 East-West Road, Honolulu, Hawaii, 96848, U.S.A.

**Chi Schive:** Professor of Economics, National Taiwan University, Taipei, Taiwan

**Somsak Tambunlertchai:** Professor, Faculty of Economics, Thammasat University, Bangkok, 10020, Thailand

**Jenn-Hwa Tu:** Assistant Research Fellow, Institute of Economics, Academia Sinica, Nankang, Taipei, Taiwan

**Shujiro Urata:** Associate Professor of Economics, School of Social Sciences, Waseda University, 1-6-1 Waseda, Shinjuku-ku, Tokyo, Japan